TORONTO
MAYORS

TORONTO MAYORS

A History of the City's Leaders

MARK MALONEY

Foreword by David Crombie

DUNDURN PRESS

Publisher: Kwame Scott Fraser | Acquiring editor: Kathryn Lane | Editor: Michael Carroll
Cover and interior designer: Karen Alexiou

Library and Archives Canada Cataloguing in Publication

Title: Toronto mayors : a history of the city's leaders / Mark Maloney.
Names: Maloney, Mark, author. | Crombie, David, 1936- writer of foreword.
Description: Foreword by David Crombie. | Includes bibliographical references and index.
Identifiers: Canadiana (print) 20230201733 | Canadiana (ebook) 20230201806 | ISBN 9781459751224
  (hardcover) | ISBN 9781459751231 (PDF) | ISBN 9781459751248 (EPUB)
Subjects: LCSH: Mayors—Ontario—Toronto—History. | LCSH: Mayors—Ontario—Toronto—
  Biography. | LCSH: Toronto (Ont.)—Politics and government.
Classification: LCC FC3097.25 .M35 2023 | DDC 971.3/541—dc23

We acknowledge the support of the Canada Council for the Arts and the Ontario Arts Council for our publishing program. We also acknowledge the financial support of the Government of Ontario, through the Ontario Book Publishing Tax Credit and Ontario Creates, and the Government of Canada.

Dundurn Press
1382 Queen Street East
Toronto, Ontario, Canada M4L 1C9
dundurn.com, @dundurnpress 𝕏 f ⊙

This book is dedicated to three very special people. They represent Toronto's past, present, and future: Virginia Williams, my beloved and closest friend, who was born and raised in Toronto and has seen Toronto's past and the multitude of changes over seven decades; Bob Richardson, a political veteran, respected on all sides of the aisle, who is publicly known as one of Toronto's 50 most influential citizens and represents the best of Toronto's present-day political engagement; and Lucas Granger, a bright young political activist passionate about urban issues and deeply committed to making Toronto a better place. That is our city's future.

Contents

Foreword

In late August 1978, I left the office of mayor of Toronto after almost six years to run in the by-election in the federal riding of Rosedale. Later, as I was walking down Parliament Street and waiting at an intersection, a lady in a motorized wheelchair, whom I knew, came up beside me, touched my arm, and said, "David, I hear you're going into federal politics."

As we crossed the street, she told me she was having a good summer, especially with her grandkids at the park with the recreation programs. Now they were getting ready to go back to school where she herself had once gone as a little girl. "But there have been a lot of changes since then," she told me. She also let me know that things were changing in the neighbourhood — some good, some bad — and that she was on her way to the library and then to Wellesley Hospital (long since closed), since she hadn't been feeling well lately. After that, she sped off.

Thinking about that brief encounter later, I realized she'd clearly understood the basic difference between local government and all the rest. For her, local government was essentially about services and not politics. It wasn't about political parties jousting in a public arena. It was more about people's needs being met by services in the community.

The list of those services is long and known and so well grounded that they're often simply taken for granted. What are they? They're schools and libraries; childcare facilities; parks and recreation facilities; roads, highways, and sidewalks; public transit; welfare and social service programs; garbage and waste management; police, fire, and emergency services; land use and environmental planning; cultural institutions of all kinds; and clean and safe water. I could go on and on.

Taken together, these services are fundamental to our existence, even to our survival. They're our connective tissues linking our private worlds and our generations one to the other in the creation of a community. They're the glue that holds us together. They also provide us with the ability to craft a platform for economic growth and form the basis for our social peace.

Of course, it requires from us that we engender a culture of caring and an understanding of the power of community, a willingness to widen the circle of inclusion, and an ambition to reimagine and reinvest in new services as we continue to maintain the usability of the old.

Considering all that I've said, Mark Maloney's new book, *Toronto Mayors: A History of the City's Leaders*, is a magnificent treasure trove of information and storytelling about the life and times of Toronto since its birth in 1834 as seen through the careers of its mayors. In terms of the quality and quantity of research, I don't think there's another book that I know of about Toronto that is so comprehensive and so detailed. It allows you to see each mayor's career reflected in the city. So if you're interested in understanding Toronto, Mark's book is a great place to start. It's a veritable time machine of the city's history.

Without doubt, *Toronto Mayors* will become an indispensable possession for scholars and practitioners alike as well as an absorbing experience for the general reader. It's not to be missed!

David Crombie
Toronto, Ontario
March 2023

Introduction

Toronto Mayors is a very modest undertaking with respect to the history of the mayors of Toronto. Indeed, for any author, the hardest part of completing a book is what has to be left out of the final manuscript. That was the case here, as well.

This undertaking does have a predecessor, though. It is Victor Loring Russell's *Mayors of Toronto*, published in 1982 as a first volume from 1834 to just 1899. My book builds upon Russell's terrific work.

For each Toronto mayor, I have tried to reflect the following:

- the mayors' formative years, including family backgrounds, education, and personal lives;
- circumstances as well as their prior work, successes, or accomplishments that led them to be chosen mayors;
- their political careers and mayoral priorities as well as issues Toronto's Council was dealing with during their terms as mayors;
- a look at what was happening in Toronto during each mayor's time and how the city was evolving; and
- the mayors' lives and careers after serving in the city's top job.

Toronto has had an amazing journey as a city — from its origins as a small, dusty colonial outpost of 9,200 hardy souls at the time of incorporation in 1834 to becoming a major global centre of more than three million residents as it approaches its 200th anniversary in 2034.

The mayoral history of Toronto is both rich and colourful. It is sometimes forgotten that more Toronto mayors have made the journey to and from City Hall by horse than have used motor vehicles. And as the *Toronto Star* once noted, there have been mayors who were "scoundrels, rogues, and socialists." One of Toronto's mayors was involved in the brutal torture of an opposition candidate. Another went insane while in office as he began to suffer from a long, slow, agonizingly painful death due to an acute third stage of syphilis.

Toronto's mayors have been curious, eccentric, or alcoholic, while others were offbeat, rebellious, or swaggering. Some city leaders have been bigots, bullies, refugees, social crusaders, war heroes, or bon vivants. Other mayors have been inspiring, still others well ahead of their times.

In today's modern world, Toronto has become Canada's major powerhouse and is the country's main hub for education, manufacturing, financial services, trade, transportation, arts and culture, media, high tech, and research. The city's mayor is a political, social, and economic leader of a respected metropolis, identified for several years in a row by the *Economist* as one of the world's top 10 most livable cities.

Today, the mayor of Toronto guides the city further into the 21st century and is also the inheritor of a rich legacy of hopes and dreams, ambitions and efforts, successes and failures that all began with William Lyon Mackenzie, the first mayor in 1834.

The office of mayor remains an unbroken link to Toronto's founding.

Mayor William Lyon Mackenzie

1834

The 1st mayor of Toronto

Occupations: Shopkeeper, merchant, journalist, publisher, Member of the Upper Canada and Province of Canada Legislative Assemblies, Toronto Council member, rebel, political refugee, author
Residence While Mayor: 19 Richmond Street (at Church Street)
Birth: March 12, 1795, in Dundee, Scotland
Death: August 28, 1861, in Toronto

—— • ——

E ccentric, mercurial, intemperate, stubborn, and passionate, William Lyon
Mackenzie was a partisan firebrand and a radical ideologue who was both
fearless and foolhardy. These were just a few of the words used to describe
Toronto's first mayor.

Born in Dundee, Scotland, on March 12, 1795, he was the only son of
weaver Daniel Mackenzie and Elizabeth Chalmers. His father died three
weeks after his birth, and he was brought up by his single mother. Somewhat
ironically, he had no interest in journalism or politics during the first 25
years of his life.

Mackenzie's mother was proud and deeply religious, and though he later
rebelled against organized religion, he nevertheless maintained a strict, almost puritanical zeal throughout his political life. Even at the age of five,
"Lyon," as he was called for much of his adult life, was a difficult boy to
discipline, perhaps a foreshadowing of his life in politics.

By 1814, at age 19, he was operating a general store 32 kilometres north
of Dundee, a business that would later fail. He then worked for a canal company, travelled in France, and lived in London, later admitting to a highly "dissipated"[1] life of gambling, carousing, and heavy drinking. In 1814,
Mackenzie fathered a son out of wedlock, and his mother raised the child.

At the age of 25, in 1820, Mackenzie sailed to Canada, first settling in
Montreal, where he found work as a bookkeeper for the Lachine Canal and
as a reporter for the *Montreal Herald*. Yet, within just a matter of months,
he moved to the small, dusty colonial outpost of York (Toronto), then a
garrison town of just 1,500 residents still recovering from the War of 1812.
Mackenzie set up shop on the still-unpaved King Street at Church Street,
across from a then small wooden Anglican church (today's Cathedral
Church of St. James).

In 1822, Mackenzie returned to Montreal to meet his mother, newly
arrived from Scotland with his son, and with Isabel Baxter, a young woman
his mother had picked to become his wife. Within weeks they were married
and went on to have 13 children. Isabel proved to be a faithful partner during an often difficult life of turmoil and turbulence.

Mackenzie soon left York to open a general store in Dundas in 1822 and then two years later settled in Queenston near Niagara (today's Niagara-on-the-Lake). Still restless, he bought a small printing press, which led to the birth of the *Colonial Advocate*, his Reform movement newspaper. Unlike other newspapers, it did not rely on government advertising and covered a host of issues: the independence of juries, the slow construction of canals, and much-needed St. Lawrence River shipping improvements.

In the mid-1820s, Mackenzie undertook a major journalistic tour of Upper Canada to examine the economic, social, and transportation needs of several towns, including Kingston, Belleville, York, London, and Niagara. His report took aim at the need for better roads. These, he noted, were "the worst feature"[2] of Canada.

His paper and its pungent criticisms were obviously being felt. The *Upper Canada Gazette* denounced him as "an insolent and wretched specimen," also noting "the total abandonment of all truth, principle, sense, and decorum."[3]

In late 1824, the strident Mackenzie moved his family back to York and found a business location and home at Front and Yonge Streets. But with a circulation of just 830, he was forced to cease publication due to crushing debts. His personal attacks — often considered scurrilous yellow journalism — did not help, such as when he publicly called a leading citizen a "pitiful mean-looking parasite."[4]

Soon, Mackenzie was himself attacked in full force. In June 1826, a group of rowdy young men in disguise raided his newspaper in broad daylight, hurling the printer's type into the harbour and effectively shutting him down. After seeking restitution, the courts awarded him a substantial settlement, and he was able to pay off debts and re-establish the paper — the opposite of what his tormentors had intended.

To no one's surprise, in 1828, Mackenzie announced he would run for the Upper Canada Legislative Assembly for York County. Electing two members, the riding took in the Town of York north of Queen Street as well as a wide swath of rural areas in York, Peel, and Ontario (now Durham Region) Counties. Many voters had emigrated from the United States and were open to Mackenzie's Reform platform.

However, having government decision-making put under the control of ordinary citizens was a novel idea in the 1820s, and Mackenzie's plank was an ambitious one: establish a university, create a less costly court system, improve shipping, and give greater powers to an elected Legislative Assembly.

Mackenzie continued his bitter attacks on the Tory establishment, cementing his status as an outsider. For months he dissected opponents in a weekly list of wrongdoings, misdeeds, and evildoings titled "The Parliament Black Book ... Official Corruption and Hypocrisy Unmasked," earning him the nickname "William Liar Mackenzie." Yet these aggressive tactics resonated with his electorate, and he and his running mate, Jesse Ketchum, won in a landslide. Now an elected figure in his own right, there was no stopping him.

It was Mackenzie who coined the term *Family Compact*,[5] one of Canada's most enduring political descriptions, denoting the elite group of conservative officials holding the cream of public appointments, including judges, sheriffs, justices of the peace, court clerks, customs inspectors, land commissioners, postmasters, and surveyors. Compact members were also deeply intertwined by way of family, religion, and economic and social status, as well as a deeply held allegiance to the British monarchy and to the institutions and way of life of Britain.

When the assembly — a modest, part-time vocation at the time — finally met in January 1829, Mackenzie soon pressed for reform of the postal service (British owned and controlled), arguing that a local authority should be established with revenues ploughed back into better Canadian service and not sent to the United Kingdom's treasury.

Mackenzie also criticized the poor state of roads and the enormous power of banks, becoming a fierce opponent of the Bank of Upper Canada. In 1829, he travelled to the United States where he secured a meeting with Andrew Jackson, the new U.S. president. As his admiration for the United States grew, so did his disdain for Great Britain and its institutions. In 1831, Mackenzie called for a radical political change — that elections be held by way of a secret paper ballot, instead of voters making an open and very public verbal declaration in front of hundreds of fellow citizens.

Ever the serious politician, Mackenzie carried out another major tour of Upper Canada, holding a series of 19 meetings that focused on strong municipal councils, giving power to ordinary citizens, and better control of public lands. Yet the Reform movement was hampered by inexperience and disorganization, and by Mackenzie's bitter personal attacks, fuelling further Tory hatred.

By late 1831, the Tory majority expelled him from the assembly and declared his seat vacant, with Attorney General Henry Boulton terming Mackenzie "a reptile." A new election was called for 1832, and though Mackenzie was re-elected, the assembly was still not ready to allow his return, ejecting him this time for "gross, slanderous, and malicious libels"[6] in his newspaper.

In 1832, Mackenzie journeyed to England to present his grievances to the imperial government in person. The sympathetic hearing he received there outraged Upper Canadian Conservatives and led to greater obstacles for Mackenzie. In November 1832, though he was still in Britain, Mackenzie was again re-elected. The next year, Canada's most famous legislator returned after 15 months away. No longer holding faith in Britain, his political orientation toward the United States grew even stronger.

The Tory majority once more refused Mackenzie his seat and yet another election was called. Again, he was elected, this time returning to the assembly with a host of supporters in tow. Denied permission to take his seat, he was dragged out by the sergeant-at-arms, and it took a direct order in February 1834 from Lieutenant Governor John Colborne to have him sworn in. Yet upon taking his seat, Mackenzie was arrested on the spot.

By now, the Family Compact had turned Mackenzie into a political martyr, ensuring his elevation just a few weeks later as the first mayor of the new City of Toronto. Worried about losing political control to a Reform mob, Tories had ensured that mayors were selected by members of the municipality's Council and not by citizens from across the town.

York became the newly incorporated City of Toronto on March 6, 1834, and on March 27, both Tories and Reformers presented a full slate of candidates for the city's first Council election. Mackenzie was successful in St. David's Ward, and by a vote of 10–8 was chosen by the Council to serve as mayor over Reformer Dr. John Rolph, who had originally been slated to become the first chief magistrate, not Mackenzie.

Urgently needed in the new city, yet still non-existent, was a basic sewer system, as well as the construction of wooden-planked sidewalks over the mud, refuse, ash, and garbage scraps that infested the unpaved dirt streets. During periods of rain, city streets turned into a mess of sloppy and impassable mud. Toronto's municipal finances were in a very weak state, and a new courthouse, jail, and market building had resulted in serious debt. Assessment was also unfair, with substantial Family Compact property owners paying taxes just slightly higher than people of modest means.

The city's Council established a new Board of Health and basic fire prevention standards, as well as regulations on public markets. It requested the Bank of Upper Canada to provide a major loan for road repairs but was turned down. The Tory-controlled bank had no desire to assist a Reform-dominated Council.

As mayor, Mackenzie also served Toronto in two judicial positions — as a chief magistrate of the Mayor's Court handling criminal matters, and as a Police Court judge dealing with minor offences such as drunkenness, disorderly conduct, liquor, and wife beating (considered to be a "minor offence" in 1834).[7] In one celebrated case, Mackenzie's puritanical outlook caused him to harshly sentence one habitually drunk woman to the public outdoor stocks simply for insulting him.

First used in medieval times, the stocks were brought to North America from Britain to render scorn, punishment, and public humiliation. A prisoner's head and hands were bound and then inserted into the large open holes of a wooden plank. Immobilized, and in an open square, the public insulted, jeered, kicked, spat, and in some cases, even urinated or defecated on a victim in the stocks.

One of Mackenzie's first acts as mayor was to tour city slums with officials to see first-hand the dire problems of shelter, housing, gambling, unlicensed alcohol, and "vice in its blackest shapes."[8] A virulent cholera outbreak struck in 1834, killing hundreds of the city's 9,200 residents. As the epidemic raged, both Mackenzie and his arch-conservative foe, Bishop John Strachan, spent time bringing the sick and diseased to hospital. Yet, as Mackenzie continued to publish his caustic *Colonial Advocate* newspaper, it was clear he was better suited being in opposition than governing.

Ironically, though he skewered the status, privilege, wealth, and public appointments of the Family Compact, Mackenzie himself doled out patronage to his own supporters, and by the fall of 1834, the Council had become ineffectual and unable to institute reforms, demonstrating that Mackenzie was more prone to attack than to attend to issues in a collegial manner.

In the Upper Canada election of October 1834, and even before completing his mayoral term, Mackenzie again became a candidate for the Legislative Assembly, winning in the second riding of York. The Tories, seeing no majority in Toronto's Council and about to lose it in the colonial assembly, sought to make Mackenzie's life more unmanageable by criticizing, disrupting, and attacking him at every turn, often denying a quorum in the Council.

Despite Mackenzie's efforts, there was little chance for reform, since the new lieutenant governor, Sir Francis Bond Head, had been instructed by the British imperial authorities not to make concessions. Originally viewed as a reforming governor, Head soon quarrelled with moderate elements in the assembly and then dissolved it. The 1836 Upper Canada election, notorious for its bribery, false enumeration, threats, and gangsterism, not to mention strong-armed intimidation at the polls, meant defeat for Reformers, including Mackenzie. The loss was a transforming event and set the stage for the 1837 Rebellion.

Mackenzie's tone began to change; he now believed in severing links with Britain and possible armed resistance to "British oppression."[9] By the summer of 1837, he was attracting large crowds and thought the only way to end Family Compact rule was to lead a substantial group of supporters to overthrow the government. In November 1837, Mackenzie's newspaper proposed a new draft constitution, one modelled after the U.S. Constitution, and he recruited a military veteran to serve as commander of the rebel forces. No violence would be necessary, he insisted, if there was truly spontaneous backing for revolution.

On Monday, December 4, 1837, Mackenzie led a scouting party into Toronto to judge the colony's preparedness. He was confronted by John Powell, sent by Lieutenant Governor Head to investigate rumours of a rebel invasion. Powell coldly murdered Anthony Anderson, a key Mackenzie ally and one of the few rebels with military training. Powell, who less than a month later became Toronto's fifth mayor, also raised his gun in an attempt to kill Mackenzie, but his pistol jammed, and Mackenzie quickly fled. For his part, Powell hastily escaped to warn authorities of the impending rebellion.

On December 6, convinced he would gain spontaneous popular support, Mackenzie led his erratic ragtag rebel army down Yonge Street. As the force neared Toronto, it was dispersed by shots from the troops of Sheriff William Jarvis. The next day, 1,000 pro-government forces marched on Montgomery's Tavern, Mackenzie's rebel staging area, easily defeating his smaller collection of hard-core and poorly armed rebels. The Rebellion of 1837 was over.

Under pain of capture and certain death, rebel leaders speedily bolted Canada for the United States. Having attempted his coup d'état, Mackenzie arrived in New York State, setting up camp on Navy Island in the Niagara River and publicly declaring it to be the "Provisional Government of the State of Upper Canada."[10] But on December 29 that year, British troops bombarded the island, destroying an American ship supplying Mackenzie's rebels.

With the total collapse of his new political regime, Mackenzie, with little income and large debts, moved to New York City where his family joined him in April 1838. With money from generous benefactors, he started a new paper, *Mackenzie's Gazette*, the next month.

In 1839, Mackenzie took his first steps toward American citizenship, yet ongoing money woes, the inability to find work, and family illness made life a misery. He was also convicted for violating American neutrality laws and sentenced to 18 months in jail. The filthy lockup on a bog containing factory effluent led to a deterioration of his health. Yet, in 1840, he was pardoned, even though still attempting to recruit "shrewd and daring fellows"[11] to burn English-owned ships, barracks, and warehouses in Canada.

With money problems continuing to dog him, in 1842, he took a job with the Mechanics' Institute and became a U.S. citizen the following year. In 1844, he authored *The Sons of the Emerald Isle*, a comprehensive biography of Irish patriots, and though having made his name as an anti-patronage activist, he secured an appointment as a clerk at the New York Customs House.

Mackenzie then published a highly critical biography of former U.S. president Martin Van Buren in 1846, and in May of that year, covered the State of New York's constitutional convention in Albany for the *New York Daily Tribune*, remaining there until 1847 when he returned to New York City to work for the newspaper as well as serve as its political correspondent in Washington, D.C.

Meanwhile, the new United Province of Canada (formed from the union of Upper and Lower Canada) was created in 1841, and an amnesty was declared for the rebels of 1837. The pull of Canada proved to be too great, and Mackenzie moved back to Toronto in 1850, continuing to write for the *New York Daily Tribune*, as well as for the *Niagara Mail* and *Toronto Examiner*. Robert Baldwin, co-premier of the Province of Canada with Louis-Hippolyte La Fontaine, resigned in 1851. He was out of step with more ardent Reformers who wanted to make the administration more democratic and responsible.

Mackenzie founded another paper, the *Message*, yet within a year it was in financial trouble. He also managed to alienate George Brown, the owner of Toronto's *Globe* and an important government critic. In 1851, Mackenzie won a provincial by-election in Haldimand County, defeating Brown, whose anti-papist views did not play well in a constituency with a large Catholic population.

Again, Mackenzie became involved in issues still unsettled from the 1830s: state aid for religious colleges, public overspending, and governmental assistance to railways. He also advocated that mayors be directly elected and supported trade reciprocity (the mutual reduction of duties) with the United States as well as a simplified legal code to allow citizens to plead their own cases. Yet times had changed, and the strong grassroots political organizer was no longer as effective.

With his financial problems worsening, Mackenzie was forced to stop publishing the *Message*. At the same time, he refused full-time positions with the *Examiner* and the weekly *Globe*. In 1856, several long-time allies raised funds to honour his contributions to public issues and to purchase a house on Bond Street close to St. Michael's Cathedral in downtown Toronto.

In August 1858, his strength failing, Mackenzie resigned his Legislative Assembly seat but publicly called for the complete annexation of Canada by the United States. Plagued by creditors and seeing little hope in the future, he experienced bouts of severe depression. In August 1861, Mackenzie suffered a fatal apoplectic seizure and died at home.

John Sewell, himself a former Toronto mayor (1978–1980), published *Mackenzie: A Political Biography* in 2002 in which he described Mackenzie as a puritan on a mission, seeking reform for virtually every cause, holding a deep suspicion of all those who had power, and displaying a fierce pride in his own solutions and independence of thought.

Mayor Robert Sullivan

1835

The 2nd mayor of Toronto

Occupations: Lawyer, Toronto Council member, author, member of the Province of Canada Executive Council, judge
Residence While Mayor: Duke Street (now Adelaide Street East)
Birth: May 24, 1802, in Bandon, County Cork, Ireland
Death: April 14, 1853, in Toronto

— • —

A brilliant legal mind and a shrewd and canny albeit alcoholic Tory, sympathetic to reforms, yet who bent his principles when it was in his interest to do so, Robert Sullivan later went on to become president of the Province of Canada's Executive Council, its most powerful governing body.

Sullivan was born in Bandon, County Cork, Ireland, in 1802, the son of merchant Daniel Sullivan and Barbara Baldwin, whose brother was William Baldwin, a very prominent citizen of York (Toronto). With his family, he immigrated to York in 1819 at the age of 17. It was a long and arduous journey, crossing the Atlantic Ocean and entering Canada at Quebec City, followed by a steamer to Montreal and again by ship down the St. Lawrence River to Kingston and finally York.

The 1907 illustrated *Commemorative Biographical Record of the County of York, Ontario* describes the young Sullivan as "a bright, intelligent boy, quick to learn, and able, to a remarkable degree, to retain knowledge he acquired."[1] His father established himself as a merchant in a store just east of the current Cathedral Church of St. James on King Street East.

As was customary at the time, boys assisted their fathers in the shop. Yet, after a promising beginning, the Sullivans' original aspirations were dashed. In 1822, Robert's father died, leaving him as head of the family at age 20. Through his uncle, William Baldwin, his extended family provided support, placing him with the Law Society of Upper Canada and securing a position for him as a librarian in the Upper Canada Legislative Assembly. He excelled in the study of law and at 26 was called to the bar in 1828.

Sullivan first took an active role in politics during the exciting Upper Canada election of 1828 as a campaigner for William Baldwin in the riding of Norfolk. Once his uncle was elected, Sullivan returned to York where he took part in helping Dr. Thomas Morrison in an unsuccessful challenge of Tory foe (and later chief justice) John Beverley Robinson, Sr., in the third riding of York County. Despite Morrison's loss, Sullivan's political and legal talents did not go unnoticed. Shortly afterward in January 1829, he returned to Norfolk County to marry Cecelia-Eliza Matthews, the 17-year-old daughter of prominent Reform leader John Matthews.

Yet tragedy once again unravelled Sullivan's personal life. Just six months after the birth of his first daughter, Sullivan's wife and infant baby died. Sullivan quit the area and returned to York to seek the support of his family. Upon his return, he established a partnership with Robert Baldwin, his cousin, and soon the firm was prospering.

On the personal front, Sullivan once more found happiness, marrying Emily-Louisa Delatre in Niagara Falls during the 1833 Christmas season. He and his wife went on to have a family of four sons and seven daughters. Sullivan did not seek a seat in Toronto's first election in 1834, but the following year ran in St. David's Ward, defeating William Lyon Mackenzie, who by then had lost interest and set his sights on higher office in Upper Canada.

The 1835 municipal election changed Toronto's political complexion. Mackenzie was no longer on the city's Council, and the calmer Sullivan exhibited a more moderate and collegial approach. The mayoralty was clearly his end goal. On January 15, 1835, he was selected by a unanimous vote of the Council.

While he leaned toward conservatism, the eloquent Sullivan proved to be a competent administrator, providing stability to often raucous Council meetings. He approached the city's problems with a less partisan and more practical outlook than Mackenzie, even donning a new set of official robes.

However, Sullivan was plagued with the same difficulties and turned his attention to the financing of the city's first major works project, a new trunk sewer. And early in its term, the Council petitioned Upper Canada's Legislative Assembly to provide "for more fair and equal Assessment of the City Taxes."[2]

The Council dealt with a range of issues in 1835: the removal of "filth and nuisances" from city streets, grants to the firefighting Hook and Ladder Company, contested election results, negotiations with the Bank of Upper Canada, creation of a Council committee on improvements to Toronto's harbour, funding to aid widows and orphans, and city payments for wood planking, lumber, candlesticks, and pistols. The Council also dealt with the regulation of the fish market, the appointment of a "Keeper of the Don Bridges," enforcement of city ordinances "against swine running at large within the City,"[3] the difficulty of collecting taxes, and the regulation of bread prices.

With no such thing yet as piped fresh water and all firefighting carried out by way of paid cartage and bucket brigades from Lake Ontario, the provision of water was an ever-present concern. The Council received a report on bringing water into the city from the Humber River, revealing that it would need a complicated series of dams, reservoirs, and aqueducts of more than 11 kilometres, and have to deal with issues of stability, leakage, and water pressure. Despite an exhaustive report, the Council took no further action.

The Council also established a committee to "report as to a proper Place for depositing Rubbish and Manure"[4] and authorized citizens to dispose of their garbage in a field at the northwest corner of Yonge and Adelaide Streets. Yet the still-unruly Council could not be convened several times in 1835 due to a lack of quorum, and there was discussion concerning whether members could be compelled to attend meetings.

What really brought citizens out every time were the public hangings held near Market Square. Great preparations were made for these ceremonies, with gallows attractively painted and decorated for the occasion. To instill respect for the law and deter schoolchildren from future criminal activity, they were excused from class to attend such events.

The second King Street East Gaol (1827–1840), northeast corner of Toronto Street, sketch by John George Howard (1803–1890). The public hangings of the Upper Canada Rebellion rebels Samuel Lount and Peter Matthews took place on gallows adjacent to the prison in 1838.

Even more visible day to day in terms of punishment and public sham-
ing during Sullivan's term were the stocks and pillory, a large, heavy timber
contraption where an offender was locked in, exposing him to mockery.
Passersby were encouraged to throw objects at them, including mud, rotten
eggs, mouldy vegetables, smelly fish, and animal or human excrement.

Council members retained the power to directly hire police officers, resulting in a local constabulary recruited through political favours. The city's
earliest police force was partisan, corrupt, and inept, with no standards for
enlistment. By March 1835, Toronto had five full-time constables — one for
every 1,850 citizens, with each a political appointment for a year.

At the end of his term, Sullivan did not seek re-election and moved on
to other affairs of Upper Canada. In 1836, actions taken by Lieutenant
Governor Francis Bond Head disappointed Reformers and plunged the colony into a constitutional crisis. Head summarily dismissed a number of
Reformers from office and proved in correspondence that he was urging
abandonment of the policy of conciliation with them. However, Sullivan
decided to accept an invitation to join Upper Canada's Executive Council,
though he was criticized by some for being a turncoat. As the *Dictionary of
Canadian Biography* has noted, "Sullivan's volte-face is without parallel."
A possible reward? A few months later he accepted another appointment as
commissioner of Crown lands. One of Sullivan's own relatives pointed out
that he was "in the midst of enemies,"[5] and for a time, he became a pariah
among acquaintances and an object of rebuke by others.

Nevertheless, Sullivan proved himself to be an able manager, and Head
defended his choice, noting that the young, well-educated lawyer was a man
of superior talents and irreproachable character. As biographer David Read
noted, "He was not a party man in the strict sense. His partyism, if he had
any, consisted in his desire to advance the interest of the Province under the
aegis of Great Britain — he was a Reformer, but not a Radical."[6]

When the armed rebellion in Upper Canada broke out in December
1837, Sullivan chose to defend the colony. While he believed that reform
was necessary, armed revolt was not the remedy. On December 11, 1837, just
days after the failed uprising, he was appointed a special commissioner to
examine persons arrested for high treason.

A natural leader in the rapidly growing city, Sullivan also served in
several other capacities, specifically as vice-president of the Mechanics'

Institute, established in 1830 to provide technical courses, adult education, public lectures, and a lending library for its members. As mayor, Sullivan also served as treasurer of the Law Society of Upper Canada and in 1837 was president of the St. Patrick's Society.

In 1838, in the aftermath and turmoil of the rebellion, Sullivan was increasingly relied on by senior administrative levels and was asked to prepare a mammoth report on the state of Upper Canada. Although he noted the strong denunciation of responsible government and an elected Legislative Council by Toronto conservatives, he also warned that the neighbouring American political culture amounted to virtual mob rule and what he termed the "tyranny of a majority."[7] He also defended the Executive Council's right to claim revenues independent of the Legislative Assembly's control.

Furthermore, Sullivan's detailed report dealt with policies on immigration, finances, and land tenure. Prosperity, he said, could only be achieved by way of large-scale immigration, a rise in the value of land, and effective new public works. Although Sullivan favoured centralization of power, he offered an eloquent defence of an agrarian society composed of independent farmers as the basis of the colony's future political stability and economic prosperity.

In June 1838, Sullivan assumed the additional office of surveyor general, and the next year was appointed to the Legislative Council of Upper Canada, the chamber dealing with legal matters, property, and civil rights. Modelled after the British House of Lords, its members were appointed for life, but it was dissolved in February 1841 when both Upper and Lower Canada were merged into the United Province of Canada.

As has been noted, Sullivan had a love of intrigue, a respect for power, and a weakness for flamboyance. In October 1842, he was involved with the newly formed government of Robert Baldwin and Louis-Hippolyte La Fontaine, a ministry made up, one harsh critic said, of "fanatics, villains, or incompetents." Considered a brilliant orator who charmed with his "Irish provincial accent," he sometimes lacked conviction and a steadiness of purpose, and in the opinion of the *Dictionary of Canadian Biography*, seemed "to have dozed through his duties as president of the province's Executive Council in 1841–1842,"[8] a situation perhaps made worse with heavy drinking.

Although a well-known Protestant, Sullivan still became a target of the Orange Order. After the legislative passage of new bills dealing with party processions and secret societies in 1843, there was a huge and furious Orange demonstration in November of that year.

In the winter of 1844–1845, Sullivan joined William Blake in a campaign to reform the judicial system of Canada West (formerly Upper Canada). He was also the author of major pamphlets on key topics: colonization, the connection between agriculture and manufacturing, and responsible government.

By the mid-1840s, rapid industrial development was viewed as the solution to Canada's economic problems, and Sullivan advocated the adoption of protective duties as a means to foster needed industry. Despite his successes in the colony, Sullivan's heavy drinking and inattention to business dealings almost destroyed his career, and by 1843, he was experiencing difficulties in collecting his accounts, in sharp contrast to cousin and brother-in-law Robert Baldwin, who was fierce in pursuing payment from wealthy clients.

In 1844, however, things looked more promising. A young lawyer, Oliver Mowat (later a premier of Ontario), observed that Sullivan had joined the "total abstinence society." Yet few in Toronto's small legal community had confidence in what they viewed as an often drunken Sullivan, and the promise of change did not last. By 1848, Robert Baldwin's property manager reported that Sullivan was in serious difficulties: "It is very generally reported here that he is broken out again."[9]

After the United Province of Canada election of January 1848, Sullivan's name was proposed for one of the 11 Cabinet positions. Despite his problems, Sullivan had preferred an appointment to the bench. Yet upon the urging of Governor General Lord Elgin, his name was included as a Cabinet appointee. Sullivan, a superb orator and incisive analyst when sober, was appointed provincial secretary, becoming one of the most senior ministers of the Baldwin–La Fontaine ministry.

When he left government, Sullivan returned to the practice of law under the firm name of Sullivan & Smith before receiving his desired reward, an appointment as a justice on the Court of Queen's Bench. In January 1850, Sullivan moved from the Queen's Bench to the newly formed Court of Common Pleas where he sat until his death.

Sullivan died at his residence on Yonge Street, just north of Edward Street, on April 14, 1853, age 51. Without question one of the most talented men to serve as Toronto's mayor, Sullivan was remembered as a superb orator with a brilliant mind and capable of incisive analysis when not drinking. In his book *The Lives of the Judges of Upper Canada and Ontario*, David Read wrote that "Mr. Sullivan has sometimes been called a Tory or Conservative, sometimes a Reformer; the fact is, he was Mr. Sullivan and that was all."[10]

Value of Toronto Homes in 1835

In 1835, the value of a Toronto home was assessed based on the following assessment criteria and the wealth that they represented:

- Cultivated land or uncultivated
- A town lot or not
- Square, two sides, one-storey pleasure
- Additional fireplaces
- Framed, brick, or stone, two storeys
- Framed, under two storeys upward
- Brick or stone, one storey
- Brick or stone, not more than two fireplaces
- Merchant shop
- Stone house
- Closed carriage, four-wheel (for pleasure)
- An open carriage
- A curricle, two-wheel (for wagons)
- Dogs, three and upward
- Horses of three years old and oxen of four years old and upward
- Milk cows
- Cattle, two to four years old

Mayor Thomas Morrison

1836

The 3rd mayor of Toronto

Occupations: Physician, Province of Canada legislator, Toronto Council member, Board of Health chair, Reformer, rebel, political refugee, professor of medicine

Residence While Mayor: 57 Newgate Street (now Adelaide Street East)

Birth: 1796 in Quebec City

Death: March 19, 1856, in Toronto

——— • ———

Thomas David Morrison was elected to serve on Toronto's first Council and was a well-regarded medical practitioner in the city. To this day the only physician ever to serve as mayor of Toronto, he was an active Reform supporter of William Lyon Mackenzie, though he opposed the armed rebellion and insurrection of 1837.

Morrison witnessed the city's birth and its earliest struggles, and his life became a turbulent one. Thrown in prison for several months, he was tried for high treason and later forced to uproot himself and flee to the United States.

The Toronto of his mayoralty was still a small frontier town with no paved roads and wild geese, pigs, horses, and chickens often running free. All travel into or from the city was carried out either by foot or by horse, wagon, stagecoach, or tall ships. Trains would not make their way to Ontario for another 20 years, and it would be another 40 years before the first electric light was unveiled in the province's capital.

Morrison was born in Quebec City in 1796 where his father was a clerk with the Royal Engineers. In the War of 1812, the 17-year-old Morrison served with the purveyor's branch of the British Army's medical department. By 1816, at age 21, he had become a clerk in the Office of the Surveyor General in York (Toronto).

In September 1818, age 23, he married Effie Gilbert (though her grave at the Toronto Necropolis refers to her as Affa Morrison). Although originally an Anglican, Morrison had become, for "conscientious motives,"[1] involved with the establishment of the first Methodist church in Toronto and later became a Methodist lay preacher.

As *The Medical Profession in Upper Canada* later recounted, Morrison was dismissed in June 1822 from his position in the Office of the Surveyor General "and cast destitute upon the world"[2] for his role in helping the Methodists. For public office holders at the time, a conversion to Methodism was looked upon as a serious deviation from the official norm of Anglicanism.

The Medical Profession in Upper Canada noted that Morrison was "a person of industry, energy, and ability"[3] and that soon after he left for the

United States to pursue a medical education. Upon returning to York, he completed his examination at the Medical Board of Upper Canada in July 1824, earning a licence to practise medicine.

In politics, Morrison played an important role in the city's progressive movement of the 1820s and 1830s. Although not possessing the incessant political drive or the reformist zeal of William Lyon Mackenzie, he was a talented orator and much in demand in a close-knit, highly politicized community in which public meetings, rallies, and demonstrations occurred frequently.

Morrison first ran for office in the Town of York in the Upper Canada election of 1828. His opponent, Attorney General John Beverley Robinson, Sr., was declared elected with 110 votes to Morrison's 93. Morrison then challenged the result on the grounds of illegal voting irregularities, but Robinson's election was upheld, though Reformers won a majority of seats in the Legislative Assembly.

The young Morrison was a popular physician, establishing a large practice in both the town and adjacent rural area. He served on a new ad hoc Board of Health formed in York during the 1832 cholera outbreak and spent much of his time courageously fighting an even more deadly cholera epidemic in 1834. In August 1832, he and two fellow physician colleagues founded the York Dispensary. Lasting just eight months, it was Canada's first system of basic pharmacare, carrying out the prescribing and distribution of free medicine to some 746 patients.

Morrison was appointed to the Medical Board in early 1836, a position he held until the winter of 1837–1838. Also active in other areas of the Toronto community, he served as vice-president of the Bible Society of York, as trustee of the Toronto General Burying Grounds, and as a school trustee.

In Toronto's first municipal election in 1834, Morrison was elected an alderman for St. Andrew's Ward, joining a Reform majority. Following intense negotiations within the City Council about who to ask to serve as the city's first mayor, Morrison supported the firebrand Mackenzie. Morrison also ran for the Legislative Assembly in 1834 and was duly elected and served until 1837. He had finally gained a seat in the third riding of York, joining Reformers who had swept the other constituencies in the county.

Morrison played an important role in the Reform movement of the 1830s. A talented orator, he was in popular demand in an environment

The Scourge of Cholera

Dr. Thomas Morrison (1836), Toronto's third mayor and a leading physician in the city, dealt directly with the ravages of cholera. In addition to unsafe water, the municipality faced enormous problems: filth, disease, horse droppings, garbage, and polluted wells. Little had been done to improve sanitary conditions.

Under Mayor Joshua Beard (1854), Toronto's Council was advised in 1854 that of 292 cases, 142 residents had died and 150 were saved. The city experienced its last outbreak of cholera in 1866 under Mayor Francis Medcalf (1864–1866 and 1874–1875).

In 1866, the Provincial Board of Health circulated an extensive 12-page report on the precautions to deal with cholera, including the use of disinfectant, increased cleanliness, greater ventilation, better drainage, the use of scavengers to remove horse droppings from streets, the cleaning of yards and stables, and not using tainted or decaying animal or vegetable foods.

where political support was publicly expressed at large rallies and demonstrations. At a time when it was common for public officials to serve simultaneously at different levels, Morrison was also re-elected to Toronto's Council in 1835 and 1836. In January 1836 when Reformers regained the majority on the Council they had lost the previous year, Morrison was chosen by his colleagues to serve for a one-year term as mayor of Toronto as well as president of the Board of Health.

Toronto was growing in size and its economy was steadily progressing. Morrison's time as mayor saw the Council take action on "lighting the streets with gas"[4] and the building of the first and still very rudimentary waterworks system. Morrison was all too familiar with the fact that water was both in short supply and contaminated much of the time, which had led to the city's devastating cholera outbreaks in 1832 and 1834.

As historian Claire Mackay notes, Toronto residents caught cholera from infected food and water. The disease first begins "with terrible diarrhea and hours of vomiting. Then all the muscles of the body cramp and the skin turns blue because it's out of oxygen. Half the people who get it die, sometimes within six hours."[5]

In addition to unsafe water, Toronto also faced enormous problems due to filth, disease, and garbage. Little had been done to improve sanitary conditions. Reform-minded newspaper owner Francis Collins of the *Canadian Freeman*, who later died of cholera, waged a campaign to appoint a medical officer to clean up Toronto: "The cleanliness of the town, or rather its filthiness, ought to engage the first attention of this officer. Stagnant pools of water, green as a leek, and emitting deadly exhalations, are ... in every corner of the town — yards and cellars send forth a stench ... from rotten vegetables sufficient almost of itself to produce a plague — and the state of the Bay, from which a large portion of the inhabitants are supplied with water, is horrible...."[6]

As with earlier councils, the city had an immense interest and preoccupation with Upper Canada's affairs. In February 1836, Morrison had presented a warm welcome to Sir Francis Bond Head, the new lieutenant governor, who, it was hoped, would secure meaningful political reform. Yet it soon became apparent that would not happen, and in late 1836, Toronto's Council passed a motion of non-confidence in Bond and his administration.

In addition, when Mackenzie was defeated in the Upper Canada election in July 1836, Reformers once again turned to using Toronto's Council as a platform. Morrison himself was re-elected to the Legislative Assembly, and upon the end of his mayoral term in late 1836 did not serve again on the Council.

Daily living in 1836 was indeed a difficult ordeal: a typical four-room Toronto home was small and made from wood. Lit with candles and later kerosene, it was heated by a central stone fireplace or by an iron cooking stove with pipes. Homes contained the most basic tables, chairs, and beds. Early schools were held either in a nearby home, a general store, or a church basement.

Sawmills were key to the well-being of Toronto residents, since they provided needed lumber to construct the city's new buildings. Blacksmiths fashioned needed implements out of iron, and their hot, sweaty, grimy job was vital to the early city. In 1836, a neighbourhood general store was both a trading centre and important meeting place, and residents often bartered items or traded crops from their own property.

The mushrooming city was laid out on the basis of the original 10-block grid of the Town of York. With early factories, industrial uses, abattoirs, stables, and warehouses built immediately adjacent to homes, development in the rapidly growing city was uneven and haphazard.

Fresh water was fundamental to the early life of Toronto in 1836. It kept families' only means of transportation, their horses, alive and also allowed them to raise food (fruits, vegetables, hogs, and chickens). Water was essential for drinking, cooking, washing, and bathing, and critical to both industry and firefighting. Yet both the supply and quality of water were unreliable and at times even dangerous. Residents obtained water from just four principal sources: wells, rainwater, streams, or Lake Ontario.

A special Council committee was struck to investigate the best method "of bringing Water into the City from the neighbouring Springs," and in mid-October 1836, it recommended that the city "aid and assist ... [the] bringing of pure, wholesome water into the city, either for domestic use or any other purpose."[7]

The 1836 Council under Morrison dealt with a diverse range of topics: a salary for the Keeper of the Don Bridge; the issue of hogs running wild; waterfront wharf fees; the regulation of meat; the construction of new wooden-planked sidewalks on Yonge, Bay, and Front Streets downtown; horses running loose; and an outbreak of hydrophobia (rabies) in dogs. The Council also discussed the selection of a new town crier, thefts carried out by police constables, a prohibition on begging, and relief measures for the destitute.

One particularly vexing issue confronting the Council was tavern licences, referred to by some as a "growing evil" caused by an "immense number of small taverns licensed to retail spirituous liquors."[8] The Council established a committee to investigate why there were so many, yet ironically the city also wanted to see street improvements paid for by funds from the issuing of beer and tavern licences.

As the demands for reform in Upper Canada intensified throughout 1837, Morrison continued to play a leading public role, especially in the Legislative Assembly. He attended a meeting of Reformers at John Doel's brewery in July 1837, signed a Reform declaration, and became a member of what was called the Central Vigilance Committee. It would all come back later to haunt him.

However, as with several other leading Reformers, Morrison refused to support William Lyon Mackenzie's plan for an armed revolt and remained at home while the abortive coup took place, telling Mackenzie "if you think to entrap me in any such a mad scheme, you will find I am not your man!"[9]

Nevertheless, after the rebellion collapsed in December 1837, Toronto's third mayor was one of the first persons arrested by the militia; he was thrown in jail and held without bail for four months until a formal trial. Although not active in the rebellion itself, he was, in April 1838, put on trial for high treason.

Morrison's trial opened under a terrible pall created by the public hanging of 1837 rebels Samuel Lount and Peter Matthews, put to death just 12 days earlier. Morrison was, in effect, in a fight for his life. His defence was further complicated by Mackenzie's firebrand pronouncements from U.S. exile, as well as by the evidence of Morrison's actual signature on the earlier Reform declaration of July 1837.

Fearing for his safety and possibly being charged with other offences, Morrison also fled into exile in upstate New York where he set up a medical practice and remained for five years. In 1843, after a declaration of amnesty for 1837 rebels, he returned to Toronto and re-established himself as a physician.

Morrison did not again seek elected office. Instead, he concentrated on his medical career, serving on the boards of the Maternity Lying-In Hospital and the Gerrard Dispensary, as well as lecturing at the Toronto School of Medicine. In 1851, Morrison was appointed to a newly reconstituted Medical Board.

Dr. Thomas Morrison died quietly of palsy at his home on Adelaide Street on March 19, 1856, at the age of 60. He was remembered as a respected and highly regarded figure who played a valuable role in the early civic life of Toronto and in the health of its residents.

Mayor George Gurnett

1837 and 1848–1850

The 4th mayor of Toronto

Occupations: Journalist, Toronto Council member, police magistrate, Orange leader
Residence While Mayor: King Street West (near John Street)
Birth: 1792 in Sussex, England
Death: November 17, 1861, in Toronto

—— • ——

As mayor, George Gurnett's views were on the opposite side of the political spectrum from those of his three mayoral predecessors who had been more sympathetic to political reform. Gurnett was less so, though he gradually evolved into a city builder over time.

He was — in the overwhelmingly male-dominated municipal world of 1830s and 1840s Toronto — very much a "man's man," an establishment Tory and High Anglican who believed in the supremacy of church, sovereign, and empire. By the end of his service on Toronto's Council, he also held the honour of having one of the longest periods of uninterrupted municipal service up to that point.

Gurnett had a rotund figure, a high, balding forehead, dark, beady eyes, and small, pursed lips on a flushed, clean-shaven, round face. With his well-tended mutton chops, he had both the look and manner of a British aristocrat.

Little is known about Gurnett's early life. He was born in Sussex, England, in 1792, and in his thirties immigrated to North America, first settling in Richmond, Virginia, then in 1826 at the age of 34, moving to Ancaster in Upper Canada — today a suburb in the City of Hamilton — where some of his family were already.

After obtaining a printing press from Albany, New York, Gurnett began a career in journalism, publishing in 1827 the first edition of the *Gore Gazette* whose motto was "All Extremes Are Error." Soon, Gurnett was known as a leading advocate and propagandist for the Family Compact, Upper Canada's conservative elite.

In 1828, Gurnett was personally involved in a case of human torture when in Dundas, Upper Canada, he took part in the tar and feathering of local Reform supporter George Rolph. Although at first it sounds benign, a tar and feathering was, in fact, a brutal form of violence dating back to the Middle Ages. In 18th- and 19th-century America, it was mostly carried out by agitated mobs intent on inflicting severe pain and total humiliation on a political opponent. It was widely employed against tax officials during the American Revolution, and in the 21st century, Amnesty International has called it human torture, plain and simple.

The target in question was immobilized, beaten to a pulp, and stripped naked. Burning hot pine tar was then poured over the victim, resulting in severe first-degree burns. While his body was still roasting with molten tar, the victim was forced onto the ground and rolled in a pile of chicken feathers so they would stick to the tar. Often the person was then paraded through town in an ox cart or tied to a rail to publicly humiliate him. The tar could last up to a week, and when the victim tried to remove the feathers, he stripped off his own skin. The effects of the beating, combined with the charred flesh and searing pain inflicted by the tar, made it an agonizing form of personal human torture.

In 1829, Gurnett moved his printing press to what is now Jarvis Street in Toronto and renamed the triweekly paper the *Courier of Upper Canada*. It soon became one of the town's major anti-Reform and Tory-supporting publications, bringing Gurnett into a very personal, direct, and public conflict with his political opponent, the radical firebrand William Lyon Mackenzie.

After Toronto's incorporation in 1834, Gurnett was first elected to the city's Council for St. George's Ward, a position he held continuously until 1851. With a band of staunch Tories, he vigorously opposed Reformers on the early councils when they were in the majority in 1834 and 1836.

In January 1837, a Tory-dominated Council selected Gurnett to serve as the new city's fourth mayor by a vote of 18 to 1. The Tory-supporting *Royal Standard* was jubilant when it spoke of the triumph of conservatism.

By now, Toronto's population had grown to 10,871, almost equally distributed to the east and west of Yonge Street. A new Upper Canada Parliament building faced Front Street at Simcoe Street, with the waters of the bay, at the time, in close proximity.

In all, Gurnett spent a total of 17 years on Toronto's Council and was selected by his colleagues to serve as mayor on four different occasions: 1837, 1848, 1849, and 1850. It was during his first term of office that Gurnett really made his mark on the city. His dominance over Council affairs was so complete that William Baldwin, a respected moderate, noted that Toronto had now become "a rotten borough under the control of an ignorant and violent faction"[1,2] — a faction, he maintained, led by Gurnett.

Under Gurnett, a few sewer and road-building projects were carried out, a second open-air farmers' market (St. Patrick's) was built, and improvements commenced on Toronto's harbour. Relief for the poor during winter months led to the formation of the House of Industry, which, Gurnett believed, would help curb "the vice[s] of Intemperance, street begging, pilfering, dissipation, indolence, and juvenile depredation of the destitute." These, he observed, could be dealt with by the re-education of children, in which they would be taught "the habits of industry, sobriety, morality, and religion."[3]

Issues dealt with by the Council in 1837 included the slaughtering of cattle, the continued absenteeism of Council members, dogs and swine running at large in the city, new carpeting for the Council chamber, and the removal of manure from city streets. That year also saw the beginning of Toronto's first cab service, begun by Thornton Blackburn, an escaped enslaved man from the United States. Although illiterate, he had wisely seen the need for a taxi vehicle and had commissioned the construction of one.

Gurnett sold the *Courier of Upper Canada*, and in September 1837 was appointed a magistrate of the Home District, and shortly after became district clerk of the peace, an office he held until 1861. Yet it was the momentous events of the Rebellion of 1837, occurring at the end of Gurnett's first term as mayor, that played a pivotal role in the city's future.

By August 1837, "The Declaration of the Reformers of Toronto" had been published in the *Constitution* newspaper, and events were starting to spiral out of control. In November 1837, William Lyon Mackenzie published his *Handbill for Rebellion*, an inflammatory pamphlet in which he called upon Toronto's citizens to revolt in opposition to what he termed an "unlawful authority."[4]

Mackenzie led his rebel forces down Yonge Street to attack and occupy Toronto, the city he had headed as mayor three years earlier. In December, a 7,500-member militia, along with 1,000 Loyalist volunteers, put down the rebellion and burned the rebel headquarters to the ground. Mackenzie fled across the American border, and all of his personal papers were seized.

During the 1840s, though no longer mayor, Gurnett remained active on Toronto's Council committees dealing with the harbour, as well as gas and waterworks, but a recommendation he had proposed in 1840 to create a waterfront park was never acted upon.

After Gurnett's first wife died in 1835, he remarried, this time to Catherine Darby of Halton County in 1841. Even though six of his children passed away in infancy, two of his daughters and his second wife survived him.

A political comeback as mayor was thwarted in 1841 when Toronto's municipal election took on an unusually vicious tone. Reformers did their utmost to get rid of Gurnett and members of the city's old guard, whom they saw as a leftover collection of inept and out-of-touch Family Compact Tories. While it was assumed Gurnett would again be selected to serve as mayor, it was suddenly revealed that he was renting out a home used as one of Toronto's most notorious whorehouses. With prostitution and brothels morally unacceptable to God-fearing councillors, George Monro was instead chosen as mayor.

Returning again in the late 1840s as mayor, Gurnett continued to show administrative skills and chaired a committee to rebuild the St. Lawrence Market. As Board of Health chair, he helped combat the serious typhoid epidemic, and his views began to moderate.

Much was happening in Canada during the period of Gurnett's second mayoralty. In 1849, the Parliament of Canada granted immunity for those involved in the failed rebellion, and former mayor William Lyon Mackenzie returned to the city soon after. Also in 1849, Parliament passed a first Municipal Corporations Act and barred the immigration to Canada of "lunatics, idiots, the deaf and dumb, blind or infirm. Persons with such afflictions arriving at Canadian ports would be deported."[5]

In the city's Council, a wide range of issues were discussed between 1848 and 1850 during Gurnett's mayoral terms: payment to carters for the delivery of water to fires, the city's future boundaries, the appointment of municipal tax collectors, conflict-of-interest provisions for members of Council, issues involving the storage of gunpowder, and a visit by the mayor to New York City. Also dealt with were liquor and intemperance matters, a new bridge over the Don River, road funding, a labour union within the Fire Department, and the inspection of firewood.

The destruction and ravages of fire were key problems the city had to face during the second Gurnett mayoralty. In the 1840s, the city's firefighting capacity was made up of a half-dozen volunteer fire companies operating from a fire hall near King and Church Streets. Firefighters pulled manual pumpers by hand, while horse-drawn tankers brought water directly from the harbour.

Along with hundreds of helpless onlookers, Gurnett could only watch the devastation that destroyed the city core on April 7, 1849. The Great Fire of Toronto, as it became known, razed the central business district and St. James Cathedral itself. Claire Mackay paints a vivid picture in *The Toronto Story*. Starting in a stable just east of Jarvis and King Streets, "it spread from the straw to the pine board floors, to the stalls, to the walls, to the wood shingled roof, to the shed next door, to the rickety stable beyond."[6] Within three hours, downtown Toronto was ablaze.

The Great Fire was massive, fed by wood, cloth, paint, oil, paper, plank sidewalks, dry goods, wooden sheds, and roof shingles, as well as stables full of hay and straw and taverns jam-packed with liquor. Volunteers were able to save little, with much of the water sent to the scene already having been spilled on the deeply rutted streets between the waterfront and King Street East. Virtually the entire downtown core of Gurnett's city — more than six hectares of the main business district — was left a charred and blackened wasteland.

Yet just 15 years after Toronto was founded, its population had grown rapidly to almost 30,000 by the time Gurnett's second term ended. Scarborough had 3,700 people, while Etobicoke had 2,900. In January 1850, the effects of alcohol and the need to control hundreds of drinking shops played a major part in civic elections. As *The Toronto Story* notes, "alcohol was by far the beverage of choice. Everyone drank, even the children. Teachers drank before they taught a class. Preachers before they gave a sermon, lawyers and judges in the courtroom, and politicians most of the time."[7] Yet even that had little effect. Most Council members were re-elected without serious opposition.

By 1850, Gurnett's final term, the Council dealt with the issue of street watering to reduce the severe dust on King Street. It also addressed the role of citizens apprehending criminals and held several discussions regarding the regulation of city stables. In terms of the city's finances, Gurnett considered a truly novel scheme to invest £100,000 in lottery tickets to pay for rail expansion. In January, he chaired a public meeting to debate the matter, and even though skeptics called lotteries a "debasing and demoralizing influence,"[8] he persuaded the Council to adopt his plan, one that depended on the approval of city electors. On June 3 and 4, 1850, a vote was held, and of the 865 votes cast just 196 supported the lottery-financing scheme, with 669 opposed.

By the end of Gurnett's mayoralty, transportation was huge in the minds of Torontonians. The city was on the verge of an explosive railway boom, one fuelled by optimism, raw capitalism, and a sense of progress, reflected in the local press and by railway promoters. The sod for the very first railway in the city was turned in 1851.

Relations with the United States were improving. At the invitation of the Council and the Legislative Assembly, some 200 prominent citizens from Buffalo were invited to visit Toronto. The streets of the city were decorated with bunting, flags, and banners.

When the provincial government decided in 1850 to establish both a police magistrate's court and a recorder's court for Toronto, Gurnett was an obvious candidate for the first post. Robert Baldwin appointed Gurnett as the first police magistrate, and the approval of the Reform and liberal press demonstrated how the times had evolved. He assumed the office in January 1851, and for a decade served with distinction, also later acting as a member of the Police Commission, which was established in 1858.

Gurnett died of a sudden stroke on November 17, 1861. Although he was seen as a "Tory among the Tories, a Church and King man first, last and every time,"[9] his political career proved to be circular, from a previously solid Tory stance to one of accepting responsible government in the 1840s. Even the Reform-minded *Globe* obituary noted that Gurnett was "highly respected by all who knew him, as an upright and honourable man."[10]

Mayor John Powell
1838–1840

The 5th mayor of Toronto

Occupations: Lawyer, militia member, Toronto Council member, judge, registrar of the United Counties of Lincoln and Welland
Residence While Mayor: William (now St. Patrick) Street at the top of Graves (now Simcoe) Street
Birth: June 19, 1809, in Lincoln County, Niagara
Death: February 24, 1881, in St. Catharines, Ontario

— • —

This three-term mayor and pillar of the Tory establishment is the only murderer ever to become mayor of Toronto. Powell played a critical role in opposing the forces of rebellion and was a leading member of the Family Compact, the powerful clique of wealthy conservative families controlling the political life of Upper Canada.

Born in the Niagara region, the son of Captain John Powell and Isabella Shaw, he was the grandson of a chief justice of Upper Canada, William Dummer Powell, on one side, and General Aeneas Shaw on the other. Shaw had fought alongside the British during the American Revolution.

Married in August 1830 to Eleanor Drean with whom he went on to have eight children, Powell was a lawyer by training. In the 1837 elections, he was first elected to Toronto's Council from St. Andrew's Ward, then a long, narrow square between King and Queen Streets, west of Yonge Street and east of Bathurst Street.

Appointed a notary public in 1834 and on the barrister rolls of the Law Society of Upper Canada after 1835, Powell practised law from an office on fashionable King Street downtown. In 1837, after his election to the fourth Council, he was appointed to the influential Finance and Assessment Committee and served on the Council until 1841.

However, it was his role in fighting the rebels that propelled Powell into the mayoralty. On the night of December 4, 1837, he left the central part of the city to ride up Yonge Street to gather what information he could about reports of rebellion to the north.

Civic officials, and indeed residents of Toronto, had heard only rumours of a possible invasion, so Powell borrowed a prize horse from Sheriff W.B. Jarvis and set off to gather intelligence. However, unknown to Powell, rebels had already captured a local armoury and were now gathered at Montgomery's Tavern, preparing to march south on Toronto.

While scouting rebel movements in the vicinity of Gallows Hill (today's slope on Yonge Street between St. Clair and Summerhill Avenues), Powell was captured and taken into custody by a rebel patrol led by Mackenzie himself. However, before he could be brought to the rebel headquarters, Powell pulled a hidden pistol from under his coat. In an act of cold blood, he shot his captor, rebel captain Anthony Anderson, who was the military brains of the uprising, killing him with a single well-aimed bullet to the head. As Anderson fell off his horse, Powell galloped away.

When Powell again encountered Mackenzie, he attempted to shoot him, but his gun jammed, and Powell fled. It was indeed a sad and cruel irony in Toronto's history: the man who just a month later became the city's fifth mayor had just tried to kill its first.

As Mackenzie biographer William Kilbourn describes, Powell then stumbled back into Queen's Park "with all two hundred and more pounds of him wheezing and puffing mightily,"[1] making his way down what is now University Avenue toward Government House. Arriving exhausted and almost incoherent, Powell was one of the first to arrive back.

The following day, December 6, Mackenzie and his 500 ragged, ill-clad, poorly armed, and untrained rebels left Montgomery's Tavern and marched down Yonge Street to take over the city. Later that afternoon, he led his troops even farther south where they met a group of 20 Loyalist volunteers led by Sheriff William Jarvis.

By December 7, forces loyal to the Crown and empire were 1,500 strong and marching north to attack Mackenzie's ragtag rebel army at Montgomery's Tavern. During the rebellion's second major "battle," the rebels were routed within half an hour. Loyalist forces burned down the tavern, proclaimed victory, and leisurely marched back to Toronto. The Upper Canada Rebellion was over.

For his actions, Powell was proclaimed a hero and "saviour of the city,"[2] further enhancing both his political reputation and career. Within weeks, the 28-year-old was re-elected to the city's Council, then on January 12, 1838, was selected by his colleagues in a vote of 10–7 to serve as mayor, a position he held for three years. At just 28, Powell remains the city's youngest mayor.

His term was a period of change in Toronto. Citizens across British North America were thrilled with the coronation of their new sovereign, the young Queen Victoria, in 1838. Yet at home, city streets were filthy mud bowls, garbage was an ongoing problem, and Toronto's market building was already too small for the new, growing, and bustling community.

The aftermath of the rebellion occupied much of the city's attention. One of Powell's main concerns, perhaps to be expected, was the matter of security in the new city. That included the posting of sentries around Toronto, organizing militias in each ward, and the selection of a new chief constable. Yet city finances also remained a major preoccupation, and the Council faced difficulties even achieving a quorum.

Powell's term as mayor, though overshadowed by the fallout of the rebellion, saw a number of important initiatives addressed, including the province's conveyance of legal deeds to waterfront lots that years later produced Toronto's downtown Esplanade district. Serious discussions were also held about municipal services such as gas and water systems in a city that had now grown to more than 12,500 residents.

Powell was no fan of the remaining rebels in Toronto, calling them "a licentious and rapacious enemy."[3] A motion was thus brought before the Council to establish a committee in each ward of the city to allow every "loyal inhabitant" to volunteer "for the defence of his country and his home."[4]

The year 1838 saw the publication in Britain of *Winter Studies and Summer Rambles in Canada*, a chatty account of life in British North America by Anna Jameson, a genteel British aristocrat who had lived in Canada for just a short time. Her travel journal described Toronto as "most strangely mean and melancholy. A little ill-built town on low land, at the bottom of a frozen bay, with one very ugly church, without tower or steeple, some government offices built of staring red brick, in the most tasteless, vulgar style imaginable; three feet of snow all around, and the grey, sullen, wintry lake …"[5]

Toronto's roads, she noted, "are breaking up, and nearly impassable; lands are flooded, and in low situations there is much sickness…. Almost all the servants are of the lower class of Irish emigrants, in general honest, warm-hearted, and willing; but never having seen anything but want, dirt, and reckless misery at home, they are not the most eligible persons to trust with the cleanliness and comfort of one's household."[6]

As for Toronto's mayor, she wrote that he "complains of the increase of crime, and of poverty, wretchedness and disease … within the bounds of the city, and particularly of the increase of street beggars and juvenile depredators, and he recommends the erection of a house of industry on a large scale."[7]

A unique and sombre event — one casting a pall over the entire city — occurred early in Powell's mayoralty. At the end of the previous year's rebellion, several hundred rebel suspects had been rounded up, including Reformers Samuel Lount and Peter Matthews. In April 1838, after a lengthy and emotional trial, both were sentenced to hang, despite a plea for mercy signed by 5,000 people and presented by a kneeling Mrs. Lount.

On the political side, a provincial-municipal struggle took place under Powell's mayoralty. In 1838, it was a conflict over security within the city's confines. The Council rejected any additional role in organizing citizens to defend Toronto, proposing instead to hire additional constables. Other issues discussed by the Council in 1838 included remuneration for the clerk of the fish market, a reorganization of the Fire Department, repairs to bridges carried away by floods, and the use of space at City Hall by volunteer militia.

Two principal political factions fought for power in Toronto at the time: the Tories, who represented the entrenched establishment, and the Reformers, who spoke for a newer and rising working class. Further complicating matters was the growing presence of a powerful secret society, the Orange Order, an ultra-Protestant movement born out of the deep Old World conflict between Catholics and Protestants. Entirely pro-British, the Orange Order believed in the holy trinity of Crown, empire, and Protestantism.

Beginning in 1839 and for the next 20 years, there were 26 riots in Toronto, virtually all involving the Orange Order in some fashion. Toronto police constables, at least half of whom were members of the order and appointed by Orange-affiliated politicians, often acted in favour of Orange factions in the riots and sometimes even participated, as well.

In the aftermath of the rebellion, Powell was on hand to formally welcome Lord Durham upon his arrival in Toronto in May 1838. Durham was there to investigate the colony's political affairs, and six months later presented his official report to the Crown. It included strategies to restore peace, ensure an English-speaking majority, strengthen the influence of citizens, and establish ministerial responsibility.

Issues discussed by Toronto's Council in 1839 included an application to build a large public bath on the waterfront, better accommodation and space for the mayor and Council, the building of an ice house, negotiating a loan for the city in Great Britain, unlawful liquor licences, the continuing matter of swine running at large in the city, the collection of a tax on dogs, and the appointments of the city's weigh master, high bailiff, housekeeper, and inspectors of flour and pork.

Of enormous importance to Toronto, however, was a proposal to move the seat of government from the city. In 1839, the second year of Powell's mayoralty, rumours swirled that tiny Kingston was to become the permanent capital of the new United Province of Canada. Indeed, contractors, land speculators, and builders all responded quickly, and overnight Kingston's population mushroomed.

Daily life in Toronto remained a major challenge. Most residents could not yet afford gas, and indoor lighting was solely by candlelight. Since there was no running water in Toronto, bathing was very difficult, and travel to or from the city was still quite primitive. Some 15 years before the first trains began operation, intercity transportation was either by foot, by horse, or on a lake schooner, and involved a difficult journey of several days.

By 1840, the selection of mayor had become very heated: four candidates from the Council were nominated, with nine ballots necessary to secure the choosing of Powell again. That year the Council dealt with a range of issues: problems faced by water carters attending fires, an inquiry into licensed inns, new wooden-planked sidewalks for Yonge Street, the appointment of a city beef inspector, setting the hour of business closings at 7:00 p.m., the discrimination faced by Toronto's Black population, and a mission to Britain by Dr. Thomas Rolph to increase immigration to the city by "loyal, industrious, and intelligent Settlers from the United Kingdom."[8]

The imperial government introduced the Act of Union of 1840, whose purpose was to unite the two Canadas, Upper and Lower, under a single Parliament and make English the sole official language. The goal was to see imperialism strengthened and British investors reassured.

In January 1841, Powell was again re-elected to the Council, but it was another colleague, dry goods merchant George Monro, who was selected by the Council to serve as mayor for 1841. Powell soon lost interest in city affairs, attended the Council infrequently, and finally, that September, submitted his resignation and retired from active politics.

As soon as the union of the Canadas took place, and a month after Powell had been replaced as mayor, Governor General Lord Sydenham officially proclaimed Kingston the new capital. Supporters of Toronto argued it was a folly to abandon existing public buildings and build new ones else-where, and would be ruinous to those who had invested in Toronto.

By then, Powell had five children under 10 years of age, and he and his wife, Eleanor Drean, went on to have another three. After retiring that year from his fifth term on the Council, Powell continued to live in Toronto for another three years, serving as a judge of the Home District Court until he was appointed registrar of Lincoln County (now part of Niagara region) in 1844. Powell then moved his growing family — he was still just 35 years old — to St. Catharines where he served with distinction as registrar of Lincoln County, residing quietly on the family estate for another three decades.

As an 1880 biographical profile pointed out, Powell was well regarded in that role. He was "prompt, faithful, and efficient in discharging its duties. He seems to have kept out of politics; has secured and retained the goodwill as well as the confidence of all parties and all classes of people; and has the warm esteem of a very large circle of acquaintances."[9] The biography noted that Powell was "in comfortable health, has a clear and active mind, and observes his hours with almost the same punctiliousness that he did when in the mid-summer of life."[10]

John Powell died at the age of 71 on February 24, 1881, and his passing was covered in the *Globe* in a mere four short lines, noting that his funeral would be at St. Mark's Church in St. Catharines. Toronto's Council approved a "resolution of respect" for the former mayor.

Mayor George Monro

1841

The 6th mayor of Toronto

Occupations: Merchant, company director, Toronto Council member, Member of the Legislative Assembly
Residence While Mayor: Palace Street (now Front Street East)
Birth: July 23, 1801, in Banffshire, Scotland
Death: January 5, 1878, in Toronto

— • —

George Monro is the only mayor of Toronto appointed to the job as the direct result of a sex scandal. Yet the scandal wasn't even his — it had to do with another mayor being caught up in a controversy concerning Toronto's most popular brothel.

In early 1841, the very able George Gurnett, who had been serving as mayor, was anxious to be chosen again by Toronto's Council but was openly challenged after it was learned he had sublet a property he owned for use as a brothel by one of the city's most notorious and best-known madams. As a result, Monro was picked instead, becoming Toronto's sixth mayor for only a single year in 1841.

The son of Alexander Monro and Margaret Taylor, George Monro was born in 1801 in Boyndie, Banffshire, a small North Sea village on Scotland's far northeastern coast. The following year, he and his family made the long and difficult journey across the Atlantic by tall sailing ship, then by riverboat, wagon, and stagecoach, finally settling in the Niagara region.

After the end of the War of 1812, Monro moved to the small, dusty Town of York, and in 1815, barely 14 years old, began work as an apprentice in the retail grocery store of John Young. Demonstrating considerable business acumen at a young age, he soon joined his elder brother to establish a wholesale dry goods company on King Street East.

In 1822, Monro wed Christine Fisher of Montreal and started a family that eventually grew to four daughters and two sons. He also took part in the community and political life of York, still a small town of fewer than 3,000 at the time.

Monro later formed a second company, also on King Street in Toronto, with his brother before deciding to strike out on his own in 1824. Upon the separation of the businesses, Monro went on to become one of the city's most successful retail merchants, branding his company locally as the "Importer of British and India Goods." It was an enterprise that continued for 45 years until he retired in 1869.

As a rising young business leader, Monro developed into one of the social and financial pillars of Toronto's early establishment. A pew holder at St.

James Cathedral and a member of the Church Society, Monro also served as a vice-president of the York Bible Society and as a director of the Home District Savings Bank. Later, he was a director of both the Bank of British North America and the British America Fire and Life Assurance Company. He was also appointed a magistrate for the Town of York just prior to it becoming the City of Toronto.

In 1833, Monro became president of the Commercial Newsroom, a unique and well-used reading room, perhaps the earliest version of what today would be an internet café. Situated on the northeast side of Market Square, it was supported by subscribers, all of whom paid an annual fee of 30 shillings. Members of the provincial Legislative Assembly who lived farther than 16 kilometres from Toronto could use the room for free while in the city, as could the ship captains of steamboats plying their traffic on Lake Ontario.

At age 33, Monro served as a member of Toronto's first City Council, and from 1834 until 1845, with the exception of 1836, was the representative of St. Lawrence's Ward. During the Rebellion of 1837, he was commissioned as a captain of the York Volunteers, a local Upper Canada militia. Monro also ran unsuccessfully for the new Legislative Assembly that same year.

In 1841, he was chosen by colleagues on the Council to serve as Toronto's sixth mayor after the previous mayor was challenged on the grounds that one of his properties was a brothel. During his mayoralty, and upon the occasion of the birth of a royal son, the future King Edward VII, Monro was picked to travel to England to present the congratulations of the City of Toronto in person to Queen Victoria.

The union of the colonies of Upper and Lower Canada into the Province of Canada signalled major changes for the young city. Indeed, February 6, 1841, was truly a dark moment in the city's history. Residents awoke to hear that the capital of the United Province of Canada would be Kingston. The news was considered ruinous, with some even predicting that the city would become deserted.

Mayor Monro and the Council sent an immediate petition of protest, arguing that the new capital should, at the very least, alternate between Quebec City and Toronto. Yet, as time progressed, and even though it was damaging to the city, the move turned out not to be the fatal economic blow many had predicted.

Indeed, the winds of change were already beginning to transform the city's makeup. In Ireland, agriculture had fallen due to a serious blight, and stricken tenant farmers who depended almost entirely on potatoes were in crisis. With hunger becoming desperate, immigration to the New World became a matter of life and death.

While London, England, in 1841 was the centre of the civilized world with 2.2 million residents, the population of New York City was 313,000. By comparison, Toronto had just over 14,000 citizens.

In *Toronto from Trading Post to Great City*, Edwin C. Guillet describes the city as having "as many as 90 four-wheeled open and closed carriages and 130 gigs and pleasure waggons returned upon the assessment rolls of the city. The churches and chapels amount to thirteen, and there are numerous benevolent and other societies: eight or ten newspapers are regularly published, three of which are twice-a-week papers, the others weekly."[1]

At City Hall, issues discussed in 1841 included an ongoing problem of cattle running at large in the city; the enormous danger of fire posed by certain downtown businesses; and the budget for wood, printing, sand, auctioneer services, candles, and the hiring of horse teams. Also discussed were rabid dogs, new gasworks, the state of public schools, the quality of meat, new fishing grounds in Lake Ontario, the appointment of a flour inspector, physical improvements to the mayor's office, and new wooden-planked sidewalks on Yonge Street downtown.

The Council also deliberated whether revenues from tavern licences could be used, as was the case in Montreal and Quebec City, for needed purposes such as overnight policing, better roads and drainage, and the provision of a new source of clean, fresh water. Other issues tackled by the Council were public riots in Toronto (considered five times), preventing the annoying ringing of "auctioneers' bells,"[2] problems with respect to city tax assessment, and the borrowing of funds for a major new public city clock.

In one of the earliest known steps to fight racial discrimination in Toronto, some 85 members of the city's Black community banded together to seek help from City Hall. They were protesting travelling musical shows portraying Black people as buffoons, simpletons, or scapegoats in what some called "nigger minstrel acts."[3]

As history writer William R. Wilson noted, social conditions in the 1840s were quite turbulent. A public inquiry reported that crime was rife because "tippling houses abounded and drunkenness was endemic. Liquor enlivened every event…. Fairs, funerals, marriages, circuses, christenings — all frequently ended in 'the rude and boisterous roar of riot.'"[4] Weekend revelries in Toronto began on a Saturday and continued unabated until Monday morning, and violence was often close at hand as alcohol-fuelled arguments degenerated into physical assaults. The city's "140 licensed drinking places provided a legal bar for approximately every 100 Torontonians…. In addition, there were reputed to be many unlicensed houses."[5]

While serving as mayor in 1841, Monro also stood as the Conservative and Constitutional candidate for the provincial Legislative Assembly in a two-member riding, openly repudiating responsible government as "anti-British and unreasonable." When all the polls finally closed, Reformers won, and Monro was in last place. The Orange Order was not pleased with the results, however, and sought to vigorously oppose any triumphal Reform celebrations. When he was asked to provide protection for a Reform victory parade, Monro quickly and emphatically responded: "You may go to the Devil."[6]

As soon as they reached St. James Cathedral, Reform paraders were attacked and pelted with dirt, feces, muck, rocks, stones, and jeers. Their horses were also clubbed. When the carriages of the successful Reform candidates passed in front of the Coleraine Tavern, shots were fired. A bystander was killed and other participants wounded. The previous mayor, John Powell, arrived on the scene and read the riot act.

Fallout was severe, and the colony soon ordered a special commission of inquiry, which concluded that the indecision of local authorities amounted to collusion with the rioters and that Monro's conduct was a "dereliction of duty."[7] Yet his reputation remained intact and was not sullied by the riot or subsequent events.

There was one bright moment toward the end of Monro's mayoralty. On December 28, 1841, a few days after Christmas on a cold, crisp evening, Torontonians travelled downtown by horse, carriage, wagon, buggy, or on foot to see a new-fangled invention never before seen on dark and gloomy Toronto nights: street lighting. Toronto history writer Claire Mackay describes it well: "They were gas lamps, set on iron poles, and there were a hundred of them along King Street. Each lamp gave as much light as 10 candles, and the gas, made from coal was sold by a company that eventually became Consumers' Gas…. Children followed the lamplighter on his evening rounds, watching in wonder as he pushed his long torch under the six-sided glass shades to ignite the wicks."[8]

Stepping down as mayor after only one year, Monro continued to represent St. Lawrence's Ward on the Council from 1842 to 1845. And from 1844 to 1845, he became the new Conservative member of the Legislative Assembly for the third riding of York (taking in present-day East York). Meanwhile, in November 1844, the new capital was moved from Kingston and re-established for a while in Montreal. Later, the capital was alternated between Toronto and Quebec City.

Indeed, Monro's election to the Legislative Assembly was by way of a curious electoral twist. Although he was defeated in the riding by James Small, he was later declared elected after Small was disqualified when claims surfaced that Small did not meet the criteria for election. The assembly agreed and declared Monro elected.

Monro again ran in the same riding in the general election of January 1848 but fell victim to a popular Reformer, William Blake, who was not even in the country to campaign for the seat. Blake, the father of Edward Blake, later an Ontario premier and federal Liberal leader, was travelling in Europe at the time. That defeat ended what was described as the "peppery political career" of George Monro.[9]

Monro retired from business in 1857, enjoying his passion and lifelong hobby of gardening. As J. Ross Robertson's *Landmarks of Toronto* describes, he sat for hours at a time amid his flowers:

> Mr. Monro was a great lover of plants and flowers, and all his life made gardening a hobby…. Opposite the house on the bay shore bank was a piece of ground owned by Mr. Monro … [who] extended his hobby for gardening beyond the surroundings of his dwelling. He bought a plot of about half an acre on Front Street, between Portland and Bathurst streets, and here in a little cottage he installed a Scotch gardener named McGrath, whom he had brought from Scotland. Here Mr. Monro would pass his evenings occasionally, while McGrath paced up and down playing the bagpipes.[10]

Toronto's sixth mayor died on January 5, 1878, leaving two sons and four daughters. Upon his death, the Council approved a motion noting that Monro had "filled for nearly half a century a position of high respect and esteem ... and filled the Civic chair as Mayor of Toronto in 1841." It also noted that he represented East York in Parliament and that "his memory will be long cherished as one of the most worthy and faithful denizens of a city in which he passed his long and respected career."[11]

Mayor Henry Sherwood

1842–1844

The 7th mayor of Toronto

Occupations: Militia officer, lawyer, business leader, Member of the Legislative Assembly, Toronto Council member, judge
Residence While Mayor: 20 Windsor Street
Birth: 1807 in Augusta Township, Upper Canada
Death: July 7, 1855, in Kissingen, Bavaria, while on an extended European holiday

——— • ———

lever, driven, and possessed of a healthy ego, Henry Sherwood had
considerable abilities as a communicator, yet lacked the political skill
to cloak his prodigious ambitions under the aura of core principles.
Affable yet unloved, even distrusted at times by both Reformers and Tories,
Sherwood was known for his attraction to business and law, as well as to
professional regulation and the church.

The eldest son of Levius Sherwood and Charlotte Jones, Henry Sherwood
was born in 1807 in Augusta Township, a rural area of Eastern Ontario. The
family was from solid United Empire Loyalist stock and was close to the
colony's Tory establishment and Family Compact. Levius Sherwood had
served as Speaker in the Legislative Assembly of Upper Canada from 1821
to 1825 and on the court of the Queen's Bench.

As a young boy, Henry Sherwood received his early education at the
Home District Grammar School under Reverend John Strachan, later the
Anglican bishop of Toronto. From his teenage years, he developed a keen
interest in politics, and in June 1826, age 19, took part in an infamous riot
in which the printing presses of Reform leader William Lyon Mackenzie of
the *Colonial Advocate* were damaged by a roving mob.

The young Sherwood articled in York in the law offices of his uncle,
Solicitor General Henry Boulton, and was admitted to the bar of Upper
Canada in 1828 at the age of 21. He then practised law in Brockville, and
as with many men from an upper-class background, speculated on the sale
of land for future development. In July 1829, he married Mary Smith of
Kingston; the *Dictionary of Canadian Biography* notes that over the course
of a 26-year marriage "they had 18 children."[1]

Although Sherwood ran for election in Leeds County in 1830 at age 23,
he finished last. Later that year, he was active in efforts to establish a branch
of the Bank of Upper Canada in Brockville and was hired as the institution's
local solicitor.

In 1833, he became a director of the Saint Lawrence Inland Marine
Assurance Company, and the following year, while Toronto was incorporated as a new city, he was a candidate for the Upper Canada Legislative

Assembly seat of Brockville, losing by just one vote. Then he shifted his attention to Toronto, moving back to the city and establishing a law office on the south corner of the market building.

Sherwood was selected to serve on the first board of the Farmer's Joint Stock Banking Company and also devoted attention to the possibility of building a rail line between Toronto and Lake Simcoe, though it would still be another 20 years before railways came to the province.

In June 1836, the ambitious Sherwood returned to Brockville to again present himself as a Legislative Assembly candidate there and this time was successful, entering the 13th Parliament of Upper Canada with the help of the Orange Lodge, whose members had settled in the riding in large numbers. Sherwood held the seat until 1840.

In his first parliamentary session, Sherwood demonstrated several qualities that shaped his later public career: constituency work, debating skills, and a mastery of procedure. Politically, he was interested in reforming the medical profession, the administration of justice, and the raising of professional standards. He also proposed the appointment of a provincial immigration agent.

At the time, Sherwood was against a political union with Lower Canada, and always an upper-class patrician conservative, also opposed responsible government and an elected Legislative Council. Yet he also rejected British interference in the colony's affairs and combined a pragmatic concern for economic growth with a concern for social well-being.

When the 1837 rebellion occurred, Sherwood was appointed an aide-de-camp to Lieutenant Governor Sir Francis Bond Head and was a part of the military force dispersing the rebels at Gallows Hill. The following year, as a newly appointed Queen's Counsel, he was involved in several of the trials arising out of the rebellion and served as a judge advocate in the court martial of 44 rebel prisoners. Sherwood was also named chair of a special parliamentary committee on the political status of Upper and Lower Canada and pressed hard to ensure that a pro-British majority in Canada prevailed.

Sherwood's own dilemma was to both resuscitate a political career and improve his personal finances. As with contemporaries of a similar background, he was used to playing a leading role in society. He was a member of the Upper Canada Club (now the Toronto Club) and gave generously to several church organizations, but with a large and ever-growing family, it was a lifestyle he could not support.

By 1838, Sherwood was claiming financial hardship, and in 1841, upon running for office, he had difficulty paying for election expenses such as posting a security deposit for an appeal of his election loss. Adding to his woes, he was cut off from performing legal work for the Crown because of stands he had taken against government spending. Sherwood did manage to keep afloat, however, with some high-profile court cases and also set about to strengthen his political base by lobbying in favour of Toronto becoming the seat of government for the newly created Province of Canada.

In the first election for a United Canadas Legislative Assembly in 1841, Sherwood stood for the Tories, alongside George Monro, a well-established merchant then serving as mayor. They enjoyed support from the Loyal Orange Lodge, the Tory establishment, and Anglican bishop John Strachan.

A major riot ensued the next day after a victory parade by Reformers was attacked by Orangemen carrying knives and firearms, brought in from Scarborough by tavern owner Samuel Sherwood, Henry's brother. In the ensuing melee, an innocent Reformer was killed, yet no one was ever charged.

In January 1842, Sherwood moved into the municipal field with his election as a member of Toronto's Council for St. David's Ward, and then, by a vote of 15–5, was chosen by his colleagues to be the city's seventh mayor. In 1843 and 1844, he was again selected mayor while also remaining active in provincial politics, becoming solicitor general in the summer of 1842, still serving as mayor.

A lover of intrigue who always sought to advance himself, Sherwood was known at times for an intense and excessive ambition, as well as possessing a prickly sense of self-importance and lapses in judgment. Yet he was also seen to be an effective chief magistrate who oversaw the regulation of the city's public markets, the paving of streets, and improved tax collection.

Under Sherwood, both King and Yonge Streets were the first to be illuminated with 94 gas streetlamps, while Toronto's first rudimentary water pipes were finally started, though a vast majority of residents would not see running water or indoor plumbing for decades. As mayor, Sherwood promoted the construction of wooden-planked sidewalks and better drainage on the city's mud-filled streets.

Several issues were discussed at the Council in 1842: a pay raise for police constables, the chronic absenteeism of Council members, the management of the new lunatic asylum, measures to restrain horned cattle from running at large, and the creation of committees to deal with a host of other matters — the building of a dog pound, allowing cabs for hire, and the state of public schools.

In May 1842, Toronto was graced by international celebrity Charles Dickens, visiting just a year before publishing *A Christmas Carol*. With his bestselling works *The Pickwick Papers*, *Nicholas Nickleby*, and *Oliver Twist*, 30-year-old Dickens was the Victorian equivalent of a literary superstar.

While in the city, Dickens accepted a dinner invitation to the home of a conservative member of the Family Compact, Chief Justice John Beverley Robinson, Sr., whose dinner guests went on at length about the disadvantages of democracy, the danger of popular representation, and the pitfalls of the Reform movement. Dickens later wrote to a friend that he was appalled by "the wild and rabid Toryism of Toronto," yet he found the city itself was "full of life and motion, bustle, business, and improvement," noting the streets were "lighted with gas, the houses are large and good, the shops excellent."[2]

Sherwood twice became solicitor general of the Province of Canada while still mayor of Toronto, yet both of his tenures in the Cabinet were short. On the personal front, by the mid-1840s, he was back on a more solid financial footing.

In a March 1843 provincial by-election, he enjoyed support from powerful "Corporation" (i.e., City) interests, the Orange Lodge, several provincial officials, and even some Roman Catholics and Reformers. In the end, he won handily.

As mayor, Sherwood observed that the city's municipal offices were already too small to accommodate the expanding civic government of a bustling city, and plans were soon drawn up to build a new purpose-built City Hall that would combine municipal offices, a central market building, and a new police station.

The solid brick building at Jarvis and Front Streets (today's St. Lawrence Market South) saw its cornerstone laid in September 1844. On the second floor were the offices of the mayor, city officials, and a new Council chamber, with a balcony as the public gallery. Yet less than six years after its completion, city engineer John Howard presented the first of several reports on the state of the building.

Basement flooding meant prisoners were often knee-deep in water. During a major storm, several city creeks flowed toward Lake Ontario and flooded the jail. Shackled to the wall in chains, desperate and unable to move, some prisoners drowned, while others were forced to remain in a toxic and contaminated mixture of garbage, debris, animal waste, and human feces, washed into the jail from sewer backups.

The Council dealt with several issues in 1843 and 1844: a call to regulate stables, the problem of wandering pigs and cattle, and a severe city revenue gap arising from numerous sources, including city fines, licences, rentals, taxes, and weigh stations. In addition, the Council grappled with the serious concern over fires caused by steamboats arriving and leaving the inner harbour with their chimneys open and ash and cinders pouring out into the wind. The Council also prevented "dangerous manufacturers," such as industrial foundries, from sprouting up in the fast-growing city.

One very colourful description of Toronto during the Sherwood mayoralty was offered by O.L. Holley in *The Picturesque Tourist*:

> A large number of elegant buildings have been recently erected, and it now presents as neat an aspect as any place in Canada. The streets are paved, and the city is well lighted with gas. Water works are also in progress, which when completed will afford every family a bountiful supply of pure water, which heretofore has been taken from the lake and distributed by carts.... King Street, the great mart for merchandize, is near a mile long, mostly built in a substantial manner with brick stores or dwellings.... The population are decidedly English in their appearance and feelings.[3]

After his final mayoral term, Sherwood continued to sit on the Council until 1849, after which he carried on with provincial affairs, his first love. Although tainted by charges of excessive ambition and a perceived betrayal of principles, he was determined to forge an ongoing political career.

Sherwood's victory was overwhelming, and he returned to the Legislative Assembly with a vengeance, attacking the Baldwin–La Fontaine administration on a range of issues. When the new assembly convened in November

1844, its majority was slim, and Sherwood stepped down as mayor at the end of the year.

While in the provincial Cabinet in 1845, Sherwood also served as a director of the City of Toronto and Lake Huron Railroad Company, a lucrative posting with one of the municipality's surging and fastest-growing enterprises. In his provincial duties, he proved to be a strong debater and one of the only government ministers to wield significant political influence. Yet he could also be touchy and self-important, and in June 1846, taking offence at the Cabinet's refusal to consult him, resigned from his position. Later, from May 1847 to March 1848, Sherwood served as leader of the government and as the co-premier of the Province of Canada with Denis-Benjamin Papineau.

Although the Cabinet was short on ability and internal harmony, it did enact several important and timely fiscal measures. Provincial tariff reforms placed a duty on both British and American manufactured goods, and warehouse and bonding privileges were also extended. Amendments to mercantile law, the Criminal Code, municipal law, and the Common Schools Act were also passed.

The 1848 provincial campaign saw Sherwood returned to office, yet his government was trounced in both parts of the new United Province of Canada. Although he was not principally to blame, the election results left him both discouraged and discredited. He did gain parliamentary support to have the seat of government alternate between Toronto and Quebec, yet encountered divisions between moderate and extreme Tories. Sherwood continued to sit on Toronto's Council until 1849, as was allowed at the time.

By 1850, his political thinking had evolved further, and Sherwood was by now advocating a single structure that would unite all of British North America. He also accepted the notion of responsible government and announced his public support for an elected Legislative Council. In the general election of 1851, divisions within the Tory vote, combined with overconfidence and the sudden and final rush of Reformers, resulted in Sherwood losing his provincial seat. Although he regained it in 1853, he was already in failing health and served for just another 15 months.

To restore his health, he left Toronto for a lengthy and expensive luxury tour of Europe (minus his 18 children). In April 1855, a Toronto newspaper reported that he was in Rome and noted, "His health is greatly improved."[4] While still on that tour, however, Henry Sherwood passed away in Bavaria in today's Germany on July 7, 1855, at age 48.

Mayor William Boulton

1845–1847 and 1858

The 8th mayor of Toronto

Occupations: Lawyer, Toronto Council member, Member of the Legislative Assembly, deputy grand master of the Loyal Orange Lodge for British North America
Residence While Mayor: Wellington Street West
Birth: April 19, 1812, in York (Toronto)
Death: February 15, 1874, in Toronto

—— • ——

Henry Sherwood's successor as mayor was William Boulton, whose downtown Toronto residence is what today is known as The Grange (beside the Art Gallery of Ontario). In the 19th century, its front gates faced onto John Street, and the family estate covered a wide area northwest of the downtown.

William Boulton is the only mayor of Toronto not even in the city when chosen to serve as chief magistrate. Boulton was in Montreal, attending a session of the Legislative Assembly of the United Canadas in his capacity as an elected member for Toronto. It would be another month before he returned to the city to assume his mayoral duties.

With both a respect for tradition and also an instinct for populist politics, Boulton understood the power and political importance of the Orange Lodge, of which he was a proud member. He was both feared and disliked by Reformers such as William Baldwin and George Brown, who did not appreciate his non-intellectual approach to issues. Boulton was known for his affable personality and the ability to enjoy either a formal dinner in the officers' mess or campaigning on the street.

Toronto's eighth mayor was the eldest son of Chief Justice D'Arcy Boulton and Sarah Robinson and belonged to a third generation of the Family Compact, the province's Protestant, pro-British Tory elite interrelated through marriage, family, society, and business.

Called to the bar in 1835 at the age of 23, William Boulton joined the prestigious legal partnership of Gamble and Boulton and married Harriette Dixon. In 1840, he acted as treasurer of one of the most important sporting events in the city, the Toronto Races, an annual two-day horse-racing competition that had begun in 1837. By 1841, it was held on the spacious grounds adjacent to The Grange. Boulton also hosted the organizational meeting of the first Toronto lodge of the Independent Order of Odd Fellows and was chosen to be its first "grand noble."[1]

In the next few years, Boulton emerged as an important figure, making use of his family influence and association with the emerging power of the Orange Lodge, whose interests he later served as deputy grand master for

British North America. In addition to its fervent advocacy for the empire and contempt for both Roman Catholics and Americans, the Orange Lodge believed in maintaining the economic status of Toronto's propertied class.

First elected to the Council from St. Patrick's Ward in 1838 at the age of 26, Boulton retained the seat until 1842, serving as a member of several key city committees: Police and Prisons, Markets, the Board of Health, and the Board of Works. After an absence of one year, he returned to serve again on the Council from 1844 until 1847 and was selected by colleagues to serve as mayor for four terms: 1845, 1846, and 1847, and then later in 1858.

Toronto's city limits at the time were Bathurst Street on the west, Dundas Street to the north, Parliament Street on the east, and Lake Ontario to the south. By 1845, the city had grown rapidly, and Sir R.H. Bonnycastle described Toronto as "a city in earnest, with upwards of 20,000 inhabitants — gas-lit, with good plank sidewalks … with sewers and fine houses of brick or stone." Toronto's main thoroughfare, King Street, was, he added, "two miles" in length "and would not do shame to any town, and has a much more English look than most Canadian places have."[2] That said, it could also be a corrupt and at times even a wild place to live, with frequent riots over political differences and religious affiliations, and more than 140 licensed taverns dotting the city landscape.

Boulton's dual career as both mayor and a representative in the Legislative Assembly began in 1844 when he stood for the Tories along with Council colleague Henry Sherwood. The *British Canadian* publication called him "shrewd, prompt, and persevering."[3] His electoral support came largely from the working classes, with *Globe* founder George Brown complaining that Boulton would continue to hold their support throughout his political career.

When Boulton entered the Legislative Assembly in 1844, a major issue was a Reform bill making King's College a secular institution, a proposal Boulton was firmly against. Coming from a strong Church of England family, he tried consistently to protect what he considered the rights and privileges of his church.

Boulton was a colourful figure with varied interests. He was an enthusiastic sportsman and was instrumental in the building of St. George's Anglican Church. Once, while the Council was debating salaries, he was informed there were some back streets in the city that could not be paved for lack of funds. So he instructed the Council to leave his salary money with the city's treasury "for the benefit of the community."[4] Yet he also had a more ostentatious side: when he was selected mayor in 1845, he ordered a gorgeous mayoral robe of scarlet trimmed with ermine. Clad in the magnificent gown, Boulton rode by horse to City Hall to preside over the deliberations of the Council.

A number of other items were considered by the Council that year: road improvements, a request for wooden-planked sidewalks on Parliament Street, and the creation of a new Council committee to regulate livery stables. Also included was a review of the mayoral power of being able to fire someone at will. Boulton had suspended Constable William Davis in December 1845 for being drunk on duty, yet the young Davis had fought back. It was, in fact, the mayor who was drunk, not him, he declared.

One of the highlights of Boulton's mayoralty was to supervise the opening of the new City Hall at Front and Jarvis Streets. By the fall of 1845, senior officials and members of the Council began working out of the new building, which remained their home until 1899.

December 19, 1846, a midway point of Boulton's mayoral term, also marked a major revolution in communications in Canada: the inauguration of the telegraph. At the time, it had the same impact on society as the internet did some 150 years later. Prior to December 1846, there had been no ability for timely communication between distant points. It was still a decade before train travel, and all communication between Toronto and other cities or towns required days of travel by horse or tall ship. The telegraph rendered contact instantaneous.

Toronto's Council considered several items in 1846 and 1847, including sewer rate charges, dealing with the problems of vagrancy, the watering of King Street, restricting the construction of wooden buildings to reduce the number of fires, improving property assessment, regulating furnaces, and erecting of tollgates.

Social concerns during Boulton's mayoralty were also reflected by Council measures "for the arrest and punishment of idle, drunken, vagrant, and disorderly persons," as well as "apprehending destitute orphans without legal guardians." The Council also dealt with the matter of "dangerous and offensive factories"[5] in the growing city and ordered that they be built of brick and stone and not wood and that factory roofs be covered in tin, tile, or sheet metal.

Terrible Typhus

In 1847, under the mayoralty of Mayor William Boulton (1845–1847 and 1858), 38,560 Irish Famine migrants emigrated from Ireland to Toronto at a time when the city's population was only 20,000.

The Irish who arrived in Toronto were unskilled labourers desperately weakened by famine and often sick with typhus contracted on the filthy, overcrowded, rat-infested ships used to transport pigs, cattle, and horses, not passengers. The fever, chills, headache, rapid breathing, nausea, vomiting, and confusion from typhus caused untreated victims to die within three to four days. Temporary fever sheds were erected downtown where more than 1,000 people succumbed to typhus and other illnesses.

Toronto was still without proper lighting, sewers, water service, or indoor plumbing, and the thousands of starving and mainly Irish Catholic refugees were unwanted and unwelcomed by many of the city's established residents.

Elsewhere, the greatest humanitarian crisis of the century — the Irish Potato Famine, in which more than a million people had died and an equal number fled their homeland — was raging. By 1847, thousands of sick, destitute, and dying Irish refugees had landed in Toronto, overwhelming the existing population and causing a health crisis. Temporary fever sheds were erected downtown, and more than a thousand people succumbed to typhoid and other illnesses.

The city was still without proper lighting, sewers, water service, indoor plumbing, paved roads, or electricity, and thousands of starved and struggling Irish refugees were unwanted and unwelcome by many in the city. The arriving Irish were unskilled labourers, desperately weakened by famine, and often sick with typhus contracted on ships used to transport pigs, cattle, and horses, not passengers. That they were mostly Catholic made them all that much more unwanted.

The Orange-controlled city had as its first order of business the ridding of as many Irish as possible. They arrived anywhere from 300 to 500 at a time, with healthy ones sent to immigrant sheds for 24 hours. Once that period expired, they were forced to move on and their rations were ended. If found on the streets begging, they were often imprisoned.

Retaining his Legislative Assembly seat in the Conservative debacle of 1847–1848, Boulton had warned electors that their interests would be sacrificed in favour of "Tobacco-smoking, Dram Drinking, Garlic Eating Frenchmen."[6] Yet he surprised his Conservative colleagues in 1850 by proposing amendments to the constitution to more fully develop an "elective system."[7]

Boulton boasted that "he owed his election to … the bone and sinew of the country, the mechanics, the artisans and labourers"[8] and to the Orange Order, grateful for his efforts to repeal the 1843 act that had restricted marches and processions. In his role as an Orangeman, Boulton had risen to become deputy grand master of British North America in 1854.

In 1858, Boulton was chosen by his colleagues on the Council to serve again as mayor. A keen interest of Boulton during his second mayoralty was the Provincial Agricultural Association, in which he played a lead role to erect a permanent exhibition building for agricultural and industrial arts. A major new structure, The Crystal Palace, was opened in 1858, with annual exhibitions held there until 1866.

Yet the city's infrastructure was unable to keep pace in 1858, as was later noted by George Ure in *The Hand-Book of Toronto*: "While we have nearly 100 miles of streets opened, there is not now in all more than 15 to 20 miles of pipe laid, and a great proportion of that is useless."[9]

The Council discussed a range of issues in 1858, including the approval of a jail plan for the city and a look into contracts awarded for construction of the new industrial farm. Alderman Robert Moodie appealed to colleagues for a crackdown on city brothels and to "provide punishment of keepers of houses of ill fame."[10]

Lighting from the city's new gas lamps was in high demand, and their installation on Bathurst, Church, and Bloor Streets was approved. The Council was also asked to do something about cows running at large, and with the severe danger of fires always top of mind, the Board of Insurers asked the city to stop the erection of wooden buildings.

During Boulton's final term, water proved to be a huge issue. The insufficient supply of it was foremost on people's minds, and the Council was advised to tread carefully when considering a purely private system.

Water was commonly available from wells and also from roof rainwater, yet a city staff report informed the Council that an increased use of coal and "rain falling through an impure atmosphere upon the soot and other filth accumulated on the roofs" were affecting the city's water supply, in addition to the "continually increasing pollution of the wells by cesspools, drains, sewer, and renderers."[11]

One major event in August 1858 had an international dimension. In a sign of substantial progress, coming barely two years after the first railway link between Toronto and Montreal, Mayor Boulton called a special meeting of the Council to recognize the completion of the Atlantic telegraph cable, linking Britain and North America with its first instantaneous communications link.

No longer would it take days to get news from across the ocean. A celebratory message from Queen Victoria to U.S. president James Buchanan was read, and the Council approved a lofty motion calling it "an event of the highest importance in the History of the Triumph of Science, [and] of incalculable value to commerce."[12] In 1858, the immediate linkage of two continents was an occasion of such importance that the Council declared a special holiday.

Boulton resigned as mayor on November 8, 1858, after a serious quarrel with Chief of Police Samuel Sherwood, brother of former mayor Henry Sherwood. He was succeeded by noted lawyer David Read, who assumed the job for a month and a half, the shortest period of any Toronto mayor.

In January 1859, Boulton chose to seek the mayoralty again in the first municipal election in the city's history in which electors voted directly for mayor instead of the Council making the selection behind closed doors. However, he was defeated by populist Reform lawyer Adam Wilson, who was supported by noted newspaper editor George Brown and his Municipal Reform Association.

After leaving politics, Boulton departed Canada to travel in England and on the Continent. He had suffered a recent string of political defeats: a failed bid for his seat in the 1857 Legislative Assembly election, his resignation as mayor in 1858, and his subsequent defeat in the first direct mayoral election in 1859. All of that led to his retirement from politics.

Boulton continued to practise law in Toronto. His former residence, The Grange, is now an integral part of the Art Gallery of Ontario and a National Historic Site.

Mayor John Bowes

1851–1853 and 1861–1863

The 9th mayor of Toronto

Occupations: Merchant, business leader, Toronto Council member
Residence While Mayor: 76 Church Street (later 296 Front Street West)
Birth: 1812 near Clones, County Monaghan, Ireland
Death: May 20, 1864, in Toronto

——— • ———

A barrel-chested Irishman with a reputation as a true man of the people, Toronto's ninth mayor, John George Bowes, was a popular figure in town and the city's longest-serving mayor of the 19th century, presiding over six one-year Council terms.

Of medium height and build, Bowes was a handsome man who enjoyed physical prowess and vigorous exercise and was praised for both his geniality and business acumen. A Council colleague, Samuel Thompson, observed that "in educational affairs, in financial arrangements, and indeed in all questions affecting the city's interests, he was by far the ablest man who had ever filled the civic chair."[1]

The son of Thomas Bowes and Margaret Speer, John Bowes was born in 1812 in Clones, a village in County Monaghan on the border of today's Northern Ireland and Republic of Ireland. He came to Upper Canada in 1833 at the age of 21 and worked for his brother-in-law, the noted York (Toronto) merchant Samuel E. Taylor, in his dry goods store at 181 King Street East.

In 1838, Bowes married Anne Hall and had 10 children with her over 18 years. When Taylor died in 1838, Bowes took the leap, and with his brother-in-law, opened his own successful wholesale dry goods business. By 1840, they were able to buy the well-established firm of Buchanan, Harris, and Company at the corner of Yonge and Wellington Streets, renaming it Bowes and Hall. It flourished over the next 10 years, and by 1851, Bowes became sole owner of the most successful dry goods operation of its day.

Two important railway positions were held by Bowes: president of the Toronto and Guelph Railway Company and an original business leader in the incorporation of the Grand Trunk Railway. He was also president of the St. Patrick's Society, president of a savings society, and director of several business enterprises.

Bowes was known for his personal generosity to both charitable institutions and needy individuals. Although conservative in his politics, his views were often more liberal in outlook. With Adam Wilson, a future mayor, he successfully oversaw the establishment of scholarships for exceptional common school graduates, allowing them to attend the Toronto Grammar School. In November 1847, he accepted an appointment by the city's Council to sit on the first Board of Trustees for the Common Schools.

With his flamboyant style, personal popularity, and optimistic attitude, Bowes was intent, by way of his many private and public dealings, to promote Toronto and its burgeoning metropolitan aspirations. In 1850, he was elected to the Council from St. James's Ward, and just a year later, in 1851, was chosen by members of the Council to be the ninth mayor of Toronto. He was again returned to that office in 1852 and 1853.

In the early 1850s, Toronto was on the cusp of change. Prior to the Irish famine, there were just 2,000 Catholics in the city. Ten years later, they made up 27 percent of the population. Irish itinerant labourers moved around the city to find work, while unskilled Catholics faced considerable racism, class bigotry, and religious prejudice, and were sometimes portrayed in the local press — George Brown's *Globe* in particular — as apes in clothes. Signs bearing a simple message, NO IRISH NEED APPLY, were commonly posted in Toronto.

To understand the Toronto of Bowes's first mayoral term, one has only to look at the composition of the city's population. Of the 30,000 residents, just over 28,000 were from the British Isles (England, Scotland, Ireland, or Wales), and the population was still overwhelmingly Protestant, pro-British, and pro-empire, as well as anti-American, anti-French, and anti-Catholic.

Toronto's Council between 1851 and 1853 was busy: it discussed 10-pin bowling, the increased watering of Bay Street, and the regulation of taverns and beer houses. Payments were approved for coffins, lightning rods, glazing, tin work, weigh scales, gas fittings, coal, stovepipes, candles, lime, wood, and coroner services.

Only three years after a raging inferno destroyed much of the city's downtown, fire remained a huge concern, with the Council discussing a range of issues on the subject: alarms, brigades, hydrants, inspectors, insurance, wooden buildings, and the cause of calamitous fires through the ongoing work of a committee on fire, water, and gas.

And though rail transport had not reached Toronto yet, it occupied an increasing amount of the Council's time: railway matters were discussed 38 times in 1851, 50 in 1852, and 94 in 1853. Yet it was on May 16, 1853, that the city was truly transformed forever. On that date, the very first Canada West (Ontario) train departed Toronto for Aurora, and in July of that year, the Grand Trunk Railway became the province's most important transportation conglomerate, formed by an amalgamation of smaller rail companies.

Indeed, it was his eye for making a profit, a knack for shrewd investments, an interest in railways, and a desire to expand commerce that led Bowes into a major conflict-of-interest scandal in 1853, called the "Ten Thousand Pound Job,"[2] a reference to British pounds. Francis Hincks, the co-premier of the Province of Canada, and Bowes were accused of manipulating the transaction for a personal advantage, and both the Council and the Legislative Assembly established committees of investigation, yet the final reports absolved the two of any dishonesty. The Council heard that while Bowes was guilty of a lack of candour he had done nothing illegal and should be exempt from further censure. Yet eight of the 28 sitting Council members were outraged and submitted their resignations.

A legal case against Bowes was brought forward by respected Toronto lawyer and future premier of Ontario Oliver Mowat to recover the share of funds Bowes was suspected of engineering. While the court did not find Bowes guilty of fraud per se, it did order him to pay back any profits. That decision was later upheld by both the provincial Court of Appeal and the Judicial Committee of the Privy Council in Great Britain. Although legally innocent, Bowes was viewed as not acting in the public good and withdrew briefly from civic politics.

While he did not seek a fourth mayoral term in 1854, Bowes's political career was far from over. During the provincial election that year, he was elected to the Legislative Assembly, defeating former mayors Henry Sherwood and William Boulton. Holding the seat until 1858, he supported an expansion of the separate school system, earning him the bitter opposition of George Brown and the *Globe*.

Bowes championed Toronto's interests in the assembly by supporting a settlement of the city's northern boundary, the building of new municipal waterworks, new waterfront development, an improved bankruptcy law, and legislation to create the British Bank of Canada.

In 1856, Bowes re-entered municipal politics as a member of the Council for St. David's Ward. By 1861, the position of mayor was a publicly elected position and no longer a secret, closed-door selection by the Council, which set the stage for Bowes's return.

Both the city and province had changed markedly since Bowes's first mayoral term. Under his watch, the railways' explosive growth had taken over the city. As Claire Mackay observes in *The Toronto Story*, by the 1860s, it was an unstoppable fact of life: "Twelve miles of track became 2,000. And all of these railroad lines came together on Toronto's waterfront. The dream — to turn the lakeside into a beautiful park, where children could swim and play, where their parents could promenade in the healthful air — was now a nightmare. The City Council caved into the pressure from the railway owners. They were, so to speak, railroaded."[3]

What the railways did, however, was spur industry, growth, and development. New factories, warehouses, "and businesses to serve the factories sprang up everywhere. Toronto bubbled with energy and wallowed in money."[4] By 1861, the population of Canada West had grown to 1.4 million residents, and a first resolution calling for the union of all British North American colonies into a single federation called Canada was circulated to senior colonial officials.

Also in 1861, the outgoing, genial, and still-popular Bowes spent lavishly on what was called Toronto's first pork-barrel style municipal election campaign, establishing, in particular, a political power base among his fellow constituents of Irish background.

With Bowes as chief magistrate once more, the city made arrangements to provide a horse and buggy for the police chief, and in September 1861 began its first-ever public transit system, the privately owned Toronto Street Railway (TSR), which used wooden tracks and horse-drawn streetcars along Yonge Street from downtown to the city's northern border. Toronto had become one of the first cities in North America to acquire this "symbol of progress and pride."[5]

Indeed, the launch date of September 10, 1861, proved to be a day that transformed the city. The first streetcar was hitched up at 4:00 p.m. and departed to the accompaniment of an artillery band and spirited cheers. Horse-drawn streetcars ran every half-hour 16 hours a day. In the winter, their frozen passengers travelled in the open with no windows, stove, or heat. Yet, under Bowes, it was a major travel improvement over the prior ruts, potholes, dust, dirt, and rotting planks that covered streets of pure mud. And in typical John Bowes fashion, the mayor himself at one time held a major financial interest in the TSR.

During Bowes's second set of three-year mayoral terms, the Council also dealt with a range of issues: the Anglican bishop of Toronto requested an extension of the time period within which wooden buildings could no longer be built, a new bylaw was brought in to govern chimney sweeps, and the Council provided aid to "the School for the Deaf, Dumb, and Blind."[6]

To encourage the manufacture of cotton and woollen goods, the Council exempted them from municipal taxes. Other matters included enacting a new bylaw to prevent "the Keeping of Gambling Houses,"[7] while Bowes was asked to issue a mayoral proclamation prohibiting the running at large of all dogs in the city. The Council also defeated a motion to pay the mayor a salary of $2,000, agreeing instead by a vote of 11–10 to $500.

In terms of daily life, a report to the Council in early 1862 from the chief constable revealed that 4,470 crimes had been reported the year before. There were 187 cases of selling spirituous liquors without a licence, 113 for vagrancy (37 of whom were women), eight for housebreaking, three for stealing cattle or horses, and one of rape.

During Bowes's final year as mayor, one of the most colourful motions ever was filed with the Council. Moved by Alderman Carr and seconded by James Smith, a future Toronto mayor, the motion asked for the creation of a select committee of the Council to "examine and report to this Council at as early a day as possible, the state of the Official Staff, Employees, Servants, and all persons receiving remuneration from the Corporation, with a memorandum of their duties, salaries, names, etc.… and how many of such persons are incompetent, inefficient, or whose services might be entirely dispensed with advantageously to the interests of the City."[8]

In January 1864, as a provincial controversy over separate schools was at its height, Bowes sought re-election as mayor, yet this time was narrowly defeated by Francis Medcalf, grand master of the Loyal Orange Lodge, who was strongly supported by the notoriously anti-Catholic George Brown and his newspaper, the *Globe*.

Bowes died in Toronto in 1864 at the age of 52, leaving a widow and nine children. His funeral was attended by a wide range of citizens from all classes. Even the opposing *Globe* noted that "as a businessman he had few

equals in the community," and that though he was "shrewd, observant, and
calculating," he was "to all, a kind, generous man."[9]

SPECIAL NOTE: Between 1851 and 1853, John Bowes was chosen as mayor
by Toronto's Council and not by citizens at large. Later, after changes were enacted, Bowes was elected by Toronto voters at large between 1861 and 1863
and not by members of the city's Council.

Mayoral Election in 1861

CANDIDATE	VOTES
John Bowes	2,189
Matthew Crooks Cameron	1,793

Mayoral Election in 1862

John Bowes	1,624
Samuel Sherwood	1,280

Mayoral Election in 1863

John Bowes	1,943
William Henderson	748
Samuel Sherwood	434
William Henry Boulton	28

Mayor Joshua Beard

1854

The 10th mayor of Toronto

Occupations: Merchant, builder, Toronto Council member, real-estate developer, school board chair
Residence While Mayor: 212 Jarvis Street
Birth: August 23, 1797, in Mottram-in-Longdendale, Cheshire, England
Death: November 9, 1866, in Toronto

—— • ——

With the exception of just three years — 1836, 1848, and 1853 — Joshua Beard was a member of Toronto's Council representing St. Lawrence's Ward for 20 years. The son of George Beard and Mary Lowe, he was born in August 1797 in Mottram-in-Longdendale, just east of the Greater Manchester area of central England. As a young man in 1824, Beard made the long voyage to Upper Canada, settling in the colonial outpost of the Town of York with the express aim of making his fortune.

He soon started his own business, and within a few years, became the largest and most successful coal-and-wood merchant in the growing community. The firm of J.G. Beard & Sons was located near the lake at the bottom of Jarvis Street and included a large wharf and grain elevator. In addition to being a considerable property holder, Beard was a local contractor, owner of an iron foundry, and held an interest in Beard's Hotel.

In September 1826, age 29, Beard married Elizabeth Jane Marsh, 23, at St. Peter's Anglican Church in Cobourg, Ontario. His wife was later described as a woman of many talents, active in charitable works, and a noted singer, as well as being the lead soprano in the choir of St. James Cathedral.

In the late 1820s, the town's economy was bustling, and in a very entrepreneurial spirit, Beard turned a corner lot used to grow cabbages into the site of an inn, tailor's shop, printing office, and grocery store. Having this desirable property at the southeast corner of what is now King and Jarvis Streets was one of the keys to Beard's success.

By 1830, the brick building he erected became a hotel called the Crown Inn, operated by local tailor and businessman Thomas Moore, who relocated his tailoring business there. With no stables attached, it was patronized mostly by local residents and tradespeople. The inn remained open for about 10 years, with other businesses sharing space in the building. From 1829 to 1837, the printing and newspaper offices of former mayor George Gurnett's *Courier of Upper Canada* were upstairs.

Beard was a deputy sheriff by 1833 and well known as the owner of extensive stove works in the town. In 1834, the year in which York became the

City of Toronto, Beard was elected to its first Council from St. Lawrence's Ward in a fall by-election to replace the original member who had died in September.

As Toronto grew, the Church and Front Street neighbourhood became a main focal point for transportation, markets, municipal and judicial affairs, hotels, and entertainment. In addition to the Crown Inn, Beard was later connected to a small wooden-framed hotel operated by B.R. Snow at the northeast corner of Church and Colborne Streets. From 1841 to the late 1840s, it was a popular and well-patronized establishment favoured by country folk coming into the city, since it was connected to adjoining stables that were quite extensive for the time.

In 1848, the original frame building was demolished, and in its place, Beard erected a new brick structure where several hotelkeepers operated what became Beard's Hotel. The new hotel was occupied successively by D.B. Snow, Robert Beard, Azro Russell (of the family that owned Quebec City's venerable Hôtel Saint-Louis), and John Montgomery, who had once been the proprietor of Montgomery's Tavern, the headquarters of the Upper Canada Rebellion of 1837.

In the days of the old Parliament of Canada, Beard's was notable for its cuisine and became one of Toronto's most popular hotels, patronized by leading merchants, business leaders, government officials, and Members of Parliament. Beard's Hotel in the early 1850s enjoyed "a great share of the patronage of the fashionable and general public" and gained even more from "the prosperity of the city of Toronto with its certain rapid advancement."[1] The hotel's upper floors were occupied by the Knights Templar, while its handsomely furnished meeting hall was considered one of the best Masonic lodges in Canada, with other rooms leased to the Orange Order.

And the city continued to evolve. In *Toronto from Trading Post to Great City*, Edwin Guillet observed that "at the middle of the century the chief places of public resort for no small section of the population appear to have been the 152 taverns and 208 beer shops which dotted the city in 1850 — the inhabitants then numbering about 30,000. Many men 'loaded up' every Saturday night (if not oftener) and spent the weekend drunk."[2]

As a member of Toronto's Council, Beard witnessed nine mayors come and go prior to assuming the city's top post himself in January 1854. With his respectability, business acumen, and length of service, he was the unanimous choice of the Council for the 1854 mayoralty, becoming the 10th chief magistrate in the young city's history.

Toronto was still reeling from the effects of the previous year's scandal, the "Ten Thousand Pound Job," and the resignation of eight Council members in protest. Yet Beard's term as mayor did not start off well. He became very ill in January 1854, just weeks after taking office, and could not assume his role as mayor for several months. John Beverley Robinson, Jr., was appointed to act in his place until Beard regained his health and was able to resume the function.

Beard returned to the mayoralty in April, whereupon he was also appointed a commissioner of the Toronto Harbour Trust. For the rest of his term, things went smoothly, much to the relief of the Council. One of the major reasons Beard had been chosen was his stature, integrity, and financial standing. With scandal plaguing the city's business dealings the year before, it was expected that Beard would be immune to the seductions and temptations of bribery, manipulation, or even coercion.

That hope proved to be right. The Council was able to get through its regular business such as planning an esplanade and dealing with rail matters, public works, and sewer construction without controversy, scandal, or problems. As the mercantile centre of Canada West in the mid-1850s, Toronto was still a growing young city whose population rose from just over 30,000 residents in 1851 to 45,000 several years later.

In the early 1850s, the Toronto Board of Trade highlighted the rapid strides of domestic industry since the 1840s, which included new foundries, tanneries, breweries, distilleries, factories, gristmills, paper mills, and manufactories, as they were called then. These were a significant change from the small, cramped, cottage-like craft industries located across the city.

The new railways spurred Toronto's first large industrial enterprises, while the steel ribbon of tracks along the lakefront also transformed the city's core. For the next decade, warehouses, rail sheds, wharves, factories, shanties, and supply houses congested the entire area. Yet, in some ways, the city was still a small town. As Reverend Henry Christmas noted in *The Emigrant Churchman in Canada*: "In Toronto, even cows and pigs are occasionally seen running loose about the town, though contrary to law, frequently pursued by half the dogs in the parish."[3]

Toronto's Earliest Issues

In its first 20 years, the City of Toronto had 11 mayors. Still a dusty colonial outpost, it had no paved streets and no lighting, sewers, piped water, or indoor plumbing. All travel to or from Toronto was by foot, horse, wagon, stagecoach, or tall ship. Trains did not arrive until the mid-1850s.

Toronto's earliest Councils regularly dealt with the problems caused by swine, dogs, wild geese, pigs, horses, cattle, and chickens running free. Indeed, in a bustling city where a horse was the principal means of transport, the streets were filthy. Droppings from thousands of horses fouled the streets and threatened public health. Spring was the worst time: filth mixed with slush and melting snow and spread across entire thoroughfares.

Life in Toronto was not easy during its earliest years. Ever-present menaces confronted city residents: stagnant water, dust and grime, horse droppings on every street, decayed garbage, rotting wooden-planked sidewalks, roads of pure mud, and danger from carts, coal deliveries, stagecoaches, or runaway horse-drawn wagons.

Toronto newspaper accounts in the 1850s paint a lurid picture of the battle against theft, assault, brawling, prostitution, larceny, and public drunkenness. The Board of Health eventually brought in new efforts to deal with the pollution of thousands of daily horse droppings, hiring seven scavenger carts to collect filth from the street.

Almost 50 years into its creation as a city, Toronto elected as mayor William McMurrich (1881–1882), who called for major streets to be swept daily and for all refuse, garbage, and horse manure to be removed. Yonge Street, he noted, was overcrowded with horses, dogs, bicycles, wagons, coaches, buggies, livery cabs, and pedestrians.

By 1890, Mayor Edward Clarke (1888–1891) and the Council were grappling with the unauthorized dumping of "night soil" — the manure droppings scraped off streets — into Lake Ontario near the city's main water intake pipe.

For those with money, handsome horse-drawn livery cabs were available to hire, while for everyone else there were slow, dusty, creaky open carriages. Toronto's first public transit system was a sluggish open-air streetcar pulled by horses on a rudimentary rail line that did not begin until 1861.

When there was a recurrence of cholera in 1854, the powers of the Board of Health were increased, particularly in light of a severe outbreak. With its profuse vomiting and diarrhea, cholera often starts just days after contracting the bacteria. Left untreated, its life-threatening dehydration has fatal consequences. In 1854, the Council was advised that of 292 cases, 142 residents had died and 150 were saved.

Cholera-related items requiring immediate payment at the city included lime, wearing apparel for patients, wages, building sheds, internments, and the transport of bodies. The Council was also informed that certain public works could not be finished because "of a scarcity of labour as a result of people leaving the city due to the cholera epidemic."[4]

The Council's Standing Committee on Fire, Water, and Gas unanimously recommended a thorough review of bringing pure water down into the city from Lake Simcoe, believing it possible to do so for the same cost as the existing method of using fresh water from Lake Ontario. Indeed, water was also a major concern when the Council accused entrepreneur Albert Furniss and his private water company of supplying it with "impure water." Another report called the bills from the water company "extortionate"[5] and cut off its supply until they could be reviewed.

A house was also found by the Council on Yonge Street to serve as a police station. The property had enough space for an officers' sleeping room, a prisoner lock-up, and a residence for the sergeants. The Council also approved two police officers being stationed on the city's main wharf to meet the arrival of every steamship coming into the city.

A former mayor, George Gurnett, wrote the city to complain about the foul air, terrible odour, and bad ventilation of the police station downtown, while the Council approved the increase of fares for horse-drawn cabs, regulations for the storage of gunpowder, and allowing the impound of roaming swine found on downtown streets.

The year 1854 was a time of change for Canada. Many believed the solution to economic woes lay in the signing of a reciprocity treaty with the Americans — the 1850s version of a free trade pact — arguing that it would improve economic trade between the two nations. The Council supported a reciprocal trade agreement between the United States and also the British colonies.

At the end of his one-year term as mayor, Beard chose to retire, with colleagues thanking him for his service and in particular for helping the Board of Health with its efforts to deal with cholera. Mayor Beard, it noted, had "spared neither time nor trouble, night or day, in attending to his important duties."[6]

Not standing for re-election to the Council in 1855, Beard shifted his priorities to an area in which he had always had a strong interest: education and public schools. He had been a member of the Board of Trustees for the public school system after it was formed in 1850, and in addition to his Council and mayoral duties, had served as chair of the board since 1852. Beard served in that position until he was forced to retire due to ill health in 1864.

As board chair, Beard was a strong, visible, and committed voice in favour of free public education supported by municipal taxes, a contentious principle in the 1850s. There was just one common school in the city in 1850, and free public education was actually viewed with scorn by many. In the very class-conscious Toronto, it implied an inability to pay, and a stigma was attached to the idea of free schooling.

The Public Schools Act, fathered by Egerton Ryerson, was passed by the Legislative Assembly, with the first school board election held in Toronto in September 1850. In the first three years, six schools were built, one in each city ward, all six identical, with sheds, fences, outhouses, and four classrooms. A teacher lived in the basement of each school to keep an eye on things. At the time, a female teacher earned $350 per year for teaching 110 children.

The schools in Joshua Beard's public board kept boys and girls apart, and several grades were combined in one room under one teacher. Cuffings (slaps around the head) and canings (hits using a cane) were common and frequent. Pupils sat on long benches, each lesson was an hour long, summer holidays lasted just a month, and there was no compulsory attendance law.

There were no kindergartens or secondary schools yet, and the curriculum went only as far as Grade 9. In 1854, there were 2,000 registered students, and by the time Beard retired as school board chair in 1864, several more schools had been built, with enrollment reaching 5,550 pupils.

For several years, Beard's sons had been helping to conduct his business affairs, and one of them, George Beard, served as a member of Toronto's Council from 1865 to 1868. After completing his term as mayor, Beard served as a member of the board of directors of the Canada Permanent Building and Savings Society, a new firm established in 1855.

Joshua Beard died in Toronto on November 9, 1866. His wife, Elizabeth Beard, who survived him by another two decades, passed away on October 10, 1890, in Toronto at the age of 86.

Mayor George Allan

1855

The 11th mayor of Toronto

Occupations: Lawyer, business leader, Toronto Council member, provincial legislator, member of the Senate of Canada, philanthropist, arts patron, university chancellor
Residence While Mayor: Moss Park, Queen Street at Sherbourne Street
Birth: January 9, 1822, in York (Toronto)
Death: July 24, 1901, in Toronto

——— • ———

George Allan of Moss Park was the son of William Allan and Leah Tyrer, United Empire Loyalist pioneers who had settled in the small, dusty Town of York. William Allan had been the city's first postmaster and customs collector for the port, and during the War of 1812 had served as a lieutenant-colonel. He also figured prominently in the community's early commercial life as the first president of the Bank of Upper Canada and was a supporter of the established Tory elite known as the Family Compact.

The Allan family's most valuable personal asset was owning land that stretched from what is today Richmond Street in the south, to Bloor Street in the north, and from Sherbourne Street over to Jarvis Street. On a vast wooded lot, William Allan began building Moss Park, a large Greek Revival mansion where young George spent much of his formative years.

Born in 1822, George Allan was first educated through private tuition during his early years and was later sent to Upper Canada College where he was one of its earliest pupils. Yet his family life was also marked by tragedy. Of George Allan's siblings, nine of the 11 children in his family died before the age of 20, many of them of the same tuberculosis that took his mother in 1848.

Allan's studies were interrupted in 1837 when the Upper Canada Rebellion broke out and a young Allan, age 15, left college to volunteer as a private in the Rifle Corps, a military unit of constables organized for the protection of private property and which helped quash the rebellion. He returned to school at the end of the following year, remaining there until his final examinations as a law student, which he passed in the senior class of the Easter term in 1839.

Before beginning a legal practice, his father encouraged young Allan to go abroad, so he had the good fortune to travel more extensively than other young men of the same age or social standing at that time. In addition to an extended tour of Europe, he journeyed up the Nile River delta to the border of Sudan, as well as to Syria, the Holy Land, Greece, and Turkey, at a time when many of these areas were still relatively inaccessible, unsettled, even chaotic. The *Globe* later reported that he met with "many exciting adventures in the lawless districts." Later, these and other extended trips, greater than any prior mayor before him, provided a lifelong appreciation of other cultures and nations. Subsequently, he became a fellow of the Royal Geographical Society of England.

Upon his return to Toronto, Allan commenced further studies in law and was called to the bar in 1846 at age 24. He first practised law with James Robinson, the son of Sir John Beverley Robinson, Sr., the chief justice of Upper Canada. Allan also married Louisa Robinson, Sir John's daughter.

His father had given the newlyweds a part of his own estate located near today's Wellesley and Sherbourne Streets and built them a new residence called Homewood. By the 1840s, the Allan family's vast forested estate was beginning to see development on both its east and its west sides.

A rising young lawyer, Allan was first elected to Toronto's Council for St. David's Ward in 1849. Tragically, however, his wife died in Rome, Italy, in 1852, and the next year, his father, the family patriarch, passed away at age 81.

George Allan did not serve on the Council from 1850 to 1853, but in 1854 was once again elected in St. David's Ward. Then a young widower, all of 32 years old, he soon immersed himself in the affairs of the city, impressing many of his elderly and more settled colleagues. He was a member of the all-important committees on finance and assessment, as well as wharves and harbours, and served as a commissioner of the Toronto Harbour Trust.

In 1855, Allan himself was selected unanimously by his colleagues to serve as the city's 11th mayor — no small feat at age 33. In addition, and without soliciting it, he was given an appointment from London to become a commissioner of the Canada Company, an office he held until his death. That same year the Council dealt with a range of issues, including powers to better regulate "Inns and Houses of Entertainment," the ability to impose a frontage tax on properties, and civic relief for the cost of providing medical certificates for "paupers and lunatics." It also sought the authority to impose a duty on all brokers and money changers (as was the case in Montreal), and for all goods, wares, and merchandise sold by auction to be subject to a 1 percent duty.

The Council also discussed damage to properties as the result of flooding, the cost of watering city streets, the problem of handcarts using city sidewalks, and held a special Council meeting to discuss "the incompetence" of the chief of police and an "absence of any system of organization or discipline in the Police." The last mentioned resulted in a motion to recruit a new chief from England. Also debated were the capping of the city engineer's salary, complaints with respect to "drunkenness and the desecration of the Sabbath," and a report by a Council committee investigating civic corruption.

Yet life in Toronto was not easy in 1855. There were ever-present menaces confronting city residents: stagnant pools of water; dust, grime, and filth; horse manure droppings on every street; decaying garbage; rotting wooden-planked sidewalks; roads obstructed by mud; and danger from runaway horse-drawn wagons, carts, coal deliveries, or stagecoaches.

Toronto newspaper accounts in the 1850s also paint a lurid picture of the battle against theft, assault, brawling, prostitution, larceny, public drunkenness, and the selling of liquor without a licence. The year before his mayoral term thousands of Toronto residents, children included, had braved the cold at the Front Street jail to view the hanging of Richard Kehoe.

During Allan's mayoral term, a major gathering, the Toronto Railways Festival, was held to celebrate the inauguration of the new Toronto and Hamilton Railway. Four thousand guests crowded a rail warehouse converted for a night into a special ballroom with bunting, decorations, gas lighting, and a clock fountain, where those assembled dined, danced, and partied until 5:00 a.m., all under the dinner chairmanship of Mayor George Allan.

Toronto's overall political orientation at the time was largely pro-British and pro-business, as well as anti-American, anti-French, and anti-Catholic. The city had become a major commercial centre within the vast British North American empire, and its key economic and political purpose post–American Revolution was to prevent further U.S. expansion northward.

It was also a city of church steeples — 24 in all — in an overwhelmingly Protestant province. About 15 percent of the city's adult population were active members of the Loyal Orange Lodge (that figure, if it were translated into an equivalent 21st-century number, would mean 450,000 Orangemen in today's Toronto).

Indeed, it was a riot based on religion and ethnicity during Allan's mayoralty that led to the first substantial reform of Toronto's early Police

Department. On July 12, 1855, an important day for Orangemen everywhere, members of the Howe Circus from the United States were visiting a local brothel, of which there were several downtown. Once there, a fight broke out between clowns and local patrons, several of whom were members of the Hook and Ladder Company, Toronto's earliest fire service. The following day, the firefighters retaliated. Circus tents were pulled down, and wagons overthrown and burned.

Mayor Allan called out members of the army from Fort York to disperse the mob and restore civil order. Later, when constables professed being unable to recall any of the accused rioters, police reform became an important local topic, one that Allan took steps to implement.

Allan did not seek a second term as mayor or seek re-election to the Council in 1856, since it was his intention to leave the city temporarily and travel once again. After stepping down, he embarked on a lengthy foreign tour.

In 1858, Allan married again, this time to Adelaide Schrieber of Essex, England, and they eventually had a family of six children: three sons and three daughters. That autumn, having returned permanently to Canada once more, Allan again entered the active political scene with his election by a large margin to the Legislative Council of the United Province of Canada for the district of York, serving in that position until Canadian Confederation in 1867.

In October 1867, George Allan was appointed a Conservative member of the brand-new Senate of Canada, one of its first members, where he served until his death. As a senator, he is best known for a long tenure as chair of the Standing Committee on Banking and Commerce.

One of Allan's great legacies is the benevolence he showed toward Toronto's homeless urchins and street children. In the 19th century, it was not uncommon to see abandoned children, some as young as 10 years old, sleeping outdoors. In 1870, Allan donated land he owned near Front Street and proceeded to build the Newsboys' Home, an early residential and health-care facility for impoverished and orphaned young street children, nicknamed "newsies," who sold daily newspapers on downtown street corners. The home became a model of care and eventually led to the founding of the Children's Aid Society of Toronto in 1891.

In March 1888, Allan was elected Speaker of the Senate, serving in that capacity from 1888 until the end of the session in April 1891, remaining a member of Canada's upper chamber until his death in 1901, a Senate career of more than 33 years. In 1891, he was also made a member of the Queen's Privy Council.

Urbane, cultivated, and well read, Allan was a Renaissance man with many interests outside politics. A patron of the arts throughout his life, he both promoted — and made a substantial financial contribution to — education, literature, science, culture, and horticulture. Allan was an early sponsor of celebrated Canadian artist Paul Kane, and his patronage allowed the young artist to travel and paint extensively in Canada.

Allan presided over several important organizations, among them the Royal Canadian Institute, the Ontario Society of Artists, the Art Union of Canada, the Toronto Conservatory of Music, and the Ontario Historical Society. He also served as chairman of the council of the Ontario School of Arts.

A friend of higher education, Allan was closely associated with Trinity College from its founding in 1852 and acted as its chancellor from 1877 to 1901. He was vice-president of the Church of England Union of Canada and the Ontario Society for the Prevention of Cruelty to Animals. In addition to the Royal Geographical Society, Senator Allan also became a fellow of the Royal Geological Society.

In business affairs, he served as a director of the Western Canada Loan and Savings Company and the North American Life Assurance Company. As an active member of a rapidly growing municipality just 40 years after its founding, Allan also served his beloved city as a member of the five-person Board of Water Works Commissioners from 1872 to 1877.

Allan was a member of the elite Conservative Club of London, England, and Ottawa's posh Rideau Club. He also had a summer home, Strathallan, on Lake Simcoe. Active in the synod of the Church of England, he was a long-time president of the Upper Canada Bible Society. In 1869, he was appointed a government trustee for the municipal bonds of the Toronto and Nipissing Railway.

With a long and deeply held passion for horticulture, Allan was president of the Toronto Horticultural Society for 25 years, seeking to foster a broad interest in the study, practice, and cultivation of flowers and fresh fruit. As such, he presented to the society the original donation of land that became the city's Allan Gardens horticultural centre.

Senator George Allan died on July 24, 1901, at the Moss Park residence where he had lived for the better part of 50 years. He was mourned by his wife and six children. The *Globe* called him "a dignified and courteous gentleman." The newspaper noted that he had had poor health and a weakened heart since the winter. His funeral was held at St. James Cathedral.

Mayor John Beverley Robinson, Jr.

1856

The 12th mayor of Toronto

Occupations: Athlete, army officer, lawyer, business leader, Toronto Council member, lieutenant governor of Ontario
Residence While Mayor: College Avenue (now University Avenue) north of Queen Street
Birth: February 21, 1820, in York (Toronto)
Death: June 19, 1896, in Toronto

——— • ———

John Beverley Robinson, Jr., was the son of one of the most eminent government figures of Upper Canada, Chief Justice Sir John Beverley Robinson, Sr., and his wife, Emma Walker. Robinson Junior had three brothers and three sisters, one of whom — Louisa — married George Allan, Robinson's immediate predecessor as mayor.

Between 1830 and 1836, from the age of 10 until 16, John Robinson, Jr., attended Upper Canada College. One of the earliest students at that noted seat of learning, he became known there for his boxing abilities and skills on the cricket field. As a later description recalled, his collegiate days were marked by a robust constitution "and an excessive fondness for athletics — characteristics which may be said to have accompanied him through life."[1]

In December 1837, during the Upper Canada Rebellion, at the age of 17, he served as an aide-de-camp to Lieutenant Governor Sir Francis Bond Head. After the defeat of the 1837 rebels, he volunteered to carry dispatches on the rebellion to the British ambassador in Washington, D.C. He left Toronto in midwinter, reaching Washington seven days later, the entire distance covered by a four-horse stagecoach. While in Washington and though just 17, he had the honour of meeting President Martin Van Buren. The trip was indeed an important one: upon his return, Head complimented him in writing and presented him with a favourite horse as evidence of official appreciation.

The young Robinson studied law with Christopher Hagerman, a prominent lawyer who was subsequently appointed to the bench, and he affiliated with Strachan and Cameron, one of the leading law firms in Toronto. In 1844, at the age of 24, he was called to the bar.

As a result of his prior government service, law clerkship, and family background, Robinson became closely connected to the ruling Family Compact. In June 1847, he married Mary Jane Hagerman, the daughter of his former law colleague, and they had three sons and two daughters.

By 1850, he began to promote a major new interest — the soon-to-arrive railway — an activity that dominated his business activities for the next several decades. That same year he sought to have the city invest £100,000 using lottery tickets to raise funds for the Ontario, Simcoe and Huron Railway, which later became the Northern Railway of Canada. The scheme, however, was rejected by voters in a referendum.

Robinson's involvement in what he termed "city railway"[2] issues eventually led him into local politics. First in 1851 and then in 1853 and 1854, he was elected an alderman for St. Patrick's Ward. Once on the Council, he actively supported railway interests and championed the pro-railway forces there, thus shaping the future of downtown Toronto for decades to follow. To Robinson, the choice was simple: railways meant significant economic prosperity, and in 1851, as chair of the Council's Standing Committee on Railways, he proposed a municipal grant for the Toronto and Guelph Railway, taken over by the Grand Trunk two years later.

However, it was the Ontario, Simcoe and Huron Railway that became Robinson's principal focus, since it connected Toronto with the nearby Georgian Bay region and with trading opportunities in the United States. From January to June 1854, with the absence of Mayor John Bowes due to a serious illness, Robinson served as the Council's president and was also appointed its director on the railway's board. For the next 25 years, he continued to be an enthusiastic promoter of the Northern Railway, and from 1862 to 1875, served as its president.

In 1856, again as a member of the Council for St. Patrick's Ward, Robinson was selected by 25 of his colleagues for a one-year term as mayor of Toronto. During his mayoralty, the Council approved the purchase of land along the Don River for a jail and industrial farm. Built between 1858 and 1864, the Don Jail boasts an Italianate style with a central pavilion, portico, and columns and is one of very few pre-Confederation structures intact in Toronto to this day.

The Council discussed a number of items in 1856, wanting to know "the most practical method of organizing and conducting an efficient Police Force"[3] and how to deal with serious concerns regarding the management of Toronto General Hospital. And even though it was just three years since the very first train departed from Toronto, railway matters were already occupying a huge amount of the Council's time. More than 70 railway items were discussed that year.

By 1856, a transportation revolution was underway in Canada. Toronto celebrated the first rail link with Montreal, directly connecting the nation's two largest commercial centres. To celebrate, the Council thanked the Grand Trunk Railway for conveying thousands of people to Montreal free of charge,[4] noting that this was in marked contrast to the stinginess shown by the Great Western Railway when it opened its first line to Hamilton.

The Council also appointed a committee to seek the authority to assess and then tax the part of the city east of the Don River. But after hearing local concerns, it also struck a committee "to enquire into the difficulties" in the same area "and the best mode of redressing grievances." The Council further considered whether "continuing burning of the Public Lamps from twilight to dawn should be continued" and if the city might "cease to consume Gas on moonlit nights."[5]

Circuses, the Council ruled, would not be permitted within city limits, and the city was advised that the raw sewage being discharged directly into the bay was increasing daily, since new sewers that had been laid had also expanded the municipality's drainage area. Another sign of how the city was booming was revealed by the 1856 census, showing a population of 41,760, the majority of whom, some 24,000, were born in the British Isles, with just 12,000 in Canada itself.

In September 1856, the Council recommended the purchase of the waterworks from business leader Albert Furniss. It was the first definitive move toward public ownership of a major civic utility, preceding the city's takeover of public transportation by 65 years.

Although Toronto had cancelled Casimir Gzowski's contract to build a major waterfront esplanade, Robinson himself supported such a project. Yet when he attempted to be appointed mayor again in 1857, he was portrayed as being too close to the Family Compact, which was seeking to hold on to privilege and power. After a flurry of shady closed-door political bargaining, Robinson lost the Council selection for mayor by a single vote to John Hutchison, who was chosen for one year in 1857.

However, Robinson remained on the Council where he continued a pro-development stance, backing a plan to link Toronto and Georgian Bay by a new canal, one in which he had a direct financial interest. In the end, though, the Council did not approve the financing for this major undertaking.

During the 1858 Province of Canada voting, Robinson and George Brown — later a Father of Confederation — both stood for election in the two-member riding of Toronto. Brown, the Reform candidate and powerful editor of the *Globe*, attacked Robinson for his allegiance to the province's co-premiers, John A. Macdonald and George-Étienne Cartier, as well as for his support of the Roman Catholic Church. Ever the established politico, Robinson relished the hurly-burly of campaigning, and his supporters appeared at Brown's rallies to disrupt them.

Nevertheless, Brown topped the polls, with Robinson elected as the second member in the riding. Historian Barrie Dyster describes Robinson as a natural politician "whose family name, wife's accomplishments, deep purse, and animal energy combined to advance him above others more gifted than himself."[6]

In Parliament, Robinson had to balance his support for the interests of Upper Canada with his backing of the government of Macdonald and Cartier, kept in power by the allegiance of Lower Canadians. On very popular issues such as representation by population, which he favoured, Robinson sought to survive politically, focusing his time, attention, work, and energy on matters of importance to Toronto.

On one major issue in 1859, however, Robinson was caught between two sides. The decision on the location of the future capital of Canada had been referred to Queen Victoria herself, and to the dismay of Toronto, Montreal, and Quebec City, she had chosen Ottawa, a sleepy backwater lumber town. It was expected that Robinson would support the queen's choice, yet he was anticipated locally to defend Toronto's economic interests. As it turned out, he diplomatically asserted that the decision had been made by the Crown and to question, refuse, or reject it would be disloyal.

Soon after retiring as mayor, Robinson applied himself to obtaining a new luxury hotel for Toronto and succeeded in collecting $134,000 toward the building of the new Rossin House. At the corner of King and York Streets downtown, it was rebuilt in 1863 after a serious fire to become one of the city's pre-eminent hotels. An 1866 guide claimed: "What the Fifth Avenue Hotel is to New York, and the Windsor is to Montreal, so the celebrated Rossin House is to Toronto."[7]

In the 1861 election, Robinson's Liberal opponent in Toronto West was former mayor Adam Wilson, who had fought railway interests on the Council. He portrayed Robinson as a tool of John A. Macdonald and an insincere advocate of "representation by population,"[8] yet Robinson won handily.

The business successes of Robinson were due in part to his role in the sale of Crown land to an English company, whose chairman was Sir Francis Bond Head, a former colleague. By 1860, Robinson had become the solicitor of the Canada Agency Association with authority to sell 178,000 hectares of land in Haliburton to the north and then travelled to Britain to arrange the sale of land to investors there.

In March 1862, in recognition of the importance of Toronto, Robinson was appointed to the Conservative Cabinet, with the role of president of the Executive Council. Brown's *Globe*, in a very pointed comment, called him the local "dispenser of Government favours,"[9] yet Robinson served for just a few months before the government fell. At the time of the next election in 1863, Robinson's political fortunes fell, as did those of his party, condemned for supporting Catholic demands for separate schools. Robinson was defeated.

After his electoral defeat, Robinson turned his attention to business and legal interests. His contacts within the Family Compact Tory establishment saw his appointment in 1864 as Toronto's city solicitor, a position he retained until 1880. And in addition to serving there, he also began a loan company, which became the Western Canada Building and Loan Association, one of the largest financial institutions in the country.

Post-Confederation, even though it appeared he might be selected in 1872 as a Toronto Conservative federal candidate, Tories in Northern Ontario sought out Robinson to be their candidate in the sprawling riding of Algoma. Known for his mining knowledge, entrepreneurial spirit, understanding of government, railway experience, and promotion of the North, Robinson was strongly urged to accept. The Northern Railway also promised to pay his campaign expenses. He accepted and was duly elected to Canada's post-Confederation House of Commons.

In January 1874, however, he chose instead to run again in Toronto West and this time was defeated. Even though he was a casualty of the national railway scandal that had engulfed John A. Macdonald's federal government, he later returned to Parliament in a November 1875 by-election. Robinson remained discreetly on the backbenches of the House of Commons until 1877 when a royal commission into the Northern Railway questioned the payment of election expenses in his 1872 campaign.

Robinson's explanations did not appear to bother voters. In 1878, his popularity actually increased from 54 to 58 percent, and he was easily re-elected in Toronto West, proving himself one of Ontario's more durable Tories. The Toronto West seat was a position he held until appointed lieutenant governor of Ontario in 1880, a position he filled with enthusiasm and a high regard for matters of protocol. Although he was a veteran Tory, it was, ironically, sometimes Robinson who had to transmit the views of Oliver Mowat, the provincial Liberal premier, to the federal Conservative administration in Ottawa. Robinson was so well regarded that his term of office was extended two years.

In 1887, he retired to Sleepy Hollow, his Toronto home on College Street near University Avenue, overlooking the city's cricket grounds. A distinguished figure who excelled in athletics, the one-time boxer retained an interest in sports throughout his life. Robinson was a member of the Toronto Gymnastics and Fencing Club and president of the Toronto Cricket Club. He helped inaugurate the Toronto Athletic Club in 1891 and served as its president until 1895. Finally, he was also a member and later president of the St. George's Society.

Robinson's very dramatic and visible death was a major blow to Toronto: on June 19, 1896, Conservative prime minister Charles Tupper, desperate to hold off a surging Liberal Party, organized a major Toronto area political gathering at Massey Hall downtown. As a former mayor of Toronto, MP, and lieutenant governor, Robinson was a respected veteran warhorse and was asked to address the highly partisan audience. Robinson, who had moved to an anteroom prior to giving his speech, suffered a sudden and massive stroke, collapsed, and died just as the meeting began.

Mayor John Hutchison

1857

The 13th mayor of Toronto

Occupations: Merchant, business leader, Toronto Council member
Residence While Mayor: 51 Church Street
Birth: 1817 in Portpatrick, Scotland
Death: July 2, 1863, in Métis-sur-Mer, Quebec

——— • ———

Born in 1817 in the small seaside village of Portpatrick in the Southern Uplands region of southwest Scotland, John Hutchison made the long, difficult transatlantic voyage of several weeks with his parents in 1828 when he was only 11 years old. The family first settled in Montreal where Hutchison grew up and went on to work with considerable business acumen for the mercantile trading firm of John Torrance and Company.

In 1847, at the age of 30, he moved to Toronto to open a new office of commission agents at Church and Front Streets called Hutchison, Black, and Company. It was an operation that relied closely on prior business connections in Montreal, then Canada's leading commercial centre. Hutchison quickly became involved in the economic, social, and political affairs of the young city and was soon investing in several local businesses.

He became a director and shareholder of a brand-new venture coming into Canada and eventually to Toronto — the railway, in this case, the Toronto and Sarnia Railway Company. He also served on the board of the Metropolitan Building Company and the Metropolitan Gas and Water Company. With his Scottish background, he also became involved with the Toronto Curling Club, serving as the organization's secretary-treasurer.

Hutchison also engaged in the political life of the city as an alderman for St. James's Ward in 1852, 1853, 1856, and 1857. He was a severe and outspoken critic of Mayor John Bowes over a major financial scandal, and in 1853 was one of the eight Council members who resigned in protest over the Council's failure to censure Bowes for his conduct.

Returning to the Council in 1856, Hutchison, as a measure of his business acumen and financial expertise, was made chair of the body's Finance and Assessment Committee. An astute manager of funds, he at times admonished fellow Council members for their lack of thriftiness. As chair of the committee dealing with the salaries of public officials, Hutchison recommended a number of reforms that proved politically unpopular and also made several unsuccessful attempts to reduce taxes. In 1857, though he had been in Toronto for just a decade and on the Council only a few years, Hutchison had built a strong personal following and was handily re-elected in St. James's Ward. He was chosen mayor that year through a curious set of circumstances.

During the January 1857 municipal elections, a riot broke out in St. David's Ward and a "mob" took over the polling station. With the election clerk unable to take a complete poll of voters, it was impossible to file a proper legal and final return. That resulted in no representatives for St. David's Ward being seated at first and also put into question the selection of mayor for 1857 by the Council. Toronto city clerk Charles Daly had foreseen the problem and sought legal opinions in advance from the city solicitor and from the province's attorney general and co-premier, the young John A. Macdonald, who later went on to great fame as Canada's first prime minister.

On January 19 at the first meeting of the new 1857 Council, 24 elected members gathered to select a mayor. It was noted that major problems had arisen as the result of an election "disturbance" in St. David's Ward. Both legal opinions that had been sought were of the view that the four representatives of that ward could not take their seats, and both stated that the Council itself would have to choose four of its members from that ward before a new mayor could be selected.

After a number of Council votes, four St. David's Ward representatives were finally chosen and seated and the vote on a new mayor was able to proceed. With all of that out of the way, Alderman Oliver Mowat, a future premier of Ontario, moved John Hutchison's name to serve as the city's chief magistrate, and what was later described as "a tired and befuddled"[1] Council confirmed him by a slim majority of just one vote.

In 1857, Toronto was still a young city, just 23 years having passed since its founding, yet it was the mercantile centre of Canada West with a strong British and Protestant heritage. An edited passage from the book *Sketches of a Tour in the United States and Canada in 1857–58* by Charles Mackay provides a unique look at Toronto in 1857 during the term of John Hutchison:

> Toronto is built upon the American principle, which loves the economy of straight lines, prefers the chess-board to the maze. The streets are long and straight. There is no more crookedness in them than there is in Philadelphia; and they all run at right angles to the lake....

There is a Yankee look about the whole place which it is impossible to mistake; a pushing, thriving, business-like, smart appearance in the people and in the streets; in the stores, in the banks, and in the churches....

Looked upon from any part of itself, Toronto does not greatly impress the imagination; but seen from the deck of one of the ferry steamboats that ply at regular intervals between the city and the peninsula that protects the harbor, it has all the air of wealth and majesty that belongs to a great city....

Its numerous church spires and public buildings; its wharves, factories, and tall chimneys, mark it for what it is — a busy, thriving, and expanding place.[2]

A respected business leader, Hutchison had followed John Beverley Robinson, Jr., into the mayoral office and was also the first, but not the last, mayor to go bankrupt while in office. And in a sure sign that the world was changing, passengers were now able to travel to Toronto by Canada's first trains, which plied daily between the nation's two largest cities. Just a few months earlier, on October 27, 1856, the Grand Trunk Railway had commenced passenger service between Montreal and Toronto, a trip that took just 14 hours.

Prior to that, intercity travel was an arduous journey by horse and wagon, steamboat, and stagecoach and usually took three days with overnight stays along the way. While the St. Lawrence River was the normal route for travel by boat, in winter it was frozen for months and there was no other choice than a stagecoach over deeply rutted and ill-kept pathways blocked by snow in winter and turning to sheer mud in spring.

Toronto was transforming in other ways as well with its first Jewish congregation, the Orthodox Sons of Israel, meeting on a regular basis. Meanwhile, Parliament passed legislation to establish the dollar as the principal unit of Canadian currency, pegged at the same value as the U.S. dollar, while one British pound sterling was worth $4.86.

Yet not everyone in Toronto enjoyed the same upward lifestyle. In 1857, almost 5,000 persons — more than 10 percent of the entire city, including 1,025 women — were arrested on various charges connected with drinking or the sale of alcohol. History writer Bruce West has noted that Toronto

Earliest Photographs of Toronto

From the earliest photographs of Toronto. Left: Looking north along York Street to Osgoode Hall from King Street West in 1856. Right: King Street East looking west in 1856. The Golden Lion, a dry goods store, was one of the city's most famous retailers. The middle of the street is a sea of mud.

When the amalgamation of Upper and Lower Canada into a single United Province of Canada took place in 1841, the new government did not have a permanent capital yet. Several cities had provided a temporary and revolving home for the colony's Parliament. The rivalry to become the new capital was intense.

In 1857, Toronto and four other Canadian cities submitted formal bids to the Colonial Office in Great Britain on why *they* should be chosen the new capital. As part of its official submission, Toronto included a set of photographs that emphasized the city's streets, commercial areas, business enterprises, public institutions, and neighbourhoods. They are the earliest known photos of Toronto.

The City of Toronto had commissioned the firm of Armstrong, Beere, and Hime, "Land Agents, Engineers, and Photographists," in 1856 to create a montage of photos at street level and from the roof of the Rossin Hotel at the southeast corner of King and York Streets downtown.

Toronto's bid to become Canada's national capital failed, and the photographs were later lost and completely forgotten. They were rediscovered by an archivist of the Foreign and Commonwealth Office Library in 1979.

developed its own slums, "shadowed, grimy, and shockingly poor … there are no backyards to these miserable hovels, and slops, filth, and dirt are thrown out in front of the doors." A few doors down there was a house with the rear room "occupied by a brigade of pigs…. An open door led to a room where people cooked, ate, and slept."[3] Beside the sleeping room was the sickening odour of a pigpen curling through the cracks of the door.

Under Hutchison, the Council dealt with a range of issues in 1857: the widening of Front Street, tree protection, a requirement for residents to number their homes, the additional regulation of taverns, and St. Lawrence Market butchers petitioning the Council not to increase their rents.

Sanitation, sewage, water, and water quality were ongoing issues during Hutchison's mayoralty. By 1857, only 10 percent of houses were being serviced with fresh water. The Council appointed a committee to study this situation, yet it took another 15 years until a public water supply was established in 1872.

Other matters at the Council included the poor state of the city's horse-drawn cab stands, a comprehensive 38-page report by Oliver Mowat into allegations of corruption by certain members of the Council, and a request from the Board of Trade for the survey of a Georgian Bay canal route. Its goal was to shorten the distance for grain and timber by 724 kilometres by connecting Toronto to Georgian Bay.

The Council approved a request to the Legislative Assembly, asking for new powers specifically to

- regulate trading agents and others visiting the city offering goods for sale,
- require witnesses to appear on matters being formally investigated by the Council,
- punish residents for using "grossly insulting language"[4] to provoke others,
- punish boarding house proprietors guilty of fraud in taking advantage of immigrants,
- have the mayor elected by citizens, and
- levy a special rate on properties benefiting from improvements.

In June 1857, the Council received the draft of an 11-page brief sent to the British secretary of state for the colonies dealing with "the grounds upon which Toronto bases her claims to becoming the permanent Seat of Government for the Province of Canada."[5] It dealt with three key areas: settlement and colonization, the economics of the situation, and the future defence of the capital.

In 1857 and 1858, British North America experienced a severe depression, and the economic downturn took a deep personal toll on Hutchison and his business. While the Anglican bishop of Toronto asked the Council to provide relief to the poor during the winter, the mayor's own firm, Hutchison & Co., a leading Toronto retailer, was suffering. Selling everything from almonds, raisins, oils, brushes, paints, and lamps to gun powder, tobacco, liquor, wine, port, and sherry, as well as the finest vintage Moët & Chandon champagne, it was in deep difficulty.

Despite all the signs of a once-booming Toronto, historians Graeme Mercer Adam and Charles Pelham Mulvany noted that "1857 will long be remembered as the gloomiest epoch in the history of the commerce and industries of the country.... Mercantile houses of long established reputation went by the board; the factories were idle, trade was stagnant, and the streets swarmed with beggars and vagrants ... and there is reason to believe that not a few deaths from starvation occurred."[6]

On November 2, 1857, with two months still left in his mayoral term, Hutchison offered the Council his resignation due to "the temporary derangement of the affairs of my firm" and that "my whole time and energies ought to be devoted for some weeks to the readjustment of my private affairs."[7] He was persuaded by members of the Council to remain in office until the end of his term, yet by the start of 1858 he had vacated his premises and left for Montreal. The former mayor never again returned to Toronto.

Hutchison died five years later in Métis-sur-Mer, Quebec, having gone there to restore his health. He was just 46. Upon his death, the *Globe* said: "Hutchison was a man of no ordinary kind. Endowed with great energy and sagacity, and an almost iron will, he brought these powers into full use in everything in which he engaged. Many citizens of Toronto will long remember his sterling worth, and his prompt and liberal sympathy towards those who required or deserved his aid."[8]

Mayor David Read

1858

The 14th mayor of Toronto

Occupations: Lawyer, Toronto Council member, Law Society
bencher, educator, historian, author
Residence While Mayor: 510 Queen Street West
Birth: June 13, 1823, in Augusta Township, Upper Canada
Death: May 11, 1904, in Toronto

——— • ———

A leading and public-spirited Torontonian, David Breakenridge Read was one of the best-known lawyers in the province, with a strong regard for public issues. Although a devout Conservative, he was not highly partisan, and some of his closer friends in later years were prior opponents.

To this day, Read's term as mayor remains the shortest of any of the City of Toronto's 65 chief magistrates, lasting just 51 days from November 11, 1858, to year's end. Read had been appointed by colleagues to serve out the final days of William Boulton's term after he resigned suddenly due to a conflict with police chief Samuel Sherwood.

Born in eastern Upper Canada's Augusta Township, David Read was the sixth child of Janet Breakenridge and John Read, a veteran on the British side in the War of 1812. Both sides of the family hailed from strong United Empire Loyalist roots.

Read was first educated in Brockville, and in 1836 at age 13 was accepted into Toronto's Upper Canada College, the school of choice for the colony's elite. Four years later, in 1840 at age 17, he was admitted to the Law Society of Upper Canada and later articled in the Brockville offices of George Sherwood. He completed his studies in Belleville with lawyer John Ross and then in Toronto with John Crawford, who later became lieutenant governor of Ontario.

Called to the bar in June 1845 at the age of 22, Read established his own Toronto firm, one that eventually became a large and successful practice. When a war with the United States loomed in 1846 in connection with the Oregon boundary dispute, Read and a colleague volunteered to serve and met nightly for military drills at St. Lawrence Hall. In September 1848, he married Emily Ballard of Picton in Prince Edward County. From this union, three sons and four daughters were born.

In the 1840s, Read had first become politically active working as an election scrutineer. Although a faithful Tory, he enjoyed lifelong friendships with people of all stripes. One of them, Liberal Oliver Mowat, was provincial secretary and had served on Toronto's Council the year Read was chosen to be mayor. Mowat later went on to serve as Ontario premier from 1872 to 1896.

Read took a special interest in legal education and lectured for more than a quarter century to students at Osgoode Hall. In 1856, the province's attorney general and co-premier, John A. Macdonald, appointed him to a commission revising the statutes of Upper Canada. In 1858, Read was first elected an alderman for St. Patrick's Ward and sat on several Council standing committees.

On March 17, 1858, there was rioting between the city's Orange and Catholic factions upon the occasion of a St. Patrick's procession during which a stabbing death had occurred. However, Chief of Police Samuel Sherwood refused to testify against a fellow Orangeman implicated in the violence and further aggravated the dissatisfaction with Toronto police when, in October 1858, he unilaterally released prisoners accused in a bank robbery.

After Sherwood let the robbery suspects go free without any questions, an enraged Mayor Boulton called for an inquiry, receiving only minimal co-operation from Sherwood. Boulton expressed strong dissatisfaction and sought to have the entire matter discussed by the Council, but Sherwood pre-empted him, sending a letter to city newspapers claiming that Boulton was convening a legal star chamber.

Boulton fought back with a letter of his own, calling for Sherwood and his deputy to either resign, be suspended, or be dismissed. Later, the Council broke into a sharp disagreement over what was said, when, and by whom. When it finally dealt with a motion to suspend the chief, the vote was 14–10 in favour of Sherwood and not Boulton. The motion on whether to accept Boulton's resignation was passed 15–8 in favour.

Embarrassed, angered, and humiliated by the Council's action and what he believed was a gross miscarriage of justice, Boulton tendered his resignation in November 1858, even though he had been planning to run for mayor just six weeks later in what would be the city's first direct election to choose the mayor by voters and not by shadowy private deals made by councillors in the backrooms of City Hall. The Council met at a special meeting on November 11 to select a replacement for Boulton, and Read, who had served just a single term on the Council yet was known as an accomplished and highly respected lawyer, was approved by a vote of 14–10.

As a caretaker for a month and a half, Read oversaw several issues during his brief term: drainage problems, police clothing, the petition for a first wooden-planked sidewalk on mud-filled Jarvis Street, the installation of three large bells for use as major city-wide fire alarms, and land for an industrial farm next to the new Don Jail.

An urgent appeal was also received from Toronto General Hospital, whose budget was sufficient to cover just 80 patients. The Council agreed to additional funding but with a major new stipulation: the hospital's funding could only be used to care for residents living within the limits of the City of Toronto. And citizens were advised that an emissary had been sent to London, England, to express the city's hope that the sovereign, or a member of her family, would visit Toronto.

Police reforms were also on the public agenda in 1858. The Legislative Assembly of Upper Canada had passed an act requiring that in each of the colony's five major cities a Board of Commissioners of Police be established. It also provided that "constables shall obey all the lawful directions."[1]

Other issues dealt with during Read's short term included the management of the exhibition grounds, dealing with the city's poorest and most vulnerable during the winter, the long-continuing economic depression, the state of the city's public markets, claims with respect to the removal of snow and ice, the delivery of gas in the city, the establishment of a committee to look into municipal corruption, and the city's upcoming and first directly elected mayoral campaign.

Yet Read also faced challenges in assembling members of the Council and with the accountability of city staff. Council meetings on December 22, 23, and 24 were all cancelled due to a lack of quorum, and the Board of Works asked the Council for an extension of its year-end report until mid-January 1859 because of the "multiplicity of accounts and the great diversity of affairs."[2]

The Council approved the purchase of a $1,000 annuity for the widow of a Toronto firefighter who had lost his life while on duty, then dealt with a report on the offer of George Allan, a former mayor, to convey land on Sherbourne Street between Gerrard and Carlton Streets to the city for the purpose of a new public park.

In December 1858, as Read's term was ending, the new provincially mandated Board of Police Commissioners sat down for the first time to plan how to replace the existing constabulary with a new police force. And just weeks later, in February 1859, the entire force from the chief down to the constables was dismissed and a new one constituted to take its place. Only 24 of the prior Toronto constables were rehired on the new police force of 51 men and seven non-commissioned officers.

Toward the end of the year, a *Globe* editorial lamented the state of poverty in the young city with the advent of winter and what was being done to relieve the suffering of the poor and destitute: "Their wants are not paraded at street corners ... they are ashamed to beg [and] with scanty clothes and ill-filled stomachs and fireless hearths their sorrows are comparatively unnoticed."[3] The *Globe* noted there was an immediate need for food, heating fuel, and cast-off clothing and called on the mayor to convene a meeting of individuals interested in tackling the problem.

Although widely viewed as a successful mayor, Read was nevertheless swept up by the winds of change. The Municipal Reform Association swept the polls in the 1859 civic election. According to the *Globe*, it was carried out at "almost no expense.... Candidates spent no money on the opening taverns, hiring cabs, or treating voters."[4] And with just 270 votes, Read was defeated in his St. Patrick's Ward council seat by Alderman Jonathan Dunn, who received 313 votes, and Dr. Michael Lawlor with 309 votes.

Read was succeeded as mayor by Reformer Adam Wilson, yet he would continue to play a central role in the legal affairs of the city and province. From 1855 until 1881, he was an elected bencher (director) of the legal profession's governing body, the Law Society of Upper Canada, and on December 23, 1858, just as he was wrapping up his service as mayor of Toronto, he was also appointed a Queen's Counsel by the pre-Confederation Province of Canada.

In his personal life, Read was active in a number of major local organizations. An avid sportsman, he was a member of the Toronto Cricket Club, the Royal Canadian Yacht Club, and the Caer Howell Bowling Club. An early member of the venerable Toronto Club, he also served as an officer with the 5th Battalion of the Toronto Militia. Read was also a supporter of two new Anglican churches in Toronto, St. John's and St. Matthias, acting in both as a churchwarden and synod representative. In addition, he helped found the County of York Law Association in 1885, serving as its historian.

Read had a deep interest in and passion for history. After his retirement in 1881, he applied himself in both time and energy to the preservation of Ontario's history through lectures, speaking engagements, and writing for leading historical journals. He served on the executive of the Pioneer and Historical Association of Ontario, which later became the Ontario Historical Society, and was an honorary member of the Women's Canadian Historical Society of Toronto, which he helped establish in 1895.

Some of Read's most impressive legacies are his historical writing. He published several scholarly texts: *The Lives of the Judges of Canada and Ontario* (1889), *The Life and Times of General John Graves Simcoe* (1890), *Life and Times of Major-General Sir Isaac Brock* (1894), *The Canadian Rebellion of 1837* (1896), and *The Lieutenant Governors of Canada and Ontario* (1900).

With a major change in judicature and procedure in Ontario completed for the most part by 1885, it was proving difficult for older practitioners and elderly judges to keep up with the significant legal revisions. Having been in practice for 40 years, it was the right time for Read to bow out gracefully. The law had been his life's work and passion.

Sadly, Read suffered an apoplectic stroke in November 1902 at the age of 79 and remained bedridden yet conscious for the final year and a half of his life. On May 11, 1904, age 81 and paralyzed, he died at his home on Breadalbane Street downtown and was buried privately at St. James Cemetery.

In the eyes of the *Globe*, he was "a public-spirited participant in municipal administration" and "a master of legal technicalities and pleading cases ... a man of activity with a special fondness for public affairs ... all traces of partisan aggressiveness passed away from him long ago ... some of his most intimate friends were former political opponents."[5]

Mayor Adam Wilson

1859–1860

The 15th mayor of Toronto

Occupations: Lawyer, Toronto Council member, Cabinet minister, judge
Residence While Mayor: Spadina Avenue (north of College Street)
Birth: September 22, 1814, in Edinburgh, Scotland
Death: December 28, 1891, in Toronto

— • —

Toronto's first mayor directly elected by the citizens of Toronto was the Reformer Adam Wilson. In the *Commemorative Biographical Record of the County of York, Ontario*, published in 1907, it was later noted that Wilson was one of Toronto's "ablest and most erudite practitioners" and "the highest type of citizen, upright, honourable and blameless, alike in public and private life."[1]

Born in Edinburgh, Scotland, in September 1814, he was one of eight children of Andrew Wilson and Jane Chalmers. In 1830, at age 15, the young Wilson made the long voyage to Canada by ocean steamer, settling in Upper Canada. He soon went to work for his uncle, Colonel George Chalmers, a former MP who owned a mill store in Halton County. Shortly after Wilson's arrival in Canada, his parents and siblings followed.

In January 1834, the same year Toronto was created, 19-year-old Wilson moved from Halton's Trafalgar Township to Toronto and began the study of law as an articled clerk in the office of Robert Sullivan and Robert Baldwin, two of the most prominent lawyers in the city. The following year, Sullivan became Toronto's mayor, while Robert Baldwin later served as a leader of the Reform movement and a key founder of democratically elected responsible government.

Wilson soon became a protege of Baldwin and for five years was his diligent and industrious student. He was finally called to the bar in 1839 and was made a partner the next year at age 26. It was a relationship that continued until 1849 when Baldwin retired. For much of his life, Wilson was known as a "Baldwin Reformer."

In May 1841, he married Emma Dalton, daughter of Thomas Dalton, the editor and proprietor of *Patriot*, a Conservative organ and one of the first newspapers to publish in Toronto. Toward the end of the decade, in January 1848, the Wilsons adopted a daughter named Julia.

With Baldwin, Wilson shared a Reformist interest, and as both of his colleagues in the firm became increasingly absorbed in political affairs, more of the firm's work fell to him. His reputation was that of a bright, well-regarded, hard-working Toronto barrister. He was elected a bencher of the

Law Society and became a Queen's Counsel in 1850. In 1856, he formed a law partnership with Christopher Patterson (later elevated to the Supreme Court of Canada in 1888), and a young Halton County barrister, James Beaty, Jr. (Toronto's mayor from 1879 to 1880). The partnership of Wilson, Patterson & Beaty lasted 18 years.

Drawn into politics in the civic elections of 1855, Wilson was elected alderman for St. Patrick's, a sprawling ward northwest of downtown where he had recently built a new home. Thrust into the swirl of municipal issues, he headed a faction opposed to powerful railway interests and the sway they held over the city. The first railway operating from Toronto had begun just two years earlier, yet the strength, power, and might of railways were already overpowering the small community.

Wilson headed a commission of inquiry that probed previous councils and their handling of a major landfill project on the harbour, known as the Esplanade, and how a consortium had obtained a highly lucrative contract for its construction. Rumours of graft, cronyism, influence peddling, and mismanagement were rampant. Wilson's commission managed to have the Council reopen and then cancel the contract.

From 1856 to 1858, Wilson temporarily departed the political arena. The Province of Canada attorney general and co-premier John A. Macdonald recruited him to serve on a commission to revise, update, and consolidate the legal statutes of Upper Canada. But a number of changes occurred to draw him back to City Hall. A new act provided for the city's mayor to be directly elected for the first time, and Wilson accepted the nomination of George Brown's Municipal Reform Association to run for the position. On December 20, 1858, three candidates were nominated to contest the 1859 mayoral election, including John Bowes and William Boulton, two former mayors.

An elected city-wide mayoral contest was a historic first, and as Victor Loring Russell notes in *Mayors of Toronto*, the campaign was both notorious and controversial. The land along Toronto's waterfront was its key issue. A January 1859 editorial in the *Globe* supporting Adam Wilson stated: "We trust that no friend of Reform will slacken his exertions today, but that every vote will be polled which can be brought up."[2]

Wilson's campaign centred on vigorous opposition to rail giveaways and railway tycoons, charging incompetence, corruption, and mismanagement and that rail interests were "the greatest calamity which has ever fallen upon the city."[3] Most of the waterfront land had been allocated by the city to wealthy land speculators and building contractors pushing for newly built rail tracks and industrial yards.

The runaway favourite in the 1859 election was Wilson, who tallied 1,928 votes to 910 for Bowes and 810 for Boulton, giving him a solid majority. Although opposed to massive public railway subsidies, Wilson was not against all rail matters. Standing for more ethical behaviour, he himself became a founding director of the North-West Transportation, Navigation and Railway Company, which had received its charter in 1858.

In 1859, the Council dealt with a wide range of issues: the purchasing of stone "so as to employ the poor,"[4] inspecting weights and measures at city markets, a rapid increase in city debt, and more effective street watering to reduce the dust, grit, grime, dirt, and horse droppings on Toronto's muddy, unpaved streets. An increasing amount of time was spent on matters related to the new railways, in operation only since 1853. Negotiations included items such as drainage, assessment issues, bridgework, rights-of-way, and financing.

Heavy smoke and ash from major industrial uses in the city resulted in a new bylaw on smoke abatement. The Council also discussed a joint proposal by the cities of Chicago and Milwaukee, as well as Canada's Simcoe County, for a new ship canal between Lakes Huron and Ontario that would save 1,379 kilometres in distance between Chicago and Liverpool. It would, the report said, secure "a commanding position upon the American continent."[5]

In August 1859, Mayor Wilson informed the Council of a major issue: the entire ground under City Hall, including the area immediately beneath the civic offices, courts, Council chamber, and market shops, "was covered with standing water to the depth of about 18 inches." The stagnant water, he said, "renders the whole building very unwholesome," noting that City Hall was "the worst drained, worst ventilated, and filthiest building in the whole city."[6] Yet with pomp and circumstance, Wilson also helped lay the cornerstone of another important public works project — the Don Jail on Gerrard Street at the Don River.

Wilson's political support remained solid, and he was successfully re-elected in 1860, winning against Matthew Crooks Cameron, a member of the Council, by 2,146 votes to Cameron's 1,546. The anti-Tory *Globe* trumpeted that "Wilson's majority is truly a magnificent one … the contest was made a political one by the corruptionists themselves."[7]

The Council dealt with a range of issues: enacting a chimney inspection bylaw, forcing local prisoners to carry out farm labour, and the setting aside of a room at City Hall for the first time for the use of Council members. Wilson observed that Toronto still lacked large "manufacturers of importance"[8] and was concerned about the drop in cross-lake shipping due to the new railways. At a time when politicians could, and often did, hold more than one office, Wilson ran for the Legislative Assembly in 1860, winning the rural seat of York North, even though his opponents sought to peg him as a Toronto candidate who would become a captive of the city's interests.

One of the true highlights of Wilson's mayoralty was the 1860 visit of His Royal Highness, the Prince of Wales (later King Edward VII), who undertook a two-month tour of Canada on what was also the first official visit to Toronto by a member of the British royal family. As he arrived by ship at the foot of John Street, the prince was greeted by an enthusiastic crowd of 60,000, greater than the entire population of Toronto itself.

During the same time, Wilson was in the process of writing a book, published the following year and called *The Constable's Guide: A Sketch of the Office of Constable*. Indeed, policing had become a top mayoral issue. The highly political constables were often considered corrupt because they were loyal to the members of the Council who had appointed them. By 1860, several new measures were introduced: standardized training, fair hiring practices, and strict new rules governing discipline and professional conduct.

Years later, in the *Commemorative Biographical Record of the County of York, Ontario*, Adam Wilson was vividly described as someone who "entered with zeal into all matters pertaining to the city's interests, and bravely met and faced the usual conflicts, being sustained by the people-at-large."[9]

Wilson urged his Council to proceed with approval of Toronto's first and very rudimentary streetcar system, a series of small horse-drawn cars that would travel from St. Lawrence Market to the outer suburb of Yorkville. However, he did not seek a third term as mayor in 1861, preferring to devote his time and energy to provincial affairs. A respected member of the legal

City Hall: Toronto's Filthiest Building

At the beginning of his term, Mayor Henry Sherwood (1842–1844) observed that the city's original municipal offices were already too small to accommodate the expanding civic government of a bustling city. Plans were soon drawn up to build a new purpose-built City Hall to combine municipal offices, a central market, and a new police station.

The solid brick building on Front and Jarvis Streets, where today's St. Lawrence Market South sits, saw its cornerstone laid in September 1844. On the second floor were the offices of the mayor and city officials, as well as a new Council chamber with a public gallery. Yet, less than six years after its completion, city engineer John Howard presented the first of several reports on the state of the building.

Basement flooding meant prisoners were often knee-deep in water. During a major storm, several city creeks flowed toward Lake Ontario and inundated the jail. Shackled to the wall in chains, desperate, and unable to move, some prisoners drowned while others were forced to remain in a toxic and contaminated mixture of garbage, debris, animal waste, and human feces, washed into the jail from sewer backups.

The situation was not corrected, and in 1854, former mayor George Gurnett (1837 and 1848–1850) complained to the Council about the foul air, terrible odour, and bad ventilation of the police station downtown. The situation persisted even until the late 1850s when Mayor Adam Wilson (1859–1860) informed the Council that the entire ground under City Hall immediately beneath the civic offices, police station, and market shops "was covered with standing water to the depth of about 18 inches." The stagnant waters, he said, "render the whole building very unwholesome," also noting that City Hall was "the worst-drained, worst-ventilated, and filthiest building in the whole city."

profession, he contested both the seat of York North as well as the constituency of Toronto West. He succeeded in holding York North but lost Toronto West to John Beverley Robinson, Jr., a former Toronto mayor.

In May 1862, along with several Reformers, Wilson entered the Province of Canada Cabinet of Co-Premier John Sandfield Macdonald, holding the post of solicitor general, but was dropped the following year, then chose to leave political life altogether. Like his colleagues, Wilson had been a prominent advocate of representation by population.

Upon his resignation, in May 1863, Wilson was appointed a judge of the Court of Queen's Bench and later a judge of the Court of Common Pleas. In 1871, he was made a member of the Law Reform Commission, and in 1876 was involved in a major public fight with *Globe* founder George Brown when he declared that a Brown letter in support of the Liberal election campaign had been written for corrupt purposes.

In 1878, Wilson was appointed chief justice of the Court of Common Pleas and was in that position when the Ontario Judicature Act of 1881, which revolutionized the court structure of the province, was passed by Oliver Mowat's Ontario government. Later, in 1884, he became chief justice of the Court of Queen's Bench, and upon his retirement in 1887, Queen Victoria made him a knight bachelor in recognition of his lifetime of service to Canada.

Until his death in December 1891, Wilson and his wife lived in a house he had built in the 1850s just north of Spadina Avenue and College Street. His pastor delivered a stirring eulogy at his funeral a few days later, noting that Wilson had "sterling qualities that distinguished his public and professional career ... fidelity, integrity, practical ability, sound judgement, courtesy, and indefatigable industry marked his conduct of affairs."[10]

SPECIAL NOTE: From 1859 to 1866 in what was a major reform, Toronto's mayors were for the very first time elected by citizens across the entire city. Yet the voting public was made up at that time of only male property owners. Women were barred by law from running for office until the 1920 civic election.

Mayoral Election in 1859

CANDIDATE	VOTES
Adam Wilson	1,928
John Bowes	910
William Boulton	810

Mayoral Election in 1860

Adam Wilson	2,146
Matthew Crooks Cameron	1,546

Mayor Francis Medcalf

1864–1866 and 1874–1875

The 16th mayor of Toronto

Occupations: Blacksmith, millwright, foundry owner, Toronto Council member, Orange Lodge leader
Residence While Mayor: 448 King Street East
Birth: May 10, 1803, in Delgany, County Wicklow, Ireland
Death: March 26, 1880, in Toronto

———— • ————

Of all of Toronto's mayors, Francis Medcalf was the most devoted member of the Loyal Orange Lodge, with the exception perhaps of a successor, Leslie Saunders, who became the imperial world president of the lodge 90 years later.

He was the son of William and Martha Medcalf who in 1819 immigrated to Upper Canada with Francis, age 16. His parents later had seven more children and settled on Big Otter Creek in Bayham Township, Elgin County. In 1823, barely 20 years old, Medcalf struck out on his own and moved to Philadelphia where he worked as a blacksmith and millwright.

He married Mary Harrison of Philadelphia in 1831 and had six children with her, four of whom were later the core of the family business. After 16 years in the United States, he returned to Toronto in 1839, age 36, and by 1843 had become a pioneer in the growing city's foundry and machinery business.

Four years later, he was Toronto's foremost millwright and machinist and opened the Don Foundry and Machine Shops on the south side of King Street East beside the Don River. It specialized in farm machinery, agricultural implements, heavy castings for gristmills and sawmills, and threshing machines and steam engines. Although it burned down five times and was insured for only one of those occurrences, his foundry still prospered and earned Medcalf the financial success and respect he sought. His residence was also close to his business — a large red-brick house on the north side of King Street near the junction with Queen Street.

By the 1860s, Canada was rife with tension between Protestants and Irish Roman Catholics, and Medcalf, a strong Orangeman, loyal Conservative, devout Mason, and faithful Anglican, saw much of his support in political life derive from his involvement in the Orange Order, the secret society opposed to the Roman Catholic Church. Medcalf was master of Lodge 275 in Toronto several times and master of the newly created County Orange Lodge from 1854 to 1862. He also served as grand master of Canada West from 1862 to 1864.

In 1860, Medcalf first ran for political office and was elected to Toronto's Council from St. Lawrence's Ward. He was off the Council in 1861 and

1862 but returned in 1863 in St. David's Ward. Medcalf's ability to exploit his rags-to-riches story led to him being given the nickname "Old Square Toes," a reference to his work boots. In his political career, Medcalf portrayed himself as an honest, hard-working, self-made mechanic, a simple man who had risen by hard toil and plain speaking. Yet he was also quite clearly the main anti–Roman Catholic candidate.

A continuing controversy over Catholic education was at its height in 1863, and John Bowes, the incumbent mayor, was seen as a defender of separate schools. Medcalf considered Bowes deceitful and far too clever. A loose coalition of Orangemen and anti-papist Tories, spurred on by *Globe* publisher George Brown, convinced Medcalf to run against Bowes. On January 6, 1864, he was elected mayor, receiving 2,276 votes to Bowes's 2,114 and depriving him of a seventh term.

In his first official address, Medcalf struck a very sobering and serious tone with respect to city finances, astounded to learn that of the $270,000 in property tax revenues owed the city, just $118,000 had been collected by year's end. He called it "a source of great evil ... caused either by neglect of duty on the part of the collectors, or an interference with them."[1] And in terms of publicly reported police offences, Medcalf noted that of the 4,124 listed, 2,441 were for various liquor charges and for being drunk and disorderly.

Medcalf's first year saw a range of issues discussed: new coal oil lamps for Queen's Park, a major review of public markets that dealt with weigh houses, butchers, the sale of meat, vendor leases, the regulation of hucksters and dealers, and the sale of firewood. The Council also expressed concern about an act that required all stores and taverns to close from Saturday evening at 7:00 p.m. until Monday morning.

In 1865, Medcalf turned aside a challenge from John Cameron, and his popularity continued to rise. He won with 2,530 votes to Cameron's 999. Surrounded by his political workers, he began a procession toward St. Lawrence Hall in a sleigh. By the time they arrived, the crowd numbered in the thousands.

Soon after, Alderman John Canavan shocked his Council colleagues when he publicly called the Board of Works a "very cesspool of corruption and extravagance."[2] The allegations were referred to staff to conduct a thorough investigation. The Council was also asked to ensure that Queen's

Park be kept as an area for public recreation and that no further pieces of land there be sold.

In 1866, Medcalf was not opposed in his bid for the mayoralty. His inaugural speech to the Council, at just three paragraphs, was the shortest in the city's history. He recommended immediate action with respect to the city's debt load and called for "a thorough cleaning of the city."[3] Yet the *Globe* commented on the sad state of local politics: "The struggle for seats in the City Council has in great part been left to inferior and incompetent men … respectable men have hesitated to allow themselves to become candidates for election."[4]

Tavern licences were also identified as a source of major civic problems. Ninety-four of the 180 licences were considered to be third-class bars: noisy, crowded, and basic working-class saloons for thousands of thirsty low-wage craftspeople, labourers, unskilled workers, and hired hands.

The Council considered several issues under Medcalf, including a Young Men's Christian Association petition asking the city to prevent steamboats from operating to the Toronto Islands on Sundays, as well as a major new effort to deal with the pollution of thousands of daily horse droppings. The Board of Health hired seven scavenger carts to collect the filth from the street and bring it to the Don Jail where prisoners spread it as manure at the city's new industrial farm.

The provincial Board of Health circulated an extensive 12-page report on precautions needed to deal with cholera, including disinfectant, cleanliness, ventilation, drainage, slaughterhouses, and the use of scavengers, as well as the cleaning of yards and stables and not using tainted or decaying animal or vegetable foods.

In 1867 and until 1873, the previous electoral reform of choosing the mayor by way of a city-wide vote came to an end and the selection reverted to secret backroom vote trading behind closed doors at the Council. Although he again won a seat in St. David's Ward in 1867, Medcalf was defeated as the Council's choice for mayor; instead, James Smith was picked. Medcalf continued on the Council and later switched to St. John's Ward from 1869 to 1871 and also threw his hat into the 1871 provincial election, running as a Conservative in Toronto East where he was defeated.

Although out of the active political world in 1872 and 1873, Medcalf again prevailed when city-wide mayoral elections returned in 1874, defeating the incumbent Alexander Manning and A.M. Smith, who had served on the Council and in the Ontario Legislative Assembly for four years. One of the issues Medcalf had championed was the establishment of chain gangs to clean city streets, noting "the largely increasing numbers of drunken and worthless men sent to gaol … calls loudly for a remedy for this increasing evil."[5] Yet his call also fell flat in the provincial assembly.

The Council also dealt with a number of concerns: the continuing erection of wooden buildings in the city, the storage of lumber piles, an inadequacy of fire hydrants, the impurities in commercial ice taken from the harbour, a request for a first comprehensive bylaw regarding the treatment of animals, and an appeal by anti-liquor forces to deal with the "alarming spread of intemperance."[6]

For the mayoralty race of 1875, the *Globe* this time opposed Medcalf, saying "that in every part of his work as Mayor Mr. Medcalf has been a disastrous failure."[7] It also went on to say: "He has not made even a decent figurehead in the council; he has been unequal to the preservation of order; he is past giving intelligent attention to business. At the Police Commission, he has been a mere cypher…. Mr. Medcalf will simply be a friend of the whiskey dealers."[8] Yet at the conclusion of the 1875 campaign, Medcalf again emerged triumphant.

The Council initiated legal proceedings against the Grand Trunk Railway for the continuing use of steam whistles on locomotives, which had become in the words of the Council, "a public nuisance."[9] It also approved the first major sewers for Parliament Street, as well as the powers needed to compel Consumers' Gas to properly repair the streets that it ripped up to lay pipes.

One of the major characteristics of Medcalf's time as mayor was his devotion to the Orange Lodge and a total dismissiveness of the Roman Catholic population. In a major public speech at Queen's Park in 1875 to celebrate the July 12 Orangeman's Day, he spoke of the "persecuting spirit of Popery" and declared that Toronto's Protestants "ought to be proud and pleased in not having been brought up under the system of Roman Catholicism. The principles of Orangemen were duty to God, fidelity to their fellow men, and loyalty to their Queen."[10]

In July 1875, Medcalf was granted a 10-week leave of absence to attend an imperial gathering of British and colonial mayors hosted by the Lord Mayor of London. While there, "Old Square Toes" sought to impress by purchasing a complete mayoral outfit with a chain of office and cocked hat. Upon returning to Toronto, he wore it just once at the Council. Wisely, Medcalf had travelled at his own expense to London for an event that was widely reported back home.

One of the defining moments of Medcalf's mayoralty was the Jubilee Riot. The year 1875 had been proclaimed by Pope Pius IX as a special jubilee year, and the city's faithful were asked to carry out several pilgrimages. Medcalf, known for his hostility toward Catholics, let it be known that would be a serious breach of the public peace.

Toronto's Catholics, long an object of scorn, were duly warned, but on a Sunday that October a procession of about 2,000 men, women, and children proceeded peacefully to St. Michael's Cathedral and encountered a hostile crowd of almost 8,000 along Church Street. As a hail of stones fell on the religious procession, shots rang out and a major fight was on. With pilgrims throwing stones in return, several drew guns and began firing.

Medcalf had easily won re-election in 1875, though even his own supporters acknowledged he was by now a worn and tired political figure and not necessarily the best choice. Although he had been forced to seek a leave of absence from the Council due to illness, he again sought re-election and was beaten in 1876 by the popular, more vigorous, and less discriminatory Angus Morrison, who captured 4,425 votes to Medcalf's 2,673. And later, in 1879, even though he had been the city's mayor as recently as four years earlier, he only received a humiliating 136 votes, coming in last out of six mayoral candidates that year.

A year later, Medcalf died in Toronto on March 26, 1880, age 76. For a man who revelled in secret societies, his long funeral procession included his beloved Orange Order as well as Freemasons, Odd Fellows, and Foresters.

It was noted that with his plain-speaking style and utilitarian boots, "Old Square Toes" had relished that very description, considering it a mark of incorruptible ordinariness. It was recalled that the only matters in life that truly aroused passion, or indeed anger, in Medcalf were perceived slurs on his cherished Orange Lodge, and the assertiveness of the Roman Catholic population of Toronto whom he considered dastardly, uppity, and disloyal.

Mayoral Election in 1864

CANDIDATE	VOTES
Francis Medcalf	2,276
John Bowes	2,114

Mayoral Election in 1865

Francis Medcalf	2,530
John Cameron	999

Mayoral Election in 1866

Francis Medcalf was unopposed and was acclaimed in office.

Mayoral Election in 1874

Francis Medcalf	2,994
A.M. Smith	2,746
Alexander Manning	476

Mayoral Election in 1875

Francis Medcalf	3,552
Andrew McCord	3,029
Angus Morrison	2 (yes, just 2!)

SPECIAL NOTE: Angus Morrison, a well-known Conservative, withdrew from the race, yet his name was still on the ballot and captured what is believed to be the smallest number of mayoral votes in Toronto's history.

Mayor James Smith

1867–1868

The 17th mayor of Toronto

Occupations: Merchant, retail grocer, Toronto Council member, insurance underwriter
Residence While Mayor: 42 Wood Street
Birth: December 25, 1831, in London, England
Death: March 9, 1892, in Toronto

—— • ——

The son of William and Anne Smith, James Edward Smith was born in London, England, on Christmas Day 1831 and had the unique distinction of being baptized in St. Paul's Cathedral. At age 10, he and his parents made the long and difficult journey to Canada, settling in Toronto. The young Smith, after receiving what was later described as a first-rate education, worked for a while in the law office of Henry Sherwood, a former Toronto mayor, but chose not to complete further legal training.

Described years later by the *Globe* as "energetic, frugal, and ambitious" and someone who "made money and friends," he turned his mind to a mercantile career. His first of several ventures over a lengthy business career was proprietor of a small wholesale grocery business, including the sale of wines and liquors, in the Village of Brockton, a small community later annexed by the City of Toronto (today, the area of College Street west of Little Italy). As one biographical account notes, he "was early trained in business and commercial pursuits. He was a man of very free and genial temperament, and made heaps of friends."[1]

The ambitious Smith was prospering, and at the age of 26, was elected to Toronto's Council from St. John's Ward, a position he held from 1857 to 1866. From the start of his municipal career, he took an active part in the proceedings of the Council. His outgoing personality, business acumen, and interest in financial matters led to his being chosen to serve as chair of the powerful Standing Committee on Finance and Assessment, an eventual stepping stone to the mayoralty.

By 1861, the firm of James E. Smith had moved to the southern end of Church Street in the city's commercial heart, specializing in the importation of wine, liquor, and grocery products. With a new reciprocity, or free trade, treaty with the United States in effect, the company thrived, leading to Smith's diversifying into real estate and financial services.

Smith became an agent for the British Empire Life Insurance Company, the Imperial Fire Insurance Company, and the City of Glasgow Life Assurance Company, a smart business move that later netted him a large fortune. With a wide circle of acquaintances and well known throughout the province, Smith was also frequently employed as an arbitrator in large real-estate litigation matters.

Politically, Smith fitted what many saw as Toronto's proper mould: a member of the High School Board, an Anglican, a Tory, and a member of the Masonic Order in which he was a past grand master of King Solomon's Lodge and active in the formation of the Grand Lodge of Canada, of which he was senior warden in 1857–1858.

Between 1859 and 1866, Toronto mayors were elected for the first time by a city-wide electorate. Yet that was short-lived, and from 1867 to 1873, the selection of the city's mayors was again done by a murky process of backroom lobbying and secret deal-making at the Council.

However, one major city-wide electoral reform did come into effect for local Council races in 1867: 33 years after the city's founding there was now for the very first time a secret municipal election ballot. Prior to that, choices for the Council had to be made in the open at a large public meeting usually held at the main tavern of each ward.

In *The Toronto Book*, historian William Kilbourn describes the city in 1867: "New Year's Day 1867 was sunny, clear and cold. That day was scattered with ice boats and cutters and prancing horses. And the streets below were filled with the sound of sleigh bells and of sleighing parties bundled in their muffs and great caps and buffalo robes." Kilbourn further notes that "young people of quality, and not a few of their elders, indulged in the practice of 'doing King,' which was to say parading up and down the north side of the street on the 12-inch board sidewalk between the hours of three and six p.m. ... King Street was the place 'where everybody meets everybody.'"[2]

On January 21, 1867, the 21 members of the Council, seven of whom were either past or future mayors, gathered solemnly at City Hall. On the seventh ballot, James Smith won narrowly 11–10 after voting for himself. In its first weeks, the new Council dealt with a range of issues, including the request for a bylaw "prohibiting the use of obscene and blasphemous language" and to deal with "persons leading lewd and vagrant lives." The Council also received word from Police Magistrate Alex McNabb complaining of "the offensive smell at the Police Court, caused by the stables underneath and adjoining the Fire Hall."[3]

A year-end account by the city's auditor was encouraging: total budget receipts were $762,755, while expenditures were just $716,175. Of major concern was a report to the mayor and a new body, Toronto's Police Commission, where Police Chief William Prince emphatically noted that "Canada is infested by criminals from the United States ... and is a harbour of refuge for felons who successfully evade arrest in Canada."[4] Prince noted that due to the treaty situation between the United States and Great Britain only certain felonies were included and thus a number of U.S. saboteurs, felons, criminals, and evildoers could operate in Canada with impunity and not be touched.

A new and expanding form of local transportation — horse-drawn cabs — was high on the chief's list for attention. To control this unregulated new business, he recommended a sweeping set of reforms: licences for all cabs with a card showing the driver's name and address, cabs all of one colour, all new drivers required to first meet in person with the chief, horses to be kept in proper condition, and drivers to be sober when driving.

On the first day of Canada's Confederation, Toronto had grown in just over 30 years from a population of 9,200 to almost 50,000, with a busy Toronto harbour as the site of flourishing grain and lumber businesses and frequently crowded with schooners loading and unloading cargo.

As Toronto historian Mike Filey describes:

> Along the water's edge wood-burning railway engines chugged in and out of the thirty-three-year-old city's not one, but three, waterfront train stations. Horse-drawn streetcars (sleighs in winter) made their way along a little more than four miles of track on two of the city's main thoroughfares.... Amenities taken for granted today were still pretty primitive in the Toronto of 1867. Most still drank water from the bay while indoor plumbing was a luxury enjoyed by a very few of its citizens. Interior illumination still relied on coal oil and candles, while a couple of streets boasted gas lights installed and maintained by Consumers' Gas (a company now known as Enbridge). There were 180 hotels in the Toronto of 1867 ... 67 butchers, 34 pawn shops, 31 bakers, 12 plumbers, 9 dentists, and 1 chiropodist.[5]

A dignified Mayor Smith presided with aplomb and decorum on July 1, 1867, as 10,000 citizens gathered at Queen's Park for a municipal celebration of Confederation and the emergence of Canada as a new nation. The event included an official review of troops, the laying of a cornerstone for a Queen's Park monument, an evening concert, a hot-air balloon ascension, and a massive illumination of Chinese lanterns, all giving the city a festive and joyous feeling.

On January 20, 1868, Smith was once again chosen as mayor, this time unanimously by all 21 councillors, with even Samuel Harman, whom he had beaten the year before, seconding Smith's nomination. The Council considered a range of items that year, including the commissioning of a report on whether the city would be better served if water were under its own control instead of by private suppliers. It was also decided to forge ahead with a petition to the Legislative Assembly for an act to allow a new public waterworks.

In a major bid to attract more jobs, investment, and trade, the Council approved $400,000 to assist two major railways. It also considered a novel idea: that the city reduce city taxes when paid on or before fixed dates, and a penalty for those in arrears. The Council set the mayor's salary at the princely sum of $1,600 per year and signalled displeasure with jail operations, asking for a detailed report on all expenses. It also agreed to a commission of inquiry into the management of Toronto General Hospital, which reopened in August 1868 after being closed for 10 months. The hospital was forced to restrict public beds to 25 in total and struggled until 1874 when the first provincial aid became available.

Cholera in Toronto had been reduced due to several factors: greater disinfection and cleanliness, vigilant staff as new immigrants arrived, the enforcement of quarantines, the forced isolation of cholera patients, and even the condition of immigrant ships coming to the New World.

In the bustling metropolis, whose principal means of transport was by horse, the streets were filthy. The droppings of thousands of horses fouled the roads and threatened good health. Springtime was the worst: the street refuse mixed with slush and melting snow spread across entire thoroughfares. And a further problem of noxious air was also noted, due to polluted basements, sewer fumes, and a huge number of rank drains.

In 1868, Smith let it be known he would not seek a third mayoral term. That November he accepted the lucrative post of customs collector for the

Port of Toronto and served in that position until 1879. He also remained on the Council in 1869 and 1870, whereupon he retired.

His earlier firm now became J.E. & W.E. Smith, and his son, Alfred, joined the enterprise. Smith's prior business interests had been a wise investment. The growth of financial, banking, and insurance needs in the last half of the 19th century saw him become a very wealthy man.

Smith was first seized by an illness in December 1890 while at worship at St. James Cathedral and shortly after visiting with friend and fellow grocer James Wheaton, the mayor of Detroit (1867–71). The malady included an attack of paralysis from which he never recovered, making him bedridden for the next 14 months. As his poor health extended into 1892, Smith's family and friends gradually realized he would never recover. Smith died on March 9, 1892, and was mourned by his wife, Josephine Pfaff, four married daughters, and a son.

SPECIAL NOTE: From 1867 to 1873, Toronto's brief experiment with local democracy ended, and the city's mayors were not elected in a city-wide election. They were again chosen by members of the city's Council in what were secret vote-trading sessions held behind closed doors.

Mayoral Election in 1867

James Smith was selected after seven ballots at the city's Council on January 21, 1867, by a vote of 11–10.

Mayoral Election in 1868

James Smith was selected by acclamation on January 20, 1868, when no other mayoral candidate was nominated.

Mayor Samuel Harman

1869–1870

The 18th mayor of Toronto

Occupations: Banker and plantation owner in the West Indies, lawyer, accountant, Toronto Council member, City of Toronto assessment commissioner, City of Toronto treasurer
Residence While Mayor: 303 King Street West
Birth: December 20, 1819, in London, England
Death: March 26, 1892, in Toronto

——— • ———

Samuel Bickerton Harman, Jr., was born in London's West End on December 20, 1819, the son of Dorothy Murray and Samuel Harman, Sr., of Brompton, Middlesex, England. Although British-born, his father was also a West Indies plantation owner who had served as chief baron of the Court of Exchequer and owned Harman's, a 48-hectare family plantation in northeastern Antigua's Saint Philip Parish.

The junior Harman had attended King's College School in London, England, and began his career as a clerk with the Colonial Bank in Barbados in 1840. Two years later, in July 1842 in Toronto, he married Georgiana Huson, the daughter of George Huson, a Barbadian planter. One of Huson's other daughters had settled in Toronto in 1835 where the Huson family also had financial interests.

Samuel Harman Jr.'s first child was born in 1843 in Grenada where he had been posted as head accountant and then manager of the Colonial Bank. In 1847, he returned to Britain to carry out some family business, yet just over a year later, Harman, age 29, and his wife settled in Canada. Over the course of their marriage, they had six sons and two daughters.

Harman had come to the city to oversee a Huson family investment in trouble, yet his efforts were not entirely successful. Although he was installed in a relatively fashionable part of the city, he was forced to return to full-time work to make a living.

By the early 1850s, he was studying law with John Hillyard Cameron, treasurer of the Law Society of Upper Canada. He received his bachelor of common laws from Trinity College in 1855 and later that year was called to the bar of Upper Canada, beginning a legal practice as a junior partner to Cameron and serving with him for 17 years.

Upon commencing the pursuit of law, Harman also involved himself deeply in community affairs. He was a member of the Council for the Canadian Institute and the New England Historical and Genealogical Society, pursuing a lifelong devotion to genealogy, heraldry, and astronomy.

In 1853, as a devout Anglican, he participated in Toronto's first diocesan synod and served as treasurer of the diocese from 1856 to 1858, diocesan

The Mayor Who Once Owned Slaves

Prior to his becoming Toronto's 18th mayor (1869–1870), Samuel Bickerton Harman was a plantation owner on the small Caribbean island of Antigua where his family had a slave-owning legacy spanning five generations.

The Harman family and other white slave owners who ruled the island were some of the wealthiest merchants of their time. The plantation was where young Harman, born in 1819 in London, England, grew up in a slave-supported life of luxury. In 1832, two years before the creation of the City of Toronto, records show that 142 enslaved people were forced into hot, grinding, back-breaking manual labour at the Harman estate.

As a result of its unlimited sunshine, enriched soil for sugar cane, and excellent harbours, Antigua had become a major source of the world's sugar. As the demand for sugar soared, the result was subjugation, bondage, and slavery, leaving a legacy of oppression, control, exploitation, and murder of people of African descent on the island.

Enslaved people, including those on the Harman plantation, were forced to work under a whip and in the tropical sun for 10 to 12 hours per day six days per week. They were forced to toil when sick and punished for not working fast or hard enough or for defying authority. Punishment could include imprisonment, whippings, even torture and mutilation.

In 1848, Samuel Harman arrived in Toronto with his wife and family to look after a family investment in Canada. Although he now lived in Toronto, *The Antigua Almanac* of 1851 showed Harman was still the owner of his family's 48-hectare Antigua plantation.

First elected to Toronto's Council in 1866, Harman was selected by his colleagues to become mayor in 1869 and 1870. Today, a Harman family cemetery still exists in St. Philip's Parish, Antigua, along with the ruins of the now-abandoned Harman sugar mill and plantation.

registrar from 1859 to 1877, and later, its chancellor. Harman also carried out legal work for Trinity College, and in 1852, helped establish the Toronto Boat Club, which later became today's Royal Canadian Yacht Club. Politically, Harman was an ardent Conservative.

He became president of the St. George's Society in 1860, the year in which the Prince of Wales and future King Edward VII visited Toronto, officially presenting the formal address of that body to the prince upon his visit. A member of the Freemasons since 1842, he also introduced the Knights Templar to Toronto in 1854 and remained a senior officer until 1882.

With his intimate knowledge of banking, finance, and accounting, Harman specialized in commercial law with a focus on legal-financial transactions and the often complex field of arbitration. Yet even though he had come from a background of wealth and privilege, including family sugar estates in the British West Indies and property in rural England, it appears that personal finances were on his mind from the very beginning of his professional career.

All through their life in Toronto, the family lived in rented premises, and in April 1862, Anglican bishop John Strachan wrote to the Legislative Council on Harman's behalf, seeking his appointment as a court clerk. Later, in 1870, the Harmans' young son, on his way to the Red River Rebellion as a member of the Queen's Own Rifles, wrote to his mother to say he hoped to send them money soon. The 1870s were also a time of deep personal loss for the Harmans: four of their children died, one after the other.

A central political issue for Harman as mayor was the supply of water to the city. "The object of the supply is three-fold," he said. "First, for the extinguishing of fires; secondly, for drinking; and thirdly, for ablutionary and other domestic purposes." He noted a major concern about "the proximity of the mouths of certain sewers to the very portion of the Bay from which the Water Company are daily filling the reservoirs." Harman called for "the appointment of a Committee to investigate ... and aided, if necessary, by the best scientific and engineering advice, to bring in a matured report as to the best steps to be taken in the premises in the best interests of the city."[1]

During his mayoralty, the Council dealt with a host of issues both large and small: a proposed bylaw to punish vagrants and disorderly persons, gas lamps on Seaton Street, a grant of $1,000 to the Dominion Rifle Association, a petition for the first sewer on Carlton Street, a move to dispense with the city's medical health officers, and legal proceedings against the private Toronto Street Railway to compel it to put "the road in proper order."[2]

In 1869, Toronto's Council petitioned the government of Canada to take action in support of the Huron and Ontario Ship Canal by appointing a special select committee of the House of Commons to "investigate the present position of the company and the practicality and advantages of the proposed work."[3] That same year Harman was appointed a "bencher," or board member, of the Law Society of Upper Canada. However, in 1871, when the society's general members were given a direct vote, he failed dismally and was not returned.

During the same period in Toronto, a young Timothy Eaton opened a new dry goods store at 178 Yonge Street in December 1869. As local history writer Claire Mackay describes, "Timothy's shopping rules were unheard of: all sales cash, no credit, no haggling — the price on the item is what you pay, and a money-back guarantee."[4]

A first August Civic Holiday was approved by the Council with a vote of 12–1. It was originally called "Citizen's Holiday," and several more years of one-time proclamations occurred before it became permanent. Soon after, in January 1870, Harman was selected to serve as mayor for the coming year, yet this time on the third ballot. Toronto was asked to contribute $100,000 to the Toronto, Simcoe and Muskoka Junction Railway and make the city's Crystal Palace exhibition space available as barracks for troops heading to quell the Red River Rebellion in Manitoba. The Council also posted a reward of $5 for any "information leading to the conviction of persons injuring shade or ornamental trees in the city."[5]

Although Toronto had a public water system by the early 1870s, most private homes were not connected yet, and residents had to draw fresh water from wells or from outdoor city water faucets shared with dozens of neighbours. In addition, primitive toilets in backyards were still the norm, and when they leaked, overflowed, or became too full, they easily contaminated nearby well water.

In addition, a number of dingy, dark, and poorly built downtown shanties teemed with impoverished tenants and had no toilet facilities whatsoever. Often, Toronto residents went outside and threw the entire contents of large, overflowing chamber pots into earthen gutters, sidewalks, mud-filled streets, or backyards, creating enormous health challenges.

From the mid-1860s onward, the bustling city's downtown port area became an even busier, noisier, and more crowded industrial precinct with additional harbour landfills extending the city shoreline a further 274 metres south into Lake Ontario. The Council agreed to have seven citizens appointed by the Board of Trade to look at securing the united action of all railway companies to build a single "Union Passenger Station" for Toronto, a task that took an additional 57 years to complete. The city's further economic expansion was spurred by a combination of several factors: an inflow of British investment; new municipal lighting, sewer, water, gas, and road infrastructure; the growth of the Toronto Stock Exchange; and the success of new railways, factories, and merchants due to an expanded national market post-Confederation.

In 1871, Chief Constable William Stratton Prince presented his yearly statistical report to Toronto's Council, covering 1870. He declared prostitution to be the second-highest occupation in Toronto, with some 688 persons identified as plying the trade. There was no explanation given how he arrived at the figure. The occupations listed were as follows:

- 1,397 labourers
- 688 prostitutes
- 140 carpenters
- 135 grocers
- 111 servants
- 103 clerks
- 102 shoemakers
- 96 tavernkeepers
- 93 moulders
- 91 sailors

The year 1871 proved to be Joseph Sheard's turn to serve as mayor, and he was unanimously chosen by members of the Council as chief magistrate. Although no longer the mayor, Harman remained on the Council until 1872 as its finance chair.

Harman's next career came about as a result of concerns expressed by the progressive wing of the Council with respect to the significant and continuing problems, inadequacies, and inequalities of Toronto's assessment situation. In November 1872, Harman was appointed the city's first assessment commissioner with a mandate to fix the problem and establish a completely new department. The princely salary of $3,000 per year made him one of the city's highest-paid officials, which greatly boosted his personal finances.

As commissioner, Harman put his organizational, business, administrative, and financial skills to great use, recruiting evaluators, training them, and ensuring there were procedures in place for consistent valuations, all completed in time for a full municipal reassessment for the 1873 tax rolls. Harman was worth his weight in gold: Toronto's assessable tax base increased from $32 million the previous year to $44 million. His work was one of the factors that forced the retirement of Andrew McCord as the city's treasurer in 1874, a position he had held for almost 40 years, since just shortly after the city's founding. Harman applied for the job and won it.

Yet there were also clouds on the horizon regarding assessment and the city's finances. In the early 1870s, properties and people worth $3.8 million — a massive sum at the time — were entirely exempt from taxation. They included government officials, the clergy, churches and burial grounds, universities and colleges, charitable institutions, government and county buildings, literary institutions, Osgoode Hall, judges, and army officers.

The mid-1870s were also a time of deep personal loss for the Harman family. After the death of their son out west in 1870, a remaining daughter died in 1874 and another son the following year.

Despite personal hardships, Harman reorganized the city treasurer's department, employing new methods and procedures and recruiting a first-rate professional staff. With the city expanding through annexation, the workload for Harman's department increased vastly.

In one of his last major undertakings, Harman displayed a definite political savvy in his efforts on behalf of the Institute of Chartered Accountants of Ontario. In 1882, the institute recruited Harman as its president for several terms, and after a high-profile lobbying campaign, he was successful in achieving a previously elusive incorporation status for it in February 1883.

At some point in the mid-1880s, however, Harman became ill. Overwhelmed, physically and mentally, he was unable to cope. Historians speculate that one cause might have been a reluctance to delegate. Harman hung on, though, continuing as the city's treasurer because he needed the salary it provided.

Eventually, during the mayoralty term of Edward Clarke, the matter ended up with a confrontation at the city's Executive Committee in the fall of 1888. Harman was forced to resign as city treasurer due to ill health, but as a measure of his service and the esteem in which he was held, he was awarded a generous annual pension of $2,000, the largest amount the city had ever paid.

Harman summed up affairs in his official letter of resignation: "It is not too much to say that civic life had become a second nature, the severance of myself from which was no easy matter."[6] He retired, but in the early 1890s his health and spirit declined rapidly and he died at his home on Peter Street on March 26, 1892, a mere two weeks after the death of James Smith, his close friend and ally whom he had succeeded as mayor.

Yet perhaps it was his last will that best provided a glimpse into the state of Harman's affairs: while merchant James Smith's estate was valued at $175,000, Harman left his heirs an estate worth less than $1,465.

Mayoral Election in 1869
On January 18, 1869, Samuel Harman was selected by members of Toronto's Council on the first ballot.

Mayoral Election in 1870
On the final ballot at the Council, Samuel Harman emerged the winner by a vote of 12–8.

Mayor Joseph Sheard

1871–1872

The 19th mayor of Toronto

Occupations: Carpenter, homebuilder, architect, Toronto Council member

Residence While Mayor: 14 Magill (now McGill) Street

Birth: October 11, 1813, in Yorkshire, England

Death: August 30, 1883, in Toronto

——— • ———

Joseph Sheard's humble roots reveal much about the man he would become. Born in the Village of Hornsea, Yorkshire, his father was an officer with the Dublin Dragoons who died six weeks after his birth, leaving four children and no means of support. Sheard later recounted a childhood of poverty, little formal education, and leaving home at age nine to work on a farm: "I hired myself to a farmer to do what I could about the farm.... I grew to be about 12 years of age. I had no greater pleasure than on a Saturday evening to give my mother my two shillings which had taken me a whole week to earn. I felt very happy ..."[1]

With no schooling and few prospects, he was forced to become an apprentice wheelwright and joiner, "a great trial," he described, one marked with "bitter scalding tears." After moving to Hull, England, and becoming a mechanic, Sheard saved enough to immigrate to North America. In April 1833, age 19, he sailed from England on a large ship, *The Foster*. It was, he said, "a very bad selection ... after I got to sea I found out that the captain was a drunkard ... after many narrow escapes the vessel arrived safe at Quebec City ... 40 days after she left."[2]

When he eventually arrived at York's Church Street wharf at about midnight on a moonlit spring evening, a major street brawl had spilled out onto Front Street. It was an inauspicious start to landing in what was still a rough-and-tumble frontier town. Sheard boarded with fellow travellers in a small rented house in Macaulaytown, a shabby working-class area near today's Bay and Queen Streets. It was a spartan, modest existence sleeping "on the softest plank I could find on the floor."[3]

Sheard quickly obtained construction work on a large frame home on Richmond Street but came down with a serious case of typhus, a combination of severe headache, high fever, rashes, and chills, as well as searing muscle pain and delirium. He was temporarily crippled, and it was six weeks before he was able to work again, by which time he had exhausted his meagre savings.

Discovering that his carpentry skills were in great demand, Sheard was able to find steady work and settled on what today is known as McGill

Street. As Sheard later recounted, "I bought a lot where I now reside and built a small frame house.... I married in the fall of 1834 and have lived in the same spot ever since."[4]

Sheard was an early supporter of William Lyon Mackenzie, later noting that the pro-British, ultraconservative Family Compact was in power during a period of Tory influence and patronage. He believed that Mackenzie was one of the few politicians that ordinary residents had confidence in and that "no situation or patronage could make him swerve from his duty."[5]

The 1837 rebellion caused a great upheaval in Toronto, with widely ranging rumours of rebel activity sweeping the city. Fearing for their safety, some residents fled to the countryside while others took to the lake, escaping on boats. For Sheard, it was also an unsettling time: "I went home and kept watch the whole night over my little property. I had only one child at that time. She was dressed, ready to start at a moment's notice." After the rebellion ended, Sheard noted that "a military display was kept up for months. Then came the days of oppression, which lasted for a very long time."[6]

Sheard is best known for a simple yet clear act of real courage, gaining the respect and admiration of Toronto residents. In early 1838, after the rebellion was over and in his capacity as foreman of public works, he refused at great personal risk to oversee the construction of the gallows being built for the public hanging of condemned leaders Samuel Lount and Peter Matthews, sentenced to die for their support of the uprising. "I'll not put a hand to it," Sheard said. "Lount and Matthews have done nothing that I might not have done myself ..."[7]

By the mid-1840s, Sheard became one of the most sought-after building contractors in the city. After going into business for himself, he took on more responsibility for the design of buildings. Architecture at the time was still considered a nominal pursuit, and anyone could call himself an "architect." It was another 40 years before the province saw a professionally regulated architectural body come into being.

In the 1840s and 1850s, trained professional designers were few and far between, though a small number of British-educated architects had established themselves in Canada. Sheard eventually assumed the title "architect" and accepted several important commissions, including assisting in the design of Canada's first Parliament Buildings in Ottawa.

The well-regarded building contractor began a lengthy municipal career of more than 20 years, serving as alderman in three different wards, first representing St. Patrick's in 1851 and 1852 during the turbulent mayoralty of John Bowes. When St. Patrick's was divided in two, he was the member for St. John's in 1854 and 1855. Finally, in 1859, he was elected in St. James's Ward under Adam Wilson, the first mayor directly elected.

Having served under seven different chief magistrates, Sheard himself was chosen by the Council to be mayor in 1871 and 1872. The Council's members were once again selecting the mayor, a major retreat from the prior reform of direct election. On January 16, 1871, Sheard was a unanimous choice of the Council.

The *Globe* reported on Sheard's selection by the Council, noting that "he wished it to be distinctly understood that so far as his position as Mayor was concerned he would know no politics, no party, no creed, no nationality, but know only the interests of the city." As the *Globe* also pointed out, "In the past, party lines had been pretty strongly marked in the council.... It had been said on the streets that the Mayor of Toronto ought to be of a certain stripe of politics. He was opposed to that opinion."[8] Being chosen by the Council was a recognition of faithful service by a familiar and well-known figure but also reflected that much of the city's day-to-day work was now being carried out by standing committees of the Council and a growing professional civic staff.

Sheard's immediate priorities were city finances, which were "not in the very best state." He called for action on needed street improvements, sanitary measures, and pure water "and plenty of it," as well as "pressing the provincial government to accept the Toronto gaol as a central prison."[9]

At the Council in 1871, a host of requests, motions, and petitions came forward: downtown citizens asking to "limit the number of licences granted for the sale of intoxicating liquors," a call by Alderman John Hallam for reduced taxes, a report regarding the purchase of cheap fuel and wood for Toronto's poor, a petition with respect to the "manufacture of manure from the Sewerage of the City,"[10] and a request for streetcar tracks on Jarvis Street from Bloor to Front Streets. The Council was advised that taxes levied the year before totalled $421,233, while the uncollected amount stood at $129,238.

In October, the mayor regretfully informed Toronto's Council that a major fire had occurred in Chicago, killing approximately 300 people and leaving more than 100,000 homeless. The Council conveyed a gift of $10,000 on behalf of the citizens of Toronto, who recalled their own downtown core going up in flames 22 years earlier.

Indeed, water for cooking, drinking, manufacturing, and fire protection was one of the liveliest issues in the Toronto of the 1870s. Fire protection was still inadequate, and the few existing hydrants could not supply the necessary water. In 1872, the Council approved a bylaw to authorize the construction of a new waterworks plant and a commission to oversee its management.

Sheard's first term as mayor was relatively quiet and uneventful, and on January 15, 1872, he was again selected unopposed by 20 of his Council colleagues for another one-year term. Yet he also faced a very public allegation that a councillor had been bribed to vote for him during the selection, and Sheard was forced to give sworn testimony for a formal judicial report. It was later concluded there was "no evidence of the payment, or evidence of any money by, or on behalf of any person, to him for his vote."[11]

Another headache Sheard faced was allegations of financial impropriety. City auditor George Barber reported to the Council that there was a suspected case of embezzlement within the municipality's treasury. In several cases, the amounts on city cheques had been deliberately altered, some departmental accounts simply did not add up, and senior staff in the all-powerful city chamberlain's — treasurer's — office were hampering a proper investigation. Chamberlain Andrew McCord had first been nominated for his post by William Lyon Mackenzie, Toronto's first mayor, almost 40 years earlier.

With Toronto's business and financial affairs becoming far more complex, the revelation of possible embezzlement led to several important reforms under Sheard: the appointment of a city commissioner in 1871, the establishment of a new Board of Valuators in charge of all assessment in 1872, and after Sheard's retirement in 1873, the appointment of an assessment commissioner.

After stepping down as mayor in January 1873, Sheard again served on the Council for a final three years until 1876. Although a loyal Liberal for almost 40 years, this is how Sheard described his political leanings in later years: "I am like an old horse who has grown old in the service of his master."[12]

Sheard died on August 30, 1883, age 69. Toronto's Council recognized his many years of service with a resolution praising "the memory of one who has so faithfully served his fellow citizens as mayor and alderman and, from his long residence, had become one of the landmarks of Toronto."[13]

Today, a small park just south of Carlton Street and a block east of College Park on Yonge Street pays tribute to the city's 19th mayor. Sheard Parkette, now surrounded by glass-and-steel high-rises, is immediately adjacent to what was the original homestead site of Joseph and Sarah Sheard — the raw land cleared from the forest where they raised their seven children.

A son, Dr. Charles Sheard, served Toronto with great distinction as the city's medical health officer from 1893 to 1910 and as a professor of medicine at the University of Toronto. He was also president of the Dominion Medical Association and the Provincial Board of Health, as well as a member of Canada's House of Commons from 1917 to 1925.

Mayoral Election in 1871
On January 16, 1871, Joseph Sheard was selected unanimously by the members of Toronto's Council.
Mayoral Election in 1872
On January 15, 1872, Joseph Sheard was selected unanimously by the members of Toronto's Council.

Mayor Alexander Manning

1873 and 1885

The 20th mayor of Toronto

Occupations: Carpenter, contractor, business leader, capitalist, corporate director, Toronto Council member, real-estate investor, philanthropist, arts patron
Residence While Mayor: 63 Wellington Avenue West
Birth: May 11, 1819, in Dublin, Ireland
Death: October 20, 1903, in Toronto

—— • ——

One of Canada's leading building contractors, Alexander Manning was also a major real-estate investor, acquiring substantial property and becoming Toronto's wealthiest citizen. His long and distinguished career extended over 30 years.

Manning was born and raised in Dublin, Ireland, and in 1834, age 15, arrived in Toronto just as the city was founded. As the legend goes, when Manning's ship entered Toronto harbour he saw in the distance a grand home on the city's western shoreline, one that looked more like a castle than a private home. Manning vowed that one day it would be his.

It might have taken 36 years, but in 1870 after he became the richest man in Toronto, he bought the same house. A few years later he was elected mayor of Toronto and began one of the stormiest political careers of any chief magistrate of the city.

The 1837 Upper Canada Rebellion took place just three years after Manning's arrival in Toronto, and the political instability it caused triggered a major economic depression, with hundreds of business enterprises across the city on the verge of collapse. After toiling as a carpenter in the midst of such uncertainty, Manning moved to the United States in 1838, age 19, and found a job with an Ohio building firm.

By the time of his return to the city two years later, he was a seasoned building contractor and the economic downturn had subsided. Toronto was on the verge of a boom, and Manning soon established himself as a builder and partner at a local sawmill. The city had more than doubled in population since 1834, and Manning won the first of many lucrative construction contracts through a combination of ambition, industry, and a serious and capable manner.

In the early part of his career, he was engaged in the construction of Lambton Flour Mills on the northeast of the bridge over the Humber River in the small community of Lambton. He also worked on the Welland Canal in 1842 and 1843, in the building of Fireman's Hall and the Mechanics' Institute in 1845 and 1846, and on retail stores designed by renowned Toronto architect John Howard in 1847. In February 1850, Manning married his first wife, Adeline Whittemore, in Toronto.

With the active help of his brother-in-law, a noted Toronto merchant, Manning became a prominent construction baron, rising to the top of his field as a reliable contractor, and while still a young man, executed a number of important contracts. In the 1850s and 1860s, some of his major projects included the Toronto Normal and Model Schools; road-building projects in Grey County; railway construction in Vermont, Pennsylvania, New York, and Ontario; and the masonry and brickwork of the new Library of Parliament in Ottawa.

Manning was elected in St. Lawrence's Ward in 1856 and re-elected in 1857 but stepped down for a decade to concentrate on his real-estate affairs, returning in 1867. After the death of his first wife, Adeline, in 1861, he married Susan Smith, the daughter of Hollis Smith, a senior member of the Legislative Council for Lower Canada.

While continuing to invest heavily in real estate, Manning was at times overextended and became the subject of some controversy. His commission to work on the Library of Parliament in Ottawa was obtained largely thanks to his close connection to Prime Minister John A. Macdonald's Conservative government, which became a source of trouble when the Liberals were elected in 1873. It took the return to power of the Conservatives in 1878 to finally get the matter resolved.

In 1867, Manning resumed his involvement in civic politics as a member of the Council for St. Lawrence's Ward, a seat he held until the end of 1873. As his wealth increased, he invested in several new business ventures, including the Traders Bank of Canada, the Toronto Brewery Company, and various real-estate developments. Construction projects were the Manning Arcade at 24 King Street West and the Manning Chambers at City Hall Square.

He became the owner of so many buildings that historian Victor Russell, in *Mayors of Toronto*, notes that Manning became widely known as "the largest individual ratepayer in Toronto."[1] For his part, historian Desmond Morton says he was "reputably, the richest man in Toronto,"[2] someone who could easily afford to fulfill his early ambition to purchase the castle he first glimpsed on his first day in Toronto.

In 1872, though he offered himself for mayor — a selection once again made by the Council and not the voting public — it was Joseph Sheard who was chosen to assume the mayoralty. However, on January 20, 1873, on the first ballot and by a vote of 13–6, Council colleagues chose Manning, now one of the city's top business leaders, to be the mayor.

Manning was able to carry out several of the goals he had set upon taking office: establishing a commissioner for public works, reform of municipal assessment and tax collection, and purchase of the privately owned waterworks. But there were also whispers and allegations regarding certain construction tender irregularities. In 1873, for instance, Manning had secured the first of several major contracts for work on the Cornwall and Welland Canals.

The Council dealt with a range of issues in 1873. Manning's own activist proposals included the sale of lands in arrears to recoup taxes owed, a plan to pave main thoroughfares, a comprehensive city-wide drainage plan, the allocation of all monies from the Police Court to go directly to the city treasury, a Council committee to study the building of a new City Hall ("the present building and offices being quite small"), and asking the Legislative Assembly to allow the city to "utilize the labour"[3] of jail prisoners on public streets.

Also moved ahead by the Council was a measure to strike a new street railway committee to look at the most likely routes, operations, and best type of roadway base. In addition, the formal conveyance of High Park to the city by John Howard was also brought forward. His gift of 66 hectares was approved by the Council by a vote of 13–2. Police Chief William Stratton Prince reported that intoxicated cab drivers (who then used horse-drawn vehicles) were exacting exorbitant fares and using abusive language. The chief also asked for enforcement of the law preventing the erection of new wooden buildings in the city and recommended that a restriction also be applied to lumberyards, as well.

For the 1874 election, Toronto once again returned to a city-wide mayoral vote instead of the Council making the decision behind closed doors. Manning sought election by popular vote but was trounced at the polls by Francis Medcalf, who scored an easy win.

As a noted patron of arts and culture, Manning had previously invested a considerable personal sum in the city's Grand Opera House, acquired by public auction. Three storeys high and with a massive pillared entrance, it could seat 1,600 patrons. In 1879, it was destroyed by a devastating fire, and though only partially insured, Manning had it rebuilt in a mere 51 working days.

Turning again to business affairs in 1879, Manning obtained the contract to build an isolated 108-kilometre stretch of the Canadian Pacific Railway (CPR) west of Lake Superior. The job proved tougher and costlier than foreseen, and rumours swirled concerning influence peddling. It took an 1880 royal commission investigating the CPR to find there was no evidence of bid rigging, though tendering irregularities were noted, forcing Manning and his partners to surrender the contract in 1883. Allegations of impropriety now dogged him continually.

Manning contested the mayoral race of 1879, coming in third, and in 1881, declined a nomination to run again. As one of the city's largest taxpayers, he served as president of the Property Owners' Association, a bullish watchdog group that challenged tax assessments and monitored spending at City Hall.

Late in 1884, 5,500 city residents petitioned Manning to run for mayor in 1885. He acceded, and with the endorsement of the local Tory machine, campaigned on a promise of clean water, businesslike government, and fiscal restraint. In what was a bitter race, he spent lavishly and won the 1885 mayoralty narrowly.

Manning once more showed himself to be an efficient mayor and able administrator who kept taxes low. His inaugural address covered a range of issues: the removal of filth from city streets, the issue of foul water, construction of a new trunk sewer, reform of local improvement charges, a review of the size of city wards, and new mechanisms to deal with complaints regarding Toronto's police force.

The conflict between old and new also became public in 1885. With the earliest electric lights — sputtering arc lamps in which a lightkeeper had to replace the light's carbon element — it was a member of the Council, Alderman John Moore, who had shockingly moved that immediate steps be taken to terminate the use of all electricity in Toronto and that all wires and poles be removed from city streets.

The Council dealt with a range of issues in 1885: construction of a stone (and not a wooden-planked) sidewalk on York Street, employment of the tramps "who fill our jail during winter months," the purchase of a new horse and buggy for the waterworks, the regulation of hawkers and peddlers, and the enforcement of the "proper cleaning"[4] of chimneys in the city.

By 1886, though, as he ran for a third mayoral term, Manning faced a changing city. Toronto had been rocked by a number of scandals, and in the eyes of many had become a more harsh, squalid, and dangerous place to live. Numerous citizens had opted to join a moral reform movement with the view that Toronto should become "Toronto the Good."

While Manning had expected to be easily re-elected, he found himself embroiled in one of the greatest upsets in the political life of Toronto. A growing number of residents were determined that their next mayor should be Reformer William Howland, a political rookie with no Council experience.

Howland was a temperance (anti-alcohol) advocate, while Manning was president of the Toronto Brewing and Malting Company. The 1886 campaign was a clear-cut choice between an establishment Tory and a crusading Reformer. Many Torontonians were outraged that with a population of just over 100,000 there were almost 1,000 liquor outlets. Reformers made sure to highlight that Manning was one of the principal stockholders of a major brewery.

Manning was stunned by his defeat. No one had charged him with any dishonourable act, and for years he had served as a conscientious, hard-working politician. His resounding defeat in 1886 ended his political career, and he retired from public life.

He remained an engaged and large contributor to several Toronto organizations such as the Home for Incurables, founded during his first mayoralty. Manning was also an active parishioner of St. James Cathedral and president of the Irish Protestant Benevolent Society. From 1886 onward, he was active with the Toronto Board of Trade and was a director of the Traders Bank of Canada and the Canadian Bank of Commerce. He was president of the Toronto Dry Dock and Shipbuilding Company, and at the time of his death was serving as the largest investor, shareholder, and president of the North American Land Company. He was also a member of the Albany, National, and Toronto Clubs.

When Manning died in 1903, he was one of the largest individual corporate taxpayers in Toronto and left an estate of approximately $800,000 to his surviving son and daughter, the equivalent of more than $27 million today. His home at 11 Queen's Park Circle was in an area of transition, and a year after Manning's death it was demolished.

Although he was from a new breed of monied men, he had also advocated financial probity in city government and improvements to municipal services. Despite being wealthy, which had brought him great influence and power, he also had a rich man's sense of duty toward his community.

Toronto Businesses, Industries, and Manufacturers in the Second Mayoral Term of Alexander Manning in 1885 but No Longer Seen in Toronto's Core in the 21st Century

Agricultural Implements	Glassware and Pottery	Patent Medicines
Biscuit Manufacturers	Hair Works	Piano and Organ
Boiler Makers	Hats	Manufacturers
Bookbinders	Hatters and Furriers	Plasterers
Brewers' Supplies	Hides and Skins	Roofing and Slate
Brick Manufacturers	Ice Dealers	Scale Makers
Broom Manufacturers	Iron Founders	Stained Glass
Carpet Manufacturers	Knitting Factories	Stone Works
Cattle Trade	Lime and Stone	Surgical Appliances
Coal Merchants	Livery Stables	Tanneries
Confectioners	Machinists	Tinsmiths
Corset Manufacturers	Marble Work	Undertakers
Crockery	Milk Dealers	Upholsterers
Engravers	Mineral Waters	Wagon Makers
Express Companies	Mouldings	Watchmakers
Fancy Goods	Nurserymen	Wharfingers
Flour and Feed	Oils and Varnish	Wool and Hide Dealers
Furniture Manufacturers	Paints and Oils	

Mayoral Election in 1873

Alexander Manning was selected by members of Toronto's Council and not by the city's citizens. Manning won on the first ballot 13–7.

Mayoral Election in 1885

SPECIAL NOTE: The mayor was once again chosen by Toronto's citizens.

CANDIDATE	VOTES
Alexander Manning	6,025
John Withrow	5,880

Mayor Angus Morrison
1876–1878

The 21st mayor of Toronto

Occupations: Lawyer, corporate director, Toronto Council member, Member of the Legislative Assembly of Ontario, Member of Canada's Parliament
Residence While Mayor: 2 Windsor Street
Birth: January 20, 1822, in Edinburgh, Scotland
Death: June 10, 1882, in Toronto

———— • ————

opular and charismatic, Angus Morrison was an athletic, barrel-chested lawyer with a fashionable mane of curly hair and stylish mutton-chop sideburns who became one of Toronto's leading citizens. He was born in Edinburgh, Scotland, in 1822, the son of Hugh Morrison and Mary Curran. In 1830, age eight, he and his older brother, Joseph, came to Upper Canada with their father who was by then a widower and recently discharged from the Royal Highland Regiment. After a gruelling voyage of several weeks, they first settled in Georgina Township in June 1830 with the intention of farming.

In 1831, Hugh Morrison married Fanny Montgomery, the sister of well-known tavern owner John Montgomery, whose establishment (in today's Yonge and Eglinton area) later became famous as the site where William Lyon Mackenzie's rebel forces gathered to carry out the 1837 rebellion. Soon after, the family moved to York and opened the Golden Ball Tavern, their own place.

Angus Morrison attended grammar school in Toronto, but when he was 14, his father was killed in an accident while at a political meeting at Market Square in Toronto. Three years later, in 1839, Angus became a clerk in the law office older brother Joseph had opened with William Blake on King Street, the commercial and business heart of Toronto.

Morrison took great interest in outdoor sports, especially rowing. He won and held the rowing championship of Toronto Bay from 1840 to 1842 and was also president of the Toronto Rowing Club for 14 years. An avid winter curler, he helped found the Toronto Curling Club where he served as president for two years.

After applying himself less to sporting activities and more to the study of law in the office of Blake & Morrison, he was called to the bar in 1845 and entered into a successful practice on King Street. A year later, in August 1846, age 24, he married Janet Gilmor, daughter of Commissary General Robert Gilmor of Trois-Rivières, Quebec, a veteran of the War of 1812. Together, they had four sons and two daughters.

Active in Toronto's St. Andrew's Society, he served as secretary of the society for 11 years and as its president for two. The *Dictionary of Canadian*

Biography observes that Morrison "parlayed his family relations, social connections, and public image into a substantial legal practice based on corporate affiliations rather than court appearances."[1]

Morrison was the solicitor for several well-known institutions, including
the Ontario Building Society, the University of Toronto, and later, after it
opened in the 1860s, the Canadian Bank of Commerce. His high profile and
personal popularity also undoubtedly assisted in his first electoral success as
a member of Toronto's Council for St. James's Ward in 1853.

In February 1854, he was also elected as a Reform member of the
Legislative Assembly of the Province of Canada but for the newly created riding of Simcoe North in Barrie. Although still living in Toronto, he
maintained a lofty public profile in his Simcoe constituency, supporting
local issues and strategically distributing patronage when possible. He was a
strong supporter of transportation projects of economic importance to both
Simcoe and Toronto, including railways, canals, navigation companies, and
roads.

Morrison was acclaimed in the 1857 provincial election, yet by 1861,
with his constituency not yet seeing expected gains in transportation, he
had to fight a vigorous campaign and came close to losing his seat. To make
matters worse, by 1863, the Northern Railway, which Morrison had served
as both a director and supporter, was in debt, causing severe financial difficulty for Simcoe County's council and providing political fodder for his
opponents. Morrison then lost the 1863 provincial election, described as
"riotous" and where "whiskey was sent into the Townships in streams."[2]

Ironically, though he was a Reformer, the popular Morrison was then
recruited by the Conservatives in the Niagara region to be their candidate
in an 1864 provincial by-election, which he won by a slim margin. Later,
in the 1867 federal general election, he won the riding of Niagara for the
Conservatives, thus becoming a member of the House of Commons in the
first post-Confederation Canadian Parliament. (Unlike today, when voting is
held on a single day, in 1867 a federal election took place over several weeks.)

Morrison was re-elected federally in Niagara in October 1872 by an
even smaller margin, this time capturing 300 votes to Liberal opponent
J.M. Currie's 298. Once returned to office, he continued his advocacy of
transportation matters as well as serving as a party whip. All told, he served
six and a half years as a federal MP.

In 1873, Morrison was made a Queen's Counsel, and in January 1874 was presented with a new and very difficult political task: wresting the federal riding of Toronto Centre from high-profile Liberal businessman Robert Wilkes. *Globe* publisher George Brown had described the prior election there as "the keenest and bitterest I ever knew." A Conservative observer agreed, noting that "the lame, the blind, and even the absent and the dead were brought out to vote …"[3]

Morrison lost Toronto Centre, but his federal defeat became the city's gain, and in late December 1875, he again entered the political fray, this time to campaign for Toronto's mayoralty in 1876, easily defeating incumbent Francis Medcalf. The *Globe* noted that Morrison's own personal popularity was a key factor in his victory. He lost only one of nine city wards, capturing 4,425 votes to Medcalf's 2,673.

Yet, even though the city-wide electors of Toronto once more had their say in choosing the mayor, the Council itself did not support that. In January 1876, it voted to ask the Legislative Assembly to again have the mayoralty decided in secret and behind closed doors by way of political horse trading or vote buying. Never mentioned, of course, were recent problems of alleged corruption and bribery.

Morrison's 1876 Council tackled several issues: fire service appropriations, a new awnings bylaw, a first sewer on Bathurst Street, the "unchecked lawlessness"[4] of young people destroying shade trees, an increase in butchers' licence fees, a visit by Council members to Rochester, New York, on the steamer *Southern Belle*, a report comparing the city's pavement conditions with those in several U.S. cities, and a request that the Council financially assist the Don Valley Railway.

Also dealt with were objections to new blacksmith forges within the city, new ward boundaries due to population growth, a proposed law to govern "the Sale of Fermented or Spirituous Liquors,"[5] the election of city water commissioners, and a request that the dust-filled streets downtown be watered down.

As mayor, Morrison enjoyed a substantial public profile. He represented Toronto at the Philadelphia Centennial International Exhibition of 1876 where he came across a large wrought-iron fountain that he bought, transported back to Toronto, and donated to the city in 1877 in honour of Queen Victoria's birthday.

A capable administrator and a very visible figure about town, Morrison was re-elected in 1877 and 1878. As *The Canadian Biographical Dictionary and Portrait Gallery of Eminent and Self-Made Men* says, "he effected many improvements in the conduct of matters connected with the mayoralty, and always in a dignified and strictly non-political manner."[6] In April 1876, Morrison led a Council delegation to New York, Chicago, and Montreal with respect to a somewhat suspicious topic: "inspecting the pavement of the streets in those cities."[7]

In terms of news reporting in the rapidly growing city, the *Toronto Evening Telegram* was launched in April 1876 under John Ross Robertson and became the voice of conservative, working-class, Protestant Toronto. As the *Dictionary of Canadian Biography* notes, "The *Telegram* specialized in presenting news in the form of a potpourri of tidbit items, trivia, maverick politics, and vigorous local political crusades … the first to emphasize municipal events by reporting on the City Council, the water commission, police courts, hospitals, sports, and crime," also pointing out that "Robertson's strident support of the Orange Order, the British Empire, and Canadian nationalism, and his anti-American, anti-Quebec, and anticlerical biases … reflected and reinforced the sentiments of much of late-19th-century Protestant Tory Toronto."[8]

In March 1876, Police Chief Frank Draper made a comprehensive report to the Council, observing there had been a rapid increase in the number of "houses of ill fame" or brothels and advocating for increased surveillance of them. He also pointed out that they were scattered all over the city and in constantly changing locations "without the slightest restraint whatever." In terms of city taverns, the biggest problems were the sales made during prohibited hours and that it was "next to impossible" to regulate these houses properly. Draper further stated that a prohibition on the sale of alcohol on Saturday nights and on Sundays was "a very wholesome provision"[9] of the law that would have a positive result.

Morrison oversaw a reorganization of the standing committees of the Council. During Toronto's first 30 years as a city, expenditures were not adequately coordinated, and by the 1860s, there were further calls to control municipal spending. A first major reform came with the establishment of an Executive Committee with oversight over every aspect of the corporation's activities and the authority to veto expenditures by any committee.

In 1877, Toronto's Council considered a range of matters: a bylaw to appoint an inspector of building stone; new carpet, stoves, and furnaces for City Hall; an investigation into the sale of unfit 120-day-old veal in the market; and asking the Toronto Street Railway to go from just a single to a double horse-drawn streetcar track on Yonge Street.

The 1878 Toronto municipal election was a lively one. Morrison captured eight of the city's nine wards and won with 3,852 votes to James Beaty Jr.'s 3,257. The new Council dealt with a host of issues: new "wood kerbing"[10] on Bathurst Street, telephone service (a brand-new invention) between the jail and police courts, and the removal of horse manure from city streets. The police chief noted that of the 6,484 offences in the city during 1878 just 33 were carried out by "coloured" residents, while 3,845 were by immigrants from the British Isles.

A year-end report from the Council's Waterworks Committee advised that with a city-wide population of 73,813 there were now 6,707 customers connected to fresh piped running water, with 2,300 of them the result of new water services laid during 1878 itself.

Although nominated again in late December 1878 to run for a fourth term, Morrison decided not to, retiring from public life for good and choosing to work with his prestigious law firm, now known as Morrison, Sampson, and Gordon.

The Canadian Biographical Dictionary and Portrait Gallery of Eminent and Self-Made Men describes Toronto's former mayor as "generous almost to a fault, naturally genial and pleasant in manner, possessing a courteous and hospitable disposition at all times, and withal a true gentleman. Mr. Morrison is a man who has many warm and sincere friends throughout the wide circle of his acquaintances."[11]

In 1879, a Grand Trunk engine proceeding westward hit the private railcar of the president of the Credit Valley Railway, with the impact causing serious injuries to all on board, including Morrison. The next year, it was noted that he was not in active practice because of the effects of injuries received in the Credit Valley accident.

Toronto's 21st mayor died unexpectedly at home the night of June 10, 1882, age 60. His funeral was that of a leading citizen of Toronto; the funeral cortège consisted of more than 90 horse-drawn carriages.

Mayoral Election in 1876

CANDIDATE	VOTES
Angus Morrison	4,425
Francis Medcalf	2,673

Mayoral Election in 1877

Angus Morrison	4,665
Warring Kennedy	3,651
James Britton	162

Mayoral Election in 1878

Angus Morrison	3,852
James Beaty, Jr.	3,257

Mayor James Beaty, Jr.

1879 and 1880

The 22nd mayor of Toronto

Occupations: Author, senior corporate counsel, Toronto Council member, Member of Canada's Parliament, chairman of the Toronto Police Commission
Residence While Mayor: 305 Church Street
Birth: November 10, 1831, in Halton County, Upper Canada
Death: March 15, 1899, in Toronto

——— • ———

Eloquent, unostentatious, and a man of true integrity; those are just a few of the words used to describe James Beaty, Jr. The son of John Beaty and Elizabeth Stewart, James was born on November 10, 1831, at Ashdale Farm in Halton County's Trafalgar Township and came to Toronto in 1849, age 18. His parents had emigrated from County Cavan in Ireland and settled in Halton where Beaty's father farmed for 50 years. John and Elizabeth Beaty had 13 children: four sons and nine daughters.

The Canadian Biographical Dictionary and Portrait Gallery of Eminent and Self-Made Men offers a picture of Halton in the 1830s: James Beaty Jr.'s parents were "intelligent people and the children were well educated according to the times.... Educational training was kept up by well-directed reading and conversation. Habits of industry and strict morality were rigorously enforced, and the practice of religious duties never allowed to be forgotten."[1]

The young James was sent to Toronto where he received private tuition for a time, and in 1850, entered the study of law in the offices of Dr. Larratt Smith and Adam Wilson, Toronto's mayor in 1859–1860. Beaty was called to the bar in 1855, then entered into a partnership with Wilson and Christopher Patterson, later a justice of the Supreme Court of Canada. As a new lawyer, and on his 27th birthday in 1858, Beaty married a cousin, Fanny Beaty, and had two daughters with her.

The Toronto law firm of Wilson, Patterson, and Beaty continued until the elevation of Adam Wilson to the bench in 1863. In 1874, after Christopher Patterson also became a judge, the firm continued under the name of Beaty, Hamilton, and Cassels, with Allan Cassels, a young student in the office, joining the partnership.

Beaty received a bachelor of common law from Trinity College in 1872 and was also made a Queen's Counsel by the federal government of Sir John A. Macdonald. In 1875, Trinity conferred a doctor of common law on him. In 1877, he was elected to Toronto's Council from St. James's Ward, and the following year was defeated for the mayoralty in his first try for the job, capturing 3,257 votes to victor Angus Morrison's 3,852.

At City Hall it was well known that Beaty intended to run for mayor again in January 1879. When Morrison chose not to seek another term, his mantle was assumed by Alderman Patrick Close. Yet the mayoral race proved to be highly competitive. In addition to Close, two other aldermen were in the running, as were two former mayors, Alexander Manning and Francis Medcalf. In the end, Beaty was the winner with 2,804 votes, to second-place finisher Close with 2,166.

Proud of his very frugal approach and ability to keep taxes down, Beaty introduced "By-law No. 793," which became known as the "Beaty By-law," changing the management of Toronto's civic affairs with the reduction of the Council's standing committees from 10 to five and strengthening the new Executive Committee.

One of the most popular public spaces built during Beaty's term was the Horticultural Pavilion at Allan Gardens. Built in 1879 at a cost of $20,000, it was soon characterized as the product of an illicit union between a pagoda and the Crystal Palace. With excellent acoustics, its spacious ground-floor gallery could seat 2,500 citizens.

In 1879, the Council dealt with several issues: the first regulations to govern passenger elevators in the city (then called "elevator hoists"), approval of $138 for a mayoral trip to Ottawa to press the city's case with MPs, and on 10 separate occasions a discussion of the city's new horse-drawn street railway. It also discussed ship canals, civic patronage, costs to the city due to gas leakages, and the quality of ice supplied by Toronto's 32 commercial ice dealers.

In September 1879, Toronto hosted an official visit of the new governor general, the Marquis of Lorne, featuring special night illuminations, a lacrosse match, a sailing regatta, and a grand ball. It was noted that Mayor Beaty managed the affair with tact, good sense, and sound judgment.

Beaty's term as mayor was also an eventful period in Canada. The very first telephone was installed in Toronto on February 13, 1879, and Canada's first phone directory was published in the city five months later, containing only 40 names. A patent for the transmission of speech over wire had been issued to Alexander Graham Bell just three years earlier.

In running for re-election as mayor in 1880, Beaty once again claimed victory, this time by more than 900 votes over Angus Morrison, who attempted a political comeback after being away from office for just a year. The final vote was 4,280 for Beaty and 3,367 for Morrison.

Early in his second mandate, Beaty's inaugural speech outlined key mayoral priorities: greater fiscal discipline and harshly pointing out that prior councils had spent "without due regard to the condition of the treasury." That, Beaty noted, was "a pernicious practice."[2] Indeed, his entire 12-page address dealt with a single topic: the state of city finances, including credit, interest paid, tax arrears, fines and fees, maintenance costs, taxation rates, the cost of major public works, local and frontage taxes, city benefits, Council governance, tax assessment, and a proposed new city charter.

Beaty also proposed a new system of governance in which nine Council members elected city-wide would form a new Executive Committee in place for a three-year term and staggered to provide for a yearly one-third turnover. In addition, two local aldermen would be elected to serve each ward.

The chief constable reported on crime in Toronto the year before. There was one attempted murder, one manslaughter, and 165 prostitution-related charges for "keeping a house of ill fame."[3] Yet, by far, the highest number of charges had to do with liquor: 2,836 for being drunk and disorderly.

The Council dealt with a host of issues in 1880, including a proposed hotel on the Toronto Islands; a request that Ottawa compensate the city for services provided to federal buildings, installations, and properties; a projected new horse-drawn streetcar line down York Street from Osgoode Hall to Union Station; and studying how Boston cleaned its streets.

In August 1880, Riverdale Park on the west side of the Don River was officially opened by Mayor Beaty. The next month, the Council heartily welcomed the mayor of Buffalo and a delegation of 120 business leaders. After a reception at City Hall, a sumptuous banquet fuelled by copious amounts of liquor led one appreciative reporter to declare: "The refreshments were of the best."[4] Also in 1880, Ontario unveiled plans for a new Legislative Assembly to be located south of Queen's Park, but the building took 12 years to finally open.

Politically, Beaty was a Conservative all his life yet was looked upon as a moderate, the result of his diverse personal connections and associations, which garnered him backing from supporters of both parties. Ironically, as the legal counsel for contractors building the Canadian Pacific Railway, he was involved in negotiations that resulted in the 1873 downfall of Prime Minister John A. Macdonald's government.

The Canadian Biographical Dictionary and Portrait Gallery of Eminent and Self-Made Men, published in 1880–1881, describes James Beaty as "moderate in his views of things, and temperate in language and argument" and said he possessed "the confidence of his fellow citizens … [with] convictions of his own on most subjects of public interest."[5] Under a pen name, Beaty wrote occasional articles for religious papers, literary magazines, legal publications, and political journals.

Throughout his career, Beaty enjoyed the support of his loving wife, Fanny, described in the "Beaty Family History" as "an active Christian.… Long an invalid she suffered from dyspepsia and consequent disorders,"[6] yet it was also noted that the Beaty home was a welcoming haven for strangers.

While still mayor, Beaty won an August 1880 by-election for the House of Commons caused by the resignation of former mayor and MP John Beverley Robinson, Jr., to become lieutenant governor. Beaty was elected as the Conservative MP for the riding of Toronto West, a constituency to the west and north of Queen Street and Palmerston Avenue. He retired as mayor at the end of the year, yet chose to remain in Parliament in Ottawa. In June 1882, Beaty was re-elected to the House of Commons with an increased majority, defeating his mayoral successor, William McMurrich, by a vote of 2,714 to 2,283. He served in Parliament until January 1887 before deciding to leave federal politics and return to his Toronto legal practice.

Beaty's legal career was rich and varied. As head of the firm Beaty, Snow, and Smith, he was involved in several important cases at the Court of Appeal as well as with several criminal cases. His large practice also included the management of client properties, and with partners, he took an active role in establishing the Confederation Life Association, which in just a few years became a major life insurance firm.

His law firm also carried out legal work for the Canadian Manufacturers Life Insurance Company (today's Manulife), incorporated in June 1887, whose president was the venerable Sir John A. Macdonald. Beaty's firm also served as counsel for the Commercial Building and Investment Society, one of the oldest institutions of its kind in Toronto. In addition, he was a director of the Scarboro Heights Hotel Company, which built a hotel east of Toronto on the Balmy Beach shore of Lake Ontario.

Upon his retirement from city politics, Beaty authored several legal and religious works: *Paying the Pastor: Unscriptural and Traditional* (1885);

Baptism: With Its Antecedents, Incidents and Consequents and Various Learned Testimonies (1889); *Learned Testimonies on Baptism and the Lord's Supper, with Essays on Immersion into Christ, and the Breaking of the Loaf* (1891); and *Civic Relief* (1895), as well as a publication of special interest to professionals, *The Elements of Canadian Law.*

He served as a bencher of the Law Society of Upper Canada from 1881 to 1891 and held executive positions in the Osgoode Club, also known as the Law Debating Society. In 1892, he attempted a comeback in municipal politics, but this time he was humiliated.

In a truly quixotic bid for the mayor's office in 1892, he ran against two high-profile candidates: railway magnate and philanthropist Edmund Osler and dry goods merchant Robert Fleming, both of whom reaped more than 8,000 votes each, with Beaty receiving only 603.

In the fall of 1898, Beaty sustained a stroke from which he never recovered. Six months later, in March 1899, he died, age 67. His funeral was a simple ceremony held at the Toronto Necropolis, and though he had once been an Anglican, it was conducted by the Church of the Disciples of Christ.

Mayoral Election in 1879	
CANDIDATE	VOTES
James Beaty, Jr.	2,804
Patrick Close	2,166
Alexander Manning	1,118
John Turner	789
James Britton	744
Francis Medcalf	136

SPECIAL NOTE: In an amazing turn of events, former mayor Francis Medcalf captured a mere 136 votes.

Mayoral Election in 1880	
James Beaty, Jr.	4,280
Angus Morrison	3,367

Mayor William McMurrich

1881 and 1882

The 23rd mayor of Toronto

Occupations: Lawyer, trustee of the Toronto Board of Education, Toronto Council member, author, community and church leader, college board member
Residence While Mayor: 55 Beverley Street
Birth: November 1, 1842, in Toronto
Death: September 6, 1908, in Humphrey (now Seguin Township), Muskoka

—— • ——

William Barclay McMurrich was born in Toronto in November 1842 and was the eldest son of John McMurrich and Janet Dickson. His father had come from Renfrewshire, while his mother hailed from Lanarkshire in Scotland.

To understand the drive, ambition, and success of William McMurrich, one needs only to look at the example set by his father, John, a principal with the firm Bryce, McMurrich, and Company, one of Toronto's main dry goods houses specializing in high-end British textiles. His father had been in business in Glasgow before coming to the New World in 1835 and establishing himself in both the mercantile and political worlds of Upper Canada.

William McMurrich was educated at a grammar school at Jarvis and Richmond Streets and at Knox Academy on Front Street. Subsequently, he studied at Upper Canada College and the University of Toronto. His field of choice was natural sciences, and he was a gold medallist in this field in 1863. Four years later, McMurrich obtained his master of arts and began the study of law in the office of John Leys.

In 1866, McMurrich married the daughter of Plummer Dewar of Hamilton and was also called to the bar. He then entered into a legal partnership with Leys until 1874 when he started the firm of McMurrich, Coatsworth & Hodgins, which later became McMurrich & Urquhart.

McMurrich first entered public life in 1868 as a public school trustee for St. Andrew's Ward, a position he held for nearly eight years (twice elected by acclamation). While a trustee, he chaired the Sites and Building Committee and in 1872 was intimately involved in preparations for the visit of Governor General Lord Dufferin to Toronto public schools. As biographer George M. Rose notes, McMurrich "took an active interest in providing education for the large number of children then wandering at large in our streets, and preparing for lives of sin and crime."[1]

As a trustee, McMurrich took his role seriously, visiting New York State and Massachusetts to investigate the workings of industrial schools there. His report was later adopted by the Board of Education, and as a result of his work, the old House of Refuge and 2.5 hectares of land were obtained for the purpose of a similar school in Toronto. McMurrich resigned from the school board in 1877 to become the board's corporate solicitor, a position he held for almost 30 years.

In 1879, McMurrich was elected to Toronto's Council from St. Patrick's Ward, receiving one of the largest majorities ever given to a city councillor up to that time. As chair of the Civic Reception Committee, he was also heavily involved in the successful visit of Governor General the Marquis of Lorne and his wife, Princess Louise, a daughter of Queen Victoria. The following year, in 1880, he was returned by acclamation and was named to two prestigious posts: the city's representative on the Northern Railway's board of directors and chair of Toronto's new Executive Committee.

While on the Council, he devoted considerable attention to a proposed new policy called "local improvements" in which a specific self-taxing levy was applied to a given geographic area to carry out much-needed improvements to local infrastructure. McMurrich had visited several American cities where it was already in place, and once Ontario gave permission, the Council introduced its own plan.

From 1874 onward, Toronto mayors were once again elected directly, and in 1881, McMurrich defeated Alderman Patrick Close by 1,161 votes, a comfortable majority obtained from all shades of the political and religious spectrums. As mayor, McMurrich urged stone pavement be put down "on streets subject to heavy traffic"[2] and urged the city to lay the foundation of a major park system, even offering a specific location — the Toronto Islands.

One issue causing major civic concern was gas from the sewer system, which was "becoming an increasing evil ... driving the foul gas into the houses and contaminating the air." And while it was no longer possible to bring in fresh water from Lake Simcoe, McMurrich said the solution to contaminated drinking water was an extension of the city's main intake pipe "into the pure water of the Lake."[3] Under his leadership, the city's financial affairs were strengthened to prevent it from being defrauded, and new measures were implemented for contractors doing work for the city.

The year 1881 showed that Toronto was on the cusp of great change: in May, R.H. Lunt applied to the Council for permission to inaugurate electric lights. He was granted temporary use of fire-alarm poles on several major streets to exhibit this new kind of illumination. On October 10, the following was approved: "That this council take means as early as possible to have the centre of the City lit up with electric light, and that a committee be appointed and named by His Worship the Mayor to get all the information necessary as to the cost …"[4]

The Council also dealt with a range of issues: a proposal for horse-drawn streetcars on Bathurst and Parliament Streets, water stations for the horses of hotel guests and patrons, a committee to look into building a new City Hall and courthouse, the need for a major revision of assessment methods, and a call to remove the fences surrounding Osgoode Hall in order "to use the grounds as a public park."[5]

A comprehensive report on all horses owned by the city was asked for by the Council, including the total number, their cost, when they were purchased, their present value, and the cost of maintaining them, including rent at the stables and insurance. And in a city without any form of medicare (an issue that took another 80 years to become a reality) and in which people paid for all medical services, those who could not afford treatment ended up at a place of last resort — the mayor's office. McMurrich reported to the Council that in this capacity he had sent 251 males and 262 females for admission to hospital in 1881, referring to them as "poor unfortunates." The mayor reported that he had also sent 13 young "foundlings" to hospital, noting they were "poor little waifs of humanity picked up in the public streets."[6]

Prejudice against Black people in Toronto also reared its head during McMurrich's mayoralty. Black people found it difficult if not impossible to stay at any of the city's major hotels. In September, the Fisk Jubilee Singers from Nashville, a group of Black U.S. musicians specializing in Black spirituals, were denied accommodation at the American Hotel.

Although Black people worked as waiters, porters, laundresses, janitors, and kitchen staff, their own hotels did not welcome them. When it became known that hotels would not accept the singers, several prominent citizens, including the mayor, offered their own homes. With the resulting bad publicity, the American Hotel backed down and withdrew its refusal. Justice had prevailed and the singers were able to stay.

When nominations opened on December 26, 1881, for the January 1882 mayoral vote, McMurrich was chosen by acclamation, and in another sign of the esteem of his fellow citizens, he was selected president of the prestigious St. Andrew's Society, a position he held for the next two years.

McMurrich's inaugural address to the Council in 1882 called for the establishment of free public libraries in Toronto "free from all political or sectarian influences."[7] He also announced that preliminary discussions had taken place regarding the annexation of Yorkville as well as planning for a proper celebration to mark Toronto's upcoming 50th anniversary, in 1884.

The mayor observed that the current City Hall was "extremely unhealthy" and that "sickness is very frequent." He also urged that Toronto develop what Chicago had — "a series of parks encircling the city and connected by broad boulevards." It could, said the mayor, "easily be carried out here."[8] McMurrich also reported on a large number of complaints about street cleaning and watering, saying that streets should be swept daily and the refuse, garbage, and horse manure removed. Yonge Street, he noted, was crowded with horses, dogs, bicycles, wagons, coaches, buggies, livery cabs, and pedestrians.

History writer George Monro Grant describes Toronto in 1882 this way:

> Crossing the Esplanade, monopolized by the railways, the traveller at once finds himself in the heart of the city.... Coaches and cabs are flying to and from the hotels. The street cars glide past, diverging, a short way on, towards various points. Pic-nicing parties or excursionists, bound for the ferries or for neighbouring towns, file by; and wagons with their burden of freight lumber along, adding to the noise and confusion. Massive warehouses and piles of buildings block in the traffic ...[9]

The year 1882 saw a visit to Toronto by Oscar Wilde, one of the world's most intriguing writers and famous for his flamboyance, style, and wit. The 27-year-old author appeared at the Grand Opera House on May 25, 1882, dressed entirely in black with a velvet coat, black knee breeches, and silk stockings.

McMurrich was a clear and forceful speaker who knew how to state a point with a certain grace, a quality missing among many public figures of the day. As an independent Liberal and still serving as mayor, he was a candidate in the 1882 federal election against former mayor James Beaty, who defeated him by a vote of 2,714 votes to McMurrich's 2,283. Later, in the

1887 federal general election and again running as a Liberal, McMurrich narrowly lost election to the House of Commons, this time by a mere 40 votes in the riding of Muskoka and Parry Sound.

In his personal life, McMurrich had joined the Queen's Own Rifles in the 1860s at a time when Canada feared U.S. military activity due to the Civil War. A staunch Presbyterian and member of the Masonic Lodge, McMurrich was an elder at Knox Church and superintendent of its Sabbath school. In addition, he was a commissioner of the Presbyterian General Assembly and was involved with a number of benevolent organizations: he was director of the Toronto Conservatory of Music, a member of the Prisoners' Aid Society, and a trustee of Upper Canada College. He also created the McMurrich Silver Medal in Natural Sciences at the University of Toronto.

In 1894, McMurrich was the co-author of *The School Law of Ontario*, a major work dealing with education, public school acts, high schools, truancy, and compulsory school attendance. He was also a curator of the Royal Canadian Institute, president of the Nipissing and James Bay Railway Company, on the board of the Victoria Club, and a member of the Ontario Artillery Association. McMurrich further served as a member of the Toronto Golf Club, the Toronto Hunt Club, and the Royal Canadian Yacht Club, as well as being president and commodore of the Muskoka Lakes Association.

William McMurrich, who lived on St. George Street in Toronto, died in Muskoka in September 1908. A special meeting of the Council was convened to honour the city's 23rd mayor, then adjourned to attend his funeral.

Mayoral Election in 1881	
CANDIDATE	VOTES
William McMurrich	4,111
Patrick Close	2,950
James Britton	590
Mayoral Election in 1882	
William McMurrich won the mayoralty by acclamation on December 26, 1881, for the 1882 term of Toronto's Council.	

Mayor Arthur Boswell

1883 and 1884

The 24th mayor of Toronto

Occupations: Lawyer, Toronto Council member, Toronto Public Library Board chair, yachtsman
Residence While Mayor: 230 Wellington Street West
Birth: January 3, 1838, in Cobourg, Upper Canada
Death: May 16, 1925, in Toronto

——— • ———

Arthur Radcliffe Boswell was the son of George Boswell, a judge of the County Court of Northumberland, and his wife, Susan Radcliffe. George Boswell became one of the leading lawyers in the province and was known as a strong supporter of the Reform movement. The Boswells were a prominent Cobourg family that had once owned a local distillery.

Born in the family's home in Cobourg, Upper Canada, on January 3, 1838, Arthur Boswell was educated in Brockville and at Upper Canada College, and like his father, chose a career in law. He was called to the bar in 1865, then practised law in Toronto. In July 1864 in Cobourg, Ontario, he married Ella Cruse, who had immigrated to Canada from Staffordshire, England. They had one child, Grace, born in 1866.

Boswell was noted for his love of yachting and had helped stage a grand regatta in Toronto harbour upon the occasion of the Prince of Wales's royal visit to Toronto in 1860. In later years, Boswell served as president of the Canadian Association of Amateur Oarsmen, president of the Toronto Rowing Club, and commodore of the Royal Canadian Yacht Club for more than 14 years where he was considered one of the best yachtsmen on the lake.

From 1877 to 1879, Boswell sat on Toronto's Council from St. George's Ward and was returned again in 1881 and 1882. In 1883, he ran for mayor in what the *Globe* called "a spirited and respectably conducted contest."[1] His opponent was former Council member John Withrow, still flush from establishing the Toronto Industrial Exhibition (today's Canadian National Exhibition or CNE). Yet Withrow had had a major dispute with the trade union movement, which cost him the election. As author Jesse Middleton notes in *The Municipality of Toronto: A History*, it was "one of the most exciting Mayoralty contests in the story of the City."[2] Boswell won by just five votes, capturing 4,289 votes to Withrow's 4,284 in the closest mayoral vote in Toronto's history.

Under Boswell, 33 councillors represented 10 wards, while the mayor received a salary of $2,000 and part-time Council members served without remuneration. With the annexation of Riverside and Brockton (the College

Street area near Dufferin) came two new city wards, and the number of
elected members of the Council now rivalled some provincial legislatures.

In outlining his priorities, Boswell pointed to a number of recent City of
Toronto accomplishments: several kilometres of new sewers, work on a main
trunk sewer, and the straightening of the Don River. He also mentioned
the extension of the city's main water intake pipe into Lake Ontario and
urged that a new city bylaw be enacted to provide for fire escapes at factories, hotels, and theatres. When Boswell later spoke of his achievements, he
always noted that 40 kilometres of streets were paved during his term. Half
a century earlier, Toronto had been widely known as "Muddy York," and
as Boswell often confessed, "it still seemed impossible to get rid of all the
mud."[3] He also authorized the building of a major stone wall to prevent the
Toronto Islands from being washed away. And when there was a tie vote on
where to build a new City Hall, it was Boswell's deciding vote that placed it
at Bay and Queen Streets (known today as Old City Hall).

Another accomplishment was the appointment of the city's first medical
officer of health, Dr. William Canniff, in 1883, who faced significant challenges. Many people in the rapidly expanding population lacked basic sanitation facilities, and serious infectious diseases such as typhoid and smallpox
had taken a heavy toll. Yet Canniff was not deterred, driven by the belief
that eradicating infectious disease was essential to social progress.

The city's Department of Public Health began house-to-house inspections, revealing wide-ranging filth and contamination, including "garbage, dangerous goods, filth, human waste, cesspools, dirty water, diseased
animals, or chemicals." Additional staff were hired to inspect dairies, slaughterhouses, grocery stores, butcher shops, and bakeries. Toronto factories were
also a major source of concern due to "the inhalation of injurious dusts,
fumes of chemicals, bad ventilation, poor light, excessively high temper-
atures, bad drains and plumbing."[4]

Furthermore, sewers drained directly into Lake Ontario, and residents
also found the lake a convenient place to dump unwanted materials. An
1884 public health report noted that the waterfront was filled with "all kinds
of decomposing organic matter, such as rotten vegetables and fruit, dead
animals and fish."[5]

And what to do with garbage was another matter. Crude and very basic
dumpsites filled up quickly, and the ever-expanding city was running out of

places to put more. Garbage was used to fill in ravines or fix uneven properties, with homes then built on top. Burning Toronto's refuse was considered
one of the better ways to dispose of garbage, since it was widely believed that
fire destroyed disease-breeding matter.

The year 1883 also proved to be an important election year thanks to a
major initiative by Council member John Hallam. For years, the Mechanics'
Institute, a voluntary dues-paying educational society, had enjoyed a 5,000-
book collection. Hallam had proposed that the city acquire it and establish free public libraries, yet had met with political resistance. No other
Canadian city at the time had a public library system, so Hallam put the
initiative on the ballot, and in January 1883, and by way of a huge majority,
Torontonians voted to adopt it.

The Council also dealt with a range of issues under Boswell: removal of
the tollgates at Avenue Road and Davenport, the creation of a new ward due
to the annexation of Yorkville, and how to manage 31 head of cattle and 14
horses impounded for wandering within the city. It also looked at a detailed
report on the city street watering efforts, noting that the $20,000 budget
was spent on multiple items: the purchase of water, wages and salaries, new
horses and wagons, veterinary bills, the repair of city stables, wheelbarrows,
hardware, horseshoes, horse feed, a hay-cutting machine, and the transportation of manure picked up on city streets to the farm next to the Don Jail.
The Council was advised that 61,141 cartloads of ash and refuse and 36,575
piles of manure and other scrapings had been removed from city streets.

In addition to the watering of city streets, the supply of fresh piped
water to residential and business customers was proving to be a very popular
service in the rapidly growing city. By December 1877, only 4,510 homes
and businesses had been connected to water, but just six years later in 1883,
16,276 customers were now served with piped water.

TORONTO HOMES WITH PIPED FRESH WATER, 1875–1887		
Year	Population	Number of Homes
1875	68,678	2,769
1876	71,693	3,512
1877	67,386	4,510
1878	70,867	6,707
1879	73,813	8,568
1880	75,110	9,582
1881	76,934	12,276
1882	81,372	14,062
1883	91,796	16,276
1884	105,211	18,363
1885	111,800	20,707
1886	118,403	22,643
1887	126,169	26,893

Source: Minutes of Toronto City Council, 1888.

Yet not all was in rosy shape when it came to matters of sanitation. In a scathing memo to council, Boswell let fly in no uncertain terms: the county attorney had brought charges against the city for permitting No. 1 Police Court and Station to remain in its present "foul, noxious, unwholesome, uncomfortable, and inconvenient state, totally unfit to confine prisoners therein." The mayor advised that upon inspecting the premises "it would be folly to defend the case" and that no prisoners should be confined in the cells, noting that "the stench is almost unbearable."[6]

In a sign of the changes to come, though it would still take another 35 years to happen, Alderman Thomas Downey proposed a revolutionary new idea: that both the Canadian and Ontario governments amend their Elections Acts "to enable women to vote for Members of Parliament, Mayors, Reeves, Aldermen, and Councilmen, on the same kind of qualification, and in the same way as men vote."[7]

For the January 1884 mayoralty election, Boswell was acclaimed, and the returning mayor spoke of his plans: further improvements to the Esplanade, the opening of the city's library system, and initial work looking into the building of a new City Hall. Toronto also saw its first electric street lights — welcomed by police and cursed by would-be evildoers. And for Boswell, sewage had taken on an increased importance. "Where does all the filth from these sewers accumulate?" he said. "In the Bay of Toronto … this cannot go on with safety, for our Bay will soon become a cesspool."[8]

Yet the true highlight of 1884 belonged to the 50th anniversary of Toronto's official incorporation. The principal celebrations from June 30 to July 5, 1884, covered six separate theme areas: municipal, military,

Front Street East looking west from Jarvis Street toward Yonge Street in 1884. Prominent in the foreground is Toronto's then City Hall, which is known today as the St. Lawrence Market.

benevolent societies, trade and industry, education, and United Empire Loyalists. Celebrations included concerts, fancy dress balls, athletic competitions, historical exhibits, parades, and evening fireworks. As historian Victor Russell notes, Boswell "was the epitome of the congenial host, attending all the events from early morning until late at night. Immaculate, yet robust and extremely enthusiastic, Mayor Boswell was the hit of the fair."[9]

Toronto's transportation service was also expanding, and its lumbering horse-drawn streetcars were now running on 10 major thoroughfares — Yonge, Queen, King, College, Spadina, Church, Front, Carlton, Sherbourne, and Parliament — serving a city-wide population of 105,211 citizens.

After Boswell was re-elected in 1884, his Council considered a host of issues: the removal of all remaining tollgates on Yonge Street, a bylaw to prohibit barbed wire fences, and whether all property tax exemptions should be abolished. The Council also discussed the sale of liquor in grocery stores, the annexation of Rosedale, and amendments to the Municipal Act to allow municipal councils to control the police budget.

For the first time, two electric lights were installed in the Council chamber, provoking a strong reaction. Alderman John Moore called them a nuisance and asked that they be removed. He also insisted "that steps be taken at the earliest possible moment to terminate the use of electric lights by the City and to secure the removal of the poles and wires from the streets."[10]

At the end of his 1884 term as mayor, Boswell chose to retire from office and continue with his law practice. He bought a grand semi-detached home at 69–71 Spadina Road where he resided with his wife, Ella. The Boswell home was in one of the new suburbs appropriated by the city, an area widely known as the Annex where the former mayor lived for another 40 years.

Boswell continued to play a prominent role in the life of the city. He accepted an appointment as inspector of insurance and registrar of the Friendly Societies and Loan Companies, was a member of the Masonic Lodge, and belonged to the city's most exclusive private clubs — the Albany, York, and Toronto. Boswell also served as a trustee of Toronto General Hospital and became chair of the new Public Library Board. Yet it was a love of yachting that remained his lifelong passion, and from 1889 to 1896 he served as commodore of the Royal Canadian Yacht Club. In 1907, he was made an honorary life member of the club and in later years was affectionately known as Commodore Boswell.

After 52 years of marriage, Boswell's wife passed away in February 1916, while her husband died in May 1925, age 87. The *Globe* described him as a "genial Tory" and "one of the finest gentlemen who ever sat in the Mayor's Chair."[11] A common thread in all newspaper stories was the role he had played as mayor in the city's 1884 anniversary celebrations.

Boswell's funeral was conducted at St. Alban-the-Martyr Anglican Church, where he had been a member, and was attended by Mayor Thomas Foster and civic officials. His remains were then transferred to Cobourg where he was buried.

Mayoral Election in 1883	
CANDIDATE	**VOTES**
Arthur Boswell	4,289
John Withrow	4,284
SPECIAL NOTE: Arthur Boswell won by a majority of only five votes, the closest mayoral election in Toronto's history.	
Mayoral Election in 1884	
Arthur Boswell won the mayoralty by acclamation.	

Mayor William Howland

1886 and 1887

The 25th mayor of Toronto

Occupations: Business leader, Board of Trade president, social reformer, philanthropist, evangelical crusader
Residence While Mayor: 2 Queen's Park Crescent
Birth: June 11, 1844, in Lambton Mills (now Etobicoke), Canada West
Death: December 12, 1893, in Toronto

—— • ——

One of the city's true reforming mayors, William Holmes Howland was elected with a strong mandate to, in his view, clean up Toronto both physically and morally. Not content to just observe a problem, Howland turned to civic politics to take action on drunkenness, poor housing conditions, filthy streets, and cleaning up a foul water supply.

The elder son of William Pearce Howland and Mary Ann Blyth, William Holmes Howland was educated at the Toronto Academy (where the Fairmont Royal York Hotel now stands), then at Upper Canada College and the Provincial Model Grammar School. Howland ended his formal education at age 16 after his father became active in provincial politics.

The future Toronto mayor's father was one of the province's most successful entrepreneurs and one of Canada's original Fathers of Confederation. In 1867, the senior Howland became the Member of Parliament for York West and minister of inland revenue. In 1868, he was appointed lieutenant governor of Ontario.

William took over his father's grain-and-milling business and quickly rose within Toronto's mercantile community. Although still a young man, he earned a reputation as a very capable business manager, becoming the president, vice-president, or director of a dozen companies, ranging from insurance and finance to electrical services and paint manufacturing.

He became president of the Queen City Fire Insurance Company in 1871 at age 27, making him the youngest insurance company head in Canada, a rise described as meteoric. In addition, he was president of Canadian Lloyds, president of the Millers' and Manufacturers' Company, and for two years, president of the Toronto Board of Underwriters.

In October 1872, age 28, Howland married Laura Chipman in Saint John, New Brunswick, and together they had seven children in 15 years. By the 1870s, Howland had become a supporter of commercial and industrial protection policies, beliefs he further advanced as the head of three influential Canadian business organizations: the Toronto Board of Trade, the Dominion Board of Trade, and the Manufacturers' Association of Ontario.

Although Howland claimed to be an independent who supported Conservative prime minister John A. Macdonald in Ottawa, he also continued to back the provincial Liberal government of Oliver Mowat in Ontario. In 1874, as a Canadian nationalist, he became chair of a new Canada First movement, helping to finance a weekly publication, the *Nation*, whose strongly protectionist and anti-American editorial positions appealed to Howland.

As an outgoing and enthusiastic individual armed with an influential name, high social standing, and strong business connections, Howland became noted for his devotion to both social and religious matters. In 1877, he founded the Protestant Episcopal Divinity School and became an evangelical Christian. As local prohibitionists sought to influence Toronto's political affairs, he also became a total abstainer from alcohol, applying himself to the growing temperance movement.

In the years that followed, Howland made a combination of philanthropy and evangelism a personal mission to the extent that his own business affairs suffered. In 1877, he launched a new evangelical publishing company as well as the International Christian Workers Association. He also started the Prisoners' Aid Association, an advocacy and penal reform group; was superintendent of the Central Prison Mission School; and chaired the Ontario branch of the Dominion Alliance, a major temperance association.

Yet even that was not enough. In 1878, Howland was appointed by the Ontario government to the board of Toronto General Hospital to assist in raising the standard of management there. He also worked with the Prison Gate Mission and Haven, a home for unwed mothers; the Andrew Mercer Reformatory for women; the Hillcrest Convalescent Hospital; and the Toronto branch of the Young Men's Christian Association (YMCA).

In addition to being a popular Sunday school teacher and frequent church speaker, he devoted weekends to relief work in St. John's Ward, an area considered by some to be at the centre of poverty and vice in Toronto. Regularly at night, Howland visited the inner city's slums and shanties, going from house to house to reach the poor, sick, alcoholic, and destitute. Other anti-poverty initiatives of Howland included the building of an alternative school for dropouts and a home for the aged and homeless poor. Years later, he served as founding chair of the Victoria Industrial School for

Boys, a training facility in Mimico whose purpose was to steer delinquent boys away from a life of crime.

Yet his evangelical work ran afoul of the established Church of England. In 1883, to further distance himself, Howland and several prominent citizens founded the non-denominational Toronto Mission Union, which ministered to the needs of the poverty-stricken, hungry, and abused in the downtown core by delivering social assistance, medical services, and relief aid. It also operated homes for seniors and those convalescing as well as providing Toronto's first-ever home nursing service.

Although already deeply involved in evangelical, community, social, and philanthropic work, Howland now turned his considerable enthusiasm, energy, and reformist zeal to municipal politics. Despite not having held public office yet, he enjoyed the advantage of significant business contacts, a highly prominent name, and a strong public profile. Supporters launched a campaign to have the people of Toronto "requisition" Howland to run. The plan worked.

In late December 1885, with the support of the Municipal Reform Association, he campaigned for the 1886 mayoralty on a platform of morality, religion, and reform. He was up against Alexander Manning, a Conservative and the incumbent mayor. Howland roused citizens to oppose Manning's wealthy brand of politics and won the endorsement of Toronto's newly organized labour movement. Despite a hard-fought campaign, Howland won handily, receiving 7,793 votes to Manning's 6,075 and winning nine of the city's 12 wards.

It was no surprise that the first major issues Howland chose to address were those of crime, policing, liquor, and law enforcement, noting that the total number of all offences in the city had reached more than 8,000 per year. He demanded an immediate reduction in liquor licences and that no new ones be issued or transferred.

On issues of health and sanitation, Howland called for Toronto to be a sanitary city, noting there had been a large increase in diphtheria and typhoid over the past year. These were recognized, said Howland, as "filth diseases ... preventable by proper sanitation." Howland also turned his attention to a host of issues: a new local improvement bylaw, unsafe rail crossings, and unsatisfactory fire alarms. "There was nothing the people feared more than fire," he said, also asking for major improvements "of a more permanent character" to main downtown streets such as Yonge, King, and Front Streets, as well as an end to municipal bonusing used to attract manufacturers to Toronto.[1]

The new mayor was taking over a city that, as historian Graeme Mercer Adam has described, was "British, and in the main, a Protestant city."[2] Among Howland's strongest supporters were evangelical Protestants, determined to preserve a church-centred Sabbath. As a result, on Sundays all streetcars and public transportation in Toronto stood idle.

And unlike any previous Toronto mayor, Howland tramped down city lanes and alleys to help feed the poor, pray with the sick, or comfort the lonely and dispossessed. With a population of just 118,000, Toronto had more than 800 bars, saloons, hotels, taverns, unlicensed "dens" and "dives," and "more than half of the eight thousand offences in 1885 were directly related to drunkenness. Habitual offenders savaged their friends, battered their wives and children, [and] forfeited their jobs."[3]

During Howland's first term, only a minority of Council members supported his municipal reform proposals. A major achievement was the appointment of a new inspector for the Police Department, David Archibald, whose new police squad would "combat cruelty to women, children and animals, to battle gambling, houses of ill fame [prostitution], desecration of the Sabbath, indecent exposure and, of course, unlicensed drinking dens."[4]

The overall crusade for righteousness and battling social evils was summed up in the phrase "Toronto the Good," coined by Howland and Archibald. While the new mayor wielded his new broom at City Hall, the clearing out of saloonkeepers and ward-heelers was implemented by the morality squad, which swept the streets of drunks and vagrants, swooped down on city bordellos, and emptied out drinking dens. There was also a special zeal to nab Sabbath breakers: on Sundays, tobogganing was prohibited, city playgrounds were closed, and police arrested boys for playing ball in the street.

Historian Desmond Morton, in *Mayor Howland: The Citizens' Candidate*, notes that due to municipal corruption, garbage collection was almost non-existent, and even City Hall's rubbish was rarely picked up. Rotting waste, as well as fouled alleyways, yards, and streets, resulted in insects, rodents, stench, and disease. The city, Howland believed, did not need more laws; it just required the enforcement of existing ones. So he ordered city officials to comply, even threatening the municipality's top civil servant for not doing so. Miraculously, garbage was soon collected.

As mayor, he challenged large monopolies, cartels, and business syndicates, forcing them to become more responsible in their business dealings. The year 1886 saw one of the city's most bitter labour disputes, with workers pitted against the private Toronto Street Railway monopoly, known for mistreating its employees. The railway lockout caused such a firestorm that after three days of rioting the militia had to be called in.

The 1887 mayoral results were a significant boost to Howland, who received 9,153 votes to David Blain's 6,958. Upon his re-election, hundreds of his supporters at the YMCA Hall spontaneously burst into applause, singing "Praise God from Whom All Blessings Flow." Because of Howland's support of both the Massey Manufacturing Company and street railway strikes, the city's workers had given him a solid mandate.

In his first major speech, Howland cited rising prosperity in Toronto, announcing that $10 million worth of new assessment had been added to the city's tax rolls. Howland publicly gave credit to God, saying, "the prosperity of this town is due to our character as a religious people." Yet social problems occupied much of his time and energy. First, it was liquor, since "the number of houses of bad character [brothels]" continued to rise. Howland also expressed strong concern over "tramps, idlers, and vagabonds" and said that in order to establish a "moral government" a reduction in saloons was necessary.[5]

A champion of reform, he called for the Municipal Act to be amended so that married women could vote. He also proposed an enlarged park on the Toronto Islands and expressed strong concern about a plan to extend the main outflow pipes of untreated sewage into the middle of the harbour, believing they would be ripped apart by strong currents and that the sewage swept back toward the city would end up in front of the main water intake pipe.

During his second mayoral term, Toronto's Council was also preoccupied with projects such as the Don River improvement scheme, the need for a larger City Hall, and improvements to street paving. With his ardent evangelical beliefs, zeal for temperance, and desire for reform, Howland continued to push for a range of familiar issues: an end to civic corruption, more control over powerful liquor interests, and the closing down of gambling dens. He persisted in his efforts to end prostitution and narcotic use and what he termed "desecration of the Sabbath."[6] A proposal to cut tavern licences by almost half did pass at the Council, but only after an acrimonious debate and furious lobbying by the opposing liquor interests.

In late 1887, age 43, and to the surprise of many, Howland chose not to run for a third term, returning instead to charity work and the Christian Alliance, which he served as Canadian president from 1889 until his death.

While Howland retired to help his ailing father with business affairs, he also sorted out his own business, personal, and financial matters and continued working with several charitable causes, including the alleviation of poverty, the fight against alcohol, and his personal desire to bring the gospel to more people. A major achievement in 1890 was persuading the Ontario government to appoint a royal commission on the prison and reformatory system. The following year, he played a role in the formation of Ontario's Children's Aid Societies.

Howland died of pneumonia in 1893 age 49. His funeral involved Anglican, Christian Alliance, and Presbyterian clergy, and despite a major snowstorm, more than 1,000 mourners on foot and from all social classes made it one of the larger funeral processions ever seen in Toronto.

A man born of privilege and a Board of Trade president so dedicated to the disadvantaged that he gave away most of his wealth, he left a minuscule personal estate valued at just $42,300. His brother, Oliver Howland, followed him as mayor 15 years later in 1901–1902.

Mayoral Election in 1886	
CANDIDATE	VOTES
William Howland	7,793
Alexander Manning	6,075
Mayoral Election in 1887	
William Howland	9,153
David Blain	6,958

Mayor Edward Clarke

1888–1891

The 26th mayor of Toronto

Occupations: Editor, publisher, Member of the Ontario Legislative Assembly, Toronto Council member, Member of the House of Commons, Orange Lodge leader
Residence While Mayor: 10 (later 16) Harbord Street
Birth: April 24, 1850, in Bailieborough, County Cavan, Ireland
Death: March 3, 1905, in Toronto

— • —

The son of Richard Clarke and Eleanor Ellen Reynolds, Edward "Ned" Clarke was born in April 1850 in the tiny County Cavan village of Bailieborough in the countryside of central Ireland. His father, a general merchant and flax buyer, gave his children the advantage of a finished education, but upon his death in 1864, the family was uprooted to North America. Young Clarke, then age 14, accompanied his bereaved mother and the family to Canada.

Following a brief sojourn in Michigan, Clarke settled permanently in Toronto after which he apprenticed as a printer with the *Globe* newspaper. Later, he practised his craft as a foreman with the *Express*, the *Sun*, and the *Liberal* and was a compositor and proofreader at the *Mail*.

In 1872, still a young man at age 22, he played a central organizing role as the leader of a major labour disruption — the printers' strike of 1872 — during which he was arrested and briefly jailed for alleged intimidation. The *Commemorative Biographical Record of the County of York, Ontario* notes that "it was the real beginning of the emancipation of labor and the final legalization of trades unions."[1]

In 1877, when a new company was formed to purchase the *Orange Sentinel*, the official newspaper of the Orange Order, Clarke was chosen as its manager at age 27, and soon after bought other stockholder shares and became the sole proprietor. It was said that this opened up the world of municipal politics for Clarke.

For several years, Clarke took an active interest in secret societies, especially the United Workmen, the Freemasons, and the Loyal Orange Lodge (LOL). He was a member of McKinley LOL No. 275, serving as master in 1873. He was also a master of Rehoboam Lodge No. 65 of the Ancient Free & Accepted Masons, treasurer of the Grand Orange Lodge of Ontario West, and in May 1887 was elected deputy grand master of the Orange Order in British North America.

Clarke was married in December 1884 at age 34 to Charlotte Scott, originally from Chesterfield, England. Together, they had eight children, and by all accounts, the Clarke home was a happy one. As the *Commemorative*

Biographical Record of the County of York, Ontario notes, "Clarke's home life was wholesome, tender and true … and to hearthstone, wife, and children he gladly turned when he could put aside for a season the great responsibilities resting upon him."[2]

At the time, elected officials in Ontario were able to hold office at both the provincial and municipal levels at the same time. Clarke served four one-year terms as mayor while also doing two terms in the Ontario Legislative Assembly.

In the provincial election of 1886, Clarke headed the polls as one of the three representatives from Toronto sent to the provincial Legislative Assembly, serving the first of two terms as a Tory MPP from 1886 until 1890. A year later, in late 1887 and while still an MPP and having no prior municipal experience, he presented himself as "the People's Candidate"[3] in Toronto's January 1888 civic election. As a Conservative intending to recapture the mayoralty from Howland Reformers, Clarke organized a brilliant campaign focused on his main power base: Conservatives, the Orange Order, and readers of the *Sentinel*.

To advocates of temperance, Clarke solemnly proclaimed he did not drink, while for newly enfranchised female voters, he was among the first city candidates to have women as political canvassers. He also appealed to the growing labour movement, highlighting his role in the 1872 printers' strike.

Capturing 7,933 votes in the 1888 mayoral election to 7,042 for Elias Rogers, Clarke was elected. The crowning blow to his opponent's campaign had come with the revelation of a price-fixing cartel of coal merchants that had included none other than Rogers.

At the beginning of his term, Clarke outlined his priorities. The first major topic was the state of city finances, with the municipality's debt load having significantly increased. And with additional debt issued for a new City Hall, it was projected to climb even further. Toronto was rapidly approaching the legal limit of its borrowing powers, he noted.

Clarke praised the construction of new sewers using day labour and reported that a new bylaw now provided for street lighting, cleaning, watering, and sidewalk improvements paid for with a new local improvement charge. One of the most important projects was a new trunk sewer to divert sewage from Toronto's harbour. Clarke emphasized the filth and sewage pollution at the foot of Yonge Street, and as a temporary stop-gap measure, called for pipes sending raw sewage to be extended much farther into the lake.

In 1888, the Council dealt with an investigation into the "whole system of tendering, awarding, carrying out, fulfilling, and inspecting contracts" and whether the system was, in the words of the Council, "defective."[4] Property tax exemptions were again raised, with a huge number of properties paying no taxes at all, including universities; Crown land; places of worship, clergy residences, and ecclesiastical corporations; schools; county properties; public charities; all federal and provincial land holdings, including those of the lieutenant governor; jails and correction houses; hospitals; and horticultural, agricultural, and literary societies.

Under Clarke, the Council appointed a group of experts to investigate various ways of supplying water to the city "so that it would be free of the contamination by city sewage." In 1888, the vast majority of residents still did not have piped water for bathing, cleaning, cooking, or drinking. With the city's population the year before having reached 126,169, the total number of homes served by clean, fresh piped water was just 26,893, with about 3,000 new water hookups carried out per year. The Council also dealt with a report on "how vagrants and tramps"[5] were handled in New York City, Boston, Philadelphia, Buffalo, and Rochester; a proposal to bury telephone and telegraph wires; and a new bylaw to govern the driving of cattle through the city.

On December 31, 1888, the incumbent Clarke was nominated for the 1889 election, and with no other nominations received, was acclaimed as mayor for 1889. Clarke headed up the Ontario Municipal Conference, the provincial voice for Ontario's cities, towns, and rural municipalities, and remained a sitting Conservative MPP of the provincial Legislative Assembly, where he served until April 1890.

Clarke's 1889 inaugural address to the Council was composed of weighty financial topics such as consolidation and conversion of the city debt, security to investors, and general debenture debt. He was noted for his strong hand — a much-needed one — since over time civic departments had become disorganized and lacked clear direction. Clarke even brought in a more efficient business approach by introducing two brand-new mechanical inventions — the adding machine and typewriter.

The 1889 Council discussed a range of issues: commercial ice cutting on the Don River, the thorny matter of requiring streets and houses to be numbered, the need for heat on streetcars during winter months, the abolition of road tolls, and a proposal to close all saloons, hotels, and taverns on public holidays. There was a request from the chief of police "for some means of controlling vagrant bands who perambulate the City late at night."[6]

In 1890, Clarke won a third term as mayor with 10,326 votes to opponent John McMillan's 8,432. In his inaugural address, he reported that the Toronto Street Railway (TSR) had applied to the Legislative Assembly "to make use of steam, electricity, cables, machinery, and other motive power" instead of horses for its streetcar lines. The Council also dealt with the issue of civic annexations, the use of day labour, the appointment of sewer inspectors, the creation of a future Board of Control, and a proposal to give veto power to the mayor. Also considered was the "unauthorized dumping of night soil"[7] — the horse manure recovered from city streets — into Lake Ontario near the main water intake pipe.

Clarke was again a Conservative candidate in the June 1890 Ontario election. Although still the top official at City Hall, he was relegated yet again to the Opposition benches at Queen's Park. In his final mayoral election in 1891, he received a foreshadowing of what might lie ahead. His opponent, Ernest Macdonald, was not taken seriously and gained little attention city-wide yet managed to capture a respectable 7,040 votes. Although Clarke won with 9,133 votes, the criticism of his dual elected roles continued. At the end of his fourth term later that year, he bowed out of municipal politics.

The newly re-elected mayor believed that attempts to have the city obtain its drinking water from Lake Simcoe, as opposed to Lake Ontario, "would be the height of folly."[8] He urged passage of legislation to allow technical schools across the province and called for a bylaw to deal with construction scaffolding. Clarke also supported several new health measures: the incineration of garbage, the drainage of stagnant pools of water, the erection of public abattoirs, and the closing of the remaining wells for water.

With the imminent expiration of the private transit franchise of the Toronto Street Railway, serious decisions regarding a new contract for the city's street railway fell upon Clarke. As Jesse Middleton notes in *The Municipality of Toronto*, by 1891, the TSR operated horse-drawn wooden streetcars on 22 streets. Of the 262 cars, 90 were enclosed while 56 were fully open. The entire operation was powered by 1,372 horses.

A new 30-year charter, first negotiated under Clarke in 1891, would be granted in April 1892 to the Toronto Railway Company. It included a maximum fare of five cents per mile, the issuing of free transfers, the city receiving a percentage of the company's gross earnings, the payment of public school taxes, the building of a new streetcar factory within the city, and a maximum 10-hour workday. Another key requirement was that electric-powered streetcars be introduced within a year and the entire system converted to electricity within three years.

In his farewell civic address, Clarke reminded residents that the physical area of the city had doubled in size, and though he had chosen not to run again for mayor in 1892, he would remain in the Legislative Assembly until 1894. MPP Clarke was among the first group of members to move into the newly built Queen's Park building.

On the personal side, Clarke served as president of Gold Ring Consolidated Mining, and in 1896 was vice-president of Toronto Western Hospital's board. He also acted as a senior executive with Toronto's Excelsior Life Insurance Company. Yet the lure of politics remained strong. In the federal general election of June 1896, Clarke was elected, along with Edmund Osler, as an MP for the dual-member riding of West Toronto, defeating two Liberal opponents. First appearing on the Ottawa political scene in August 1896, Clarke's first major address was a stirring protest against a government resorting to the "spoils" system.

Heading the polls in the Toronto West federal riding in November 1900, Clarke was re-elected, receiving just 28 percent of the vote in a hotly contested five-way race. Four years later, with the redistribution of Toronto seats in the federal general election of November 1904, he was elected the MP for Toronto Centre with 52 percent of the votes. Altogether, Clarke's federal political experience in the House of Commons spanned eight years and eight months.

In the House of Commons, Clarke was regarded as a serious parliamentarian and a convincing debater, described as "one of the clearest and most logical speakers [with] a manner that spoke of sincerity in every word." Although a dedicated Orangeman who favoured a stronger British Empire, "he enjoyed the friendship of a large number of the Roman Catholic clergy."[9]

Sadly, Clarke was stricken with an illness and died at home in March 1905, age 54. One account said that he knew his death was near and how in touching language the last words to his family were "those of affectionate farewell."[10] Messages were received from every region of the country. A private service was first conducted at his home at 383 Markham Street, followed by a public service at the Broadway Tabernacle, attended by a huge throng. His funeral cortège was one of the most imposing in the city's 70-year history, and a final graveside committal service was carried out under the auspices of the Loyal Orange Lodge.

Prime Minister Wilfrid Laurier noted the House of Commons had lost one of its most prominent members, also expressing "sincere admiration for his many great qualities and our deep sorrow at his loss." Opposition Leader Robert Borden also paid tribute: "He was gifted with the unusual powers of clear and vigorous expression yet with all his intense convictions and earnestness no word of his ever caused any sting of bitterness in the hearts of his political opponents."[11]

Mayoral Election in 1888	
CANDIDATE	VOTES
Edward F. Clarke	7,933
Elias Rogers	7,042
Daniel Defoe	2,003
Mayoral Election in 1889	
Edward F. Clarke was acclaimed.	
Mayoral Election in 1890	
Edward F. Clarke	10,326
John McMillan	8,432
Mayoral Election in 1891	
Edward F. Clarke	8,133
Ernest Macdonald	7,040

Mayor Robert Fleming

1892–1893 and 1896–1897

The 27th mayor of Toronto

Occupations: Business leader, temperance crusader, merchant, Toronto Council member, corporate director
Residence While Mayor: 325 Parliament Street
Birth: November 23, 1854, in Toronto
Death: October 26, 1925, in Toronto

—— • ——

n his epic *The Municipality of Toronto*, history writer Jesse Edgar Middleton is unequivocal in his admiration for Robert Fleming: "He has exercised a strong and beneficial influence upon his time and holds a respected place in many circles of Toronto life."[1]

Fleming's family roots were on a farm near Dromore, a tiny village in County Tyrone in the north of Ireland. His immigrant parents, William Fleming and Jane Cauldwell, left Ireland with eight children on the transatlantic sailing ship *Sesostris*. With 428 passengers on board, all were seeking a new and better life in North America.

On their difficult and stormy ocean passage to Canada, three of the Fleming children, including a nine-month-old baby, died at sea, while 11-year-old Eliza passed away from typhus upon their arrival at Grosse Isle, Quebec. She was buried in an unmarked mass grave with dozens of other immigrants.

Born a few years after his family had settled in Toronto, Robert Fleming became a veritable Horatio Alger success story. His father was a licensed carter, hauling wood from the forest near St. James Cemetery and moving the family nearby so the children could attend Park School. It was in Cabbagetown "that Fleming first won his reputation as a scrapper."[2]

When he was 12, he quit school to help support his family and got a job as an office boy and stoker for a coal-and-wood merchant. Before electricity arrived, the stoker was seen as an important office fixture, hired to keep the fires going in numerous individual fireplaces throughout a workplace. While in his teens, Fleming was a regular member of the local Methodist church and later became a staunch temperance advocate.

The future mayor went on to attend business school at night, and being highly ambitious, entered the wood, coal, and feed trade in the mid-1870s. Discovering a flair for commerce, he also moved into the world of real estate. Fleming's sister lived on Parliament Street, and her popular store offered credit to poor working-class immigrant families, something that many of the established retail concerns did not. Fleming himself lived above the store after his mother's death in 1871.

The Agony of Typhoid

Within days of exposure, typhoid causes a fever of up to 40 degrees Celsius and can result in delirium, agitation, dehydration, hemorrhaging, and pneumonia. In Toronto's case, the disease was caused by unsafe drinking water from Toronto's harbour.

In 1886, Mayor William Howland (1886–1887) noted a huge increase in both diphtheria and typhoid over the past year. These, he said, were "filth diseases ... preventable by proper sanitation." For his part, Mayor Robert Fleming (1892–1893 and 1896–1897) said that hundreds of deaths in Toronto in the 1890s were due to typhoid, as citizens drank disease-laden water from the city's harbour where raw sewage was flushed into the bay in proximity to cracked water intake pipes.

Later, under the mayoralty of Reginald Geary (1910–1912), unsafe water remained a huge problem, with 739 cases of typhoid contracted because of contaminated water from the harbour.

First married in December 1879 in Montreal to Margaret Breadon of Montreal, Fleming saw his wife die tragically while giving birth in March 1883. In October 1888, he remarried, and with his new wife, Lydia Orford, had four sons and five daughters.

At age 31, in 1886, he first won election as an alderman for St. David's Ward, urging that gas and light be immediately provided to 16 poverty-stricken families in the ward. Social reform and Christian principles were strong elements in Fleming's life.

A close ally of Mayor William Howland, he was an articulate crusader against liquor interests, the evils of demon rum, and the city's hundreds of taverns, succeeding in having a bylaw passed to significantly reduce the number of drinking establishments. Many believed it would cost him votes among the city's solidly hard-drinking, working-class Irish, but Fleming was such an engaging figure that he was easily re-elected to the Council for three one-year terms (1887–1889).

In 1892, with some Liberal support, he successfully won the mayoralty by a majority of 350 votes, defeating Edmund Osler on a mildly Reformist platform that included opposition to the Toronto Railway Company, the city's secretive, privately held transit monopoly. He immediately raised the salaries of all civic labourers, saying they had always been grossly underpaid, and awarded them a raise of 25 cents per day, a handsome sum in that era.

For his 1892 inaugural address to the Council, Fleming adopted a businesslike approach, calling for fewer city committees and a reduction in the municipality's staff. Assessment, he said, was an area needing reform, a theme he carried out over his entire mayoralty. He also predicted that major change would soon come to the streetcar system as it evolved from horse-drawn to electric vehicles.

On the afternoon of the 1892 Civic Holiday in August, Toronto's new electric streetcar system was finally inaugurated. Numerous dignitaries assembled at City Hall (then on Front Street) for a successful 3:00 p.m. first run. Yet not everyone was happy. Strong opposition had come from horse buyers and suppliers who said electric trolleys would drive horse-drawn carriages off the streets, decrease property values, and increase the danger to life.

In terms of jobs and growth, Fleming supported a proposal to reclaim and then sell land at Ashbridges Bay, insisting it was "a public work of vast importance."[3] The Council soon dealt with a range of issues there, including flooding, sanitation, soil conditions, pollution, land reclamation, sewage disposal, and property improvements. Water also emerged as a serious concern in 1892. In December, a bad break in a conduit pipe bringing fresh water into the city caused a considerable section of it to float to the surface.

Issues discussed at the Council included new wooden sidewalks, a new horse-drawn fire truck, the inspection of bread, the "suppression of vice,"[4] an extension of municipal voting hours so workingmen could vote, providing heat on city streetcars, the abolition of tollgates, and having Toronto exhibit at Chicago's World's Columbian Exposition.

In 1893, Toronto's civic election results were far more conclusive: Fleming's vote total of 11,736 was more than 3,000 ahead of Edmund Sheppard's 8,618. As historian Jesse Edgar Middleton notes, "Generally speaking the administration of Mr. Fleming was vigorous and efficient ..."[5]

Fleming recommended that water management be placed under the Board of Works and shot down proposals to bring Toronto's water in from Lake Simcoe. In terms of enhancing cross-lake shipping traffic, he recommended improvements to the docks, a wharf extension, and the leasing of land for new warehouses or light manufacturing.

He expressed support for a bylaw "to exempt all manufacturing plants from municipal taxation" and a leaner city by amalgamating departments and dispensing with "unnecessary officials."[6] City hiring should be done solely on merit, he said, and not based on prior friendships, personal relations, acquaintanceships, place of origin, religion, fraternal lodges, or membership in secret societies.

In 1893, the Council dealt with a host of issues: tax collection, a new swing bridge at Cherry Street, the conversion of the streetcar system from horse-drawn to electrical power, and asking the Legislative Assembly to allow married women the same right to vote as unmarried women and widows.

The municipal election of 1894 proved to be a vigorous contest, with the Conservative establishment putting forward Warring Kennedy. For his part, Fleming combined his Reformist Christian ideals with an unpretentious manner and a scrappy, entertaining style, earning him the nickname "the People's Bob," yet it was Kennedy who prevailed with 13,380 votes to Fleming's 9,306.

In 1894, Fleming served as president of a national conference on the complete prohibition of alcohol, and in 1895, he headed the Dominion Prohibitory Alliance, actively working for the banning of liquor. As local historian Jesse Middleton later observed, Fleming was "a most zealous champion, and he has fought the liquor traffic with courage and tenacity born of deep-felt conviction."[7] With both a strong personal and political popularity, Fleming again contested the mayoralty in 1896, and after a gap of two years, was re-elected, carrying all six wards. Fleming received 10,364 votes to John Shaw's 8,561.

A hard-nosed realist, Fleming advised the Council that "nothing should command the attention of the people more than the finances of the city." He also attacked the Consumers' Gas monopoly which, he stated, "only cared about the interests of its own shareholders."[8] In one interesting new proposal, the returning mayor urged that space be set aside on every street for bicycling. He noted there was still too much drunkenness in the city and that water rates were unjust. Fleming also called for better access to the Esplanade and was highly critical of the new City Hall construction project at Bay and Queen Streets.

In April 1896, during Fleming's third mayoral term, a significant reform of city government took place: the province amended the Municipal Act to establish a Board of Control in cities with populations greater than 100,000. The board's function was to prepare the city's budget and oversee the civic bureaucracy. A two-thirds vote of the Council was needed to overturn a board decision.

Issues at the Council in 1896 included the state of manufacturing in the city, a proposed reduction of city salaries, hosting the world conference of the Women's Christian Temperance Union, and the illicit sale of liquor on the Toronto Islands. It was noted that hundreds of deaths in Toronto in the 1890s had been due to typhoid, since citizens drank disease-laden impure water caused by raw sewage floating into the bay in close proximity to cracked water intake pipes.

In 1897, Fleming received 11,987 votes for mayor against George McMurrich's 10,364. In what would be his fourth inaugural address, he spoke of extending a new electric streetcar line to the Toronto Islands, urged the creation of a bureau for the unemployed, and pushed for "relief of the destitute poor"[9] in terms of food, fuel, and necessities. Fleming championed a minimum wage for public workers and said the time had come for Toronto to advertise itself widely as a major convention destination in both Great Britain and the United States.

Toronto was also changing in other ways. By way of a special vote held on May 15, 1897, citizens reversed two previous referendum decisions and voted to allow streetcars to operate on Sundays. It was the third attempt for approval on this polarizing issue.

A detailed report titled *Of Toronto the Good: A Social Study* looked at a hidden side of Toronto society and was published during Fleming's term. Provocatively named chapters included "Street Walkers," "Detectives," "The Poor of the City," "Gambling Houses," "Drunkenness," "Imposters," "Crooks," "Pickpockets," "Thieves," "Quack Doctors," "Churches and the Clergy," and "Swindlers."

Personally and financially devastated by the real-estate collapse of the 1890s, Fleming let it be known that he would consider the role of assessment commissioner if approached. In August 1897, he resigned from the mayor's chair and accepted a salary of $4,000 to assume the post of assessment commissioner.

Yet, soon after, he left that job to accept highly contentious employment with the Toronto Railway Company. With a yearly salary of $10,000, he was now able for the first time to begin paying back monies owed from the collapse of his real-estate business. For 16 years, from 1904 to 1921, Fleming was a central figure in the battles with City Hall and the transit-riding public. Yet for Fleming, his focus was crystal clear: to have the company turn a profit. He cut the number of vehicles and reduced service in some areas of the city.

Eventually, Fleming managed or served on the boards of several other firms, including Toronto and Niagara Power, the Electrical Development Company, and the Toronto Electric Light Company. Yet, by 1921, the private-sector streetcar franchise was not renewed and the entire transit operation became a new city-owned public entity called the Toronto Transportation Commission (today's Toronto Transit Commission).

On a personal front, Fleming re-entered the real-estate, stock, and mining markets, serving as a director of the Gold and Silver Mines Development Company and Rossland Gold Mining. In 1921, he also became a director of the Toronto Board of Trade and Toronto Harbour Commission.

Fleming had always led a rather understated life. After neighbours in Cabbagetown complained of the cattle at his Parliament Street home — a leftover from when his parents had kept livestock — he moved to a larger estate near Bathurst Street and St. Clair Avenue where the presence of his Jersey cows continued to draw criticism.

In 1923, a full 30 years after his last run for mayor, Fleming decided again to contest the city's top position, losing to incumbent Alfred Maguire by a healthy margin. The campaign focused on Sir Adam Beck's proposal for a new electric railway along the length of Toronto's waterfront. The sitting mayor favoured the plan, while Fleming was vigorously opposed. Maguire was re-elected with 40,795 votes to Fleming's 39,802, a margin of less than 1,000 votes.

Fleming's years with the Toronto Railway Company, specifically as a corporate director, had been financially rewarding for him. By 1923, after selling his St. Clair Avenue–area home, he retired to Donlands, a 386-hectare farm in Don Mills. That was where, in the autumn of 1925, Fleming caught a severe cold that turned into pleurisy. In October 1925, he died at the farm, leaving an estate of more than $1 million ($17 million today).

The *Globe* noted that Fleming had been one of the best-known and most personally popular figures in the city. Mayor Thomas Foster ordered flags to be flown at half-mast. Fleming was buried at Toronto's Mount Pleasant Cemetery, with Foster stating, "He gave his best for the city and her interests at all times."[10]

Mayoralty Election in 1892	
CANDIDATES	VOTES
Robert Fleming	8,622
Edmund Osler	8,272
John McMillan	4,746
James Beaty	603
Mayoralty Election in 1893	
Robert Fleming	11,736
Edmund Sheppard	8,618
Mayoralty Election in 1896	
Robert Fleming	10,364
John Shaw	8,561
Mayoralty Election in 1897	
Robert Fleming	11,987
George McMurrich	10,364

Mayor Warring Kennedy

1894 and 1895

The 28th mayor of Toronto

Occupations: Retail merchant, Toronto Council member, Baptist church leader
Residence While Mayor: 200 Beverley Street
Birth: November 12, 1827, in County Down, Ireland
Death: June 25, 1904, in Toronto

— • —

Warring Kennedy was born in County Down, the easternmost part of Northern Ireland. As a young boy, he attended grammar school in Londonderry before becoming an apprentice in the dry goods business in the town of Kilrea. It was also where he wed Jane Macaw in March 1855, eventually having seven children with her.

The couple then moved to Belfast where *The Canadian Biographical Dictionary and Portrait Gallery of Eminent and Self-Made Men* reports that Kennedy earned "a reputation second to none for intelligence, undivided application to, and thorough knowledge of business."[1]

At age 30, in 1857, Kennedy immigrated to Toronto where at first he was unable to find positions that were "commensurable, either in salary or position, with what his business qualifications fairly entitled him to expect." However, with "his indomitable energy, his untiring industry, his exemplary character, his devoted attention to, knowledge of, and regularity in his business … [he] soon attracted the notice of commercial men."[2]

Kennedy first worked for Robert Walker at the Golden Lion, a dry goods emporium on King Street East, then joined the J. Macdonald & Co., a well-known wholesale importer at Wellington and Front Streets. In 1869, Kennedy left there to form a partnership with two fellow employees in a new business, Samson, Kennedy & Co., which was soon ranked as one of the leading dry goods firms in the country.

Repeatedly solicited to accept a nomination for a seat in the House of Commons, the usually quiet and sedate Kennedy instead chose a different route. In 1871, he was elected alderman from St. John's Ward with one of the largest votes then on record, yet served just a single year. He was also a trustee of the Toronto General Burying Grounds Trust (today's Mount Pleasant Cemetery), a position he held from 1876 until 1904. Later, in 1889, he was appointed its chair.

In 1877, Kennedy first opposed Angus Morrison, the popular incumbent mayor, for the mayoralty, capturing 3,651 votes to Morrison's 4,665, even though he had not actively canvassed. It had been an unsolicited nomination in which Kennedy had simply allowed his name to be placed in contention.

Kennedy remained deeply involved in the community as a member of the Toronto Board of Trade, as president of the Irish Protestant Benevolent Society in 1872, and as treasurer of the Upper Canada Bible Society. Kennedy also served as a trustee of the Necropolis burial ground.

A founder of and for many years a trustee of the Victoria Industrial School for Boys in Mimico, he was also a director of the House of Industry, the Home for Incurables, the Newsboys' Home, the Yorkville and Toronto Christian Temperance Mission, and the Irish Protestant Association, as well as secretary-treasurer of the Toronto Orthopedic Hospital.

Kennedy took a leading part in the formation of the Commercial Travelers Association in 1873 and was chosen as its first president. He was a director of the Saskatchewan Land and Homestead Company, and for several years, was on the board of the Real Estate and Loan and Debenture Company.

Devoted to the Methodist Church, Kennedy was a class leader, preacher, trustee, and superintendent of the Elm Street Sabbath School from 1866 to 1878, and was a delegate to the General Conference, the church's highest body. He was a strong public speaker, indeed one of a handful of Toronto business leaders at the time with the ability to express themselves in public with ease.

Before he was nominated for the mayoralty in the January 1894 election, Kennedy had held only one publicly elected office as a member of Toronto's Council for St. John's Ward, yet in 1894 as the personal choice of fellow Orangeman Edward Clarke, he defeated incumbent mayor Robert Fleming by 4,070 votes.

The campaign was characterized by misrepresentation and vilification, which was not the usual case in city elections. For his part, Kennedy disclaimed any responsibility for the harsh, unkind attacks on Fleming.

An Ontario-wide plebiscite on prohibition was held on January 1, 1894, in conjunction with municipal elections. Eligible citizens in Toronto voted on a question dealing with alcoholic beverages and the possible implementation of prohibition. The question was this: "Are you in favour of the immediate prohibition by law of the importation, manufacture, and sale of intoxicating liquors as a beverage?"[3] In Toronto, the majority in favour of prohibition was 2,463 votes.

In a detailed inaugural speech, Kennedy observed that 22 years earlier when he was elected an alderman, the city's population was 57,000 but was now more than 188,000, noting that Toronto had a growth rate exceeded only by Chicago's. The Fire Brigade, said the mayor, was now 122 members strong. He also pointed out that complaints had been raised that the outskirts of the city were "too well lit"[4] with electric lights.

Kennedy maintained that a great deal of work was still needed for the conversion of streetcars from horse to electrical power. He also drew attention to the deteriorating water quality in the city, with 46 new typhoid cases in the past two years. Kennedy believed it had been a mistake to expand the municipality's boundaries so widely and said that it was unwise to offer companies inducements to locate in the City of Toronto.

With both Fleming and then Kennedy in office, the power of the Orange Lodge continued to expand. Toronto was, in effect, an old boy's club controlled by a Council reflecting 10 very similar characteristics: well off, white, Protestant, middle-aged, English-speaking, business-oriented, property-owning, male, Anglo-Saxon, and a homeowner.

In 1894, the Council dealt with a host of issues: future industrial and manufacturing uses at Ashbridges Bay; continuing problems with the cleaning of manure on Yonge Street; the removal of wooden telephone poles; and building streetcar extensions on Front Street, Avenue Road, and Dovercourt Road, and into High Park.

The Council also discussed topics such as regulating bicycles to protect the public from injury, an invitation to have Toronto host a major convention of the Deep Waterways Association the following year, and a complaint from the Toronto Island Association decrying a lack of ferry service.

Yet Toronto was experiencing a severe economic depression, and 1894 was one of the most unsatisfactory business years since Confederation. In an environment of shrinking volumes, reduced profits, and fewer customers, business failures increased by 40 percent.

In January 1895, amid continuing economic uncertainty, Kennedy stood for re-election, once again against former mayor Robert Fleming. Yet this time his prior 4,000-vote margin over Fleming was reduced to fewer than 50 votes.

It had been less than a banner year. A judicial investigation of civic graft and corruption in 1894 by a respected county judge revealed that several aldermen had tried to sell their votes on street-lighting matters to the Toronto Electric Light Company, one of the three firms seeking to install lighting in the city, thus creating an even greater pressure and need for municipal reform and accountability.

In what was a wide-ranging inaugural address, the mayor cautioned members of the Council about the city's debt of $17.9 million and reviewed the financial situation in great detail, urging them "not to get distracted by proposals from every dreamer." He pointed out that there were "many miles of cedar roadway so decayed, worn, and defective"[5] that the city was liable for accidents and also provided some further bad news: another 111 deaths in the previous year due to typhoid.

Kennedy also spoke about the less fortunate in the city. At a time when there was no employment insurance, social programs, or welfare, he reported that charities had given out 1,074 metric tonnes of coal and wood and 54,449 loaves of bread, as well as 4,153 kilograms of groceries.

Issues in 1895 dealt with by the Council included a wide range of topics: a request that all saloons, taverns, and shops selling liquor be closed at 9:00 p.m.; asking Ottawa for legislation to compel the underground burial of all telephone, telegraph, and electrical wires; the inspection of factories for health and labour conditions; an offer by the Georgian Bay Ship Canal and Power Aqueduct Company to supply the city's fresh water; and impure commercial ice being sold in the city.

Also discussed was a request from Alderman Andrew Bates that city departments only hire married men who were municipal ratepayers, grants to the Ontario Rifle Association and the Ontario School of Art and Design, and a $3,000-per-year salary for Toronto's police chief (the city's six police detectives were each paid $1,000 per year).

In December 1895 in the twilight of Kennedy's term, the Council approved a new body that revolutionized how city spending was carried out. A Board of Administration was created, which later became the provincially mandated Board of Control.

In purely human terms, the final year of Kennedy's mayoral term proved to be a personally disastrous one. With the country still in the grip of a severe economic recession in 1895, Kennedy was forced to put his company into receivership, and all of its stock and merchandise was bought by the T. Eaton Company.

Virtually bankrupt, Kennedy retired from public life following the total collapse of his business and the state of his own personal finances.

From 1897 to 1899, he was employed as an insurance agent for Mutual Reserve Fund Life Assurance of New York and later as secretary-treasurer of Toronto Orthopedic Hospital, a position for which he received a modest remuneration.

Early in the morning of June 25, 1904, Warring Kennedy passed away at the home of his sister in Parkdale and was survived by five of his seven children. His wife, Jane, had died in 1889. Two days later, he was honoured by Toronto's Council. Controller William Hubbard stated that the former mayor was known for his "integrity and sterling character ... and in this way became known as a leader in all works of benevolence, charity, and philanthropy."[6]

Mayoral Election in 1894	
CANDIDATES	VOTES
Warring Kennedy	13,380
Robert Fleming	9,306
Mayoral Election in 1895	
Warring Kennedy	10,260
Robert Fleming	10,212
SPECIAL NOTE: The final results followed a judicial recount.	

Mayor John Shaw

1897–1899

The 29th mayor of Toronto

Occupations: Lawyer, City of Toronto alderman and controller, Member of the Legislative Assembly of Ontario
Residence While Mayor: 222 Bloor Street West
Birth: May 13, 1837, in Toronto
Death: November 27, 1917, in Toronto

———— • ————

The 1907 *Commemorative Biographical Record of the County of York, Ontario* states: "In every community, great or small, there are found men who, by reason of personal attributes, enterprising spirit, and natural ability, have arisen above their fellows in business, social or public life. Toronto has numerous examples, and one of these is John Shaw."[1]

George Shaw and Laura Jackson, John's parents, left the British Isles in 1832 for York where George pursued carpentry as a trade and became a well-known local builder. John Shaw was born in the very midst of the newly renamed Toronto's most turbulent time — the 1837 rebellion.

Shaw was educated at Upper Canada College and Victoria College. He later read law and was an apprentice with the firm of Patterson and Harris, the practice of the late Chief Justice Robert Harrison, who himself had been a runner-up in Toronto's 1867 mayoral race.

In 1870, Shaw established his own law practice and for many years was a solicitor on Toronto Street in the heart of the city's downtown. Later, he had a partnership with John Blevins, who went on to become city clerk.

In Shelburne, Ontario, in October 1889, Shaw married a widow, Elizabeth McClellan, who was already raising a young daughter, Isabelle, from her first marriage. Both Shaws wanted another child, so they adopted Mabel.

Upon the death of his father, Shaw inherited a considerable amount of money and for several years lived, as if already retired, in a large cottage on Bloor Street West in what was the still-quaint Village of Yorkville, north of the city. When Yorkville was annexed by Toronto in 1883, Shaw's friends persuaded him to run for public office. The following year, he was elected to the Council in the newly created St. Paul's Ward. By then, Shaw was 47 and a respected figure and easily won the election. In fact, except for a single year's break, he was on the Council continuously from 1884 until 1900 and came back post-mayoralty in 1904 and 1905 for an additional two years of service.

While a member of Toronto's Council, Shaw chaired the Fire and Light, Works, and Executive Committees. In 1895, when Mayor Warring Kennedy was absent in England, he assumed the role of president of the Council and was responsible for chairing meetings in the mayor's absence to ensure the proper functioning of the municipality's business.

During Kennedy's time away, the city's drinking-water intake pipes unexpectedly rose in Lake Ontario, completely shutting down Toronto's supply of fresh water. Shaw took decisive action to make certain large casks of water were brought in, many delivered to homes by horse-drawn wagons. He also presided over and kept on top of the six-week period needed to repair the intake pipes.

Shaw first ran for mayor in 1896 but was defeated by incumbent Robert Fleming, who received 10,364 votes to Shaw's 8,561. Fleming was again re-elected to office in 1897, while Shaw returned to Council as an alderman for Ward 3. Yet it was a completely unexpected decision in August 1897 that led overnight and without prior warning to Shaw becoming the city's 29th mayor.

Surprisingly, Fleming announced he was resigning to accept a position as the city's new assessment commissioner, so the Council was obliged by law to select one of its own to serve as mayor for the balance of Fleming's term. After an extensive procedural debate, the final vote was taken at 2:00 a.m. that night and Shaw emerged the winner.

The true highlight of 1897, though, was not a municipal one; it was the celebration of Queen Victoria's Diamond Jubilee. At the very height of the Victorian era, Toronto was a British, Orange, and Protestant city. In fact, of 786 municipal employees, only 41 were Catholics.

The 1898 mayoral election was challenging. Ernest Macdonald, a wealthy developer, promoter, and land speculator, had spent a fortune on several prior election campaigns and was desperate to become mayor. Considered to be erratic and unpredictable by many on the Council, he brought forth renewed charges of corruption against certain councillors.

As the *Toronto Evening Star* pointed out, "he succeeded in stirring up excitement in the city which dearly loves scandal."[2] The wily Macdonald won the vote of organized labour, while Toronto's middle-class Protestant males, still a majority of the city's electorate, continued to support Shaw.

In the 1898 election, Shaw made two key promises: cheaper electric power and the building of a great railway to link Toronto with the North. It was a vision and dream that captured the imagination of Toronto, placing the city at the centre of a huge commercial empire. That would, Shaw said, make Toronto one of the richest cities on the continent, with the new line extending more than 1,609 kilometres through northern boreal forests to link Ontario's capital with Hudson Bay.

When the 1898 election dust settled, Shaw had received 12,648 votes to Macdonald's 8,401. To further his goal, the new mayor formally established the Toronto and Hudson Bay Railway Commission to determine the feasibility of the new link and also tapped several of the city's wealthiest and most influential citizens to serve as commissioners. Today, the City of Toronto Archives has boxes of official reports and papers documenting plans for the Toronto and Hudson Bay Railway Company. Yet not widely known at the time was that Shaw was also a principal financial proponent behind the scheme and stood to make millions of dollars.

Although he was successful at the polls, Shaw's grand dream soon collapsed once it became clear that other major rail companies, especially Canadian Pacific, were also planning to build a line to the North. Toronto reluctantly withdrew from the race.

In his inaugural address to the Council, Shaw outlined a number of issues: city finances were in a better condition, debt was being reduced, and Toronto's credit rating on the money markets was "a matter for congratulation."[3] He noted that one of the most important factors in the development of a manufacturing base was the cheap supply of power and that Toronto now had an energetic assessment commissioner and former mayor whose duty it was to encourage the establishment of new industries. Assistance continued, he said, in the form of building sites, exemptions from municipal taxes, and cheap water.

Shaw advised the Council that raw sewage being discharged into the bay in a city of 200,000 was "not wise or judicious." He urged that immediate steps be taken "to ascertain the best method of disposing of this sewage, either by purification, chemically according to the best modern practice, or by treating it in some other way."[4] City staff visited Massachusetts, Rhode Island, and Pennsylvania to look at sewage treatment options for a rapidly growing city. The Council also received detailed information on how Paris, Berlin, Danzig, Glasgow, and Manchester treated raw sewage.

By 1899, the economic downturn of the early 1890s was over, and there were now abundant signs of renewed prosperity. Exports had increased, bank clearings and the circulation of currency had risen, and the pace of manufacturing in Toronto had accelerated. For the 1899 civic election, there was another heavy vote, yet by this time Shaw's popularity had waned and he was re-elected with a majority of just 863 votes. What was the most surprising was the unexpected strength of Ernest Macdonald, who captured a stunning 10,532 votes.

In his inaugural address to the 1899 Council, Shaw called for improvements to the St. Lawrence Market, an enlargement of the Cattle Market, and harbour upgrades that included an extension of the Eastern Channel and a diversion of the Don River. He also noted that by the end of 1903 "Toronto will be one of the most lightly taxed of the larger cities of North America."[5]

On the eve of a new century, Toronto's Council dealt with a range of issues: city wage rates, the censorship of street posters, a city deputation to Ottawa in support of the James Bay Railway Company, and the hosting of a major gathering of cities, towns, and counties from across Ontario to discuss matters of common interest such as exemptions from municipal taxation, city assessment, policing issues, bonusing to attract industry, fire services, good roads, school-related matters, licensing, and different methods of taxation.

It also looked at a request to have the College-Carlton streetcar line extended as far as Broadview Avenue in the east and heard from unions supporting a new bylaw to limit the hours of work on city contracts to just nine hours per day. Council members were advised that in the 1899 municipal election 6,662 women had been eligible to vote (at that time only widows and single women were allowed to vote; married women were not), yet only 1,676 women had actually turned out.

As late as March 1899 during Shaw's final term, the Council was still examining the work needed to complete the signature new courthouse and City Hall. Still to be approved were tenders for a cash vault for the treasurer, portable furniture, a clock for the tower, and the building's electric lighting plant, as well as sodding and grading, decoration, artwork, and even the iron in the bars for the courthouse prisoner cells.

Toronto's third City Hall was finally completed later that year, and at the official inauguration of the new building — described as the new symbol of a dynamic city's pride and confidence — Shaw opened its main front doors

The last meeting of Toronto's Council in the municipality's first purpose-built City Hall (1844–1899) in the St. Lawrence Market before moving to what is now Old City Hall at Queen and Bay Streets.

with a ceremonial gold key, saying, "Great buildings symbolize a people's deeds and aspirations."[6] Completed eight years after its cornerstone had been laid, the new City Hall was significantly overbudget.

Now installed in the spanking new City Hall, Shaw, to his credit, kept taxes at a minimum and left the mayoralty after his 1899 term was completed only to be succeeded by Ernest Macdonald, his old foe and political rival. Upon his retirement as mayor, a Council resolution stated: "His manner was that of a cultured gentleman; he was distinguished by his kindness and politeness to those with whom he came in contact."[7]

Although defeated in 1904 for the city's powerful new executive, the Board of Control, now elected city-wide, Shaw was successful in both 1905 and 1906. In 1907, he failed to get a position on the board, and in January 1908, both Shaw and former mayor Robert Fleming were beaten.

A few months later, in June 1908, Shaw returned to public life as an elected member of the Legislative Assembly for three years at Queen's Park as the Conservative MPP for Toronto North. He served on three standing committees in the assembly — railways, municipal law, and private bills — and remained an MPP until November 1911, after which he retired from elected life. His final public service was his appointment as an official of the County Court of York in 1915.

Shaw was a member of the elite Albany Club, the McKinley Loyal Orange Lodge 275, and a Masonic lodge. Both Shaw and his wife were devout Conservatives as well as followers of the Anglican Church, and from 1877 to 1904, they lived at 222 Bloor Street West in a low-roofed cottage-like home built decades earlier by Robert, his brother.

In November 1917, Shaw died at his home at 49 Roxborough Avenue, age 80. Although he was a former controller, mayor, and MPP, Shaw's passing went virtually unnoticed. Newspapers were filled with reports of the First World War, and an entire new generation scarcely remembered his name, even though he had been an ardent champion for Toronto to become a major North American commercial and industrial centre.

In *The Municipality of Toronto*, Jesse Edgar Middleton calls him a substantial mayor: "There came to John Shaw opportunities for splendid public service ... he won a measure of regard and esteem that constituted eloquent tribute to his standing in the community ... his career was crowned with all that is most worthwhile in life."[8]

Mayoral Election in 1898	
CANDIDATES	VOTES
John Shaw	12,648
Ernest Macdonald	8,401
Mayoral Election in 1899	
John Shaw	11,395
Ernest Macdonald	10,532
George McMurrich	3,675

Mayor Ernest Macdonald

1900

The 30th mayor of Toronto

Occupations: Builder, land developer, promoter, real-estate speculator, journalist, Toronto Council member
Residence While Mayor: 35 Grenville Street
Birth: November 1, 1858, in Oswego, New York
Death: December 18, 1902, in Toronto

— • —

Born in Oswego, New York, in 1858, Ernest Albert Macdonald immigrated as a young boy to Brockville, Ontario, with his family. His father, Simon Macdonald, and his mother then moved to Toronto in 1861 with their three-year-old son. The young "E.A.," as he was often called, was educated in the city as well as in Davisville, then a small rural countryside town. He also received some later training at the Kingston School of Gunnery.

With a strong entrepreneurial streak, Macdonald made his first venture into business with children's toys and novelties for a firm called Juvenile Manufacturing. By 1884, age 26, he became the owner and manager of the Toronto and Leslie Land Company, a modest building-and-land development firm, hoping to prosper from the growth, expansion, and economic boom of Toronto in the 1880s.

Macdonald was involved in the marketing of several real-estate projects east of the Don River from 1884 to 1889. As with several other real-estate speculators of the era, the ambitious Macdonald quite naturally became involved in civic politics, though first and foremost it was to promote his own interests.

His first major land venture in the mid-1880s was to advance, finance, and build a new residential suburb located on a former 60-hectare market garden near the Village of Chester to the north of today's Riverdale. On the former W.L. Taylor farm, Macdonald laid out large development tracts, built expensive homes, graded the streets, installed septic sewage systems, and even constructed wooden-planked sidewalks, all at his own expense.

Although it would still be another 30 years before the Chester area and Danforth Avenue were connected across the Don River to Bloor Street by a bridge, Macdonald's homes sold at a considerable profit. Dubbed the "Baron of Chester," he even built a local church for the community, which was later annexed by Toronto and given the ward name St. Matthew's.

The young developer earned a small fortune from his real-estate projects. In the book *Toronto, Old and New*, Graeme Mercer Adam included Macdonald in a chapter titled "Real Estate, and Those Who Traffic in It."

It was said that by the late 1880s Macdonald was worth millions of dollars, yet disaster loomed on the horizon.

In 1890, Macdonald began a new development in the Bellamy area of Scarborough, aiming to turn it into a true suburb. Residents could commute into the city using train service on the main rail line linking Montreal and Toronto. While the market was booming when the project started, within two years the bubble had burst. As one observer noted, all of Macdonald's equity — his land and properties — vanished "like frost before the sun."[1] The disaster cost Macdonald his entire fortune. He had both made and lost millions by the age of 32.

To advance his own real-estate projects, Macdonald entered municipal politics and was first elected to Toronto's Council in 1886 from St. Matthew's Ward. His success was mixed, however, as the tide of his popularity ebbed and flowed. From the 1880s until his final mayoral race in 1901, he was a candidate either for the Council, the mayoralty, or the Ontario Legislative Assembly in 18 different campaigns, winning seven and losing 11. And just as with his business fortunes, his political career was one of turbulent ups and downs.

In 1896, while it appeared he had won a seat on the Council for Ward 1, he was unseated in April of that year by a judicial review. He later said it was because the judge held a personal grudge. Macdonald's refusal to answer questions in the judicial review landed him in jail for three months.

His next venture in the mayoral field was in 1898 when he ran against and was defeated by incumbent John Shaw, the final tally being 12,648 to Macdonald's 8,401. The following year, Macdonald again ran for mayor in a sharply defined three-way race between old foe Shaw and veteran alderman George McMurrich. Once again, Macdonald lost, this time coming in second with 10,532 votes.

During an intense time in the public eye, Macdonald also sought to become a journalist in the competitive field of Toronto's newspaper dailies, yet both ventures lasted only a matter of weeks. The first promoted a grandiose pet project called the Georgian Bay Ship Canal and Power Aqueduct Company. As historian Jesse Edgar Middleton notes, "Macdonald talked of making an artificial channel between Lake Simcoe and Lake Ontario, building four great locks and dams and generating electric energy, besides bringing Lake Simcoe water to the City."[2]

A second Macdonald newspaper, the *Sun*, established in 1891, promoted Canada's annexation to the United States and had one definite consequence. As a result of his active lobbying to join the United States, he was stripped of his commission and rank as a lieutenant in the 12th York Rangers.

In January 1900 in an open multi-candidate election caused by John Shaw's retirement, Macdonald was finally elected mayor of Toronto, capturing 11,912 votes to 9,229 for Edward Clarke, a bitter and long-time rival then serving as MP for Toronto West.

It was clear that change was in the air. As the *Globe* noted, Macdonald "was bold and aggressive in his methods and he had the knack of keeping himself in the public eye." One reporter wrote that Macdonald's supporters would repeatedly say, "Give him a chance; let us see what he can do."[3]

Macdonald announced his first priority was to deal with the Toronto Railway Company (TRC), the secretive private monopoly operating the overcrowded yet highly lucrative streetcars. Figures tabled a week later revealed that the TRC's revenue of $5 million in 1899 was up from $4.5 million the year before.

Although appearing to be at the peak of his political career and having captured the city's top job, Macdonald was never allowed to enjoy his success. Quite simply, he was seen as an outsider, a troublemaker, and a maverick. Councillors viewed him as erratic and thoroughly unpredictable. And to further complicate matters, he vehemently assailed city employees and politicians of all stripes.

Macdonald spoke of waste, poor government, and mismanagement in virtually every area of the city's administration. While popular with voters, such invective angered top city managers, and when it came time for his inaugural address just days after his election as mayor, city staff vividly demonstrated just how they planned to deal with him. City department heads, for the first time in the city's history, broke tradition by refusing to provide the new mayor with even basic information on matters in their respective areas.

The new mayor referred to it himself in the first sentence of his inaugural speech: "It is usual for the Chief Magistrate of this City, upon assuming his annual duties, to review the situation of public affairs with respect to municipal government.... I made application through the Acting City Clerk to the heads of the various departments for such information as they could render me, concerning the condition of their respective charges. I did not get the information I sought, except in part, and for that reason I will not attempt a complete review or a lengthy address, but will confine myself to several public questions of great moment …"[4]

In that first speech, the combative mayor denounced the head of the Toronto Railway Company, questioned the efficiency of the Crown attorney, and openly rebuked the general public for having supported construction of a new City Hall. Macdonald soon found that he had to go it alone. From the beginning of his mayoralty, Toronto Council members, civic employees, managers, and the city's inner circle sought to obstruct virtually his every move.

Macdonald's priorities included a reform of the still unelected Board of Control, the creation of an elected people's auditor, strong support for a new technical school, and asking the Legislative Assembly to nationalize electric power and telegraph services in Canada.

Under Macdonald, the Council dealt with a range of items: the quality of asphalt pavement, a report from the provincial inspector of asylums and prisons, an increase in telephone rates by Bell Canada, harbour improvements, better enforcement of the city's early-closing bylaw, efforts to close down gambling dens, and regulations for the driving of cattle and horses on city streets.

By the summer of 1900, the political situation for Macdonald had become hopeless. One newspaper account stated with great irony that civic government in Toronto was actually in better shape than a year before. Why? The Council, many said, was so busy trying to keep the mayor from doing anything that it had no time to get into mischief itself. The more Toronto residents saw of the mayor they had elected in 1900, the less they wanted him to continue in office. By this time, too, the mayor was already beginning to suffer the effects of a disease that first rendered him insane, then killed him.

In his bid for re-election in 1901, Macdonald observed that tradition in Toronto dictated that a sitting mayor be given a second term. "British fair play" is what he called it, so he took out ads with that very slogan, which were ignored when several opponents came forward to challenge the politically weakened Macdonald. Yet he was also physically enfeebled. Before his term was over, an illness to which he eventually succumbed had started to make noticeable inroads. The disease that no one knew about and that was slowly rendering him insane was syphilis.[5]

Predictions Made in 1900 About Life in North America in the Year 2000

Adapted from an article by John Elfreth Watkins in The Ladies Home Journal, *December 1900.*

- **There Will Be No Streetcars in Large Cities:** All hurry traffic will be below or high above ground…. In most cities it will be confined to broad subways or tunnels, well lighted and well ventilated, or to high trestles with "moving-sidewalk" stairways leading to the top.
- **Trains One Hundred and Fifty Miles an Hour:** To go from New York City to San Francisco will take a day and a night by fast express…. Along with the railways, there will be no smoke, no cinders, because coal will neither be carried nor burned.
- **Automobiles Will Be Cheaper Than Horses Are Today:** Automobiles will have been substituted for every horse vehicle now known.
- **There Will Be Airships:** But they will not successfully compete with surface cars and water vessels for passenger or freight traffic.
- **To England in Two Days:** Fast electric ships crossing the ocean at more than a mile a minute will go from New York City to Liverpool in two days.
- **Coal Will Not Be Used for Heating or Cooling:** It will be scarce but not entirely exhausted … electricity manufactured by water power will be much cheaper.
- **Ready-Cooked Meals:** Food will be served hot or cold to private houses in pneumatic tubes or automobile wagons.
- **Hot and Cold Air from Spigots:** Central plants will supply this cool air and heat to the city house in the

same way as now gas or electricity is furnished. Rising
early to build the furnace fire will be a task of olden
times.

- **How Children Will Be Taught:** A university education
  will be free to every man and woman.... Poor students
  will be given free board, free clothing, and free books.
- **Store Purchases by Tube:** Pneumatic tubes instead
  of store wagons will deliver packages and bundles ...
  perhaps for hundreds of miles.

Although attending an incredible number of public rallies and candidate meetings at which he continued his political attacks, Macdonald was
unceremoniously thrown out of office by an electorate that preferred Oliver
Howland, a fresh new candidate with a famous last name but no municipal
experience. Howland received an overwhelming 12,310 votes to 8,153 for
Francis Spence and just 3,303 for Macdonald.

The mayoral defeat of 1901 ended Macdonald's political career. He was
considered by many to have lost his grip, and the election trouncing may
have hastened the end of his life, as well. As the press reported at the time,
"Before the year was out the malady of which he died had made marked
inroads upon his health ..."[6]

Macdonald's flamboyant, relentless lifestyle had taken a heavy toll.
Within a few months of his election loss, Macdonald was ill with "nervous
prostration" or what the *Toronto Star* termed "a tedious mental illness."
What the public did not know is that he was completely bedridden and for
six months suffered a slow, agonizing death, the result of paresis, a form of
paralysis also known as neurosyphilis that affects the brain, central nervous
system, and spinal cord, eventually causing insanity.[7] It was believed that
Macdonald had exhibited the first stages of the insanity while serving as
mayor.

As the third stage of syphilis, paresis saw Macdonald, once one of
Toronto's most active and vital citizens, succumb to a lengthy period of
psychosis, progressive dementia, extreme pain, and agonizing inflammation
of the brain (meningoencephalitis), as well as the loss of all bodily functions.[8]

Many people said it was a blessing that his suffering ended upon his death at his Grenville Street home in December 1902, age 44. As a headline in the *Globe* noted, Macdonald "Passed Away After a Tedious Mental Illness."[9]

Macdonald had married at the age of 20, but little was known about his wife, Alferetta Guild, whom he had wed in Mallorytown in July 1877 and who had predeceased him in 1887. A son, Victor, born in September 1879 was at the time of his father's death in active service with the mounted police in South Africa.

Upon the day of his funeral service, Macdonald's cortège left his residence at 2:30 p.m. and took him to Mount Pleasant Cemetery for a ceremony under the auspices of the Masonic Order. As the *Globe* observed:

A life of tremendous strain was followed by a collapse of his faculties, ending, as we see in a premature death. That he was a man of no ordinary character need scarcely be said…. His courage and spasmodic energy were Napoleonic, whether they were always well applied is something that need not be discussed…. Mr. Macdonald achieved the mayor's chair when all possible circumstance was against him. On one side he had, in an eminent degree, the qualities of a great public man; on others he was strangely weak and his whole personality was such as to baffle or perplex …[10]

Mayoral Election in 1900	
CANDIDATES	VOTES
Ernest Macdonald	11,912
Edward Clarke	9,229
John Hallam	5,181

Mayor Oliver Howland

1901–1902

The 31st mayor of Toronto

Occupations: Lawyer, author, corporate leader, Member of the Legislative Assembly of Ontario, president of the Union of Canadian Municipalities, deep-lake water advocate
Residence While Mayor: 55 Isabella Street
Birth: April 18, 1847, in Lambton Mills
Death: March 9, 1905, in Toronto

————— • —————

The history of the Howland family in North America can be traced to the landing of the *Mayflower* at Plymouth Rock in 1620. Of this prominent and accomplished family, two of its number, William Holmes Howland and his younger brother, Oliver Aiken Howland, both became mayors of Toronto.

Oliver Howland was born in Lambton Mills (in what is today's Etobicoke), the son of Mary Ann Blyth and William Pearce Howland (later Sir William Howland), who served in the Province of Canada's Legislative Assembly and the federal House of Commons. He was also the second lieutenant governor of Ontario as well as president of the Ontario Bank, Confederation Life, Canada Life, and the Toronto Board of Trade.

Educated at the Model Grammar School, Upper Canada College, and the University of Toronto, Oliver Howland studied law with Matthew Cameron (later a chief justice) and was called to the bar in 1875. As a prominent member of the bar of the County of York, he was nominated a King's Counsel by the short-lived Conservative administration of Prime Minister Charles Tupper in 1896.

Howland enjoyed a large and lucrative law practice and appeared before the British Privy Council in several important cases. He acted as a solicitor for the London Canada Company and for the holder of a major U.S. patent to modernize the milling process. In 1892, he chaired a committee of the Ontario centenary celebrations and was a senior member of the Howland and Arnold law firm until 1897.

A director of Bishop Ridley College, Howland was also a vice-president of the Canadian Bar Association in 1896 and served on the council of the Canadian Institute from 1892 to 1894, taking an active part in its literary and scientific programs. He chaired the institute's historical section and inaugurated the Canadian Historical Exhibition of 1897, a show commemorating the 400th anniversary of John Cabot's landing in Canada.

Howland only ran twice for public office, as much from an aristocratic sense of duty as from any driving political ambition. In June 1894, he won the provincial riding of Toronto South for the Conservatives, 2,070 votes ahead of Charles Moss (later Justice Moss), and served in Ontario's eighth Legislative Assembly until January 1898. He was also among the first group of MPPs to sit in the brand-new Legislative Assembly building at Queen's Park that had opened in 1893, serving on the railways, municipal law, and legal bills standing committees.

He was a pioneer in the earliest efforts to develop the St. Lawrence Seaway, which took another 60 years to complete. In 1894, he was elected president of the International Deep Waterways Association, a business-and-trade group pushing for a St. Lawrence Seaway link from the Great Lakes to the Atlantic. Howland presided over its 1895 annual conference in Cleveland where almost 500 delegates from the scientific, business, engineering, diplomatic, and commercial sectors assembled. Succeeding Howland as its international president was U.S. industrialist John D. Rockefeller.

In recognition of his extensive work in this area, Howland was appointed one of three Canadian members of the International Commission on Deep Waterways and Lake Levels. Members of this federal commission presented a final report in January 1897, which U.S. president Grover Cleveland transmitted to the U.S. Congress 10 days later. The same year, in a paper delivered at the annual meeting of the Canadian Bar Association in Halifax, Howland was one of the first persons in the world to advocate for an international court of justice, starting with Canada, the United States, and Great Britain.

Howland's first bid for public office was in 1901 when he ran for mayor despite having no prior municipal experience. A founder of the Municipal Reform Association, he had championed an elected Board of Control, and with the help of Conservative supporters, captured 12,310 votes for mayor out of 25,014 cast. The second-place contender, Frank Spence, got 8,153 votes, while the beleaguered incumbent, Ernest Macdonald, only received 3,303.

As one of the first mayors of the 20th century, Howland was decidedly uncontroversial. In his 1901 inaugural address at the Horticultural Pavilion at Allan Gardens, the new mayor pointed out that he had already met with every member of Toronto's Council and expressed indignation at the prevalence of gambling in Toronto, calling it "a great and destructive moral evil" that should be stamped out. He urged holding the line on taxes, pointing out that the amount of money handled by Toronto exceeded that of several provinces, and also urged action to tackle "the lack of equality"[1] in the method of property assessments.

The Council established a committee in 1901 to report on the affairs of the Toronto Industrial Exhibition (renamed the Canadian National Exhibition in 1912), which led to the city taking over all its assets and assuming responsibility to erect new buildings. The following year, the city sought to secure legislation allowing Toronto to purchase and distribute electricity, resulting in a 1903 meeting attended by 90 municipalities and featuring Adam Beck, the key proponent of a public hydro system in Ontario.

Always the epitome of decorum, Howland chaired the dramatic Council meeting of January 23, 1901, called to mourn the death of the beloved Queen Victoria, head of the world's most powerful empire. No one in Toronto under the age of 64 had known any other monarch, and the city showed a profound sadness over her death. Special newspaper editions were printed, flags on buildings downtown were lowered half-mast, the Council chamber was draped in black, and the bells at City Hall and St. James Cathedral tolled in mourning.

In the rapidly growing city of 208,000, the police chief reported that while there were 55 cases of fraud, 19 of horse stealing, and 19 related to fortune-telling, the vast majority of Toronto's crimes were still connected to the ravages of alcohol, with 4,269 cases of drunk and disorderly conduct. The Police Department had 295 staff, and the entire 1901 salary allocation was only $113,900 ($4 million today).

Statistics regarding Toronto's homeless youth provide a vivid glimpse into the raw underside of a bustling, fast-moving city. Its five local police stations temporarily housed dozens of homeless, forsaken, abandoned, or orphaned young street children living on the street with nowhere to go. Under the heading "Return of Waifs Provided with Shelter," the police chief advised the Council in 1901 that 328 street youth had been temporarily housed at police stations the previous year.

In August 1901, thanks to the efforts of Mayor Howland, a convention of senior municipal representatives from Ontario and Quebec met in Toronto, providing cities with a first united voice on significant issues as well as furthering the principles of municipal ownership and public control of utilities. The meeting adopted the name Union of Canadian Municipalities (known today as the Federation of Canadian Municipalities). Howland was chosen as its first national president in Toronto in 1901 and was re-elected to that post at the organization's annual meeting in Montreal the following year.

A major highlight of Howland's term was an October 1901 royal visit by the Duke and Duchess of Cornwall and York (later King George V and Queen Mary), who toured Canada coast-to-coast for a month as part of an empire-wide voyage to the British colonies.

Having succeeded the fractious maverick and political loner Ernest Macdonald as mayor, Howland garnered general approval for the stability of his administration, as shown by his re-election in 1902, sweeping every ward with 13,425 votes out of 22,885 that were cast. In his 1902 inaugural address, Howland announced waterfront improvement measures, including a proper trunk sewer, and noted an application for special provincial legislation to allow four members of the newly created Board of Control to be elected on a city-wide basis.

Sadly, a few months later, a serious fire destroyed the city's original Horticultural Pavilion, the site of special meetings of the Council and large city gatherings. Although a very basic structure of wood and glass, the pavilion at Allan Gardens had been a popular auditorium and community gathering spot.

Howland was mayor when one of the city's worst labour disturbances, a major street railway strike, took place, forcing him to call out 1,400 members of the local militia to protect non-union replacement workers. Working conditions at the Toronto Railway Company (TRC) were arduous, with long hours and low pay in either blazing heat or freezing conditions, as well as inflexible rules requiring streetcar operators to stand for their entire shifts or to pay for broken trolley poles out of their own pockets. The TRC was indeed ripe for labour strife.

The re-elected mayor also took an active personal interest in an improved waterfront to repair some of the major damage caused since the 1850s by the sprawling railways. It included the acquisition of the Garrison Commons at a much-reduced cost. Externally, Howland also participated in the bicentenary of Detroit and represented Toronto at the Pan-American Exposition in Buffalo in 1901, leading a delegation for a special Toronto Day event at the exposition.

The Council under Howland discussed a range of issues: the abolition of all municipal tax exemptions, a request to the province to bring in a two-year term for Toronto's Council members, the regulation of bakers, new wooden-planked sidewalks for John Street (where Metro Hall stands today),

Bell's ability to erect telephone poles without obtaining city permission, and a call endorsed by 140 other Canadian municipalities asking the federal government to regulate lower telephone rates. Also discussed was a proposal to stop future contagious disease hospitals being built within 46 metres of an inhabited dwelling, along with powers to allow both the city and the police to "stop an immoral or indecent play, sketch, or performance in any theatre, hall, or other public place."[2]

Having been easily re-elected in 1902, Howland saw his support slowly erode, and by 1903, he was opposed by aldermen Daniel Lamb and Thomas Urquhart. This time a vigorous Urquhart prevailed, capturing 8,636 votes to Howland's 7,869. Although nominated for the mayoralty again the following year, Howland graciously declined to become a candidate in 1904.

Widely known for his integrity, fairness, dignity, and hospitality, Howland was also distinguished for being unostentatious and possessing unfailing courtesy. After a career in politics, he was in demand as a celebrated and popular dinner speaker and was notable for being "never more at home than presiding at a social function." He was a member of the Toronto Club, the Royal Canadian Yacht Club, the Rideau Club in Ottawa, and the St. George's Club in London, England. For a number of years, he was also a churchwarden at Toronto's St. James Cathedral.

Howland was already well known as an author of great ability, having earlier published two major volumes, *The Irish Problem as Viewed by a Member of the Empire* (1887) and *The New Empire: Reflections upon Its Origin, Constitution, and Its Relation to the Great Republic* (1891), as well as writing articles such as "The Life of Sir John Thompson," "Art Spirit," "The Copyright Question," and "The 400th Year of Canadian History" in the *Canadian* magazine.

A lifelong bachelor, Howland developed a lingering illness over the 1904 Christmas season, one that rendered him progressively weaker. He was suffering from Bright's disease, an illness of the kidneys that causes pain, fluid buildup, and acute inflammation. First hospitalized at Toronto General Hospital, he returned home but remained bedridden for another nine weeks. During his final two weeks, he never regained consciousness and died peacefully at his Isabella Street home on March 9, 1905. Coming just 15 months after serving as mayor, his death was widely considered a significant loss.

Controller William Hubbard said that Howland's administration had been marked by "dignity, faithfulness, and sterling integrity."[3] Prior to the 3:00 p.m. funeral that day at St. James Cathedral, a brief family service was held at the residence of his father, Sir William Pearce Howland, who lived across the street. The younger Howland's funeral casket was then taken to the cathedral for a service led by senior Anglican canons.

Mayoral Election in 1901	
CANDIDATES	VOTES
Oliver Howland	12,310
Francis "Frank" Spence	8,153
Ernest Macdonald	3,303
John Shaw	992
Charles Woodley	220
Mayoral Election in 1902	
Oliver Howland	13,425
William Maclean	8,818
Charles Woodley	642

Mayor Thomas Urquhart

1903–1905

The 32nd mayor of Toronto

Occupations: Retail merchant, municipal clerk, lawyer, City of
Toronto alderman, Baptist church leader
Residence While Mayor: 81 Albany Avenue
Birth: April 16, 1858, in Wallacetown, Elgin County, Canada West
Death: February 16, 1931, in Toronto

—— • ——

Thomas Urquhart was born in Wallacetown, Canada West, the son of Alexander Urquhart, a Scottish settler who had come to Canada in 1847. Alexander established a tailoring and merchant retail shop serving the greater Elgin County, and in 1853, married Sarah McCallum, whose family had immigrated to Canada from Argyllshire, Scotland, and had settled in Dunwich Township. Young Thomas Urquhart was born five years later in April 1858.

As a boy, he attended public school in Wallacetown until 1871 and then, from the age of 13, spent the next 10 years working with his father as a clerk in the family's general store. Dealing with the public, he developed an interest in community affairs and political issues. In 1879, age 21, he was appointed municipal clerk for the Township of Dunwich. Later, he became secretary of the Agricultural Society of West Elgin, and even more significantly, secretary of the West Elgin Reform Association.

At age 23, the ambitious Urquhart decided to pursue a career in law, and despite a lack of formal education, wrote and passed the Law Society's matriculation examination in 1881. After working for the firm of Farley & Doherty in St. Thomas, Ontario, for a little less than a year, Urquhart moved to Winnipeg, but the city was not to his liking and he returned to Ontario four months later. Moving to Toronto, he joined the predecessor of what is today's Osler, Hoskin & Harcourt firm, after which he graduated from Osgoode Hall. He then entered into different partnerships over the next several years, finally forming one with his brother, Daniel Urquhart, in 1892.

In July 1899, Urquhart married Margaret McDonald of Peterborough, then a teacher in Toronto's public school system. A daughter, Isabel, was born in November 1902 but died in infancy. The Urquharts lived at 81 Albany Avenue, just north of Bloor Street, for most of their lives.

Urquhart took a strong interest in local affairs and was elected to Toronto's Council in 1900 for the west end Ward 4 and re-elected in 1901 and 1902. In fact, in a brief yet very energetic political career between 1900 and 1906, he conducted nine different campaigns for office at the municipal, provincial, and federal levels.

In 1902, Urquhart was the Liberal candidate in the provincial riding of Toronto West against Thomas Crawford, a popular local Conservative MPP, and was defeated. But his luck changed for the better when, age 44, he was elected mayor of Toronto in January 1903 over incumbent chief magistrate Oliver Howland. Torontonians awoke on January 6 to read a large front-page banner headline in the *Daily Star*: "Urquhart Is the Mayor." The story noted he had won the mayoralty in a hotly contested three-cornered fight.

A *Toronto Daily Star* editorial stated: "The election of Mr. Urquhart is a surprise to most people" and it was "a triumph for organized labour in Toronto…. They threw themselves into the scale in his favor and decided the contest. The Trades and Labour Council declared in his favor the day he entered the field."[1]

The new mayor's inaugural address touched on several issues: the need for new streetcar lines and increased service on existing ones, dealing with the chronic fuel shortage and the need for Consumers' Gas to be brought under the control of the city, and the securing of land to build new parks and playgrounds ("breathing places," as Urquhart called them).

Also considered was a new proposal that Urquhart called "consulting the people," in which if enough people petitioned the city on a specific matter, it could be submitted to a public vote before the Council made a final decision. Examples included major waterfront improvements, a proposed new streetcar link to the Toronto Islands, matters of public safety, and issues regarding telephone service. Indeed, Bell Telephone's service and policies had provoked significant anger among local officials, with the Council publicly slamming the company in July 1903 by a vote of 20–2 for high rates as well as poor staffing, equipment, quality, and service to customers.

As mayor, Urquhart soon earned a reputation for being an untiring worker and having a businesslike approach to city government. The Council considered the significant offer of $350,000 in funding by prominent U.S. industrialist Andrew Carnegie to build a new library building, discussing it 14 times. And ironically, less than a year before Toronto experienced its most devastating fire ever, one that wiped out the entire downtown business core, the Council sought to control the smoke and cinders issuing from factory chimneys as well as reduce pollution, clean the air, and lessen the danger of sparks from combustible materials.

Toronto's day-to-day life was still evolving. In 1903, hot and cold running water and indoor toilets were still considered luxuries and were not yet commonplace. In a city of more than 200,000 residents, just over 40,000 homes were hooked up to the city's supply of piped fresh water. During Urquhart's term as mayor, Toronto continued to be a major transportation hub where the railway was king, and during a 12-month period, steam engines carried more than 22 million passengers in Canada.

In January 1904, Urquhart was returned as mayor, this time by acclamation. In the same year, a major new electoral reform was brought in — that year onward four members of the Board of Control were elected city-wide to sit as the Council's executive oversight body. For almost 70 years, the board would be the city's dominant, most powerful political and executive body as well as serving as the preparation ground and strategic stepping stone to the city's mayoralty.

A Toronto councillor since 1894, William Hubbard became the first non-white councillor elected city-wide in Toronto's history.

In 1904, William Hubbard became the first non-white councillor elected on a city-wide basis in Toronto's history by virtue of becoming a member of the Board of Control. He had been a local councillor since 1894, and as the *Toronto Daily Star* noted, it was "considered a marvellous achievement for the plucky little Alderman from Ward 4 and the prospects for a splendid year of civic business are reassuring with his presence on the Board of Control."[2]

A central issue confronting Urquhart during his mayoralty was the Great Fire of 1904. On April 19, a bitterly cold and windy night, a roaring fire swept through downtown, destroying most of Toronto's central business core. In just under 10 hours, it consumed 100 buildings on both sides of Bay Street from Front Street to where Commerce Court sits today. City firefighters were hampered by the clutter of overhead wires strung on poles above street level. More than 250 firefighters from outside the city responded to a special appeal by the mayor and began to arrive by train from surrounding suburbs and other cities.

Bay Street looking north from Front Street West after the major fire of 1904 destroyed Toronto's downtown core. The tower of Old City Hall at the top of Bay Street is visible in the distance.

With Toronto's downtown destroyed, the complete devastation of the city's core resembled that of a major war zone. Miraculously, no one died, though dozens of firefighters suffered temporary eye damage due to ash, smoke, and cinders. The financial losses were staggering, estimated at more than $10 million (more than $270 million today), with 5,000 downtown workers immediately losing their jobs.

Later in 1904, while still serving as mayor, Urquhart was unsuccessful as the Liberal candidate for the federal riding of Toronto North against Conservative Sir George Foster in the November 3 federal general election, garnering 4,310 votes (49 percent) to Foster's 4,422 (50 percent).

During Urquhart's mayoralty, the most common mode of transport for Toronto citizens was still overwhelmingly the horse. Ontario reported that there were only 182 automobiles in the entire province, yet the city experienced explosive growth within less than a decade. As Claire Mackay notes in *The Toronto Story*, Toronto was forced to revise its laws governing street traffic: "The speed limit was 15 miles an hour in the city, unless you were within 100 yards of a horse-drawn vehicle, in which case it was seven miles an hour. If your car scared a horse, you had to pull into a side street, park, and go back and calm it down, or be fined $25."[3]

As York University marketing professor Alan Middleton notes in a *Toronto Star* article by Nancy J. White, a name in the phone book in 1904 "was a tangible sign of prestige, of being wealthy enough to afford a telephone. A breezy 'Call me — I'm in the book' had a certain ring to it. There was a bit of class snobbery ... unwashed immigrants didn't have phones."[4]

In January 1905, Urquhart was re-elected mayor, defeating well-known local business leader George Gooderham, a member of one of Toronto's most prominent families, who were the founders of Gooderham & Worts. Urquhart received 15,184 votes to 13,064 for his challenger. The *Globe* noted that the mayoral vote was the largest in the city's history.

The *Toronto Daily Star* observed that "Toronto has had one of the best administrations in her history."[5] Ironically, Urquhart did not bother to open a campaign headquarters or distribute election materials. Four of Toronto's daily newspapers endorsed him, and as the city's *Evening Telegram* editor J. Ross Robertson pointed out, it was a victory for public ownership, progress, and non-partisan civic government.

In his third inaugural address to the Council in 1905, Urquhart praised those who had come through the Great Fire, saying, "The loss has been large and the disaster long,"[6] and praised the determination, resilience, and courage of businesses that had immediately re-established there.

The Council dealt with a number of major issues: the need for more affordably priced homes, improvements to the supply of clean water, a reduction of liquor licences, the expropriation of land on Front Street for construction of a new Union Station, the necessity of a larger Toronto General Hospital, and the streetcar situation, which the mayor called "intolerable," and in particular how the city might cancel the contract with the Toronto Railway Company. Urquhart also upheld high personal standards as mayor, maintaining that no municipal council could legally spend money for entertainment or reception purposes on a Sunday. "This city shall not take any part in desecrating the Lord's Day,"[7] he declared.

In 1905, still a strong Liberal, and a bare three weeks after his re-election as mayor, Urquhart became his party's nominee in the provincial riding of Toronto West against incumbent MPP Thomas Crawford (later the Speaker of the Legislative Assembly from 1907 to 1911). That year the Council received an upbeat report that Toronto was now "the nerve centre of the Province of Ontario,"[8] that a new Union Station was in sight, and that Canada's financial capital was now Toronto, not Montreal. The population had increased from 188,000 in 1893 to 262,000 in 1905.

Later in 1905, when Urquhart announced he would not seek re-election as mayor for the 1906 term, an *Evening Telegram* editorial stated: "Thomas Urquhart has done well. Toronto has been well and faithfully and zealously served.... The Tory bigotry of Toronto did not prevent Mayor Urquhart's election in his first contest. Conservatives have no cause to regret the support given to Thomas Urquhart. No better Mayor ever sat in the City Hall …"[9]

In February 1906, just weeks after stepping down as mayor, Urquhart was defeated yet again as a provincial Liberal candidate, this time in a by-election in the riding of Toronto North. In later federal elections, Urquhart supported the Union Government of Conservative prime minister Sir Robert Borden in 1917, but in the election of 1921, he backed the Progressive Party, a collection of Prairie farmers and dissident Liberals.

In his personal life, religion was of enormous importance to Urquhart. First entering the Baptist faith at the age of 27 through a formal baptism at the Beverley Street Baptist Church, he went on to become a respected church leader, active with the Walmer Road, Mount Pleasant Road, and later, Aurora Baptist churches. In 1908, he was elected president of the Baptist Convention of Ontario and Quebec.

Urquhart continued to practise law in Toronto for many years, and though he was sometimes seen publicly supporting a political candidate, he remained more or less a private citizen until his death. In 1925, his wife of 26 years died, but in 1927, he found happiness again when he wed Mary Ellen Hall.

In February 1931, after taking ill at his office, Thomas Urquhart was taken to his home at 136 Hillsdale Avenue. On February 16, 1931, he died from influenza and was buried two days later in Mount Pleasant Cemetery.

Mayoral Election in 1903	
CANDIDATES	VOTES
Thomas Urquhart	8,636
Oliver Howland	7,869
Daniel Lamb	6,473
Robinson Conway	912
Charles Woodley	410
Mayoral Election in 1904	
The incumbent mayor, Thomas Urquhart, was returned by acclamation.	
Mayoral Election in 1905	
Thomas Urquhart	15,184
George Gooderham	13,064
William McPherson	1,134

Mayor Emerson Coatsworth

1906–1907

The 33rd mayor of Toronto

Occupations: Carpenter, lawyer, business leader, Member of House of Commons, City of Toronto alderman, licence commissioner, judge, community leader
Residence While Mayor: 218 Carlton Street
Birth: March 9, 1854, in Toronto
Death: May 11, 1943, in Toronto

——— • ———

Twenty years after Toronto's incorporation, Emerson Coatsworth was born on March 9, 1854, in his family's home on the city's Ontario Street. He was shaped by his family's roots and its mix of strong pioneer backgrounds: hard-working immigrant farmers, thrifty storekeepers, strict Methodists, loyal public servants, and ardent Conservatives.

Emerson Coatsworth's father, also named Emerson, and his mother, Janet (Jennette) Taylor, were natives of Yorkshire and Scotland, respectively. On his father's side, the family had immigrated to Canada in 1832, settling in St. Catharines. On his mother's side, they arrived the same year and put down roots in the Peterborough area. Both families were pioneer farmers and storekeepers.

Coatsworth was educated in the public schools of Toronto and at the British American Commercial College and learned the trade of carpentry in his father's employ before entering the field of law. His brother and cousin continued the business until 1875 when the firm dissolved. That year he studied law in the offices of John Rose (later a judge) and completed his courses in 1879 when he worked in the downtown firm of Rose, Macdonald, Merritt & Coatsworth. In September 1883, age 29, Coatsworth married Helen Robertson, daughter of John Robertson of DeCew Falls, Ontario. Together, they had four children: Emerson, Vida, Cuthbert, and Helen.

Continuing his studies at the University of Toronto, Coatsworth earned a law degree in 1886. He first practised alone, then for almost 35 years was the senior member of Coatsworth & Richardson's large general practice, connecting him to much of the litigation taking place in Toronto. It was said that Coatsworth prepared his cases with great care and that his devotion to client interests was, in the words of one writer, "proverbial."

In his business life, Coatsworth was a director of the Continental Life Insurance Company and Toronto Exhibition Association, as well as a governor of Victoria Industrial Schools and a charter member of the People's Tavern Company.

Coatsworth was first elected to the House of Commons in May 1891 as the Conservative MP for Toronto East when he captured 3,520 votes (63 percent) to Liberal Alex Wheeler's 2,056 (36 percent). He was an MP for more than five years until he was defeated in June 1896 by J. Ross Robertson, running as an independent conservative and receiving 4,631 votes (60 percent) to Coatsworth's 3,012 (39 percent).

Largely on a major political issue of the day — the public funding of Manitoba separate schools — Coatsworth lost his bid for re-election. Opponent Robertson was a notable Canadian newspaper publisher who had founded Toronto's *Evening Telegram* in 1876, a paper that had become the voice of working-class, Conservative, Protestant, and Orange Toronto.

In 1904 and 1905, Coatsworth returned to public life as alderman for Ward 2. In mid-December 1905, he announced his candidacy for the 1906 mayoral term and published a pamphlet titled *The Municipalization of Street Railways in Toronto*. In 1906, he was also a convener of the Western Municipal Niagara Power Union.

For the 1906 mayoral campaign, Coatsworth advocated for Ashbridges Bay to be reclaimed, noting that its 161 hectares would be worth millions. He supported the city's Western Cattle Market, observing that it kept down the price of meat, and that 1,500 cattle, sheep, and hogs passed through there every day. He also declared: "I am opposed to corporations using our streets and not paying for it. The telephone company and the electric light companies should be compelled to pay for the use of our streets."[1]

In the end, the final vote for mayor was a decisive one. Coatsworth received 16,371 votes to Frank Spence's 12,328. Two issues were also on the ballot: reducing the number of tavern licences to 120 and cutting those of liquor stores to 40, yet both measures were defeated. In an editorial, the *Globe* said that "the combination of the Tory machine and the liquor trade machine in municipal affairs" was the main factor.

In his inaugural address to the Council, Coatsworth mentioned two specific matters: significant waterworks improvements to protect Toronto from destructive fires and a new 68.2-million-litre municipal plant that was now in operation. He noted that the city's population had increased by 12,600 in just a year, that the municipality's credit stood high, and that any new debt issued would be to acquire parks, improve Toronto General Hospital, build schools, and provide better fire protection.

Coatsworth advocated a comprehensive new scheme for the south end of the city where the railways and waterfront intersected. He said it should include proposed viaducts, street railway extensions, rail crossings, shipping facilities, the improvement and preservation of the harbour and islands, and the construction of a major trunk sewer.

A list of issues put forward by the Board of Trade in 1906 is illustrative of the municipal concerns of the day. It called for an improved water-and-sewage system, safe and easy access to the waterfront, adequate railway entrances into the city, and a new central railway station and post office. The board foresaw a population of a million in Toronto by 1931 and called for a major street-widening initiative and a beautification program.

The Council dealt with a wide range of topics in 1906: a proposal to elect Council members for a two-year term and the abolishment of individual wards, a new pavilion at Allan Gardens to replace the one destroyed by fire, a call for a new ferry service from the foot of Sherbourne Street to the Toronto Islands, and a suggested streetcar line on Adelaide Street to relieve serious congestion on King and Queen Streets.

Also discussed by the Council were extending Bloor Street East to the Don River, a request to Bell Telephone (discussed 13 times) to bury all overhead wires, a petition against cows running at large just south of Pape and Danforth Avenues, the rate of payment for cart operators hired by the city, preventing the installation of overhanging signs downtown, and the appointment of a commissioner of industries to attract new manufacturers as well as the branch plants of companies already established elsewhere.

Coatsworth served first as a vice-president, then as president of the newly formed Union of Canadian Municipalities in 1906–1907 and was a vice-president of the League of American Cities in 1907. His administration was characterized, in the words of historian Alexander Fraser, for its "promptness, efficiency, and fidelity in the dispatch of municipal business, and by a spirit of reform and improvement that the general public acknowledges."[2]

With the District Labour Council, Coatsworth appeared before the provincial Cabinet to ask for the power to borrow money to build homes for workingmen. He also opened Scarboro Beach Park, a major new recreation attraction in The Beaches, and welcomed U.S. philanthropist Andrew Carnegie on his visit to Toronto.

Re-elected to a second term in 1907, Coatsworth declined to serve a third term, choosing to again concentrate on his legal career. Indeed, his victory in 1907 was against an interesting mix of candidates: James Lindala, a well-known socialist; James O'Hara, a dedicated radical; and Robert Noble, a humorist and entertainer. Coatsworth was re-elected with 13,795 votes, but runner-up Lindala's strong showing of 8,277 votes in staid and Tory Toronto caused a major stir within establishment circles.

In his 1907 inaugural address to the Council, Coatsworth covered a range of issues: growth, city finances, the public works department, public engagement in city affairs, and reaching out to organized labour. He also referenced matters that required what he called wise and vigorous action, including the railways, the harbour and Ashbridges Bay, city parks, the street rail system, sewage, electricity and the supply of power, commerce, and roadway extensions. Coatsworth urged the Council to be both mindful of and to follow the city's motto: "Industry, Intelligence, and Integrity."

The Council engaged with a range of issues in 1907, including higher penalties against the Toronto Railway Company for not conforming to its legal agreement, the location of a new Union Station, a new smelter at Ashbridges Bay, the regulation of hand laundries, not allowing blacksmith businesses to operate in residential areas, reviewing which suburbs should be annexed, and a strategy on how to advance Toronto's interests as the commercial, transportation, and financial centre of Ontario. It also dealt with the free use of Exhibition Park for the Loyal Orange Lodge's July 12 annual picnic where only God-fearing Protestants were welcome as well as a request to study the cost and revenues of constructing and operating an underground street railway system under Yonge Street downtown.

Coatsworth bowed out of the mayoralty race at the end of 1907 and was honoured at a special meeting of the Council. His departure, it was remarked, was due to a "condition of health [that] makes it imperative for His Worship to retire for a time from active public life."[3] After a period of convalescence, Coatsworth returned to public and municipal affairs: first as chairman of the controversial Board of Licence Commissioners (1908–1915) and later as a senior member of the judiciary. One of his licensing tasks was to carry out the instructions of the Council to reduce the number of liquor licences in Toronto.

In 1908, Coatsworth was made a King's Counsel and in 1914 was elevated to the bench as a junior county judge for the County of York. Coatsworth was also appointed by the federal minister of labour in 1916 to head up a major inquiry into unrest within the mining industry in Cobalt, Ontario.

The three-member commission included both management and labour representatives. In 1919, he was elevated to senior county judge, serving until 1929. In addition, from 1925 until 1934, he was a senior police magistrate for the City of Toronto.

In his personal life, Coatsworth attended Berkeley Street United Church for more than 50 years, serving as a Sunday school superintendent for 15 years. He was also a member of Loyal Orange Lodge 781 and was chair of the Alexander Muir Memorial Commemoration Committee. Like many Toronto Orangemen of his time, Coatsworth had also served in the Queen's Own Rifles as a young man.

Coatsworth lived to the age of 89, later residing at 1 May Square in Rosedale. Over the span of a lengthy and distinguished career, he also belonged to the Masonic Order, the Independent Order of Odd Fellows, the Ancient Order of Foresters, the Benevolent and Protective Order of Elks, the Yorkshire Society, Toronto's elite Albany Club, the Royal Canadian Yacht Club, the Don Rowing Club, and the Thornhill Golf and Country Club.

Emerson Coatsworth passed away on May 11, 1943, and Toronto's Council, already convened at a special meeting to discuss the city's coal situation during the Second World War, passed a heartfelt motion of condolence.

Mayoral Election in 1906	
CANDIDATES	VOTES
Emerson Coatsworth	16,371
Francis "Frank" Spence	12,328
Mayoral Election in 1907	
Emerson Coatsworth	13,795
James Lindala	8,277
Robert Noble	1,337

Mayor Joseph Oliver

1908–1909

The 34th mayor of Toronto

Occupations: Carpenter, lumber merchant, Toronto Board of Education trustee, City of Toronto alderman and controller, sovereign grand sire of the Independent Order of Odd Fellows
Residence While Mayor: 598 Sherbourne Street
Birth: November 7, 1852, in Erin, Wellington County, Canada West
Death: January 8, 1922, in Toronto

——— • ———

J oseph Oliver was born in Erin in Wellington County, the son of John
Oliver and Hanna Drenna, Irish immigrants who had come to Canada in
1850. When he was three years old, his family moved to Toronto, settling
in Cabbagetown. Not much else is known about Oliver's childhood, and it
seems that he received little formal education. He later said that as a youth
he became a working carpenter.

By 1885, Oliver was in business for himself, operating the Oliver Lumber
Company and taking a leading role in the business community. For several years, he was involved with the Commercial Travelers, Mutual Benefit
Society, serving as the association's vice-president, and was also for many
years an active member of the Toronto Board of Trade, for which he was
later honoured with a life membership.

Oliver's political career began in the late 1880s as a school trustee for St.
Thomas's Ward. Re-elected to that position in 1890 and 1891, he then served
on the high school board from 1892 to 1894. Oliver was elected to Toronto's
Council for Ward 2 in 1895 and was again elected from 1901 to 1903. At the
alderman level, Oliver was already viewed as someone to watch — a clear-
headed businessman able to grapple with difficulties.

Selected by colleagues on the Council to serve on the Board of Control
in 1903 (just prior to it becoming a city-wide elected position), Oliver then
entered the race for the first public election for controller in 1904, only to
lose by 12 votes to veteran councillor (and Toronto's first Black Council
member) William Hubbard. Although he ran again city-wide for the board
in 1905 and 1906, he was once more defeated.

Yet, with the support of R.C. Steele, president of the Board of Trade, and
Thomas Urquhart, a former mayor, Oliver won the mayoralty in a landslide
in 1908, even though five strong candidates were in the race, including organizers Dr. Beattie Nesbitt (referred to by many as "Boss"), Miles Vokes,
and even two future Toronto mayors, Reg Geary and Jimmy Simpson.

The day after the election it was reported that it took Oliver three hours
to get to the office because there were so many well-wishers. By noon that
day, the new mayor had already received more than 50 congratulatory

telegrams. Many were happy about the defeat of backroom political operator Beattie Nesbitt. Oliver, however, claimed he was not out to defeat anyone; he had simply wanted to get himself elected.

The newly elected Oliver said he would announce his mayoral plans later, the reason being that he did not want to say anything for which he would later have to change his mind. The press duly reported that he "was a man of caution," also noting he was "a citizen of the utmost good nature."[1]

Oliver had a businesslike manner and in the lumber industry from Duluth to Boston was "known favourably." He was seen to be "honest to a fault," having a deep and pleasant voice when greeting the public and "a manner that puts a stranger instantly at ease ... there is little starch in his makeup but plenty of backbone."[2]

He was sworn into office with a solemn vow to clean up the city, and unlike later mayoral successors, it was no mere political slogan. Oliver really meant it. In his January 1908 inaugural address, he announced that his top three priorities were clean water, building a trunk sewer, and ensuring a pure milk supply for Torontonians, insisting that the "establishment of a milk standard of the highest possible percentage [was] of the utmost importance."[3]

The new mayor's inaugural speech also highlighted several other proposed measures: new streetcar routes, acquiring the plant of the Toronto Electric Light Company, reviewing the recommendations from the medical officer of health regarding a filtration plant, seeking action from the rail companies on building a new Union Station, having a chartered accountant examine the city's bookkeeping methods, enacting a new contract with Bell Telephone or establishing a new independent phone system, and asking the government of Canada to compel railway companies to reduce their fares.

In Toronto, the horse and buggy still ruled city streets that were still, for the most part, dusty, rutted, and unpaved. Roads in the surrounding countryside were in an even more primitive state. In the nation's second-largest city, car registrations had climbed from fewer than 200 in 1903 to just over 2,000 by 1908. Change was certainly in the air, and within another two years, the number of vehicles again tripled, even though the horse and buggy and horse-drawn wagons were still the most common and popular form of transport.

Toronto's major new central library opened in October 1908 at the corner of College and St. George Streets, thanks to the generosity of multi-millionaire U.S. industrialist Andrew Carnegie, who had offered the city $350,000 (almost $10 million today) to build three new libraries.

A significant improvement to the city's water supply came about in 1908. On June 27, 1908, a special vote of all qualified electors took place, and city residents voted to approve a bylaw to raise $2.4 million ($64 million today) toward the construction of major intercepting sewers and a new sewage disposal plant. For the first time in its 74 years as a municipality, Toronto would stop discharging filthy, untreated, disease-causing raw sewage into Lake Ontario.

In addition, a brand-new 1.8-metre water intake tunnel was completed in 1908 to provide fresh drinking water to the city. It would first be drawn from Lake Ontario and sent to the existing island filtration plant through a new steel pipe that replaced the rickety wooden one formerly in use and prone to breaking apart. It was then pumped to the mainland via the secure new brick-and-concrete intake tunnel.

At the Council, several issues were dealt with under Oliver's mayoralty: new regulations to govern hand laundries, a spur rail line to serve industry at Ashbridges Bay, the annexation of East Toronto, and a City Hall reception for the (then named) Ontario Association of Deaf and Dumb. The Council also received the final report of a substantial investigation by County Court judge John Winchester into improper practices by the Parks Department and its commissioner. These included city employees doing work for private citizens, improper purchases made by the commissioner, the splitting up of accounts to avoid detection, falsifying pay sheets, and an oversupply of items that later simply disappeared.

The Council discussed "an application to the Hydro Electric Power Commission [Toronto Hydro] for the delivery of ten thousand horsepower, at or within the city limits, which will be necessary for us to distribute throughout the City, by means of the plant at present owned by the Toronto Electric Light Company ... or, if not, by an independent civic system to be established in the immediate future."[4]

The police chief reported in 1908 that 9,896 "waifs" — defined as homeless, abandoned, abused, forsaken, or orphaned children — had been given overnight shelter at one of the city's eight police stations. And a major local issue was also raised: the construction of a possible major bridge across the Don River. In fact, the idea of extending Bloor Street over to Danforth Avenue by a viaduct had first been discussed in the late 1890s but was contentious and resulted in a war of words between competing Toronto newspapers.

Easily re-elected to a second term in 1909, Oliver polled just over 26,400 of the 35,000 votes cast. A divisive question on the 1909 municipal ballot asked electors — still overwhelmingly middle-aged, middle-class, property-owning males of British heritage — if they supported cutting the number of licensed bars from 150 to 110 to preserve the city's health and morals. It was a vigorous, hard-fought issue on both sides. A strong effort to reduce the number of liquor venues was mounted by anti-liquor temperance leaders, local clergy, and the Women's Christian Temperance Union.

The *Toronto Daily Star* published a major post-election editorial titled "Notice to the Liquor Interest," pointing out that licence reductions were caused by the "increase in open drunkenness in the streets of this city."[5] For its part, the *Evening Telegram* said men and boys could not walk the streets of Toronto without being lured into or seduced by what was called the "wicked attraction" of a barroom. The temperance forces prevailed, ensuring that pro-reduction candidates won a majority of Council seats. While downtowners supported keeping bars open, the outer residential wards voted in favour of a reduction, which carried city-wide by just 846 votes.

In his inaugural address to the Council in 1909, Oliver predicted that within a decade Toronto's population would exceed half a million people. He noted that bank clearings had reached $1.1 billion ($29 billion today) and urged the Council to consider further suburban annexations with the greatest of prudence. The mayor also pointed out that a new high-pressure firefighting system would help to lower burdensome insurance rates following the massive downtown fire of 1904. He also told the Council that more than 4.8 kilometres of lakefront public property between Bathurst Street and the Humber River had been acquired for a new transportation artery (today's Lake Shore Boulevard).

Outside City Hall, transit remained a top issue in 1909, with the Toronto Railway Company's private franchise lasting until 1921. Yet it was losing the public's favour, the result of equipment often broken or in disrepair, a failure to meet the ridership needs in a rapidly growing city, and the serious deterioration of its track roadbed. Friction between the city government and the street railway had increased and was continual. Interestingly, a committee appointed by the Board of Trade recommended banning all but public vehicles in Toronto's central business area, defined as the area bounded by the waterfront and Church, Queen, and York Streets.

Under Oliver, the Council applied for legislation to raise the standards of milk for consumption and allow the medical health officer to carry out the proper inspection of dairies. The Council also discussed the need to purchase an automobile for the assistant city engineer, with councillors advised that because "the City covers such a very large district a machine is very much more serviceable than a horse and buggy."[6]

Also dealt with was a request from alderman and future mayor Sam McBride, "praying that steps be taken for the suppression of gambling activities among the Chinese of the City."[7] And 15 years before Canada's first zoning bylaw was brought in by Kitchener in 1924, Toronto's Board of Control made a basic attempt to regulate land use by approving a "residential district" in two small areas of downtown.

At the end of 1909, Oliver chose to bow out of politics and not contest the mayoral campaign in 1910. However, he did make a brief foray into provincial politics in November 1911 as the Liberal candidate for North Toronto, only to lose to sitting MPP and attorney general James Foy.

As a private citizen, Oliver remained involved in the community, serving on the board of the Canadian National Exhibition, beginning in 1901, and as its president in 1914. He was also a member of the Granite and Kew Beach Bowling Clubs and was a lifetime member of the Toronto Board of Trade. Oliver was a devoted member of several of the city's fraternal orders, including the venerable Orange Order from the age of 16, and was most active in the Independent Order of Odd Fellows, first joining it in 1872.

Indeed, at the time of his death in Toronto in January 1922, Oliver was the Sovereign Grand Sire, the highest international office of the Odd Fellows. His funeral at St. Andrew's Presbyterian Church was described as a spectacular parade of fraternal regalia. He was mourned by his wife, two daughters, and two sons, and a private family service was held at their home, followed by a large formal church service in the care of the Odd Fellows.

Because of Oliver's global position, his funeral was the equivalent of that for royalty. Such was the power of the fraternal Odd Fellows that Oliver is still the only mayor of Toronto to receive a personal message from a U.S. president upon his death (in Oliver's case, Warren G. Harding).

Mayoral Election in 1908	
CANDIDATES	VOTES
Joseph Oliver	14,003
Reg Geary	7,162
Dr. W.B. Nesbitt	6,523
James Simpson	3,691
Miles Vokes	974
Mayoral Election in 1909	
Joseph Oliver	26,485
Thomas Davies	9,233
James Lindala	1,640
Joel Briggs	350

Mayor Reginald Geary

1910–1912

The 35th mayor of Toronto

Occupations: Lawyer, Toronto Board of Education trustee, City of Toronto alderman and controller, corporation legal counsel, army colonel, Member of the House of Commons, federal minister of justice
Residence While Mayor: 184 University Avenue
Birth: August 12, 1873, in Strathroy, Ontario
Death: April 30, 1954, in Toronto

—— • ——

Reginald "Reg" Geary was born in Strathroy, Ontario, in August 1873, the son of Mary Goodson and Theophilus Geary, a small-town druggist who died when Geary was nine years old. After being left a widow in 1882, Geary's mother moved the family to Sarnia where young Geary attended public school.

In 1884, age 11, he was sent to Upper Canada College in Toronto, and later, after studying law at the University of Toronto, was called to the bar in 1896, age 23. After graduation, he first practised law with J.T. Scott, a colleague from law school, then formed a partnership that later became Macdonnell, McMaster and Geary, garnering a solid reputation in litigious negotiations.

Geary was first elected to public office in 1903 as a school trustee from Ward 4, and at age 29, was one of the city's youngest school board members. Then, from 1904 to 1907, he won election as the alderman for Toronto's Ward 3.

He represented the federal government before the newly established International Joint Commission and carved out a specialty in tax matters in 1910 as the Canadian representative to the International Tax Association and secretary of the Dominion of Canada International Tax Committee. Although he established himself as a leading corporate counsel, Geary knew his true calling was public service.

In 1908, by then a well-regarded Conservative, Geary was nominated and ran for mayor but lost to Joseph Oliver, a Liberal, in a four-person race. Although Geary came in second, "Boss" Beattie Nesbitt, a self-styled mover and shaker, had presented himself as an "independent conservative," splitting the anti-Oliver vote. The next year, Geary won election city-wide to the new Board of Control, setting the stage for another run at the top job.

Upon Oliver's retirement as mayor, Geary was elected to his first term in January 1910, age 36, defeating fellow Orangeman Horatio Hocken by 4,000 votes. Hocken was a founder of the *Toronto Daily Star* and had made a subway his main election plank. Voters in 1910 were asked if they agreed to seek the "power to construct and operate a municipal system of subway."[1]

Residents voted heavily in favour, with 19,376 in support and 10,696 opposed. Yet Geary had opposed a subway because of the massive potential costs. A newspaper report years later indicated that Geary had run on a less-pretentious platform: lower taxes.

The young, still single Geary soon became known as the city's "bachelor mayor." In his inaugural address for 1910, he noted it had been six years since the Great Fire, which had "rendered possible the acquirement of a desirable site for the erection of a new Union Station,"[2] though there was still no indication when the railways would proceed.

Geary observed that major changes were about to take place, with electricity finally coming to the city and serious attention being given to overhead wires "filling our streets with a tangled mass." He also warned of the "dust nuisance," in which unpaved streets were "either dust-laden if unwatered, or veritable seas of mud if watered."[3]

Looking ahead, the new mayor said the Council could now apply to the Legislative Assembly for authority to build a subway but that plans must be submitted to taxpayers. Strategies were also announced for a new board to oversee the waterfront: "We have a magnificent harbour, but we have failed miserably," he said. In addition, Geary stated that the private Toronto Railway Company, which operated the streetcar system, had engaged in "violation, evasion, and subterfuge."[4]

In 1910, Geary was Toronto's official representative at the funeral of King Edward VII and also served as a board member of the newly formed Union of Canadian Municipalities. Always at the office by 7:00 a.m., he was one of the hardest-working of Toronto's mayors, though others pointed out that was not remarkable, since he had no family.

His support in the press also increased. The *Daily Star* observed that Geary was the ideal young man for a "youthful" city, one of the fastest growing on the continent. The population had risen dramatically from 208,040 in 1901 to 376,538 in 1911, a result of growth, immigration, and suburban annexations. At the time, the population of Los Angeles was just 225,000.

Under Geary's mayoralty came one of his greatest legacies: Dr. Charles Hastings, the medical officer of health from 1910 to 1929. The pioneering doctor saw Toronto become the first Canadian city to require milk to be pasteurized. Unsafe water also remained a huge problem, with 739 cases of typhoid contracted because of contaminated water from the harbour.

The Council had asked engineer James Forgie of New York City to report on a possible underground transit system. His 1910 report recommended three lines stretching 18 kilometres, extending from Front and Yonge Streets, at a cost of $23 million ($625 million today). And just prior to the city receiving its first electricity from Niagara Falls, the brand-new Toronto Hydro arranged for a first preview of electric street lighting. On a mid-November evening, some 38 lights were demonstrated on Charles Street downtown.

At the end of the year, the *Toronto Daily Star* urged readers to "Vote for Geary," while the *Globe* called on citizens to give him "every possible vote," saying that "he is an upright, clean, capable young Canadian who does the city credit."[5] Geary was re-elected by a landslide on January 2, 1911, capturing 31,007 votes, a 27,000-vote plurality, against two minor opponents, making him the most popular mayor in the city's history up to that point.

In his inaugural address in 1911, Geary trumpeted increased assessment growth, bank clearings, customs revenues, and building construction. The Council dealt with the erection of new fire halls and police stations, while as a result of the dead carcasses, kitchen refuse, decayed fish, poultry, and eggs disposed of in various city dumps, Geary called for "the most sanitary, economical, and effective method"[6] of garbage disposal.

Times were also changing. With the horse vital to the entire North American economy, the impact of change was enormous, affecting an entire industry and thousands of jobs. Facing doom were Toronto wagon builders, harness makers, buggy repair companies, livery and stable operators, horse-drawn deliveries, buggy whip manufacturers, saddle-makers, horseshoe manufacturers, horse-drawn fire vehicles, carriage builders, horse shows, blacksmiths, wheelwrights, horse-feed companies, hitching post manufacturers, horse breeders, and an army of nighttime City of Toronto street cleaners.

In the fall of 1911, the Council pressed forward on a subway, calling tenders for the construction of cement tubes for a 4.8-kilometre line running from Bay and Front Streets to St. Clair Avenue. The lowest bid came in at $2.6 million ($69 million today), but with the additional cost of tracks, signals, electrical power, subway cars, and needed land, the price tag would be double. On January 1, 1912, it was put to a public vote, and in the face of cold, harsh reality, citizens were not so willing to embrace a subway. Weary of taxes, and with four of the five daily newspapers against the measure, electors turned down a subway by a vote of 11,645 against 8,223 in favour.

Yet 1912 marked the return of Geary when no opponents came forward, and he was acclaimed as mayor. The Council dealt with a range of issues, including a call for several auto-related reforms: lights on all passenger-carrying vehicles, a requirement for horns and lamps, and a minimum age limit for all drivers. Also discussed by the Council were slum housing conditions, congestion on Yonge Street, future suburban annexations, serious streetcar overcrowding, and the burying of telephone wires.

Midway through the fall of 1912 during his third term, Geary surprised friends and supporters by announcing his resignation as mayor. With the city becoming increasingly embroiled in court cases involving various public corporations, Geary believed his skills, training, temperament, and knowledge of corporate law could best serve the city as its in-house corporation counsel. He held this position until 1932, spanning the terms of eight mayors elected after him.

Surprisingly, with the outbreak of world war in 1914, the 41-year-old former mayor was one of the first Torontonians to enlist in the armed forces, even though he had no prior military experience. In January 1915, he received a commission as a lieutenant with the 35th Battalion of the Canadian Expeditionary Force. Later, he was transferred to the 58th Battalion and served overseas until May 1919. Sent overseas on active duty, he was initially attached to military headquarters in London, England, then helped locate 300 missing Canadians captured and interned in Switzerland, later noting that the Germans were no match for the British.

And unlike Toronto mayors before him, Geary actually saw the horror of war first-hand and in a deeply personal way. In the dank, dark trenches of the Western Front, he was badly gassed, and as with many other veterans, rarely talked in subsequent years about his life in the war.

Serving with distinction, Geary was promoted to major and was mentioned in military dispatches. He was awarded the Military Cross, was made an Officer of the Order of the British Empire (Military), and in a rare distinction, was awarded the French Legion of Honour. On March 24, 1919, Geary was finally discharged from the army, and upon his return, served as commander of the Royal Grenadier Regiment in 1924 and 1925. In civilian life, he resumed his position as the City of Toronto corporation counsel and became active in the Great War Veterans' Association.

In 1925, Geary was elected to the House of Commons as the Conservative MP for Toronto South by a vote of 68 percent to his opponent's 28 percent. In the general election of 1926, he increased his margin of victory to 75 percent. The following year, in March 1927, age 54 and very much in love, Geary married prominent Montreal socialite Beatrice Caverhill, who had served with the Red Cross in Europe.

That same year, Geary became the heir to an unexpected fortune when a rich uncle died and left him $170,000 ($2.9 million today). Geary soon bought a stately home at 124 Park Road, naming it Caverhill. Originally built in 1855, it was one of the first great homes erected on the Jarvis estate and remained in the Geary family until the 1980s.

Geary continued his winning streak in the July 1930 federal general election, capturing 60 percent of the vote. In the R.B. Bennett Conservative government, he chaired two House of Commons committees, one dealing with railways and another looking into charges of alleged prime ministerial corruption.

While holding his seat through the worst of the Great Depression, Geary was repeatedly mentioned as a potential candidate for the Cabinet, yet was only appointed minister of justice and attorney general just weeks ahead of the 1935 federal election. This time he ran in the westerly downtown riding of Trinity, but after nine years as an MP, was finally defeated.

Tragically, in 1935, Geary's wife, Bea, died at their home on Park Road. Deeply affected by her death and now in his sixties, it was unclear if he would ever return to public life. Yet five years later, as world war again raged in Europe, Geary attempted to win back a seat in the House of Commons but lost in Trinity in the 1940 federal election. With a vote of 54 percent for the Liberals to Geary's 42 percent, it was not even close.

Geary retired from active politics but continued to practise law in Toronto for several more years. An Anglican, he was an active church-warden of St. James Cathedral and a proud member of Cameron Loyal Orange Lodge 613. Over many years, he was involved with the Independent Order of Odd Fellows, the Sons of England, the Knights of the Maccabees, the Foresters, the Knights of Pythias, and the Irish Protestant Benevolent Society. Geary was also a member of the very exclusive York, Albany,

University, and Toronto Hunt Clubs, and was active with the Alpha Delta Phi fraternity.

Toronto's 35th mayor died of coronary thrombosis at Caverhill, his Park Road mansion, on April 30, 1954, age 80, and was buried at St. James Cemetery in Toronto. He was survived by his daughter, Mary, and son, Richard.

Mayoral Election in 1910	
CANDIDATES	VOTES
Reginald Geary	18,996
Horatio Hocken	14,999
Thomas Davies	644
Robert Noble	102
Joel Marvin Briggs	92
Mayoral Election in 1911	
Reginald Geary	31,007
Herb Capewell	2,709
Robert Noble	526
Mayoral Election in 1912	
Reginald Geary faced no opponents and was acclaimed as mayor.	

Mayor Horatio Hocken

1912–1914

The 36th mayor of Toronto

Occupations: Printer, reporter, editor, author, City of Toronto controller, Member of House of Commons, Canadian senator
Residence While Mayor: 340 Palmerston Avenue
Birth: October 12, 1857, in Toronto
Death: February 18, 1937, in Toronto

——— • ———

Horatio Clarence Hocken was the son of Amelia Thompson and Richard Hocken. His father immigrated from Cornwall, England, in 1835 and settled in Toronto where Horatio was born in 1857. It was from his father — a quiet, reserved custom shoemaker with an interest in history and politics — that young Hocken inherited a lasting love of the printed word and a lively interest in political affairs.

By age 12, Hocken was a regular reader of parliamentary reports published in the *Globe* and worked briefly in Edward Dack's shoe factory before becoming a 16-year-old apprentice compositor at the *Globe*, whose founder, George Brown, was still running the newspaper. Hocken quickly became a top-notch typesetter, a function requiring strong mental and manual dexterity to keep on top of fast-moving events. In Toronto's highly competitive news environment, Hocken excelled and was given the nickname "Race," which friends called him for the rest of his life.

"Race" Hocken, with a well-earned reputation as one of the quickest typesetters in the city, was hired away from the *Globe* in his early twenties to become the composing room foreman at the *News*. But when the paper introduced a new automatic typesetting machine, Hocken and the Toronto Typographical Union led printers on a prolonged strike there. It later resulted in the start of an opposition paper, the *Evening Star* (today's *Toronto Star*), in 1892, with Hocken becoming its first business manager. Created almost overnight by 21 printers who had been locked out during the labour dispute, the *Evening Star* intended to publish a serious journal and teach the *News* a lesson. The bright new four-page broadsheet eventually became Canada's largest daily newspaper.

After the strike, Hocken left the *Star* and returned to the *News* where he was appointed City Hall reporter in 1893 and managing editor in 1895. In 1902, he purchased the *St. Thomas Times-Journal*, which he operated for only a short time before returning to Toronto the following year.

Upon the death of Edward Clarke, a leading Orange leader and former mayor in 1905, Hocken purchased his Sentinel Publishing Company and became editor of the *Orange Sentinel*, a large-circulation weekly newspaper serving supporters of the Loyal Orange Lodge. As its editor, Hocken rose to prominence within Orange circles, and even while serving in public life, remained editor of the *Sentinel* until 1931. He sold the weekly in 1928 to the Grand Lodge of the Loyal Orange Association of British North America.

This was a time when Toronto with its large Protestant Irish population was referred to as "the Belfast of Canada." Back then virtually all prominent politicians at City Hall belonged to the Orange Order. Soon after buying the *Orange Sentinel*, Hocken startled friends by announcing he was entering city politics in an unprecedented way. Running for the Board of Control instead of first becoming an alderman on the Council, Hocken was helped by the fact that he knew every influential person at City Hall and that his prior civic election work had already earned him the nickname "Kingmaker."

In 1907, Hocken was indeed elected to the Board of Control. His years at City Hall for the *News* were considered a suitable apprenticeship, and in 1908 and 1909, he was easily re-elected to the board while also serving as deputy grand treasurer of the Grand Orange Lodge of British North America. Hocken was the author of *Twenty-Five Years of Protestant Progress* and a political pamphlet, *The Duty of the Hour*, which created some political excitement in the 1908 federal general election.

Hocken ran against Reg Geary in 1910 for the mayoralty but lost a competitive race. He had campaigned on a plan to alleviate downtown traffic congestion by building an underground railway (known as a "tube") from Front and Bay Streets, the site of a proposed new Union Station, north to Yonge Street and St. Clair Avenue. Geary captured the mayoralty with 18,996 votes to Hocken's 14,999.

In 1911 and then again in 1912, Hocken was elected to the Board of Control, and with Geary's resignation in October 1912, Hocken was appointed to succeed him as mayor. As a newspaper editorial commented, "Mr. Hocken will make a six-cylinder Mayor ... he is full of energy, full of optimism, and full of faith in Toronto."[1]

The city was also changing in terms of its built form. In 1912, Toronto's earliest apartment buildings were viewed as a significant departure from the North American ideal of an owner-occupied, single-family home. Not only were apartments publicly condemned as being against the family, they were viewed as an unsanitary threat to property values, morals, neighbourhoods, and society, as well as an undermining of the city's economic and social fabric.

Transportation was also a defining issue of the Hocken mayoralty. A referendum vote allowing a new bridge across the Don River was finally approved on January 1, 1913, with 14,756 in favour and 5,520 opposed, a stark change from the 59-vote majority in opposition only a year before. The Bloor-to-Danforth bridge plan was now put into motion, and in the words of York University professor Ann Marie F. Murnaghan, it was "a momentous time for the city."[2]

During Hocken's two mayoral terms, several reforms took place. Parks with supervised recreation were opened up, with Hocken believing they took young boys out of playing in back alleys. Other public health measures included public baths, a sewage treatment plant, major new sewers, public health nursing, and the distribution of fresh milk to infants in slum housing.

Hocken was elected mayor in January 1913 to his own first term in a landslide, capturing 28,112 votes to opponent Thomas Davies's 9,159. Quite rare at the time was the support for Hocken by all of the city's leading newspapers.

Substandard downtown living conditions in 1913. The hovel pictured here is where the ice rink at Nathan Phillips Square is today. The west side of Old City Hall is in the background.

In his 1913 inaugural address, Hocken noted that the modern Toronto was now 85 square kilometres, and its population had reached 470,000. While just five years earlier, the Toronto Railway Company had carried 89.1 million passengers, by 1912 that had risen to 132 million.

The business climate remained positive through 1912, though by the end of 1913 dark clouds were gathering. The first warnings appeared when banks and financial institutions exercised greater caution, leading to reduced production, tighter credit, less construction, and higher unemployment.

In the January 1914 mayoral election, the *Evening Telegram* supported alderman Fred McBrien, while Hocken, one of the founders of the *Toronto Daily Star*, was strongly backed by that paper. Just as he had a year before, Hocken captured the mayor's chair by a healthy margin, receiving 21,387 votes to McBrien's 16,651. History was also made with the election of Lou Singer as the first municipal representative from Toronto's growing Jewish community.

In his inaugural address, Hocken dealt with several pressing concerns. He noted that a new bridge across the Don and new Danforth streetcar line would create pressure for the city to annex additional suburbs. Hocken pointed out that would require a connection to the city's sewage system and involve huge infrastructure costs. The mayor also noted the enormous majority recently given by electors in support of married women having the right to vote (in the same way that widows and single women — or "spinsters," as they were called could), and that it would "strengthen the hands of Council in pressing that change upon the provincial authorities."[3]

Hocken observed that initial work had started on the construction of a "Lake Front Boulevard," the first step of an eventual route to knit together a system of playgrounds, parks, squares, and open spaces. Yet the mayor also sounded caution about the city's rapid industrial progress, noting that a dust-laden atmosphere, combined with the danger of poisoning from lead, phosphorus, brass, mercury, and wood alcohol, presented a danger to workers.

During Hocken's term, the city's complexion was also changing. It was reported that a record number of immigrants — 400,870 in all — had arrived in Canada the year before. And to understand how different the world of 1914 was compared to the city over a hundred years later, one only has to look at the city's *Municipal Handbook*, distributed widely to business leaders, politicians, and city staff, to see that it included the home telephone number (Main 222) and home address (71 Clarendon Avenue) of Toronto police chief H.J. Grasett.

In 1914, the Council dealt with a wide range of issues, including the appointment of delegates to the National Conference on City Planning and providing the Council with all the information concerning electric lighting and power rates. Also in 1914 the Fire Department, up to then using only horse-drawn equipment, acquired its first motorized vehicle — a new hook-and-ladder truck. In June of the same year, a large delegation of Toronto business leaders made an excursion by chartered steamer to Detroit, Cleveland, and Buffalo, returning much impressed by progress there with respect to the development of parks.

By the end of his second term in late 1914, Hocken had had enough of municipal politics; the federal sphere now occupied his political interests. In 1917, he was elected MP for Toronto West, receiving 12,648 votes to just over 3,000 for his opponent. He then held his House of Commons seat for the next 13 years. In the following election in December 1921, Hocken received 51 percent support, and in what was a brand-new development in Canadian politics at the time, he ran against one of the very first female candidates in the nation, Harriet Prenter, who received 15 percent.

As historian Donald Jones notes in a *Toronto Star Saturday Magazine* article, Hocken, upon his arrival in Ottawa, had been a surprise to French-speaking members of Parliament: "Instead of the 'ogre' they expected, they found this small, somewhat fatherly figure, with the gentle voice, barely 5 feet high."[4] Hocken remained in the House of Commons until 1930, then in December 1933, after a quarter century of public life, was appointed to the Senate by Prime Minister R.B. Bennett. Although 76 and frail, the former mayor and his wife continued to be visible public figures in Toronto and occupied a large summer home on the Toronto Islands.

Hocken was a devoted Methodist and member of the Orange Order, belonging to Lansdowne Loyal Orange Lodge 469 and Queen City Loyal Orange Lodge 857. He served as the grand master of the Grand Orange Lodge of Ontario West in 1917–1918 and was grand master of the Orange Order in Canada from 1918 to 1922.

In February 1937, Hocken caught a cold that quickly developed into pneumonia, and within a few weeks was dead, age 79. Donald Jones described him as "one of the more complex and often misunderstood figures in Toronto's political history,"[5] and despite his religious biases, was a champion of many worthwhile causes.

As Jones noted, "You may not see things from his point of view, but you are blind if you don't perceive that what he sees, he sees sincerely, and that he describes it without fear, favor or affection."[6] Horatio Hocken left behind him a legacy of both infrastructure and social reform.

Mayoral Election in 1913	
CANDIDATES	VOTES
Horatio Hocken	28,112
Thomas Davies	9,159
Mayoral Election in 1914	
Horatio Hocken	21,387
Fred McBrien	16,651
Alf Burgess	3,692

Mayor Thomas Church

1915–1921

The 37th mayor of Toronto

Occupations: Lawyer, Toronto Board of Education trustee, City of Toronto alderman and controller, Member of House of Commons
Residence While Mayor: 98 Binscarth Road
Birth: January 30, 1873, in Toronto
Death: February 7, 1950, in Toronto

Thomas "Tommy" Church was born in January 1873, the son of Elizabeth and John Church. His shoemaker father, from County Sligo in northwestern Ireland, had first settled in the close-knit east end Cabbagetown neighbourhood. Young Tommy was educated at Dufferin School and Jarvis and Parkdale Collegiates, then attended Trinity College at the University of Toronto before graduating from Osgoode Hall Law School. He was called to the bar in 1897.

Entering civic politics immediately after being called to the bar, he was elected a member of the Toronto School Board from 1898 to 1904. From 1905 to 1909, he served Ward 2 as a city alderman and then as a controller from 1910 to 1914.

In 1915, when Horatio Hocken, the incumbent mayor, chose not to run again, two prominent members of the Board of Control vied to replace him: Tommy Church and Jesse McCarthy. A life insurance manager, McCarthy was a Liberal and the first major political figure in Canada to identify himself openly as a member of the Bahá'í faith.

As with other political races, it became a serious contest between rival daily newspapers, with the *Globe* and *Daily Star* supporting McCarthy, while the *Evening Telegram* backed Church. In the end, with 26,047 votes, Church easily defeated McCarthy, who received 19,586.

Indeed, Tommy Church became a mayor of Toronto unlike any other, as the *Toronto Daily Star* described decades later: "The secret of his success lay probably in the fact that he liked people [and] was interested in people,"[1] while the *Globe and Mail* noted that "if it could not be said that he was the best Mayor this city ever had, there can be no doubt of his genius in projecting himself as a warm and friendly representative of all the people."[2]

Over 1.8 metres tall and slightly stooped as well as a bit deaf, Church was at times so gaunt that he was compared to an Irish wolfhound. It was said that his outstanding trait and chief political asset was his "punch-card memory." The legend was that once he saw a face he never forgot it. He could remember names, nicknames, and family backgrounds and relationships.

Bloor Street Viaduct under construction in 1917, looking east toward Danforth Avenue.

Even a new arrival to Toronto just off a ship or train felt after that first encounter that he had known "good old Tommy" all his life.

In his inaugural speech, Toronto's 37th mayor dealt with a wide range of issues: new factories in the city, hydroelectric service, a proposed bridge from Bloor Street to Danforth Avenue, the future of local annexations, and construction of a new Union Station on Front Street.

Church became known as "the Soldier's Friend," creating a plan whereby Toronto men fighting overseas would be insured for $1,000 ($25,000 today) if they died. And virtually no train carrying troops off to war departed the city without the mayor at the station to wish them well. The same applied to veterans returning home. It was reported that during the First World War Tommy Church was everywhere, visiting troops in training, listening to their problems, giving them aid. And when news of casualties arrived in the city's homes, the mayor was often the first to call on grieving families.

In January 1916, Church had been mayor for just a year when the *Daily Star* declared that year's mayoral race was "a joke," given his sole opponent had never held office. Church was returned with 28,557 votes to Henry Winberg's 9,890. The re-elected mayor singlehandedly took credit for the turnaround in the city's finances, saying they were now "in excellent condition and all the difficulties have been met, overcome, and solved."[3] He called for far shorter meetings and the preservation of "the dignity" of the Council. Also handled by Church was the state of Toronto's harbour and the need to care for the "feeble-minded."

Church dealt with progress on a major new roadway from Toronto to Oshawa, noting a land survey had been carried out, the plans done up, and a proper estimate obtained. He also advised that a meeting of the munici- palities between Toronto and Barrie had taken place to convince the prov- ince to build a major new roadway there. High on the list of Council issues for 1916 were critical war-related matters. It was noted that 40,000 local residents had enlisted in the war, and the Council was asked to establish a special office at City Hall to look after all matters relating to Toronto soldiers serving overseas.

First elected two years earlier, Church won the mayoralty by acclamation in 1917 when no one chose to oppose him. With several years still to go be- fore the end of the private and highly secretive Toronto Railway Company (TRC) franchise in 1921, Church stated that active preparations must begin, publicly asking the Legislative Assembly for powers to compel the TRC to build 200 new streetcars.

The Council discussed a range of topics: a civic commission to prepare for conditions postwar, Esplanade improvements, construction of a new Don Destructor (garbage incinerator), and that a brand-new registry office needed to be "absolutely fireproof." Church also urged that a top city official be appointed specifically to locate new industries in Toronto.

On January 1, 1918, Church was re-elected to a fourth consecutive term, capturing 27,605 votes and earning a reputation during the war years for putting in an appearance anywhere he was needed and at any hour of the day or night. Supporters called him a veritable "human hummingbird."

In 1918, Canada's population was eight million, of which 490,000 lived in the City of Toronto. And while 4,904 Torontonians had died as a result of the war between 1914 and 1918, another 1,750 had passed away due to the Spanish flu. Indeed, Toronto in 1918 was different from the future city of the 21st century: many immigrants spoke no English and others were illiterate. There was no publicly funded health care, sick pay, or employment insurance. Families and individuals depended on survival from neighbours, their ethnic or local communities, or places of worship for survival.

The city's financial shape and greater efficiencies in revenue collection took centre stage in the mayor's inaugural address in 1918, as did the municipality's coal situation and appointment of a coal commissioner. Church also grappled with the conduct of Council meetings and the reform of outside boards and commissions.

On January 1, 1919, the mayor was elected to his fifth consecutive term with 26,020 votes after being opposed by several credible opponents, including controller John O'Neill vying to become the city's first Roman Catholic mayor, who received 16,230 votes. Toronto's 1919 Council was decidedly Tory, with 25 Conservatives, three Liberals, one independent, and a sole member from the labour movement.

Issues discussed at the Council between 1915 and 1921 under Mayor Church included the following:

- a restriction of traffic on Bay Street due to increased congestion
- the widening of Broadview Avenue
- a move to reduce municipal salaries
- establishment of a civil service exam at the City of Toronto
- a possible change of name for Danforth Avenue
- Toronto's participation in the Dominion Association of Police Chiefs
- a protest from the Board of Education with respect to Council interference
- an official inquiry concerning the price of bread
- the regulation of donations to municipal campaigns
- the licensing of ferries to the Toronto Islands
- the nuisance caused by city-owned abattoirs
- allowing apartment buildings to be built in residential areas
- underground telephone wiring
- Toronto's participation in the Ontario Municipal Association
- the sale of newspapers from stands on city streets
- the regulation of steam whistles on train locomotives
- licence fees for motor vehicles

- the widening of Bloor Street from Sherbourne to St. George Streets
- a prohibition on the carrying of weapons by "aliens"
- the yearly inspection of cartage vans
- licensing of where candies could be sold in Toronto
- the deportation of "alien" enemies
- the regulation of hand laundries
- lighting on motor vehicles at night
- participation in the Union of Canadian Municipalities
- a Teamsters Union wage increase
- the regulation of boarding houses
- matters affecting the Orange Order in Toronto
- the high cost of foodstuffs
- the Toronto Railway Company (discussed 49 times in just one year)
- a host of war-related matters, including the care of disabled soldiers, Christmas presents for Toronto soldiers abroad, grants for recruitment purposes, the welcoming of returning soldiers, grants to aid Canadian prisoners held in Germany, an appeal for contributions by the British Red Cross, the enlistment of civic employees, and a preference for the hiring of returning soldiers

In his first address to the new Council in 1919, Church reported that the previous year had seen "the most satisfactory tax collection in the history of the city.[4] Success was defined as an 85 percent collection rate. Toronto could now begin to do away with heavy war expenditures, and the employment of returning war veterans was of paramount importance. Sadly, Church revealed that the city's insurance plan for soldiers who had died while serving overseas had covered 4,168 deaths and paid out $4.1 million ($64 million today) to surviving spouses, families, and dependents.

The mayor declared that there was "no more important or far-reaching" issue facing the city than the upcoming acquisition of the TRC in 1921, noting it demanded more "care and thought, constructive effort, and efficient guidance" than any other issue. He said that due to slippery legal manoeuvring, the TRC had "been allowed all these years to escape just and fair taxation."[5]

Topics dealt with by the Council in 1919 included municipal arbitration, harbour improvements, the city's credit rating, a deepening of the Welland Canal, and the reforestation of Toronto. An important priority, said the mayor, was "the doing away of slum districts," and he also took a swipe at the Toronto Board of Education for "too many fads and frills."[6]

On January 1, 1920, Church was elected to a sixth consecutive term in office. He was opposed by labour-backed candidate, controller, and future mayor Sam McBride, and though re-elected with 25,720 votes, it was not an overwhelming win, with McBride capturing 20,818 votes. One historic development that received no attention whatsoever at the time was the election of Constance Hamilton, the first woman member of Toronto's Council and also the first woman in Ontario to be elected at either the city, provincial, or federal level.

The Council dealt with bylaw reform, waterworks improvements, the purchase of new animals for the Riverdale Zoo, the city's popular new streetcar service over the Don River to Broadview Avenue, a new municipal art gallery, a lowering of the tax rate, and the need for a new detention centre.

In the January 1921 municipal election campaign, the *Toronto Daily Star* backed mayoral challenger Sam McBride, pointing out that Church was seeking a seventh term and was making the mayoralty a career. And in a direct appeal to veterans, women, and labour, the *Daily Star* hailed McBride's support of women having a vote, a city hiring preference for returning soldiers, and the drive to achieve an eight-hour workday.

Yet, in the end, it was Tommy Church, with 35,939 votes, who was again re-elected by a wide margin over long-time political rival McBride. And with almost 56,000 voters casting a ballot, it was the highest vote total in the city's history.

The year 1921 was indeed a momentous one for the citizens of Toronto. On September 1, the TRC's franchise expired and the newly created, city-owned Toronto Transportation Commission (TTC) took its place. The first task of the TTC was to rebuild, replace, and otherwise upgrade the tracks, electrical plant, and infrastructure the TRC had allowed to deteriorate during the remaining years of its franchise.

In 1921, the Council dealt with numerous matters: ongoing problems with the new Union Station, education standards, city debt levels, the promotion of new industries in Toronto, unemployment, relations with the federal government, and the need for new rental housing.

In December 1921 while still serving as mayor, Church was also elected the Conservative MP for Toronto North and did not return again to the Council after the end of his seventh mayoralty, though he made another unsuccessful attempt for that office in 1924.

Indeed, Church served as an MP from 1921 until his death in 1950 except for four years (1930–1934) when he suffered one of his only political setbacks. In fact, Church represented five different Toronto ridings in the course of nine federal election contests and 24 years as a federal MP.

An Anglican and an Orangeman whose family had come from Northern Ireland, he became one of the city's best-known MPs, especially for his characteristic speech style. The *Globe and Mail* later noted that his rapid-fire political speeches dazed and anaesthetized his fellow MPs. "There was nothing quite like the Church style of speech-making. He ... often confused and bewildered the Commons members and the press gallery." The experts who took down the debates for Hansard were often left reeling and groggy. "It was said that there were three languages in Canada, English, French and Tommy Church."[7]

After complications due to asthma, Tommy Church died at Wellesley Hospital in January 1950, age 77. A lifelong bachelor, Church resided on Binscarth Road and was particularly devoted in the care and well-being of his sister, Rebecca Mary Church.

Upon his death, the *Globe and Mail* reported on the many qualities of Tommy Church, the city's longest-serving mayor up to that point. Toronto, it noted, had lost a good friend, "a man who symbolized in his person a vigorous era of growth.... No man in Canada had stronger love for the British connection ... he left the imprint of his personality on every facet of civic life.... He himself became a legend in his own lifetime ... he was Tory Toronto personified."[8]

Mayoral Election in 1915	
CANDIDATES	VOTES
Thomas Church	26,047
Jesse McCarthy	19,586
Mayoral Election in 1916	
Thomas Church	28,557
Henry Winberg	9,890
Mayoral Election in 1917	
Thomas Church won the mayoralty by acclamation.	
Mayoral Election in 1918	
Thomas Church	27,605
Robert Cameron	17,995
Mayoral Election in 1919	
Thomas Church	26,020
John O'Neill	16,230
William Shaw	3,772
Thomas Foster	2,180
Mayoral Election in 1920	
Thomas Church	25,720
Sam McBride	20,818
James Ballantyne	5,589
Mayoral Election in 1921	
Thomas Church	35,939
Sam McBride	19,993

Mayor Alfred Maguire

1922–1923

The 38th mayor of Toronto

Occupations: Lumber and coal merchant, insurance executive, City of Toronto alderman and controller, Ontario Hydro commissioner
Residence While Mayor: 74 Oriole Road
Birth: May 24, 1875, in Toronto
Death: October 14, 1949, in Toronto

—— • ——

A lfred Maguire was born in his family's home at 70 Gerrard Street West in 1875, the son of James Maguire and Elizabeth Brown. His father had come from County Armagh in Ireland, age 16, while his mother was a native of Toronto.

Maguire was educated in Toronto at Elizabeth, Victoria, and Wellesley Public Schools and started work in 1890 as a clerk at the offices of Love and Hamilton, agents for the Lancashire Insurance Company. He then went into business with his brother, William, at Maguire Brothers, a well-known supplier of coal, wood, and building materials that prospered during the construction boom that spurred the city's growth at the beginning of the century. In February 1900, Maguire married Lillian Cusack, 23, of London, Ontario, and they had a son, Herbert, born in 1910.

Concentrating on establishing an insurance business, Maguire formed a partnership with William Connon in 1905. Eventually, Maguire and Connon took over the firm of Kay, Banks, Love, and Hamilton, the representative of Royal Insurance in Toronto as well as in York County.

Maguire first entered municipal politics in 1909 when he was elected alderman for Ward 3. He was re-elected in 1910, 1911, and 1912, and in November 1912, was appointed by Toronto's Council to the Board of Control to replace Horatio Hocken, who had become mayor upon the resignation of Reg Geary.

In political life, Maguire was generally but not always a Liberal and unsuccessfully pursued both federal and provincial seats. In 1911, he ran as a Liberal candidate for Sir Wilfrid Laurier in the September federal election in the riding of Toronto Centre. Maguire lost badly, capturing only 36 percent of the votes to 63 percent for the Conservative candidate. Yet Maguire later ended up running in the provincial riding of St. George for the Conservatives.

In the municipal election of January 1913, he lost his bid to remain on the Board of Control but returned to the Council the following year, serving from 1914 to 1917 as an alderman for Ward 3. In 1918, he again moved up, and from 1918 to 1921 was elected to the powerful city-wide Board of Control as its vice-chair.

Maguire became mayor by acclamation on December 21, 1921, when no other nomination was received for the 1922 term. At the inaugural meeting of the 1922 Council, he pointed out that a significant debt load of $130 million ($2.1 billion today) had been caused by a number of issues: the acquisition and rehabilitation of the now publicly owned Toronto Railway Company (TRC), new buildings at the Canadian National Exhibition, upgrades to both the city's hydro and waterworks, new local improvement charges, and new housing allocations.

With pride, Maguire noted that as of 1922 the Fire Department now had 31 motorized vehicles and that just 13 of its vehicles were still horse-drawn. He pointed out that while there were 342 men in place in 1918, that number had increased to 632 by 1922.

Similarly, the Police Department, which had fallen to fewer than 500 during the First World War, was now at a strength of 827. In fact, the Council received a comprehensive report in 1922 on criminal activity in Toronto the year before. There had been 38,278 crimes, including those by 9,009 people who broke the Motor Vehicles Act, which had not existed 15 years earlier.

Upon taking office, Maguire outlined an ambitious program for his mayoralty, reiterating his determination to build rail links to both the east and west ends of the city, construct a new rail viaduct to the waterfront, maintain a low tax rate, and authorize a number of capital improvements that had long been deferred.

By the 1920s, swimming in Lake Ontario had been popular for more than 30 years, and in June 1922, Maguire opened the Sunnyside Bathing Pavilion to assist bathers changing for a swim in the lake. Constructed of concrete at a cost of $300,000 ($5 million today), each wing held an outdoor changing area, lockers, showers, and a roof garden.

Unlike the year before, a mayoral acclamation was not in the works for 1923. Maguire, like his predecessor Thomas Church, was an ardent and aggressive advocate of public ownership, especially of hydro, and had supported the establishment of the publicly owned Toronto Transportation Commission (TTC), as it was then called, to replace the unpopular, highly secretive, privately held TRC.

When the official City Hall nominations for the 1923 mayoralty were opened, opposition surfaced in the person of former mayor Robert Fleming

(1892–1893 and 1896–1897). Fleming had previously been general manager of the TRC, the monopoly liquidated to make way for the publicly owned TTC. The race was close, and "the People's Bob," as he had earlier been known, came close to winning the office once more.

Maguire minced no words slamming the TRC and its operations. The purpose of that firm, he said, had been to make all the profit possible while the comfort and convenience of passengers and compliance with the city's transit contract were only secondary.

The 1923 election campaign focused on Sir Adam Beck's proposal for an electrical radial railway line along the Toronto waterfront and farther into neighbouring cities. Maguire was in favour of the controversial plan while Fleming was opposed. Ironically, the radial railway plan was voted down in a referendum during the civic election, but Maguire was re-elected mayor.

In the end, the results were much closer than expected. Maguire captured 40,795 votes, while Fleming, who had been out of active elected politics for a quarter century, came close with 39,802, a difference of just 993. Maguire's total was the largest number of votes ever received by a Toronto mayoral candidate up to then.

Maguire proudly stated in his inaugural address as mayor in 1923 that "taxes collected last year were the greatest in the history of the city," cautioning that city debt had climbed to $145 million ($2.4 billion today) and noting that "debt is growing faster than the population and wealth of the city warrant."[1]

He remarked that Yonge Street from Summerhill Avenue to the city's northern city limits would finally be paved and that the newly minted TTC was now serving 320 kilometres of the city. Maguire also pointed out that the assets of the TRC were the subject of arbitration that had lasted for 158 days of hearings thus far.

The city assessment was now up to $828 million ($13.9 billion today), Maguire said, and was made up of four key areas: land, buildings and improvements, business, and incomes. He warned that several areas of the city were "in pressing need" of children's playgrounds and urged action. Maguire added that a new police headquarters was needed, that motorized police vehicles were a real improvement, and that "citizens are surprised at the quick response."[2]

He indicated that unemployment was down and that infant mortality was half of what it had been just 12 years earlier. Torontonians were also using ambulance services in record numbers. In the previous year, 987 citizens had been transported to St. Michael's Hospital, 709 to Toronto General Hospital, 625 to Toronto Western Hospital, and 354 to the Hospital for Sick Children.

In July, the Liberal government of Prime Minister William Lyon Mackenzie King clamped down on Chinese immigration into Canada, passing the Exclusion Act and making Chinese the only group specifically excluded from Canada solely on the basis of race. (Between 1923 and 1947, when the act was repealed, fewer than 50 Chinese were admitted into the country.)

The Council dealt with a range of issues during Maguire's mayoralty. It agreed to a motion by councillor Joe Singer for a comprehensive review of civic salaries, but by a vote of 14–13 declined to investigate allegations that major corporations had carried out a campaign against the hydro radial project in Toronto during the previous election. Maguire and city controllers also looked at four possible sites for a new east end hospital.

Toronto's population had now reached 538,771, making it the largest city in Ontario by far. The closest cities in population were Hamilton with 120,945 and Ottawa with 117,239.

In *The Municipality of Toronto*, Jesse Middleton describes the city during the Maguire mayoralty of 1923:

> Undoubtedly there is no other city of comparable size where the population is as homogeneous as in Toronto. Mention has been made of foreign citizens, but the colonies are not large.... In outward semblance Toronto is an American city. Plate glass abounds. The shop windows are dressed in the alluring New York manner. The crowds are well garbed and vivacious ... downtown offices for the most part are luxurious palaces of marble and mahogany, with hardwood floors and beautiful lighting.... In a word Toronto is British in the North American manner.[3]

At the final meeting of his mayoralty, Maguire was honoured by the Council, which expressed "unqualified appreciation of the energy, ability, and zeal" he had displayed. He was praised for his endeavours on behalf of public ownership and for Toronto's reputation as a centre of public ownership in power, heating, lighting, and transportation.

Maguire retired from city politics in 1924 but for several years was a member of the province's Hydro-Electric Power Commission. He had previously served as vice-president of the Hydro-Electric Railways Association and as a member of the executive of the Hydro-Electric Power Association. Maguire briefly came out of retirement to run for the Conservatives in the downtown St. George riding in the 1937 Ontario provincial election but was defeated by the Liberals.

A member of the Knights of Pythias, Maguire was affiliated with several other Toronto fraternal organizations: the St. Andrew's Lodge of the Free and Accepted Masons, the Cyrene Preceptory of the Knights Templar, and the Occident Chapter of the Royal Arch Masons. In addition, he was a member of the Rameses Temple, the Ancient Arabic Order Nobles of the Mystic Shrine, Loyal Orange Lodge 778, McKinley Loyal Orange Lodge 275, and Royal Black Preceptory 292, a Protestant fraternal society known as the Imperial Grand Black Chapter of the British Commonwealth. As well, Maguire was a member of the Ontario and Oakwood Lawn Bowling Clubs, while in matters of personal faith he was a Presbyterian affiliated with Deer Park Church near his home at 74 Oriole Road.

Maguire died in Toronto on October 14, 1949. A future mayor, Leslie Saunders, brought forward a resolution to the Council that said: "He was a man of likeable personality, warm-hearted, sincere, and approachable as befitting one whose character was based on ability and fineness of feeling for his fellow man."[4]

Mayoral Election in 1922	
CANDIDATES	VOTES
Alfred Maguire was elected by acclamation.	
Mayoral Election in 1923	
Alfred Maguire	40,795
Robert Fleming	39,802
SPECIAL NOTE: The above final vote totals followed a judicial recount.	

Mayor William W. Hiltz

1924

The 39th mayor of Toronto

Occupations: Teacher, builder, property developer, Toronto Board of Education chair, City of Toronto alderman and controller, philanthropist
Residence While Mayor: 682 Broadview Avenue
Birth: November 2, 1872, in Erin, Wellington County, Ontario
Death: February 26, 1936, in Toronto

— • —

William Wesley Hiltz (born Hilts) was descended from the Hilts family that had emigrated from the Palatinate area of Germany as the result of European wars and famine. The Hilts family came to North America, arriving in the United States in the early 18th century, first settling in the western part of New York State. As a result of the American Revolution, members of the family relocated to Canada in 1779, settling in Upper Canada where an ancestor received a land grant.

William Hilts was born in Erin, Wellington County, Ontario, in 1872, and his parents, Edward and Margaret, had another nine children. For personal reasons, William Hilts changed the spelling of his surname to Hiltz before entering public life.

Growing up in an environment of rural poverty, he finished public school and worked on the farm as well as in a brickyard operated by his father. He attended both Brampton and Georgetown High Schools, Milton Model School, and Hamilton Normal College. Although he wanted to study law, all the money available went into the family farm.

Hiltz secured a third-class teacher's certificate and began teaching at the age of 18. He was first appointed a schoolteacher in Halton County from 1891 to 1893, in Wellington County from 1895 to 1896, and later in Toronto where he taught for several years, eventually becoming principal of Weston Public School from 1899 to 1901. On Christmas Day 1899, age 27, he married Annie Laidlaw of Barrie, Ontario.

He was assistant principal at Hamilton Street School in the Broadview and Dundas area from 1901 to 1907. In 1904, his school was destroyed by fire, and students were taught temporarily in Sunday school classrooms nearby. A new school was built in 1905 and renamed Queen Alexandra (the wife of King Edward VII).

During this time, Hiltz also decided to completely change careers. In 1907, he went into the building industry, starting with the construction of new homes close to Danforth Avenue in Toronto's east end. The switch had come about following his marriage: Hiltz needed a larger home and sought to have one built according to his specifications, yet it was not completed on time and he was forced to renew an existing lease.

Once his new home was finished, Hiltz sold it at a substantial profit, giving him first-hand experience in development, real estate, and construction. After building and selling a second house for a tidy sum, it became clear that this could be a rewarding and profitable career, affording greater opportunities than his teacher's salary. So Hiltz resigned from teaching and entered into real-estate development full-time.

After a modest start in the business, he embarked on a larger scale with his father-in-law, John Laidlaw, eventually leading to the formation in 1920 of the realty and building firm W.W. Hiltz and Company at 739 Broadview Avenue. Several decades later, he had "constructed more than 500 houses in the east end of the city and played a prominent part in developing apartment and business properties"[1] in the Danforth area.

Hiltz first became involved in politics as a member of the Board of Education from 1911 to 1913, serving as board chair in 1913. The following year he was elected alderman from Ward 1, only to be defeated in 1915.

Returning to Toronto's Council in 1916, Hiltz captured the Ward 1 seat until 1920, chairing the Works Committee in 1917 and 1918. In 1920, he was asked to chair a special Juvenile Court Committee created to work on court improvements. Its recommendation was to build a new observation home to be comprised of court offices and space for the Big Brothers and Big Sisters community-based agencies.

Hiltz was elected to the Board of Control for 1921–1923 and was asked to oversee city budget preparations, sit on the Canadian National Exhibition board, and examine the city's hospital needs and report back to the Council on the best ways to tackle them. His election advertising reflected the sunny optimism of the Roaring Twenties: "He is a tried municipal legislator. He is one of Toronto's big taxpayers, and his honesty and ability have never been questioned. He believes 'A Greater Toronto' is progressive, optimistic, and public-spirited."[2]

In what was a reflection and symbol of the growth and expansion of Toronto, Hiltz was elected vice-president of the Ontario Town Planning and Housing Association in 1922. Its principal concerns were the need for a Provincial Bureau of Town Planning, a new provincial housing code, establishment of minimum housing standards, and for the province to provide capital funding.

In December 1923, Hiltz formally announced his candidacy for the 1924 mayoralty. The yearly mayoral race in the 1920s was mercifully short, lasting from the mid-December nomination to an election day on or close to New Year's Day. Hiltz had hung back to allow the incumbent Alfred Maguire the opportunity to run again, yet when there was still no word, Hiltz decided to put his name forward.

He faced two opponents: Colonel John Currie, a defeated Conservative MP from Simcoe North who had been elected to the Ontario Legislative Assembly in 1922, and Tommy Church, the city's long-serving former mayor who, after just two years away, had decided he wanted to return. In the end, it was between Hiltz and Church, with the *Toronto Daily Star* declaring that Church's "insatiable demand for office is not satisfied."[3] With both the *Daily Star*'s and *Globe*'s editorial backing, Hiltz captured the largest vote ever given to a mayoral candidate up to that point, yet just a year later he was defeated.

At the Council's inaugural meeting, Hiltz set out to "lighten the burden of taxation."[4] With the city facing several issues — long-term debt, a major arbitration award, and a new sewerage system for North Toronto — Hiltz asked the Council for a reduction in municipal taxation and an early budget. His priorities included better public health, a new hospital for the mentally ill, planning for an eventual population of a million, and the care of what were then termed "defective children." He also asked the Council for greater decorum, including not reading newspapers in the middle of a meeting.

Hiltz advocated for the attraction of new industries, "the life-blood of any city,"[5] and also called for a cleanup of local improvement charges as well as an expansion of the Canadian National Exhibition, pointing out that it had evolved from a provincial fair to a major national exposition. The new mayor also took pride in a 40 percent increase in rush-hour streetcar service, a tangible result of the popular 1921 takeover of the Toronto Railway Company.

With a 1924 strength of 847, Toronto's police force had hit an all-time high, and Hiltz called for a new police headquarters and court building, which had outgrown the 25-year-old City Hall. The issue of a downtown grade-separated rail corridor was a major victory during Hiltz's term. For more than 20 years, successive Councils had sought an agreement with the

Looking north toward downtown from the waterfront at the foot of the Yonge Street wharf in 1924.

railways for a viaduct infrastructure project to raise the tracks over major north-south streets and allow better access to the waterfront.

After the largest external lobbying effort Toronto had ever mounted in Ottawa, an agreement was finally reached, permitting access to a large southern portion of the city badly cut off. A bridge over the tracks would be built at Spadina Avenue with underpasses at York, Bay, Yonge, Jarvis, Sherbourne, Parliament, and Cherry Streets. Federal Cabinet ministers were impressed with Hiltz's sincerity and by the argument that Toronto had gone the limit in an effort to arrive at a settlement.

An increasingly urbanized Toronto was in a period of tremendous growth. At the beginning of Toronto Hydro in 1911, there were just 13,000 hydro users connected to the system. By the end of 1923, that had increased to 131,000, yet concern was expressed about the safety of electric heat replacing coal furnaces in residential homes.

While in 1900, Toronto's population was 200,000, by 1924 it stood at 542,000, growing by 8,000 to 9,000 new residents per year. And of the 23,000 business licences issued by City Hall, there was still a very poignant reminder of life in the 1920s: despite increasing prosperity, 1,794 licences were issued to "peddlers and rag collectors."

A 1924 personal profile of Hiltz said that he "cares neither for swell clothes nor swell expenses ... he has remembered, amid the magnificence of the City Hall, that a great and opulent Toronto is peopled by folks who in the main came from places not so very different from the farm in Wellington County where he was brought up." The journalist even interviewed a local Communist Party member about Hiltz and reported that "one of the redder reds of the town paid him the warmest sort of compliments as a candidate."[6]

Hiltz himself was strongly in favour of alcohol prohibition. Two years earlier, he had given the opening address to the major international convention of the World League Against Alcoholism, a key reason he had received such strong backing from the *Toronto Daily Star*, which slammed what it called liquor "moderationists."

In his 1925 bid for re-election, Hiltz was up against a surprisingly vigorous campaign from veteran controller Thomas Foster, whose municipal service had begun more than 30 years before. In his campaign, Hiltz claimed an active record of success: a lower tax rate; a favourable settlement of the long drawn-out viaduct matter; and though a supporter of public hydro, opposition to Sir Adam Beck's plan for "hydro radials," a series of electric streetcars connecting Toronto with other cities.

Yet a major turning point occurred when Foster declared during a period of prohibition that workingmen should be able to have their beer. It had the effect of switching a large number of votes among the city's common workingmen, lunch-bucket labourers, and daily-wage earners, securing Foster's victory by 2,600 votes.

Hiltz left politics following the 1925 defeat, devoting himself to his construction firm. Over the course of 15 years, he built hundreds of apartments above stores and houses to the north and south of Danforth Avenue and accumulated so much real estate that he became one of the city's highest-paying taxpayers.

In 1928, Hiltz was stricken with a serious case of coronary thrombosis, severely curtailing his activities. Resolving to make the best of a lengthy recovery, he opted to study English literature and history, grew hundreds of flowers, and put down his thoughts for all to see, publishing *Verses of a Convalescent* (1929) and *More Verses* (1931).

In his personal life, Hiltz served as superintendent of the Sunday school of Danforth Methodist (later United) Church from 1908 until his death in 1936, and for a time one of the largest such schools in Canada. He also served as a governor of Toronto East General Hospital, chairman of the Management Committee of the Toronto Industrial School Board, and president of the St. Matthew's Lawn Bowling Club.

Hiltz was a member of the Torbay Orange Lodge, the Imperial Masonic Lodge, the St. Patrick's Chapter of the Royal Arch Masons, and the Independent Order of Odd Fellows. He also served with the Methodist Union, the Methodist Sunday School Association, and the Riverdale Ratepayers' Association. The former mayor was also director of the Broadview YMCA and an executive member of the National Council for Boys' Work.

On February 26, 1936, Hiltz died suddenly of a heart attack at his home at 682 Broadview Avenue and was survived by four daughters and three sons. His funeral service took place at his beloved Danforth United Church.

A newspaper obituary stated: "Hiltz gave Toronto excellent service, for he was a citizen of sterling worth and fine ideals, a man of the highest integrity of thought and practice…. Hiltz won the respect even of those who disagreed with him, for his honesty of purpose was known to all. His life was an open book in which the best motives were ever apparent."[7]

Mayoral Election in 1924	
CANDIDATES	VOTES
William Hiltz	44,265
Thomas Church	33,975
John Currie	4,311

Mayor Thomas Foster

1925–1927

The 40th mayor of Toronto

Occupations: Butcher, realtor, City of Toronto alderman and controller, Member of House of Commons, philanthropist
Residence While Mayor: 45 Seaton Street
Birth: July 24, 1852, in York Township, Canada West
Death: December 10, 1945, in Toronto

———— • ————

The son of John and Frances Foster, originally of Yorkshire, England, Foster was born in July 1852 in a small house in the area of Vaughan Road and Dufferin Street, then part of York Township. Foster's family first settled in Ontario County (now Durham Region). Foster's father and grandfather were proprietors of a hotel at Leaskdale north of Uxbridge and were also farmers at different times. A few years later, the family moved to the east end of downtown Toronto.

At 15 years old and living in very modest circumstances, Foster entered the workforce, apprenticing with a neighbourhood butcher on Queen Street East. By 1874, he was an errand boy for a popular Cabbagetown retailer and then moved on to open his own business nearby. Widely known as hard-working, he earned the nickname "Honest Tom," and his butcher shop became one of the most successful in Toronto.

The young entrepreneur prospered through shrewd investments such as a timely purchase of land south of the Queen East and Coxwell area, which the city later expropriated for a new sewage treatment plant. Supporters later called it his big stroke of fortune. Foster also bought several houses in various parts of the city, keeping an eye on things by collecting the rents in person. If work was needed on plumbing or clogged drains, he got a set of tools from his car and did everything himself.

By 1890, Foster had sold his meat business and was devoting full attention to his real-estate portfolio. He belonged to a new generation of citizens acquiring prominence not because they were leaders of industry but as the result of real-estate holdings increasing in value with the city's growth.

With an 18-year record in business, enormous personal popularity, and a high profile in the community, Foster commenced a quarter century of involvement in municipal politics. Elected first in 1891, he served on Toronto's Council in St. David's Ward, then won only three of nine contests in 1891, 1892, and 1894. In 1893, he married Elizabeth McCauley, and they had a daughter the following year.

From 1900 to 1904, his political fortunes changed for the better and he was elected to the Council from Ward 2. In 1905, he campaigned for city-wide office as a member of the Board of Control, only to lose and find himself once again out of office. Two years later, he returned to the Council as an alderman, successfully holding this seat in two subsequent elections. Foster once more chose to run for the Board of Control in 1910. He was elected that year, only to be defeated in 1911, re-elected in 1912 and 1913, unsuccessful in 1914, and re-elected to the board from 1915 to 1917.

Foster was drawn into the federal election of December 1917 as a candidate for York East, a sprawling east end constituency from Pape Avenue out to Scarborough. A supporter of the Unionist federal government, Foster won the seat with 51 percent of the vote. But in 1921 he lost the party nomination, and running as an independent, failed to be elected in the adjoining riding of Toronto East from Sherbourne Street to Pape Avenue.

Yet in just a matter of weeks, Foster was again back in local politics, successfully winning election again to the Board of Control, leading the polls in 1922, 1923, and 1924, and becoming its vice-chair. A future Toronto mayor, Nathan Phillips, later observed that Foster voted against anything that cost money. His tight-fisted utterances were music to the ears of many tax-weary voters.

Thus, in 1925, following a vigorous campaign, the now 73-year-old Foster challenged and defeated William Hiltz, the incumbent mayor, capturing 33,883 votes to Hiltz's 31,408. During his years as a senior city controller and later as mayor, Foster became known widely as the "Watchdog of the Treasury" with a strong reputation for frugality. When the Toronto Police Department asked for an increase in its budget and more officers, Foster argued that it would cost the city less to simply reimburse merchants and residents for the amounts that had been robbed.

In his first inaugural address in 1925, Foster was emphatic that city finances would be his key priority, with action on a new waterworks and curtailing the usage of city-owned automobiles. He noted that new sources of electrical power, including the St. Lawrence River, were needed to develop industry and that a Toronto "Metropolitan Area" had been proposed at Ontario's Legislative Assembly. Foster was opposed, saying contributions to outer municipalities were "unjust and unjustifiable" and that Toronto residents "will not agree to the taxes of our citizens being handed over to other municipalities."[1]

The Council dealt with a range of issues in 1925: summer home rentals on the Toronto Islands for the princely seasonal sum of $100 ($1,700 today), the purchase of coal for emergency distribution, and meeting with 125 members of the Brooklyn, New York, Chamber of Commerce on a "goodwill" tour of Canada. Other matters included a motion that "no aliens shall be employed in any capacity in the city's services";[2] an inquiry into the city's bread supply; prohibiting the use of horses for deliveries made by hand laundries, butcher shops, stores, or manufacturers; and the regulation of gas stations — a brand-new phenomenon in mid-1920s Toronto.

Foster was handily re-elected mayor on January 1, 1926, and even though he had first been elected to the Council in 1891, he was running for only a second mayoral term. His inaugural address touched on several issues. With Toronto as a leading centre of manufacturing, Foster said, "we must not weaken that position by making taxation too heavy." He also advised the Council that "active negotiations with some thirty industries"[3] were underway for land upon which to build plants and factories.

In 1926, the Council dealt with a number of issues: the installation of sprinklers in the roof of City Hall, a proposed new "high-speed" 96 kilometre-per-hour electric railway between Toronto and Hamilton, fees charged for public showers, serious traffic congestion at Bay and Queen Streets, and a judicial investigation into possible graft and corruption by Council members. A staff report recommended that city department heads be required to attend every Council meeting to answer questions and that the city's budget estimates be more closely reviewed prior to their submission to councillors.

A month later, in January 1927, the aging Foster withstood a serious challenge from both past and future mayoral hopefuls Sam McBride and William Robbins as he ran for a third consecutive term. The election was marked by a concerted campaign by the *Evening Telegram* to discredit McBride with a steady barrage of critical articles and news headlines.

The most damaging was a dramatic photo of McBride in the *Telegram* just days before the mayoral election, showing him getting into his personal chauffeur-driven, U.S.-made Packard limousine with a story that it was worth $4,200 ($70,000 today), yet McBride's municipal income tax levy had been just $15.96 ($271 today) in 1925.

In his inaugural address for 1927, Foster called Toronto a "rapidly growing and progressive city," saying that the municipality "is on the eve of real prosperity,"[4] and yet true to form warned of higher taxation. The main uncontrollable, he said, was debt charges, with the gross debt now at $167 million ($2.8 billion today). Foster stated that the city had committed to a number of major public works: rail grade separations, harbour improvements, a new waterworks system, and a new North Toronto sewerage system. While work on the largest train station in Canada, Toronto's new Union Station, first began in 1914, its construction had been mired in problems and delays until it finally opened in 1927.

The Council discussed a range of issues in 1927: police protection for the Toronto Islands, the possible conversion of Casa Loma into a hotel, and the establishment of Toronto's first airport. And in what was a shameless political stunt, the mayor flew over the city in a plane, dropping $1 bills with special Union Jacks attached. Each $1 with a flag recovered below was then personally redeemed by Foster for a crisp new $5 bill ($84 today).

After seeking a fourth mayoral term in 1928 at age 76, Foster was defeated by Sam McBride by more than 15,000 votes. Even though Foster was first elected to the Council in 1891, McBride swept every ward. After his defeat, Foster lived in a large, sprawling 10-room home on Victor Avenue in Riverdale and announced he was quitting politics for good to travel the world, which he did, carrying just a small satchel and an extra hat.

During one of those global trips, the idea of a Foster Memorial was born. In 1936, at a cost of $200,000 ($4.1 million today), Foster had a replica of India's Taj Mahal designed and built as a family mausoleum on property he owned just north of Uxbridge, Ontario. Although he had spent millions on a huge family memorial, the former mayor refused to spend money on his own home. As history writer Donald Jones reports, "The drapes became bleached by the sun. The stuffing bulged out of holes in the furniture and the wallpaper turned grey with age."[5]

Almost a decade after building his own customized crypt, Foster died in December 1945, age 93. A few years earlier, he had specified that upon his death his estate of more than $1.5 million ($25 million today) should be divided among a very eclectic group of local causes: an endowment for the repair of Salvation Army musical instruments, cash gifts for women who cleaned Toronto office buildings at night ("charladies," as they were termed then), money to purchase movie projectors for patients of the Toronto Home for Incurables, funds for teenage street-corner newsboys ("newsies," as they were called), money for an Orange Lodge seniors' home, and cash for "the Anglican Mission for Eskimos."

Foster also provided funds for a diverse range of other causes: yearly tree plantings on major arterial roadways coming into the city, the feeding of wildlife on the waterfront during winter, and money for the apprehension of poachers around the city and to provide clowns, ice cream, music, and pony rides at an annual picnic for needy children on the Toronto Islands.

Yet perhaps the strangest bequest made by Foster was money for a series of "stork derbies," cash prizes to mothers having the greatest number of children in a 10-year period. As the *Toronto Star* reported in May 1974, the last winner was identified in 1964; she gave birth nine times during the previous decade.

A Presbyterian and a member of the Sons of England, Foster was also a proud member of the Orange Lodge and a life member of the St. George's Society. After his death, he was first taken to the funeral home on Danforth Avenue owned by future mayor Ralph Day.

Mayoral Election in 1925	
CANDIDATES	**VOTES**
Thomas Foster	33,883
William Hiltz	31,408
Henry Winberg	2,265
Samuel Fieldhouse	282
Mayoral Election in 1926	
Thomas Foster	47,863
Robert Cameron	38,084
Samuel Fieldhouse	919
Mayoral Election in 1927	
Thomas Foster	42,617
Sam McBride	38,447
William Robbins	6,317

Mayor Sam McBride

1928–1929 and 1936

The 41st mayor of Toronto

Occupations: Newsboy, carriage painter, lumber merchant, business leader, City of Toronto alderman and controller
Residence While Mayor: 351 Palmerston Avenue and 335 Inglewood Drive
Birth: July 13, 1866, in Toronto
Death: November 14, 1936, in Toronto

— • —

The son of Eleanor Anderson of Hoggs Hollow (in today's North York) and Bammel McBride, originally of Montreal, Sam McBride attended Elizabeth Street Public School, leaving at the age of 13 to work as a street-corner newsboy to sell the *Toronto Leader* newspaper. He also began working with his father who had once run a schooner on Lake Ontario, but by then was operating a wood-and-coal business.

In the rough and tumble of 1870s and 1880s Toronto, McBride learned politics "ward style" on the streets adjacent to his father's business, where political rallies, speeches, debates, or meetings might turn into fistfights and spill out into the open. As history writer Donald Jones later noted in the *Toronto Star*, "Sam McBride had only one ambition. He wanted to be Mayor of Toronto."[1]

After his father's death in 1882 when he was 16, McBride continued working at a number of jobs, including several years in the Toronto offices of a Hamilton-based lumber company. In 1885, McBride learned the trade of carriage painting with the firm of Hutchinson and Burns, then found employment with the *Toronto World* newspaper. Later, he joined S.C. Kanaly and Company, a wholesale lumber dealer, remaining there until 1889. After that he was in sales for Robert Thompson, a well-known lumber dealer, eventually ending up with his own lumber company by the 1890s.

Yet it was the condition of streets in his Ward 3 neighbourhood, in particular the area known as The Ward (Queen Street to College Street and Yonge Street over to University Avenue), that prompted his initial entry into local elected politics. They were in such poor shape that McBride's employees found it almost impossible to transport heavy orders of coal, lumber, or timber.

With an outgoing, gregarious personality, McBride was keenly combative and had a deep interest in local affairs. Elected alderman for Ward 3 from 1905 to 1908, he suffered a minor setback in 1909 after losing a rowdy 10-candidate election race. Although it was his first political defeat, it proved to be a valuable political lesson.

In 1910, he returned to do battle and was elected once more to the Council, serving from 1910 to 1916, including an acclamation in 1912. In

1917, McBride was defeated in his first attempt to join the city-wide Board of Control, coming in sixth for one of the four available seats. But in both 1918 and 1919, he was elected to the board.

McBride unsuccessfully challenged the popular incumbent Mayor Tommy Church in 1920, then running in his sixth mayoral campaign. The *Toronto Daily Star* was effusive in its praise, saying, "Sam is a vigorous, virile citizen who fights with all his might, and who never harbors a grudge afterwards."[2] Others, however, considered McBride too erratic, boisterous, self-opinionated, and hobbled by both friendships and intense dislikes to be entrusted with directing Toronto's Council.

He took a break from politics, not running for any elected office in 1922, but plunged back into the political world the next year when he ran for the Board of Control and was narrowly edged out of the fourth spot by Joe Singer, the city's first Jewish councillor.

In 1924, McBride made a political comeback, this time as an alderman in an eight-candidate race in the politically active Ward 4 (Kensington and the Garment District). Always ambitious, in 1926, McBride again campaigned to join the Board of Control. With his 36,223 votes city-wide, he captured the second spot.

Known for a gruff, no-nonsense, aggressive, and streetwise political style, McBride was popular with fellow Irishmen, and at times his colourful personal style and fiery speeches boiled over. In one fit of anger, he rushed across the Council chambers, grabbed an alderman by the collar, and banged him against the wall until he was almost knocked unconscious.

In late 1926, McBride took the plunge once more in his quest to become mayor against incumbent Thomas Foster. This time he sought to appeal to women, veterans, and left-of-centre voters. But he lost the race after the *Evening Telegram* published a photograph of him getting into his personal chauffeur-driven limousine (worth $70,000 today), with an accompanying story that McBride's 1925 municipal income tax bill had been a mere $15.96 ($271 today). A large headline screamed, "Can You Afford a Car Like This on an Income Tax Bill of $15.96?" Yet another blared, "Now Is the Time for McBride to Explain His Income Tax ... Only Chance That Ratepayers Will Have to Find Out Why It Is So Small."[3] In the end, Foster was elected mayor with 42,617 votes to 38,447 for McBride.

14   THE EVENING TELEGRAM, TORONTO, WEDNESDAY, DECEMBER 29, 1926

CAN YOU AFFORD A CAR LIKE THIS ON AN INCOME TAX BILL OF $15.96?

This is Sam McBride's made-in-the-U.S.A. car, and $15.96 is Sam McBride's made-in-Toronto income tax bill for 1925. Sam McBride, wealthy lumber merchant, photographed by The Telegram during the present mayoral contest, as about to enter his $4,200 Packard car, driven by his liveried chauffeur, presents the picture of a man whose assessable income, according to the Toronto Assessment Department, has averaged only $510 per annum for the past twenty years, and whose assessable income for 1927, including $2,500 received as Controller, is only $2,752. Mr. McBride's assessable wealth for 1927, according to the Toronto Assessment Department, is: Land, $4,500; house, $6,000; business, $450, and income, $2,752.

In December 1926, Sam McBride lost the election for mayor due in part to this newspaper photograph implying he was a tax cheat.

A year later, though, McBride was described as the city's most colourful municipal figure and as a swaggering, two-fisted, red-blooded go-getter. In 1928, he became the city's highly combative, pugnacious, newly elected mayor, finally defeating the aged Thomas Foster with a convincing 50,736 votes to Foster's 35,087.

Years later, the *Toronto Daily Star* pointed out that McBride's "emotions were easily stirred: emotions of pity, of sympathy, of affection — of anger too. This emotionalism in its various manifestations both helped and hampered him in his political career."[4]

In what was the shortest inaugural speech in years, McBride's first mayoral address outlined several areas of concern: a need for greater policing, completion of the North Toronto sewerage project, and an expansion of the city's existing waterworks. During his first term, the city's financial shortages were addressed, a property tax increase was tempered, and the Police Department was reorganized. As well, an Industrial Commission was established and a new Advisory City Planning Committee was created.

The Council dealt with several issues in 1928: the proposed widening of Bay Street downtown, a grant of $125,000 ($2.1 million today) to Toronto East General Hospital, the regulation of gas stations, asking the Police

Commission to hire from within when choosing a new police chief, and a first grant to a novel new organization, the Toronto Flying Club. Councillors also received a communication from the city's Ku Klux Klan "in relation to the employment of Orientals and foreigners."[5]

On January 1, 1929, McBride was re-elected, defeating former alderman Brook Sykes by a wide margin. A central issue was the plan to extend University Avenue south to Front Street, with McBride supporting the plan. In his 1929 inaugural address, he urged a hold on additional municipal annexations and proposed a new 26-metre-wide bridge over the Humber River. And since Toronto's existing garbage incinerators were "unsurpassed and inspected by delegations from all quarters of the globe,"[6] he promised another one to serve North Toronto.

The hard-driving, florid-faced McBride distinguished himself as one of the most combative mayors in the city's history, simply beating up councillors he didn't like, knocking them around the Council chamber, pinning them against the wall, or swatting them with sheaves of Council documents.

In 1929, the Council dealt with a range of political issues: major criticisms of the Assessment Act and the huge number of existing tax exemptions, the widening of Davenport Avenue north of Bay Street, and a bylaw proposed by future mayor Bert Wemp to ban the discharge of any gun, firearm, or fireworks within the city. A report to the Council advised that Greater Toronto's population was 733,000 but also publicly speculated that it was closer to 800,000 in actuality. The Council discussed the establishment of a new night court, a call for residential building restrictions in the Annex, and a motion that all candidates for municipal office be required to declare a list of all properties they owned or leased and that they not have any tax arrears.

All through 1929, McBride pushed for the adoption of a major downtown improvement plan requiring a huge expenditure of public funds. Yet with the 1930 election taking place just weeks after the stock market crash, the ballot question to approve $19 million ($316 million today) was turned down by a wary public who failed to see the benefits.

In 1930, several factors — a major loss of public confidence, continuing financial turmoil, a well-orchestrated campaign by the *Evening Telegram*, and the vigorous mayoral campaign of Bert Wemp, one of the newspaper's senior editors — cost McBride the mayoralty. When the votes were counted, Wemp received 54,455 votes to McBride's 50,598.

Down but not out, the feisty McBride ran again for mayor in 1931 upon the news that Wemp would not seek re-election after just a year. This time, however, he lost to William Stewart in a very close contest, with only 300 votes separating the two main contenders. Biding his time, McBride returned as a controller from 1932 to 1934. The next year, he again ran for the Board of Control, vaulting this time to the top position in the midst of the Great Depression. A spirited mayoralty battle had also unfolded in 1935, with Jimmy Simpson the eventual winner as the first socialist elected to the city's highest office.

Most telling, however, and stoking the fires of a further mayoral ambition in 1936, was the fact that McBride, with his 71,325 votes city-wide, had received almost 17,000 more for the Board of Control than the victorious Simpson. The next year, the pugnacious McBride finally won the mayoralty once again, with incumbent Simpson dropping to third place.

And though Toronto was still in the midst of the worst economic depression in its history, the topics of policing, town planning, sewage, waterworks, and pavement widenings were all addressed in McBride's inaugural address. It was noted that 90,942 individuals were either on a voucher (welfare assistance) or on relief from the House of Industry. Issues at the Council in 1936 included an inquiry into the Police Department, the appointment of a Town Planning Commission, and the city's application for legislation to allow for the "rehabilitation and general cleaning up"[7] of unsatisfactory neighbourhoods.

Early in his final term, however, McBride's health began to fail and his public appearances declined. By June 1936, he was unable to attend City Hall, and by September, his personal physician "strongly urged" the mayor not return to his duties. McBride was accorded a leave of absence, and on November 10, just a month and a half before the 1937 mayoral election, he lapsed into a coma and died four days later from complications of a stroke.

In the city's 102-year history and 40 previous mayors, none had died while in office, so Sam McBride was accorded a rare public honour — a civic state funeral. His body lay in the main lobby of City Hall, with Ontario premier Mitchell Hepburn and nine former mayors serving as honorary pallbearers. A huge procession from City Hall to Mount Pleasant Cemetery was witnessed by thousands of citizens.

In his private life, McBride was a harness-racing enthusiast and a founding member and director of the Canadian Standardbred Horse Society, serving as the organization's president in 1919–1920. In addition, he was a founding director of the Canadian National Trotting and Pacing Harness Horse Association. McBride also enjoyed a summer cottage on the Toronto Islands and at one point even represented them as their alderman. He was also instrumental in ending a tunnel to the islands to serve the new airport.

A worshipper in the United Church of Canada, McBride was a member of Harmony Masonic Lodge 438, Queen City Loyal Orange Lodge 857, and the Independent Order of Odd Fellows Rosedale Lodge. He also belonged to several clubs: the Granite, Lions, Kiwanis, and Ontario Jockey Club.

Mayoral Election in 1928	
CANDIDATES	VOTES
Sam McBride	50,736
Thomas Foster	35,087
Mayoral Election in 1929	
Sam McBride	46,009
Brook Sykes	30,347
Mayoral Election in 1936	
Sam McBride	48,978
Harry Hunt	43,381
James Simpson	32,777
SPECIAL NOTE: Sam McBride died in office on November 14, 1936.	

Mayor Bert Wemp

1930

The 42nd mayor of Toronto

Occupations: Royal Canadian Air Force aviator, Toronto Board
of Education trustee, City of Toronto alderman and controller,
journalist, newspaper editor
Residence While Mayor: 45 Playter Boulevard
Birth: July 3, 1889, in Tweed, Ontario
Death: February 5, 1976, in Toronto

—— • ——

Bert Sterling Wemp was born in a wooden farmhouse outside Tweed, Ontario, in July 1889, the son of Fred Wemp and Louisa McCamon of United Empire Loyalist stock. On his father's side, the family roots were Dutch Protestant, and on his mother's, French Huguenot.

Although Wemp's ancestors had come to North America in the 1600s, the family split after the American Revolution, with one side choosing to settle in Canada's Bay of Quinte region. After his birth in Tweed, Ontario, Wemp moved with his family to Toronto's Cabbagetown where he attended Dufferin Public School and then Jarvis Collegiate. He worked with the Fred Victor Mission and as a volunteer leader in the athletics department of the Central Young Men's Christian Association.

In 1905 at age 16, Wemp got his first job as a copy boy, thus beginning a lifelong career with Toronto's *Evening Telegram*. At that time, the paper had just six reporters, and one day when news of an escaped convict and gun battle in the east end reached the city desk, the editor dispatched Wemp, the only person available. The enterprising lad scrambled behind a roadblock and interviewed the police in the middle of the battle going on. He then raced back to the office with the breaking story. The following day, Wemp was made a full-time reporter.

Although Wemp took classes at Victoria College and seriously considered becoming a Methodist minister, he remained a reporter and editor with the *Telegram*, specializing in local and civic affairs during 59 years as the paper's suburban editor, city editor, and head of its courts bureau. His writing style was quieter than the often colourful, bombastic hyperbole usually seen in the newspaper. Colleagues noted that his journalistic accounts were detailed, cautious, and meticulously researched.

In 1914 as war broke out in Europe, Wemp was 25 and decided to enlist as a pilot. The only way Canadians could join the United Kingdom's new air service was to pay for their own flying lessons, obtain a certificate from a qualified training school, and enlist in Britain. Early on, Wemp enrolled at an airfield in Long Branch. Upon graduation, he became the first Canadian accepted by the Royal Naval Air Service and was assigned to a North Sea squadron.

During the First World War, Wemp was a commander with the 218th Squadron and flew numerous missions. Involved in pilot training, he taught young men how to fly and later led them on daylight bombing raids over France.

In April 1918, the amalgamation of the Royal Flying Corps and Royal Naval Air Service to create the Royal Air Force resulted in Wemp becoming a squadron commander and flying anti-submarine patrols for raids on German naval bases in Zeebrugge and Ostend in Belgium. He carried out a combination of reconnaissance and aerial photography of enemy installations and became the first Canadian to win the Distinguished Flying Cross, awarded by the Prince of Wales.

After the war, Wemp returned to his job at the *Telegram* and once again became involved in civic affairs, not only as a journalist but also as a budding politician. In addition, he was instrumental in founding the Toronto Flying Club, seeking a $5,000 ($65,000 today) grant from the city for a first-ever "aerial convention." By welcoming 350 delegates, its principal goal was to see Toronto become Canada's aviation centre.

At the age of 31, Wemp stepped into politics as a candidate for the school board to push what he called "first things first," a no-nonsense campaign against educational frills. In January 1921, he defeated Dr. John Noble, the veteran chair of the Board of Education in Ward 2. Wemp served as a school trustee in 1921 and 1922, opposing what he termed a "spend money like water" group on the board. In 1924 and 1925, he successfully became a member of Toronto's Council for Ward 2, chairing the Civic Property Committee, and from 1927 to 1929, was on the Board of Control, the city's training ground for future mayors.

Canadian aviators announced in 1927 that they wanted to form a Canadian Air League modelled after the Air League of the British Empire. It was estimated that by 1927 there were 2,000 Canadians with flying experience. Toronto newspapers reported that an offer of 200 hectares had been made to establish an airport for Toronto.

In January 1928, however, it was lumber merchant Sam McBride who was elected mayor of Toronto, defeating incumbent Thomas Foster by a wide margin, while Wemp received the highest number of votes for controller. The next year, McBride was again on top as mayor with 46,009 votes to former alderman Brook Sykes's 30,347. A key 1929 issue was a proposal to extend University Avenue south to Front Street, with McBride supporting it. Wemp became the Board of Control's vice-chair. Throughout the 1920s, he also pursued his journalistic career, and in 1928, while a member of the Council, was promoted to city editor of the *Telegram*. Wemp was in a unique position — both making and covering the news at the same time.

Encouraged to challenge mayoralty incumbent Sam McBride in 1930, Wemp did so but had to resign from the *Telegram*. His mayoral platform included several new measures: a cleanup of the eastern beaches, no increase in home electricity bills, and a major reorganization of the city's Finance Department.

The most controversial issue was the mayor's multi-million-dollar road redevelopment plan downtown. The *Telegram* was opposed, with no editor more strongly against it than Wemp himself. Voters were asked to approve $19 million ($316 million today), with Wemp believing scarce public funds should be spent on more urgently needed roads. Few believed he could win against the brash, outspoken, opinionated, and highly visible McBride running for his third term.

Yet it was the uttering of a single word shouted in the heat of the moment at a political rally at Keele Street Public School that turned the tide. In a furious exchange with hecklers, McBride lost his temper and publicly shouted that Wemp was a political "coward." The very next day, the *Telegram* hit back hard, running a full-length front-page photo of Wemp in his First World War uniform with pilot wings, medals, and Distinguished Flying Cross. Overnight, the campaign centred on McBride's slur, the newspaper claiming it was "an insult to every soldier who fought in the Great War."[1] The result was both immediate and dramatic, with supporters of Wemp quickly mobilizing and arranging a special pre-election flyover of the city.

Like most veterans, Wemp rarely talked about his wartime experiences, and city residents who knew him as an editor and controller suddenly realized he was a true war hero. The single word shouted by McBride cost him the election; Wemp won handily with 54,455 votes to McBride's 50,598. The downtown redevelopment plan itself lost when residents from outlying areas of the city voted against it.

In his inaugural address, the new mayor reported that the city now had a population of more than 600,000 and spoke of the need for a new police headquarters, a new Humber River bridge, additional grade separations, development of the eastern beaches, new road infrastructure, and funding for the Board of Education. With new vehicles purchased and track bed laid, the transit system had improved, and 86 percent of the city's 1930 population was now using streetcars.

In December 1930, a major report on the future of Toronto's city planning was presented by councillor and future mayor Nathan Phillips. It dealt with issues such as older residential neighbourhoods, zoning and land use, transportation arteries and widenings, property acquisition, community improvements, detailed local planning, growth and population increases, and public recreation.

Yet Wemp's single year in office was not as successful as he might have wished. The severe constraints of the Great Depression hamstrung his administration, so he bowed out, the result of health issues and disabilities suffered in the war as well as being scheduled for major abdominal surgery. Wemp was one of the first single-term Toronto mayors since the 1850s.

After five weeks in the hospital and a brief period of post-operation convalescence, Wemp returned to the *Evening Telegram*, again becoming city editor. Creation of a first airport for Toronto had been a major interest of aviator Wemp, and in 1929, an island airport plan was unveiled by the Toronto Harbour Commission. Starting with an air harbour for seaplanes, it would necessitate the acquisition of existing parkland, a hotel, an amusement area, and more than 40 summer cottages. The plan only proceeded after the death of Mayor Sam McBride, who had vigorously opposed it.

In January 1931, the Council unanimously approved a motion calling Wemp a man of "unfailing courtesy" who displayed "energy, enthusiasm, ability, courage, and vision."[2] After returning to life as a newspaper editor, Wemp supported the formation of a Toronto Better Business Bureau in mid-1935 to provide protection against business fraud, misrepresentation, and malpractice.

When world war broke out again in Europe in 1939, Wemp returned to France as a war correspondent for the *Telegram*, reporting on actions in North Africa, Holland, and France. He was with the Allied forces during the invasion of Italy, and at the end of the war, was awarded the Order of the British Empire. Covering the war from the front lines was not an easy task: a reporter's copy might be written on a beach or in a trench with the army, then conveyed to outriders who got it onto an aircraft to be relayed back home.

On the front lines, writes Bruce West in his book *Toronto*, "Bert Wemp's standard opening question 'Is there anybody here from Toronto?' became a familiar greeting wherever Canadians were stationed"[3] on the battlefield, and many of his stories read like a Toronto telephone directory. While Wemp might have been criticized by a few outsiders, the old maxim that "names make news" paid off, and *Telegram* readers eagerly searched for Wemp's copy, so much so that the *Toronto Daily Star* ordered its war correspondent to do the same.

As the war concluded, Wemp arrived home after serving as a correspondent for three years. One newspaper even noted he had achieved a record for uninterrupted coverage of Canadian troops by any Canadian correspondent, reminding readers that the former mayor, aviator, and war hero had commanded a squadron of the Royal Air Force in the First World War. Wemp once more returned to his duties at the *Telegram*.

In June 1955, Toronto's Council honoured Wemp with an engraved silver tray to recognize his 50 years with the *Telegram* along with a special celebration at the Royal York Hotel. It was not until 1964, upon reaching 75, that he finally retired.

Wemp then devoted much of his time to gardening, watching baseball, and working with the Shriners' crippled children's committee. He was a member of the British Imperial Association, the Army and Navy Veterans Association, the Soldiers' Rehabilitation Committee, the St. Clair Horticultural Society, and the Scarborough Golf Club. As well, he was vice-president of the Royal Naval Association and a member of the Canadian Legion and British Empire Service League. A United Church of Canada congregant, Wemp was a Mason and a member of the Orange Order.

During his later years, he moved to the Oakridge Villa Nursing Home in North York, and on February 5, 1976, died, age 86, the result of emphysema and a series of major heart issues. Upon his death, the *Toronto Sun* observed that Wemp was probably the first man to launch himself from a newspaper city desk to the mayor's office in a city the size of Toronto. As *Globe and Mail* columnist Bruce West observed, "He was one of the most colourful Torontonians, while at the same time giving the superficial appearance of being quiet, bland and altogether unimpressive. Small of stature and usually rather serious of mien, he sometimes seemed almost prim as he looked at you over the rims of his glasses."[4]

Mayoral Election in 1930

CANDIDATES	VOTES
Bert Wemp	54,455
Sam McBride	50,598
Albert Hacker	3,210

Mayor William Stewart

1931–1934

The 43rd mayor of Toronto

Occupations: Funeral director, City of Toronto alderman, Member and Speaker of Legislative Assembly of Ontario
Residence While Mayor: 309 Kennedy Avenue
Birth: February 13, 1889, in Toronto
Death: September 28, 1969, in Toronto

A lifelong citizen of Toronto, William James Stewart was born in a house on Manning Avenue on February 13, 1889. The son of Albert Stewart and Sarah Hughes of Scottish-Irish descent, he attended Manning Avenue Public School, Ryerson Public School, and Shaw Business School.

In his early life, Stewart joined the labour force as an office boy with the Cleveland Bicycle Shop on Queen Street. Later, he reminisced about leaving school at an early age, working in a warehouse, and attending night school to take business courses. In August 1910, Stewart married Ethel Huff of Dresden, Ontario, and they had five children.

The future mayor went on to become a respected, well-known funeral director on Queen Street in Toronto's west end. Stewart opened the Toronto Embalming School, using the preparation room of his business to teach students how to embalm corpses. In 1930, he became the new owner of Bates & Dodds Funeral Services, which he expanded to include a chapel seating 100 people. Although not remaining in the family, the business continued to operate on Queen Street West for another 85 years.

Stewart had been president of the Ward 5 Conservative Association and first sought office in 1924 as a member of Toronto's Council for that ward, a position he held until becoming mayor in 1931 when incumbent Bert Wemp decided not to seek re-election after only a single year. Challenging a resurgent Sam McBride, Stewart won a close mayoral battle, capturing 57,600 votes to McBride's 57,287, a win of just over 300 votes out of 114,600 cast. Stewart became the first Council member elected mayor without first being on the Board of Control since its establishment in 1904.

He received strong editorial support from the *Globe*, which wrote about Stewart, "Few men in the city are so well informed on the city's business.... There is none who has given it more conscientious study, or who brings calmer judgment to its consideration."[1] The *Globe* also noted it was a difficult moment in the city's history: "The new Mayor will preside over civic business at a time when the whole world is in a disturbed condition — and when earnest leaders in all walks of life are making every effort to restore order out of disturbance, and replace depression by prosperity."[2]

In his 1931 inaugural address, Stewart observed that Toronto now had a population of 621,000 and an assessment value of just over $1 billion ($19 billion today). He pointed out that he was a strong advocate of public ownership, hydro in particular, and also noted that a lawsuit had been filed to stop a proposed new road link from Bloor at Jarvis Street north to St. Clair Avenue (today's Mount Pleasant Boulevard).

Numerous issues were discussed at the Council, including road widenings on Bloor Street and Avenue Road, the need for a new police headquarters, a first airport for Toronto, the Toronto Islands ferry's operating loss, new development in the eastern beaches, and a campaign to promote goods "Made in Canada."

As Clare Dale notes in *Whose Servant I Am*, Stewart brought a no-nonsense administrative style and "became known for his business-like approach to politics. Acting on his view that the city was a corporation and its people its principal shareholders."[3] Stewart's insistence that the public should be consulted on all questions of major importance was characteristic of that approach.

A Tory with both a business sense and social conscience, Stewart helped institute several Depression-era initiatives for the needy and unemployed, one of the most practical being a series of special depots where the city's poor and destitute could obtain food, fuel, or a place to sleep six days of the week. He also proposed a coordinated appeal of charitable funds and the establishment of a community chest to encourage even greater philanthropy.

In 1932 as the Depression raged, Stewart won the mayor's chair by acclamation, and in 1933 and 1934, turned back weak challenges from lesser-known civic officials. In his 1932 inaugural address, he noted the severe and very dire worldwide economic conditions and also cautioned about taxpayers' financial ability to pay and the need for balance.

Stewart put forward several major projects: University Avenue continuing southward, hydroelectric improvements, and $2.7 million ($56 million today) allocated to unemployment relief. Toronto was still in an excellent financial position, he stressed, though new construction was down and there was a 2 percent decrease in tax collection.

In the 1933 election, Stewart was returned with massive support, with broad backing also given to a ballot question to reduce the size of the Council. Stewart announced a thorough review of the city's financial structure and its collection methods as well as a search for all possible channels for added revenue.

A serious racial incident marked 1933 — the riot at Christie Pits. Torontonians were shocked by the violent ethnic clash at the end of a softball game. Stewart questioned the police response, which was inadequate, despite earlier warnings of possible violence, and stated that displaying a swastika would be liable to prosecution.

Stewart's image of fairness and openness was greatly enhanced by his "Mayor's Sunday Radio Broadcasts," in which he fostered a sense that something was actually being done about the difficulties caused by the Depression. In addition to his Sunday radio broadcasts, he was active with the Citizens Friendship League.

In 1934 at the very height of the Depression, he was easily re-elected with 72,687 votes to main opponent H.L. Rogers's 17,222. As the *Globe* wrote, "Mayor Stewart has given his entire times to the duties of office since first elected which means he has been on the job day and night. His service has been conscientious and energetic ..."[4]

In his 1934 inaugural address, Stewart pointed with pride to the city's 100th birthday. Even though still in the depths of the Depression, a gala dinner was held at the King Edward Hotel, attended by Prime Minister William Lyon Mackenzie King, grandson of the city's firebrand first mayor. The city's centenary was an unquestioned success with parades, exhibits, fireworks, community, street, and neighbourhood celebrations, as well as religious services attended by thousands of residents.

In the end, Stewart chose not to seek re-election in 1935, clearing the way for what was a surprise outcome: the election of Jimmy Simpson, Toronto's first socialist mayor. Stewart "was by all accounts a popular and successful mayor"[5] with many noting upon his departure that he had been one of the best mayors the city had ever had. Stewart soon moved into provincial politics, and in 1936, offered himself as a candidate for the leadership of the provincial Conservative Party. In the May 1936 convention at the Royal York Hotel, he lost badly, placing third behind Earl Rowe and George Drew. The bitter experience set the stage for a rivalry and uneasy relationship with second-place finisher and future Ontario premier Drew.

In October 1938, Stewart handily won a provincial by-election, becoming the Conservative MPP for Parkdale. His service as an MPP spanned two separate periods from 1938 to 1948 and from 1951 to 1959. As a back-bencher from 1938 to 1943, he was on seven standing committees of the Legislative Assembly. In August 1943, with a Tory return to power under Premier George Drew, Stewart won re-election in Parkdale. The newly re-named Progressive Conservative (PC) Party had finally broken the Liberal hold on the province to begin a 42-year dynasty.

Stewart was Speaker of the assembly from February 1944 until the 1945 election. Yet the task was a difficult one, with the Tories securing only a mi-nority government. Defeated on a vote of confidence in 1945, the province again went to the polls, and Stewart was easily re-elected with 13,875 votes to a Liberal opponent's 7,716. Although the PC Party had won a convincing majority of 66 seats, Stewart was not offered a post in Drew's Cabinet and again became Speaker in July 1945.

As Clare Dale notes, a time of stormy relations between the premier, his government, and the Speaker was about to commence.[6] Long an opponent of saloons and beer parlours, Stewart had previously threatened to resign over the granting of provincial beer licences. Then, in a dramatic row with the minister of highways over the inconsequential issue of guest seating in the Speaker's Gallery, Stewart resigned as Speaker in a dramatic flourish, submitting a letter consisting of a single sentence.

Dale further notes that the resignation came about "after the ideological conflict between the Speaker and the Premier reached an intolerable level."[7] Long a behind-the-scenes opponent of Drew and his pro-liquor-related poli-cies, Stewart had clashed with him before, part of the long simmering and deeply held rivalry between two powerful Ontario political figures.

Stewart's service as Speaker lasted three years and 27 days, during which he oversaw debate on a wide range of issues: wartime housing, milk qual-ity, labour rights, cheese and hog subsidies, slot machines, venereal dis-ease, a reorganization of the Department of Public Welfare, and a new Fuel Commission of Ontario.

In the June 1948 Ontario general election, Stewart lost to noted civil liberties activist Lloyd Fell. His prior resignation as Speaker, com-bined with Drew's unpopularity and the strength of the Co-operative Commonwealth Federation (CCF), forerunner of today's New Democratic Party, all took a political toll, and Stewart was defeated by 650 votes in Parkdale.

Premier Drew lost his own riding of High Park to CCF anti-liquor crusader William Temple in the Ontario general election of 1948. Yet instead of
seeking another seat in a by-election, Drew left provincial politics altogether
to run for the leadership of the federal PC Party.

Now outside active politics, Stewart became chairman of the Toronto
Board of Assessors in 1948, overseeing the difficult task of properly evalu-
ating every property in Toronto. In 1950, he was also named chair of the
Toronto and York Civil Defence Committee.

Although he had been defeated in 1948, Stewart regained his seat in
the 1951 provincial general election, serving as the Conservative MPP for
Parkdale from 1951 until 1959. As a Toronto backbencher during the 1950s
under Premier Leslie Frost, Stewart remained out of the Cabinet but served
on 11 standing committees of the Legislative Assembly. The PC government
of which Stewart was a member oversaw a major expansion of schools, highways, and public investment, including hospital insurance; the 400 series of
superhighways; the first legislation to deal with racial, ethnic, and gender
discrimination; creation of a regional government for Metro Toronto; and
the introduction of provincial sales tax.

Stewart remained an MPP in the Legislative Assembly until the 1959
provincial election when his Parkdale seat was captured by the Liberals.
After his defeat, he was appointed to the Ontario Parole Board in 1960, only
to resign a few months later.

An avid historian, Stewart was active with the Toronto Historical
Committee, predecessor to the Toronto Historical Board, and wrote a historical pamphlet titled *From Wigwam to Skyscraper*. While mayor, he had
been instrumental in urging the city to restore Fort York as a civic centennial project in 1934. Active in the Queen's York Rangers (1st American
Regiment), he served as the unit's honorary colonel.

A member of Runnymede United Church, he was a master of the Ulster
Masonic Lodge, a past master of Loyal Orange Lodge 657, and a member
of Loyal Orange Lodge 3271. And from 1961 until his death in September
1969, Stewart was chair of the Toronto Historical Board.

Stewart died in Toronto on September 28, 1969, age 80, leaving his
second wife, Thelma Standeaven, whom he had married in 1957 after the
death of his first wife, Ethel Huff, in 1955. He was also survived by two sons
and two daughters.

Mayoral Election in 1931

CANDIDATES	VOTES
William Stewart	57,600
Sam McBride	57,287

Mayoral Election in 1932

William Stewart was re-elected mayor by acclamation.

Mayoral Election in 1933

William Stewart	85,691
Robert Leslie	26,754
Richard Tuthill	1,867

Mayoral Election in 1934

William Stewart	72,687
H.L. Rogers	17,222
Albert E. Smith	8,298
Albert Hacker	6,440

Mayor Jimmy Simpson
1935

The 44th mayor of Toronto

Occupations: Printer, journalist, trade unionist, Toronto Board of Education chair, delegate to the International Labour Organization, City of Toronto controller
Residence While Mayor: 91 Indian Road
Birth: December 14, 1873, in Lindal-in-Furness, England
Death: September 24, 1938, in Toronto

——— • ———

To the dismay of Toronto's most powerful business establishment as well as the city's Liberal and Conservative partisans, Jimmy Simpson became the mayor of Toronto in 1935. It was, to put it mildly, a complete political shock. A Methodist, prohibitionist, trade unionist, and socialist — Simpson was all of these and was now a mayor unlike any before him. With a solid build, round face, and perpetual smile, he was known as Jimmy, never James.

James "Jimmy" Simpson was born in Lancashire in rural England in 1873, the son of British stonemason Edward Simpson and Christina Brockbank. He attended a Church of England elementary school, worked for a shilling a day picking potatoes, and age 10, began selling newspapers. Simpson then worked for a local grocer at 13, carrying bags of sugar and unloading carloads of coal for a pittance.

Later, Simpson recalled that after his staunchly unionist parents picked up and moved the family to Canada when he was only 14, he regularly sang in the church choir and was good at running, bicycling, pole vaulting, rugby, soccer, and cricket.

The family settled in Cabbagetown where Simpson eventually worked at a metal-and-tinware factory in which the hands or fingers of many employees had been cut off. Working 12 hours per day at age 16, Simpson had a range of functions: making stove boards; spinning brass, lead, and copper; applying lacquer; decorating toilet seats; and dipping bicycle parts in red paint. *The National Encyclopedia of Canadian Biography* notes that it was "a dirty job: at night his arms were covered with paint to the elbows, and besides, he was intoxicated with the poisonous fumes of the benzine with which the paint was mixed."[1]

Simpson and his family lived at Dundas and Ontario Streets. Like his father, young Simpson spoke out against diabolical factory working conditions and at temperance meetings. A Sunday school mentor found him work as an apprentice at the *Toronto Daily News*. During a major strike and under the guidance of fellow Orangeman Horatio Hocken, Simpson joined labour efforts against the *News*. The strike led to the founding of today's *Toronto Star*.

In the 1890s, Simpson rose quickly as a journalist with the new *Daily Star*. In 1892, Toronto was a bustling city of 180,000 with six newspapers competing for readers as well as advertisers. This new seventh daily, a self-styled "Paper for the People," was started by the 21 printers and teenage apprentices locked out by the *News*.

Simpson had also gone back into the bicycle assembly business — this time to work at Richard Simpson and Company, his brother's firm. Yet when it merged to create the CCM bicycle firm, Simpson returned to the *Star* where he joined the editorial staff and remained until 1918. Learning city issues first-hand, he was one of the *Star*'s main City Hall reporters, later calling it his apprenticeship for public office.

In June 1899, Simpson married Alma Barton from Beeton, Ontario, and had two children with her: Ruskin (later deceased) and Maxine. The next year, Simpson and eight others started Toronto's Ruskin Literary and Debating Society, which became a well-regarded debating group whose topics included literary, social, political, and economic questions.

Simpson served three separate terms as vice-president of the Trades and Labour Congress of Canada from 1904 to 1909, 1916 to 1917, and 1924 to 1936. By 1900, it had become national in scope and was the forerunner of today's Canadian Labour Congress. Simpson was also a founder of the Labour Temple in Toronto, and as a union reporter, covered the great coal strike of Cape Breton in 1909.

At age 28, Simpson first sought elected office in 1902 as a member of the Toronto Technical School Board, then in 1905 was elected a trustee of the Toronto Board of Education. In 1908, the young and very brash union organizer threw his hat into the Toronto mayoral race, offering himself as the socialist candidate and placing a distant fourth.

Returning to the Toronto Board of Education in 1910, he became its chair and that same year was appointed a commissioner of the seven-member federal Royal Commission on Industrial Training and Technical Education, which examined key issues such as industrial training, federal policy for people in rural communities, secondary school vocational training, apprenticeships, and household sciences.

In 1911, Simpson ran for the Board of Control with the support of organized labour on a program of municipal hospital services, city coal and gas distribution, a civic greenbelt, and more parks for a thickly populated city.

Although he lost in 1911, he was finally elected to the board in 1914 with the highest vote total ever given a candidate up to that time: 20,503 votes city-wide, 3,500 ahead of incumbent controller Tommy Church.

The *Toronto News* said he had "strength, courage, and rugged power in debate … real sympathy for the 'underdog' and an earnest desire to improve living conditions. He also has a strong leaning towards Socialistic declarations which tend to alarm the electorate." Yet despite his strong showing, Simpson was defeated just a year later but ran for controller another eight times in the next 15 years before securing a Board of Control seat once again in the 1930s.

Simpson was also busy on a much broader front, representing Canadian labour at several international meetings: the American Federation of Labor in Boston (1903), the Convention of International Workers in Vienna (1914), and the British Trade Union Congress in Birmingham (1916). As a member of the Royal Commission on Technical Education, he toured seven large American cities, later attended the British Commonwealth Labour Congress in London (1925), and was a Canadian delegate to the Conference of the International Labour Organization of the League of Nations in Geneva (1926 and 1928).

To his official duties, Simpson also added several lecture tours in Great Britain, the United States, and New Zealand, and for 10 years served as managing editor of the *Industrial Banner*, the official publication of the international trade union movement. With his labour expertise, he helped settle an International Garment Workers strike; achieved a pay increase for Toronto's fire, parks, property, and street-cleaning employees; and obtained better working hours for Toronto's retail, clerical, and wagon-driving workers.

As a committed socialist and founder of the original Canadian Labour Party, Simpson also ran several times in the 1920s as a candidate for the House of Commons on a reform platform that included the nationalization of banks and public utilities, a major extension of social and labour legislation, and lower taxes for the working class.

By 1930, the *Toronto Daily Star* had written that "he is one of the most travelled, ablest and most internationally known men in Toronto's public life. The city is fortunate to have his services at its command."[2] Simpson was finally elected a controller once again as a well-known member of the Co-operative Commonwealth Federation (CCF).

He turned down the opportunity to become president of the national Trades and Labour Congress of Canada in 1934 to run instead for mayor of

Toronto the next year. Known as the "People's Jimmy," he campaigned as a veteran socialist at the very height of the Great Depression.

In running against fellow Orangeman Harry Hunt for the 1935 mayoralty, the only daily newspaper to support him was the left-leaning *Daily Star*, a position it reversed the following year. The other Toronto dailies, as well as Conservative and Liberal Party supporters, accused the CCF of being anti-British and under communist influence.

In 1935, age 62, Simpson was elected mayor with 54,422 votes to Hunt's 51,028. Simpson's community activity and an effective on-the-ground labour organization made the difference. He successfully knit together Depression-era supporters of the CCF with colleagues from the temperance community and education sectors to get out the vote.

At the inaugural meeting of the Council, the destitute and efforts to deal with homelessness, hunger, and deep unemployment were front and centre. Unpaid city taxes had now reached $11.5 million ($244 million today), while welfare costs were $8.8 million ($187 million today) for direct relief in the form of food, fuel, shelter, clothing, and medical services.

Aware of his reputation as a free-spending social advocate, Simpson pledged "high standards, discipline, and efficient service — economically delivered,"[3] while also noting that infant mortality was 33 percent lower than in 1929 and there had been major water improvements, including significant progress on a new sewage treatment plant to serve the projected city population of 1.6 million by 1970.

Yet, as Toronto's popular "socialist" mayor for only a single year, Simpson ended up having limited impact on the actual administration of city affairs, clashing publicly with Tim Buck and members of his Communist-backed Labor-Progressive Party and with Liberal premier Mitchell Hepburn on matters of relief for the unemployed.[4]

It was also a dark time for Toronto. Local citizens witnessed polio epidemics, the massive social and economic dislocation of the Great Depression, bigotry from the Orange Order, and the rise of Nazism and blatant anti-Semitism in Europe. Simpson supported a campaign to boycott the 1936 Summer Olympics in Berlin in Nazi Germany.

The Council also discussed a range of other topics in 1935: bicycle licensing, rooming houses, new bathing pools, improvements to housing, the regulation of second-hand junk shops, allowing new gas stations, a ban on automobile honking at certain hours, and an examination of the number, location, and cost of possible new public housing units. Also dealt with was an emerging issue: an "air harbour" seaplane base on the waterfront, with Simpson reporting there was now one arrival and one departure each day.

Yet, ironically, at the very height of the Depression came the city's purchase for $2,800 ($59,000 today) of a brand-new seven-passenger Cadillac limousine for the mayor. The city had also solicited bids for a Packard, Lincoln Continental, Pierce-Arrow, and two Buicks.

In December 1935, Simpson unveiled a detailed re-election program for 1936: establishment of a social planning commission; comprehensive slum clearance; a reduction in the interest rate on city debt; the municipal distribution of milk, bread, and coal and that the relief become a federal responsibility; that municipal voting be extended to tenants; and a surtax on the wealthy, defined at the time as anyone making over $3,000 per year ($63,000 per year today).

Yet Simpson's inclusion did not necessarily apply to everyone in his own city. In 1936, Simpson lost his re-election bid partly because of his anti-Catholic views and statements. Despite his populist, left-wing, social democratic background, Simpson was intensely opposed to the Roman Catholic Church, which was one of the factors that cost him the support of the *Toronto Daily Star* in 1936.

In the 1936 mayoral race, former mayor Sam McBride prevailed, capturing 48,978 votes to 43,381 for second-place finisher Harry Hunt and just 32,777 for incumbent Simpson. After losing to the combative McBride and coming in third, Simpson retired from active city politics.

During a lengthy public career, Simpson dealt with a wide range of causes, issues, and community interests as vice-president of the International Harbour and Deep Waterways Association and as a board member of the Ontario Municipal Electricity Association, the Ontario Safety League, the Ontario Red Cross, and the Ontario Hygiene Council. He was also a vice-president of the Ontario Municipal Association and a member of the executive of the Canadian Employment Council.

On the personal side, Simpson was president of the Toronto Methodist Young People's Union, the Riverside Soccer Football Club, the Excelsior rugby football team, and the Ramblers Bicycle Club. Ironically, though he was the city's first socialist mayor, Simpson had relied on his very entrepreneurial wife to pay the bills by selling real estate.

Tragically, in September 1938, the car Jimmy Simpson was driving collided with a streetcar at the intersection of Bay and Harbour Streets and he was killed. The vehicle was so badly wedged underneath and Simpson so badly injured that rescue personnel did not immediately recognize the city's former mayor. In the end, he was identified by a gold watch presented to him by the city.

For years, the Simpsons had lived in an unpretentious and comfortable home with a broad veranda at 91 Indian Road, just west of Roncesvalles Avenue. Funeral services were held at Howard Park United Church on Sunnyside Avenue, and flags were lowered half-mast on all city buildings. Toronto trade unionists formed a marching contingent headed by members of the Allied Printing Trades Union.

Mayoral Election in 1935	
CANDIDATES	VOTES
James "Jimmy" Simpson	54,422
Harry Hunt	51,028
J. George Ramsden	16,732
Albert E. Smith	4,666

Mayor William Robbins

1936–1937

The 45th mayor of Toronto

Occupations: Streetcar conductor, transit union leader, City of Toronto alderman and controller
Residence While Mayor: 750 Logan Avenue
Birth: May 8, 1874, in Bristol, England
Death: March 25, 1952, in Toronto

——— • ———

William Dullam Robbins was born in Bristol, England, in 1874 and came to Canada with his parents a year later. The family settled in Ontario's Durham County where Robbins attended public school and the Collegiate Institute in Bowmanville. In 1895, he moved to Toronto and began work as a streetcar conductor for the Toronto Railway Company (TRC).

Robbins soon developed both a profile and reputation as an ardent labour advocate, though he also referred to himself as a "loyal Orange Conservative." In 1893, two years before Robbins's arrival in Toronto, workers on the street rail system formed a local of the Amalgamated Association of Street Railway Employees of America. Robbins soon got involved, and in 1908, became the first general secretary of the Toronto local of the union, a position he held for more than 30 years.

The background to Robbins's union involvement has a rich history. Until the early 1900s, drivers had to pay for their own uniforms, stand at all times, and drive their streetcars out in the open, directly exposed to rain, snow, freezing rain, hail, wind, and sun. The TRC had, in the words of the union, fought "tooth and nail" against a covered area for drivers, claiming that a windshield would obscure their vision.

In 1902, a few years prior to Robbins becoming its secretary, the union called its first strike, with the company asking for the militia to be called in. Yet solid picketing and a strong show of public support won the day, with the secretive private franchise agreeing to a wage increase just three days into the strike. The well-regarded Robbins also became a significant player in other labour improvements, successfully advocating for an eight-hour workday and pressing for the passage of the Workmen's Compensation Act.

Robbins first sought elected office in an August 1912 by-election, winning as the alderman for Ward 1 and was re-elected from 1913 to 1917. Although the First World War halted union wage gains, after the war's conclusion, a wave of major strikes swept across Canada, including the famous Winnipeg General Strike of 1919.

As a vocal advocate for the public ownership of civic utilities, Robbins was involved, both as a labour leader and as a member of the Board of Control, in negotiations that led to the city's takeover of the TRC in 1921 and the formation of the municipally owned Toronto Transportation Commission.

Over the next 25 years, Robbins was involved in almost every annual civic election but with mixed results, recording 18 wins and seven defeats. The 1930s proved to be the peak of his political career.

Robbins was elected to the Board of Control in 1932, 1933, and 1934, and in January 1935, at the height of the Great Depression, his friend and labour-backed colleague, Jimmy Simpson, won a surprise victory as mayor, becoming the first socialist elected to Toronto's highest office.

Yet, in 1936, restless voters tossed out Simpson and returned Sam McBride to the mayoralty. Colleagues nominated Robbins to be vice-chair of the board and unknowingly set the stage for him to become acting mayor during McBride's lengthy and debilitating illness. By June 1936, McBride was no longer able to carry out his mayoral duties, then died in office in November.

Upon McBride's death, Robbins was appointed interim mayor on November 18, 1936, mere weeks ahead of the 1937 campaign. As the 1937 mayoralty race approached, a very public negotiation process took place between Robbins and possible contender Ralph Day. In the end, Day agreed to step aside and allow Robbins to have a clear field for 1937, anticipating that Robbins would simply retire at the end of a year-long term.

Robbins's brief mayoralty was marked by continuing economic hardship. Both Toronto and Canada were seriously affected by the worldwide depression. By the mid-1930s, 30 percent of Canada's labour force was out of work, with one in five Canadians dependent on relief or government assistance for survival.

The problems of restless, single, out-of-work, and homeless men became so severe that prior to Robbins's mayoralty the federal government established a national series of unemployment relief camps run by the Department of National Defence. In return for a bunkhouse residence, three meals, work clothes, medical care, and 20 cents per day, these "Royal Twenty Centers" worked a 44-hour week clearing bush, building roads, planting trees, and constructing public buildings. By the time the camps were closed in 1936, they had been home for 170,000 men.

Just weeks after Toronto's Council appointed him mayor, Robbins faced city electors. The 1937 municipal vote had been moved up from a traditional New Year's Day election and instead was held in December 1936. Robbins was elected with a huge majority, capturing 74,959 votes to principal opponent John Laidlaw's 22,202.

In his inaugural address to the Council, Robbins revealed a very personal side when he said, "I have long aspired to the Chief Magistracy, as I believe everyone who enters Council should." The Depression, he added, had led to "problems of the first magnitude," explaining that when it came to senior levels, "Toronto paid the most in revenue, and received proportionately the least in return."[1] The city, he reported, had recently asked Ottawa for $1 million ($20 million today) for park grading, pavement widening, grade separations, and the new island airport.

Robbins called for the city to be given a portion of the gasoline tax and automobile licence fees, pointing out "that residents of Toronto used approximately 100,000,000 gallons of gasoline each year."[2] He also indicated that Toronto was lagging behind other cities with respect to air transportation. Indeed, further action to obtain an airport had been a key pledge of Robbins's campaign and became a defining issue of his mayoralty, setting the course for Toronto to become the nation's leading airline hub decades later.

For several years, the city's business and corporate leadership had pressed Ottawa for a bridge or tunnel to the Toronto Islands but without success until 1935 when Conservative prime minister R.B. Bennett, facing a crucial election, sought to ensure a win in the Toronto seat held by Reg Geary, his justice minister, and chose his own brand of stimulus funding in the building of a tunnel.

Toronto's Council accepted the government's offer, and in August, by a vote of 17–7, approved both a tunnel and the airport project. Yet the reason it didn't proceed was the subsequent election victory of William Lyon Mackenzie King's Liberals. Facing deep budgetary problems, King had no desire to give millions to what was then a very Tory Toronto.

Although a tunnel was dead, political and civic leaders remained committed, and an advisory committee was struck under the guidance of Billy Bishop, the First World War air hero tasked with choosing the best airport location. Its final recommendations, made during Robbins's 1937 mayoral term, were that a future main airport should be on the islands with a "supplementary" airport at Malton in Peel County. In July 1937, work began in earnest to create the new island airport.

Issues discussed by the Council in 1937 included a proposed workweek of five eight-hour days, the extension of Mount Pleasant Road south to connect with Bloor Street, relief for single men, the registration of all men looking for work, and the establishment of an unemployment insurance plan.

Also discussed were ending hydro and water disconnections due to non-payment of bills, licence fees paid by members of the Toronto Hand Laundries Association, a limit on the number of gas stations, the daytime delivery of milk, an increase of the business tax on chain stores, and a strong condemnation of both communism and Nazism.

The fate of Casa Loma and the headache of what to do with it were also discussed in a lively fashion. Civic patience had run out in 1934 as the city assumed its ownership. Some councillors sought to tear it down, yet the demolition cost would be higher than the profits obtained from selling the rubble. One suggestion was to simply blow it up until dynamite experts reported that the ensuing blast would shatter glass throughout the west end of the city.

Proposed Casa Loma schemes included a military museum, medical centre, business exhibition space, movie studio, tea room, youth centre, rare art museum, annex for the Hospital for Sick Children, or even a new North American home for the pope. In the end, an agreement was struck with the West Toronto Kiwanis Club to operate Casa Loma as a tourist attraction.

In May 1937, Robbins and his wife represented Toronto at the coronation of King George VI in Westminster Abbey after Edward VIII sought to marry a divorced American socialite, then abdicated the throne. The year 1937 also marked the first full year of a new Toronto newspaper, the *Globe and Mail*, formed as the result of a merger of the *Globe* and the *Daily Mail and Empire*.

During his term, Robbins served on the Toronto Board of Health, as a trustee of Massey Hall, and director of the Canadian National Exhibition, the Children's Aid Society, and Consumers' Gas.

A convergence of political, economic, community, social, and budgetary issues in a Depression-weary city all came about to deny Robbins a second term. As a percentage of city expenditures, welfare had gone from 7 percent in 1930 to 16 percent in 1936, while city tax arrears increased from $5.4 million in 1930 ($90 million today) to $10 million in 1936 ($207 million today). In the 1938 election, the younger and more popular controller Ralph Day garnered 64,837 votes for mayor to 50,786 for incumbent Robbins.

In January 1938, the Council motion following his stunning defeat described Robbins as a "highly respected and deeply beloved colleague." He was, it said, "an ardent advocate of the sound principle that social progress must keep pace with economic progress."[3]

The Bureau of Municipal Research released a number of recommendations, including further amalgamation of departments, more centralized purchasing, standardizing rates of pay, reducing the size of the Council, and town planning that included zoning, housing, and a planning commission.

In 1939, Robbins sought a political comeback in an effort to rejoin the Board of Control, yet by then the writing was on the wall. In January 1939 — and on the same day as Ralph Day was himself re-elected mayor with a massive 93,211 votes — Robbins lost badly for controller when all four sitting incumbents were re-elected. Surprisingly, well ahead of Robbins by almost 20,000 votes for a position on the board was Communist Party firebrand Tim Buck.

Robbins retired as general secretary of the railway union in 1941 and celebrated both his golden wedding anniversary and the 50th consecutive Labour Day Parade in 1949. In his personal life, Robbins was a member of the Empire and Canadian Clubs, as well as Boyne Loyal Orange Lodge 173, the Ulster Masonic Lodge, the Knights of Pythias, the Withrow Park Bowling Club, and the Independent Order of Odd Fellows.

William Robbins died on March 25, 1952, age 77, and was survived by his wife, Jane Snead, a daughter, and two sons. A condolence message from Toronto's Council called him "a man of affable and friendly disposition, who took everything in life with a philosophical outlook, yet with a trait of character that showed persistence and a tenacity of purpose."[4]

Toronto's former mayor was described as a labour moderate who was both genial and kindly and painstaking rather than brilliant. A newspaper editorial obituary noted: "Robbins came to the council as a representative of labour and earned a solid reputation for his devotion to the interests of the property-owners of the city ... Mr. Robbins earned a permanent place in the annals of the city."[5]

Mayoral Election in 1937	
CANDIDATES	VOTES
William Robbins	74,959
John Laidlaw	22,202
Robert Harding	3,963

Mayor Ralph Day
1938–1940

The 46th mayor of Toronto

Occupations: Soldier, funeral director, City of Toronto alderman and controller, Toronto Parking Authority chair, Toronto Transit Commission chair
Residence While Mayor: 4 Castle Frank Drive
Birth: November 24, 1898, in Toronto
Death: May 21, 1976, in Toronto

——— • ———

R alph Carrette Day was born near Eastern and Broadview Avenues in the city's east end in November 1898, the son of sign manufacturer William Day and Evelyn Carrette. He was raised on Sumach Street in Cabbagetown and attended Park and Withrow Avenue Public Schools and then Riverdale Collegiate Institute.

In February 1916, age 17, he left high school to enlist in the 169th Battalion of the Canadian Expeditionary Force (CEF) to fight in the First World War. In England, he was transferred to the 116th Battalion, rising to the rank of lieutenant and serving in France. The CEF was created for service overseas and was a highly respected fighting unit, having such combat efficiency that Germans nicknamed its members "storm troopers." It also became so revered by Allied commanders that Canadians spearheaded the final campaigns of the war.

In April 1917, Day was involved in the Battle of Vimy Ridge, one of the war's defining moments. Fighting three divisions of the German 6th Army in northern France, the 116th Battalion, as part of the CEF, was involved in counter-battery fire against enemy guns and smashing German positions. Over four days of bloody trench warfare, Canadians were able to overrun Vimy Ridge at a cost of more than 10,600 killed and wounded. Later, in June 1917, Day was wounded in the capture of Avion, France, and spent nine months in hospital before being attached to the 8th Reserve Battalion as an instructor.

After the war, Day attended preparatory courses at the University of Toronto but didn't complete a degree, then worked briefly for his father's firm, the Day Sign Company. In 1921, he decided to completely change occupations by going to work with a local undertaker, and by 1929, bought his own funeral home, which later became the Ralph Day Funeral Home on Danforth Avenue. The business continued until October 2007 when it became part of the Heritage Funeral Centre on Overlea Boulevard, the largest single-level funeral home in Canada.

Day first became involved in Toronto civic politics in 1927 when he was elected a member of the Board of Education for Ward 1, a position he held until

1930. From 1931 to 1934, he was an alderman for the same ward, then from 1935 to 1937 was a member of the powerful four-member Board of Control.

Even though he was senior controller in 1936 (polling the highest number of votes in the city-wide vote), Day was passed over in late 1936 as interim mayor following the death in office of incumbent Sam McBride. The Council instead picked William Robbins.

In December 1936 — the election date for the 1937 term — Robbins was elected mayor while Day was chosen a controller with 56,781 votes citywide. When Robbins announced he would seek a second term, Day threw his hat into the ring for mayor, and on December 7, 1937, easily defeated the lacklustre Robbins for the 1938 term. Day came from behind to win by a significant margin, with 64,837 votes to Robbins's 50,786, winning all but two wards of the city.

With Day's decision to run for mayor, the most interesting city-wide race turned out to be the close contest between alderman Douglas McNish and Tim Buck, Canada's most prominent Communist Party leader, by then released from prison. Although McNish won narrowly, Buck came within 200 votes of capturing a seat on the Board of Control.

In his 1938 inaugural address, Day covered a range of topics, noting that free dental nursing and medical services would be made available to indigent and low-wage earners. Housing, he pointed out, was a "national problem" and Toronto would continue to press for low-priced housing. He lauded the city's two new airports, saying they would put Toronto in a better position to obtain new investment and provide speedier mail delivery.

The Council received a scathing report from Dr. G.P. Jackson, the medical officer of health, who said complaints had been received regarding "sewage floating on the surface of the water of the Island Lagoons"[1] close to public beaches. He noted the 344 cases of typhoid in the previous decade.

Issues dealt with by the Council in 1938 included a tax on beer sold in hotels; the National Steel Car Corporation's new airplane-manufacturing facility in Toronto; the use of city parks on Sundays; an upcoming goodwill visit by the mayors of Detroit, Buffalo, and Chicago; a proposed new tax on department stores; allowing parking tickets to be paid at a neighbourhood police station; and the location of second-hand stores and junkyards.

The Council also discussed reducing the salaries of Board of Control members, as well as a decrease in the eight chauffeur-driven vehicles used by city controllers and department heads. Included also was a candid assessment of the current 18 city chauffeurs and their employment hierarchy based on years of employment; seniority; wages paid; whether they were married, single, or had a family; whether they had served in the First World War; and what was their actual war service or disabilities, or if they were already in receipt of a war pension.

With his efficient and businesslike manner and administrative skills, Day was easily re-elected mayor in January 1939, receiving 93,211 votes to chief challenger Lewis Duncan's 53,490. Day had outlined several priorities in the campaign, including a new courthouse, saying that City Hall could no longer host both the courts and municipal departments. He also noted that unemployment was the city's most serious issue and that it "undermines the morale of our people [and] breeds discontent."[2]

Issues discussed at the Council included a protest by the Labour Council against the closing of beverage rooms at 10:00 p.m., the allegation of "communist schools" or "Italian Fascist Schools" in the city, and a lofty resolution adopted by the Canadian Federation of Mayors and Municipalities calling for a major new program called "Moral Re-Armament." The Council was also advised that Toronto's 30,000 passenger vehicles in 1921 had grown to almost 125,000 by 1938, causing a workload increase due to traffic and parking matters, the inspection of vehicles, protection of children at crossings, and the investigation of thousands of accidents.

As mayor, Day presided over the enormously popular and successful 1939 royal visit of King George VI and Queen Elizabeth (the parents of Queen Elizabeth II), making a six-week, coast-to-coast tour, the first such royal visit to Canada.

Later that year, Britain and France declared war against Germany, with Canada following suit a week after that. A deteriorating international situation had prompted Toronto's Council to call an emergency session in late August. Day, a respected veteran of the First World War, asked that troops guard the city's public utilities, so militia units were immediately placed on 24-hour duty at water and filtration plants, hydro stations, and electrical transmission facilities. The province announced that employees wishing to serve would be granted an immediate leave of absence, and major employers promised that jobs and seniority would be protected in the event of war.

In January 1940, incumbent Day garnered 62,019 mayoral votes to Lewis Duncan's 58,432. A ballot question to suspend municipal elections for the duration of the world war lost by a huge margin of 84,570 against 19,378 in favour.

As mayor in 1940, his final one-year term, Day addressed a number of important issues at City Hall, saying, "We face a most difficult year, made more so by the uncertainties arising from the war." Civic relief cases had fallen as a result of increased economic activity due to the war, but unforeseen expenditures arose with the need to guard public utility plants and facilities. The mayor noted a reduction in debt charges and an unusual new opportunity in the midst of a war — tourism. With Europe closed to visitors, "the possibilities of developing the business in Canada are tremendous,"[3] he said. As a first step, he advocated that all businesses in the city adopt a uniform rate of exchange for U.S. currency.

At the end of 1940, Day left public office following his third mayoral term and returned to his business interests. Although he made an unsuccessful attempt to win a seat on the Board of Control in 1942, he did not return to any public role until 1952 when he was appointed to the newly formed Parking Authority of Toronto, becoming its first chair.

The Parking Authority became North America's largest such organization, and Day actively promoted more off-street parking and suburban commuter parking lots while opposing any city taxation of Parking Authority properties. He was also instrumental in developing the massive new parking lot built under Nathan Phillips Square in 1965, still one of the largest garages in the downtown core.

In 1963, the Metropolitan Toronto Council appointed the former mayor to the board of the Toronto Transit Commission (TTC), and in March of that year, he was elected chair by his fellow commissioners to replace former mayor Allan Lamport. He was again selected chair in 1964 and held that position until 1972. His years at the TTC were eventful ones, indeed. He was a strong opponent of political interference in TTC operations, and unlike the stormy and often blustery Lamport, Day was a quietly efficient administrator who worked hard to bring the TTC under sound financial control. By 1967, the commission reported a profit.

Approval was given to a new subway from Union Station going north on University Avenue to join the Bloor-Danforth line at St. George. With Day at the helm, the TTC also opened the Bloor-Danforth subway in February 1966 from Keele Station in the west to Woodbine in the east.

Once the line was in full operation, construction of further extensions to the Bloor-Danforth subway also began under Day's chairmanship. The expansions to Islington Station in the west and Warden Station in the east were overseen by Day and opened simultaneously in May 1968.

Under Day, the commission also lengthened the Yonge Street subway from Eglinton Avenue to Finch Avenue and decided to proceed with the Spadina subway where the transit corridor generated much debate. In 1969, Day opposed a move to make the TTC a Metropolitan Toronto department reporting directly to the Metropolitan (Metro) Council.

In what was seen as a controversial move at the time, Day was not re-appointed to the commission in 1972 and retired to private life. Just three months later, he suffered a severe stroke that paralyzed his left side and confined him to his Dale Avenue home in Rosedale.

In his personal life, Day was known to enjoy golf, curling, hunting, and fishing, and enjoyed a summer cottage on Lake Simcoe. He was a member of the Riverdale Kiwanis Club, the Canadian Legion, the St. George's Society, the Scarboro Golf Club, and for more than 40 years, the 11th Battalion Association.

The former mayor died at home on May 21, 1976, and was survived by his wife, Vera; daughters, Marie and Shirley; and son, Glen. Funeral arrangements were, of course, entrusted to the Ralph Day Funeral Home. Day and his wife shared three grandchildren with former mayor and TTC chair Allan Lamport. Day's son, Glen, had married Lamport's daughter, Jane.

A member of the St. Barnabas Anglican Church on Danforth Avenue in the Chester Avenue neighbourhood for more than 50 years, Day was laid to rest at the Necropolis, a familiar burial site for some of the city's most renowned citizens, including firebrand William Lyon Mackenzie, the municipality's first mayor.

SPECIAL NOTE: There was no Toronto municipal election held during 1938 itself. Toronto's Council for the 1938 term was elected in December 1937. But for the following Council term (1939), the annual civic election reverted to being on or close to New Year's Day, thus the 1939 Council was decided on January 2, 1939.

Mayoral Election in 1938

CANDIDATES	VOTES
Ralph Day	64,837
William Robbins	50,786
Carlo Lamberti	2,749
Robert Harding	2,135

Mayoral Election in 1939

Ralph Day	92,211
Lewis Duncan	53,490

Mayoral Election in 1940

Ralph Day	62,019
Lewis Duncan	58,432

Mayor Fred Conboy

1941–1944

The 47th mayor of Toronto

Occupations: Dental surgeon, Toronto Board of Education chair, editor, City of Toronto controller
Residence While Mayor: 1043 Bloor Street West
Birth: January 1, 1883, in Toronto
Death: March 29, 1949, in Toronto

— • —

Frederick Joseph Conboy was born in the west end of Toronto on January 1, 1883, one of five children of James Conboy and Sarah Smith, who at the time owned a market garden farm at Bloor Street West and Ossington Avenue, then a semi-rural area.

Years later, a Toronto Council resolution paid tribute to Conboy's up-bringing, noting "a great measure of his success may be attributed to his background of Irish Ancestry and the instilling into his youthful mind by his God-fearing parents, the importance in life of those attributes of honesty, perseverance, sympathy, and tolerance...."[1]

Indeed, Conboy was educated at public schools in Toronto, including Dovercourt, Dewson, and Givens, then attended Humberside Collegiate. The young Conboy graduated from the Royal College of Dental Surgeons' School of Dentistry, the forerunner of the University of Toronto's Faculty of Dentistry, in 1904.

Conboy originally rose to prominence in his profession through his advocacy of dental hygiene programs in public schools. In 1905, he began a dental practice on Bloor Street, a block west of Ossington Avenue, that lasted 21 years. In 1905, he also married his first wife, Katherine McBrien of Orangeville, Ontario, and had one son with her, Alvin Frederick.

Coincidental with the growth of the public health reform movement in Toronto, led by Dr. Charles Hastings, the city's medical officer of health, Conboy personally devoted one day a week to organize dental services in schools, which led to his election to the Board of Education, where he served six one-year terms as a trustee for Ward 6 from 1909 to 1914. Conboy was also chairman of the board in 1912, taking a leading part to bring about medical and dental inspections, auxiliary classes, and open-air schools.

Although Conboy, by then in his mid-thirties, did not see active military service during the First World War, he was on the advisory committee to the Canadian Army Dental Corps. Appointed a professor at the University of Toronto, Conboy continued to be very active in writing for various dental journals and newspapers on his favourite topic — public dental hygiene.

For a time, he was editor of the *Booster*, the official journal of the Ontario Dental Association (ODA), which later changed its name to the *Journal of the Ontario Dental Association* and subsequently the *Ontario Dentist*. A member of the ODA for many years, Conboy was its president in 1923–1924 and secretary-treasurer from 1925 to 1943. Later, he received an honorary lifetime membership.

From 1925 to 1936, Conboy was the provincial director of dental services for Ontario and was once again an ardent advocate of dental inspection in public schools. He served as president of the Canadian Dental Association, president of the Canadian Dental Research Foundation, a member of the executive of both the Canadian Dental Hygiene Council and the International Dental Federation, and a fellow of the International College of Dentists.

In 1926, under Conboy, October 20 was designated as "Dental Health Day," featuring free dental clinics, radio addresses, presentations to service clubs, retail displays, and a public dental health educational film distributed to movie theatres across Ontario. In one innovative measure, Conboy arranged for a dental booth at the province's largest summertime event, the Canadian National Exhibition. Visitors there received free dental X-rays forwarded to their own dentist. In later years, the booth also included a full dental examination.

Conboy served as president of the Community Welfare Council, was a member of the Ontario Social Service Council, and was chair of the Toronto Airport Committee. Possessing a strong social conscience, he served as president of the Ontario Provincial Association for the Care of the Feeble-Minded and was a professor of psychology, economics, and history, as well as jurisprudence and ethics, at the Royal College of Dental Surgeons in Toronto.

To further encourage dental education, Conboy helped organize a joint meeting in 1932 of the Ontario, Canadian, and British dental associations at the Royal York Hotel in Toronto. With additional dentists representing the United States, Australia, and New Zealand, it was one of the world's first major international dental conferences.

Near the end of his tenure as the provincial director of dental services for Ontario from 1926 to 1936, Conboy was elected alderman for Ward 6 in the municipal elections of 1935 and 1936 and served as a member of the Toronto

Board of Health. Conboy worked tirelessly to better the welfare of Toronto's working class, and his agenda included slum clearance, relief works, public health education, and the development of the island airport.

The top controllers elected city-wide for the 1937 term of the Board of Control were Ralph Day and Fred Conboy. In 1938, the popular Conboy topped the polls on the four-member board, and by January 1940, received 79,361 votes for controller, 17,000 more than for the mayor himself.

Upon the retirement of Mayor Ralph Day in late 1940, Conboy sought the 1941 mayoralty and ran against fellow controller Douglas McNish. Conboy won with 55,729 votes to 33,069 for McNish and went on to serve four one-year terms. Conboy's election brochures for mayor spoke of the man himself, ensuring that voters knew he was "Dr." Conboy and urging "a continuance of sane progressive civic administration and energetic leadership in all war efforts."[2]

As the world war continued to rage in Europe, affecting almost every facet of Toronto life, Conboy was emphatic in his 1941 inaugural speech. There were, he said, "only two groups — those who are with us, and those who are against us ... we must give our wholehearted support to a supreme effort in men, money, and material."[3] Conboy also dealt with decreased tax assessment, sea wall rehabilitation, foreign exchange costs, increased capital spending, and speeding up production at war-related industries. Yet the new mayor also struck an optimistic note, asking that Toronto prepare for the postwar period.

Issues discussed at the Council included gas rationing, the conscription of men, the delivery of coal, a call to shorten the hours for sale of "all intoxicating beverages,"[4] and experimental wartime blackouts of the city. Also discussed were objectionable advertising signs and billboards, the licensing of cigarette machines, housing for low-wage earners, the construction of a four-lane highway to Oshawa, and asking the federal government to grant pensions to the widows of war veterans killed in action.

Yet there was also a side of Toronto not likely seen by the dignified and courtly mayor of Toronto or his Council. According to a range of racy tabloids, the Toronto of the early 1940s possessed "screwballs, chumps, dingbats, morons, boozers, blackmailers, and playthings." It was a vividly colourful place, and in the salty language of the street, was a scandal- and crime-filled city full of "vice, thuggery, robbery, fraudsters, racketeers, crooks, stool pigeons, gangsters, saps, gyps, sugar daddies, welshers, and leeches." The fiery tabloids reported on the saucy and hidden world of Toronto "pimps, perverts, dopesters, bookies, trysts, hussies, nymphs, and swingers." Readers of the day were fed a spicy diet of racist and misogynistic and homophobic stories about "Chinamen, chinks, frogs, dames, queers, cripples, and homos."[5]

Issues in the mayor's 1942 and 1943 inaugural addresses included city debt, tax arrears, the loss of revenue due to private plants being taken over by the federal government, food relief, the promotions of city staff based on merit, and traffic congestion. The Council's topics included finances, taxes, sewage treatment, civilian defence, and appeals to curtail city expenditures. Councillors formally recognized days dedicated to soldiers, next-of-kin, the army reserve, and the creation of the United Nations. Alderman Gordon Miller also proposed sending a gift of cigarettes to all enlisted Toronto men serving overseas. The ravages of liquor were also a central concern.

Toronto's Racy, Racist, Sexist Tabloids

There was a hidden side of Toronto, one not seen by the dignified, proper, and courtly mayors of Toronto or their Councils. According to a range of racy tabloids such as *Hush*, *Broadway Brevities*, and *True Crime*, the Toronto of the 1940s was a fearsome, forbidding place. In the salty, vividly colourful language of the street, it was a crime-filled city of "thuggery, robbery, fraudsters, racketeers, crooks, stool pigeons, gangsters, saps, and welshers."

The racist, misogynist, and homophobic tabloids reported on a salacious world of "dopesters, bookies, trysts, nymphs, swingers, and homos." Readers were transfixed by stories of "Chinamen, chinks, dames, and cripples," a city of "tootsie-bait, lotharios, gigolos, playboys, cheating wives, and sex capers," a municipality of "pansies, pimps, perverts, queers, and sodomists." It was a nightmarish, gang-ridden underworld of "vice, dope, love nests, orgies, white slavery, bawdy houses, and gambling dens."

Restrictions on the consumption of beer, the closing of women's beverage rooms, and an outright removal of all chairs and tables in men's beverage rooms were considered.

By 1943, the City of Toronto's population had reached 669,130 while the suburbs boasted another 243,247. TTC commissioners forwarded an ambitious plan of transportation improvements to the Council: a new high-speed roadway using the Don Valley ravine system, a first subway under Yonge Street, and a possible subway under Queen Street. Conboy also spearheaded a delegation to secure the Sunnybrook Farm in North Toronto as the future site for a much-needed veterans' hospital.

The Council also dealt with postwar housing, a prohibition of "gypsy fortune-telling" establishments, rising juvenile delinquency, the purchase and storage of wood and fuel, island ferry service, sanitary conditions at the Don Jail, traffic safety, a redistribution of city wards, the establishment of a Toronto Reconstruction Council, expansion of the island airport airplane/seaplane base, and providing returning veterans with postwar employment.

In the January 1944 municipal election, Conboy, the incumbent mayor, defeated the popular and high-profile controller Lewis Duncan, who had led polls for the Board of Control. With his 78,995 mayoral votes, Conboy came in almost 20,000 votes ahead of Duncan.

His 1944 inaugural address focused on the need to adopt a comprehensive master plan for the city, a 30-year scheme of improvements to take the city into the 1970s. It was comprised of seven key elements: low-cost rental housing, zoning, a city-wide system of parkways and superhighways, the correction of congestion, street widenings, and the "elimination of unsightly places in the downtown area." In 1944, in addition to serving as president of the Canadian Federation of Mayors, Conboy championed Toronto as the future centre of aviation in Canada, saying the city was "destined to become a great aviation centre."[6]

The 1945 mayoral election featured a vigorous contest for the city's highest post. Although Conboy had been a good mayor, both the *Toronto Daily Star* and the *Globe and Mail* opted to support fellow Orangeman Robert Saunders, his chief opponent. Conboy was defeated in January 1945 by Saunders, who received 68,992 votes to only 36,389 for the incumbent mayor.

It was a crushing defeat for the well-regarded Conboy. Newspaper coverage noted that the loss was the result of an end-of-the war desire for a fresh new face and a younger, more active and dynamic chief magistrate. A Council resolution after his defeat noted that Conboy was one of the most dignified mayors in Toronto's 110 years.

In 1948, Conboy re-entered the political arena as the provincial Progressive Conservative (PC) candidate for the Bracondale riding in the 1948 general election. Just east of Dovercourt Avenue, the riding was a long, thin sliver extending from the waterfront to St. Clair Avenue. Although Premier George Drew's PC government was re-elected with a majority, Conboy was defeated by the Co-operative Commonwealth Federation's candidate.

In his personal life, Conboy was an avid golfer and served as president of the Wasaga Beach Golf and Country Club, was president of the Whitney Club, and was a member of the Argonaut Club. He was also a member of Clark Wallace Loyal Orange Lodge 961, Britannia Loyal Orange Lodge 1388, St. Andrew's Ancient Free and Accepted Masons, and the Independent Order of Odd Fellows. He was active with the Sigma Delta Fraternity and Kiwanis International, was superintendent of the Westmoreland United Church School, was honorary president of the Ontario Religious Education Council, and was a member of the executive of the Toronto Red Cross and the Toronto Branch of the Health League of Canada.

His health declining in late 1948 and early 1949, Conboy was struck by a car and admitted to Wellesley Hospital where he died on March 29, 1949. The *Toronto Daily Star* wrote: "This country needs more citizens of the Conboy type who will not begrudge time and effort in rendering service to the people in the realm of municipal government."[7]

Upon his death, a unanimous Council motion called Conboy "an outstanding citizen of his native city, a man of many parts, endowed with boundless energy, a great organizer, and a keen student of municipal government." It also lauded him as "a true leader of the people"[8] and paid tribute to the strength of his religious convictions. Conboy was married twice, and after the death of his first wife, Katherine McBrien of Orangeville, he married Lillian Edmondson in 1940.

Mayoral Election in 1941	
CANDIDATES	VOTES
Fred Conboy	55,729
Douglas McNish	33,069

Mayoral Election in 1942

City elections were held on January 1, 1942, and incumbent Fred Conboy was acclaimed as mayor.

Mayoral Election in 1943

City elections were held on January 1, 1943. For the second time in a row, incumbent Fred Conboy was acclaimed as mayor.

Mayoral Election in 1944	
Fred Conboy	78,995
Lewis Duncan	59,042

Mayor Robert Saunders

1945–1948

The 48th mayor of Toronto

Occupations: Criminal lawyer, City of Toronto alderman and controller, Ontario Hydro chair
Residence While Mayor: 100 Burnside Drive
Birth: May 30, 1903, in Toronto
Death: January 16, 1955, near London, Ontario

——— • ———

T all, ruggedly handsome, and impeccably dressed, the dynamic young
Toronto lawyer Robert Hood Saunders was Toronto's most charismatic
mayor, combining substantive policy and solid public relations with an
attractive and outgoing manner. As the first mayor at the conclusion of the
Second World War, he was a fitting symbol of Toronto's postwar hopes and
aspirations.

Saunders was born in Toronto in 1903 into a family of United Empire
Loyalists. The son of firefighter William Saunders and his wife, Rebecca
Barrisdale, he attended King Edward and Hillcrest Public Schools and
Oakwood Collegiate. An excellent orator and athlete, Saunders excelled in
rugby at Oakwood, yet was also interested in paddling, becoming a member
of the Toronto Canoe Club, where he later coached (1929–1931). He also
made a name for himself nationally as a championship canoeist.

After graduating from Osgoode Hall Law School in 1927, he entered
a law practice with Edward Murphy, and as a dashing young specialist in
criminal law, made a reputation for himself due to several notorious and
high-profile murder trials.

First entering municipal politics in 1935 when he was elected alderman
for Ward 4, Saunders held the seat until 1937. Then, for two elections in a
row, he was an unsuccessful candidate in city-wide runs for a seat on the
Board of Control. In 1940, he returned to Toronto's Council as an alderman,
and between 1941 and 1944, was finally successful in joining the Board of
Control.

Saunders served as senior controller and vice-chairman of the board in
1944, and in what was also an unspoken tradition at City Hall, was a member of the Loyal Orange Lodge, where he was a master. As well, he was a
member of the Colonati Masonic Lodge.

In 1945, at age 41, Saunders won the mayoralty, decisively beating the
much older veteran incumbent Fred Conboy, who had been mayor since
1940 and was seeking a fifth term. With 68,757 votes for Saunders and
36,299 for Conboy, the vigorous new mayor trumped his rival by more than
32,000 votes.

In the mid-1940s, it was recognized that the region's overall future growth would take place on vacant lands in the Etobicoke, North York, and Scarborough suburbs. Saunders, however, was ahead of the curve. In his 1945 election campaign, he presented a detailed, well-considered 29-point proposal for both the immediate and long-term planning of Toronto. Noting the city's enviable financial situation in his inaugural address to the Council, he announced that the city was "in a position to take care of proper expansion and a proper postwar program."[1]

His ambitious platform included reform of the civic administration, a new city master plan, and a major increase in public works, especially road improvements, as well as "slum" clearance and new public housing. He called for a comprehensive traffic plan, a new and revised Assessment Act, the elimination of industrial smoke problems, new Canadian National Exhibition facilities for a broader 12-month use, and the purchase of snow-removal equipment, a popular call after a crippling snowstorm on December 13, 1944.

Ironically, the January 22, 1945, edition of *Time* magazine put Toronto on the North American political map, not because of its dynamic new mayor but due to the publication's blazing headline, "Red Controller," which profiled Stewart Smith, the new Communist Party member of the Board of Control. According to an incredulous *Time*, Toronto had "elected a man who two years ago was an outlaw."[2] Indeed, polling over 41,000 votes in a city still considered a bastion of Protestant Conservatism was a remarkable showing for a leading Communist.

Saunders exhibited his active "can-do" spirit on his first day in office when he called the new Board of Control into session the very next day, instead of waiting the customary week. He wanted "an all-out push" to deal with snow clearing and the removal of more than 4,000 tonnes of garbage and ash that had been delayed by weather.

Interestingly, new ideas brought to the Council were not solely the brainchildren of Saunders, nor did he seek to take credit. Even in his inaugural address — a testament to his political skills — he highlighted various Council members involved with specific issues. What he did do successfully was claim credit for keeping various schemes, plans, and proposals moving.

As the city transitioned into the postwar era, a high-energy leader was needed, and the intelligent, popular, hard-working Saunders was a mayor who even though abrupt at times had the flourish of a showman. A later profile noted that he "had developed a technique of talking boldly, raising and lowering his voice for effect ... and subdues people who come to his office to bawl him out. Humour often lies behind his sternness.... Despite the fact he is a Tory mayor of a definitely Tory city, he has become noted for his reforms and his progressiveness."[3]

If there were two defining moments in 1945, they were the official ends to hostilities in Europe and the Pacific. Toronto erupted into a joyous celebration as perfect strangers danced, kissed, sang, drank, unfurled flags, waved banners, and threw streamers. Crowds poured into the streets and formed jubilant parades on Bay and Yonge Streets to celebrate the end of the war.

By 1946, Saunders had done so well that he was acclaimed mayor. His appeal to the electorate was a distinctive personal style, good public relations, and a dramatic flair. Some important questions were voted on that year, including building an extension to link Boor Street to North Toronto (today's Mount Pleasant Road) and constructing a new artery in the Don Valley (today's Don Valley Parkway). Both received strong support.

In his inaugural address to the 1946 Council, Saunders pledged continued action on several fronts, noting that of 19 prior commitments for immediate action made the year before, 14 had been carried out. Saunders vowed action on what he called "the nuisance of smoke" caused by steamships and railway locomotives, publicly calling for conversion to diesel or electric power. He called for an end to all level crossings in the city, the building of a brand-new courthouse, for Toronto to receive a portion of the gasoline tax, for better coordination of services with adjacent municipalities, and the elimination of wires and poles from city streets over several years. Saunders pointed out that streets had been laid out to accommodate horse-drawn vehicles, not 150,000 automobiles, so he called for an immediate review of congestion and parking.

Major postwar projects underway in 1946 included the TTC's "rapid transit subway" under Yonge Street after its overwhelming approval on the municipal ballot. A proposed 20 percent federal funding share never did materialize, so the original plans were reduced, with the line then estimated to cost $32.4 million ($522 million today) for both construction and subway cars.

With little serious opposition in the 1947 municipal election and seeking a third term, the increasingly popular Saunders received more than 92,000 votes in January 1947 against two token candidates who barely scraped up a combined 13,000 votes between them. By now, the charismatic Saunders had become the city's most popular political leader.

As the returning mayor, he pledged increased safety for the explosion of young postwar families and schoolchildren. He pointed to a variety of improvements, including the addition of more school crossings, 54 supervised playgrounds, 22 community centres, and 24 skating rinks. He pledged further progress on the Don Valley Roadway, as it was then called, and stated that hospitals should become a full provincial public responsibility.

Toronto's 1947 civic election also featured two important referendum questions that had a significant impact on the city for generations to come: the building of Regent Park housing just east of downtown and the purchase of all properties on the northwest corner of Bay and Queen Streets for a new City Hall and major municipal square that would take almost 20 more years to realize.

By 1948, Saunders was at the height of his popularity as mayor, receiving 118,097 votes to the Trotskyist Revolutionary Workers' Party candidate Ross Dowson's 15,008. Saunders's 1948 result was the highest total ever recorded for any municipal candidate in Toronto up to that point.

Continuously cultivating a political image as just an "ordinary good guy" and known to everyone simply as "Bob," the mayor seldom lost an opportunity to recount his days as a hard-working newsboy on College Street, his days as an athlete, or that he had married childhood sweetheart Marjorie Rennie.

Saunders also befriended New York City's dynamic and colourful mayor, Fiorello La Guardia ("the Little Flower"), who early on learned the political advantage of using broadcast media to communicate widely. In a bustling city where television had yet to arrive and would not become a household item for another decade, Saunders launched a Sunday radio program styled after that of New York's mayor. Saunders's show, *The Mayor Reports to the People*, was a combination of politics, information, commentary, and local issues, and La Guardia himself was the honoured first guest.

On a political level, there was a great deal of substance to Saunders. Although a Tory, he cut across political party lines and was known as a friend of Prime Minister Mackenzie King. He communicated a message of political inclusion — interested only in the development of the city and willing to co-operate with any worthy proposal, even, it was noted, if it were from Stewart Smith, the Communist Party member of the Council.

Saunders successfully styled himself as a friend of labour and signed the first closed-shop agreement with the civic employees' union. It was noted that organized labour, which had initially backed the mayor's opponent in 1945, had by 1948 swung around to support him.

Yet just a month and a half into his fourth term as mayor, Saunders received an offer he could not refuse. He announced that Premier George Drew had appointed him as the new chair of the Hydro-Electric Power Commission (Ontario Hydro) and that his resignation as mayor would take effect on February 23, 1948. The premier had convinced Saunders to come to the aid of an ailing provincial agency that needed strong, clear, and focused postwar direction.

For the next seven years, Saunders continued with a high-profile style as the public face of Ontario Hydro and also as its chief promoter, overseeing a major public corporation that was experiencing significant expansion in a province coping with its own growth challenges. Toronto's Council publicly lauded Saunders for "his capable and energetic leadership," noting that "outstanding progress was made in the development of additional hydro generating facilities to meet a critical shortage of electrical energy."[4]

One of Saunders's most important tasks was to develop hydro power along the St. Lawrence River corridor. Through his energy, persuasiveness, and ability to work with all levels, both in Canada and the United States, plans were brought to fruition and a start made on the construction of the St. Lawrence Seaway and Power Project, a gigantic joint international maritime venture.

Saunders travelled the length and breadth of the province as Ontario Hydro chair. On January 14, 1955, he boarded the plane after a speaking engagement in Windsor, Ontario. It was with a sense of deep sadness that the citizens of Toronto rose the next day to learn that the plane carrying their dynamic and popular ex-mayor had crashed upon its approach to London, Ontario, and that Saunders had died as a result of injuries.

For several days, Toronto newspapers highlighted Saunders's accomplishments, including his pivotal role in the August 10, 1954, official sod-turning of the St. Lawrence Seaway, brought to completion under his watch.

During his life, Saunders was a member of several city clubs: the Granite, Canoe, National Yacht, Optimist, and Lions. In 1946, he was also made a Commander of the British Empire. At the time of his death, Saunders was serving as the president of the Canadian National Exhibition, having been chosen to lead the board there in 1954. Saunders was also a member of St. Columba and St. George's United Church.

Mayoral Election in 1945	
CANDIDATES	VOTES
Robert Saunders	68,992
Frederick Conboy	36,389
Mayoral Election in 1946	
Robert Saunders was acclaimed mayor.	
Mayoral Election in 1947	
Robert Saunders	93,220
Frank O'Hearn	9,402
Murray Dowson	3,201
Mayoral Election in 1948	
Robert Saunders	122,927
Ross Dowson	15,423

Mayor Hiram McCallum
1948–1951

The 49th mayor of Toronto

Occupations: Newspaper clerk, commercial printer, City of Toronto alderman and controller, Canadian National Exhibition general manager
Residence While Mayor: 275 Glen Manor Road
Birth: August 14, 1899, in Caledon East, Peel County, Ontario
Death: January 13, 1989, in Toronto

——— • ———

Hiram Emerson McCallum was born on a farm near Caledon East in
Peel County in 1899, but his family moved to West Toronto two years
later. McCallum attended Western Avenue Public School, Humberside
Collegiate, and Central Technical School. As a young boy in Toronto,
McCallum pointed out years later that both he and his brother, Frank (later
a mayor of Oshawa), were proud of being "newsies," hawking daily newspapers on downtown street corners.

After completing high school, he became a clerk with the *Mail and
Empire* newspaper in 1918, and the next year moved with his family to a
ranch near Bow Island, Alberta. But in 1922, he returned to Toronto, becoming a salesman with the *Farmer's Sun* newspaper, a publication of the
United Farmers of Ontario, a new political party. In 1923, he took over as
the paper's business manager. And though he had been raised in the city's
west end, McCallum moved to the east end after his marriage in 1925 to
Margaret Dinsmore, his childhood sweetheart.

In 1926, he was appointed sales manager of Ontario Press, owned by
former mayor Horatio Hocken, gaining further practical experience in
the printing business. Five years later, despite the suffering of the Great
Depression, McCallum struck out on his own to establish McCallum Press
Ltd., a commercial printing company. Although he later recalled that the
first two years were indeed tough, McCallum soon found himself at the head
of a thriving business.

As a moderately successful businessman in the 1930s and with no plans
for a political career, McCallum became part of a small neighbourhood
group that banded together to do something about the pollution fouling
Toronto's eastern beaches. His first involvement in civic affairs was the need
for a sewage plant, the biggest issue in Ward 8.

Although first defeated in 1940 for Toronto's Council, he was successful during the next three years and was elected alderman in Ward 8 in
1941–1943. McCallum was able to help push through plans for a new sewage treatment plant, which he claimed had been held up by "obstructionist
elements."

In 1944, McCallum was defeated for a position on the city's Board of Control but gained election to the board in 1945, capturing its fourth spot, just behind the Communist Party's Stewart Smith. However, the following year, McCallum turned the tables, claiming the top spot on the board.

In 1946–1948, McCallum won the board's top position, becoming its vice-chair. Upon the resignation of Mayor Robert Saunders to become chairman of Ontario's Hydro-Electric Power Commission in 1948, McCallum was unanimously appointed mayor by the Council and became active with the Association of Ontario Mayors and Reeves. It was agreed by all that McCallum was the right person for the job, and in a reflection of the mood of the day, he pledged to carry on the Saunders-initiated program of improvements.

Years later a local publication, *Toronto Calling*, highlighted that McCallum's "fairness as a presiding officer, his good judgment in matters coming before the Board of Control and in council, his broad grasp of public questions, his wide vision and enthusiasm for the future of Toronto have inspired public confidence in his leadership."[1] Yet challenges abounded. Toronto's postwar prosperity brought with it a host of challenges, including transportation, traffic, housing, public health, welfare, social services, and budgetary needs.

Municipal elections were held on January 1, 1949, and McCallum was chosen on his own merit to a first full term, facing just minimal opposition from Trotskyist Ross Dowson, who captured 20 percent of the popular vote, one of the best results of any Communist mayoral candidate in a North American city.

During McCallum's mayoralty, the Toronto of the late 1940s and early 1950s was a stable and quiet yet somewhat drab city. Having fun in Toronto did not extend to Sundays when the city's "blue laws" left tourists scratching their heads. Conservatives, Prohibitionists, Protestants, and the Lord's Day Alliance left a strong mark on the city.

In his 1949 inaugural address, McCallum stated that traffic congestion was the city's worst problem. He lauded progress on a number of municipal initiatives, pointing out that 148 postwar projects were now underway, including the Ashbridges Bay sewage treatment plant, and referred to the splendid work of the new permanent Planning Board, first set up in 1946, noting that new street lighting would make Toronto the best-lit city in

North America. McCallum also proposed that Toronto open district offices to deal with licences, taxes, water bills, and recreation programs.

He publicly called for a new metropolitan-area form of government, for a greater share of the provincial gasoline tax, and for social welfare costs not to be borne by property taxes. McCallum also continued a program of mayoral Sunday radio broadcasts for Toronto — a growing city still very much a Protestant, British, and Orange enclave in a rapidly changing world.

Toronto's very first shopping centre was built in 1949. Sunnybrook Plaza was a small strip mall of 17 stores at the corner of Bayview and Eglinton Avenues. Meanwhile, construction of the Yonge Street subway finally got underway. The thoroughfare was marked by deep open trenches along its entire length, but residents still had to wait another five years before they were able to ride the new transit system. Progress also continued on Regent Park, described at the time as "the first public housing project in Canada," and in 1949, McCallum laid a cornerstone for the first of 56 units.

Construction of the Yonge Street subway, looking south toward Front Street from just south of King Street in 1949.

In January 1950, McCallum captured 132,839 votes to just 19,733 for Charles Mahoney, his closest opponent, with newspapers reporting it was the highest vote in Toronto's history for a winning mayoral candidate. It also marked another watershed moment: a ballot question asked voters if they were "in favour of the City of Toronto seeking legislation to make amateur, professional, and other forms of commercial sport legal on Sunday."[2] It narrowly won.

McCallum took dead aim at a number of political opponents in his 1950 inaugural address, denouncing what he called "communistic agitators" and declaring that "loyal Canadian citizens would not tolerate being governed by Russian-inspired and -controlled candidates." Proudly claiming Toronto as "one of the best governed cities in North America," he called for a hotel tax and for greater home ownership, noting that owners "have a stake in the community." Again, he pushed for a better structure to deal with region-wide metropolitan issues, including traffic, health, sewer, water, planning, and the location of industries in what he called "Greater Toronto." McCallum also tackled the need for new day nurseries, the intolerable condition of the city's court system, and the necessity to review the governance and administration of the Canadian National Exhibition (CNE) to ensure the ongoing success of what he called "the largest annual fair in the world."[3]

In December 1950, McCallum was almost defeated for the 1951 mayoral term, with 86,672 votes to controller Allan Lamport's 85,065. Although McCallum had faced just token opposition in previous elections, the vigorous Lamport came surprisingly close. The hotly contested mayoral fight was marked by a range of unrelated city-wide issues: a concerted effort to defeat the Communists on the Council and the strong election interest of Roman Catholic voters due to the candidacies of two highly outspoken Orangemen for the Board of Control.

In his 1951 inaugural address to the Council, McCallum stated that "war clouds are heavy in international skies ... the so-called 'Cold War,' which we have been experiencing for some time has thrown a cloak of uncertainty over world affairs."[4] He also dealt with civil defence and how Toronto should properly prepare itself for a possible nuclear attack.

The newly re-elected mayor again maintained that "much of the present-day difficulty stems from the efforts of Communism to gain control of the world ..." He referred to the 1951 civic election, pointing out that it had been a bitter campaign "of lies, insinuations, and half truths" and that Torontonians "must be continually on the alert to confound the efforts of the agents of Communism."[5]

McCallum called for the amalgamation of Toronto and its 12 neighbouring municipalities, proclaimed that city wage settlements were excessive, and said that a recent police arbitration was too high, pointing out that a new five-day police workweek would require hiring an extra 110 men. The mayor called for a new City Hall, new ferry docks, the burying of overhead wires, and a new lakeshore arterial expressway (later to become the Gardiner Expressway).

In 1951, it was reported that a deep, dark plan was about to be foisted on the citizens of Toronto: the city's very first parking meters. As a *Toronto Daily Star* editorial noted, "city council should turn down the proposal to install parking meters on a trial or any other basis. They do not solve the parking problem. Their supervision entails additional expense. The police have something better to do than read meters."[6]

And Ontario also witnessed some broad new changes. Premier Leslie Frost introduced the government's Fair Employment Practices Act, "the first measure of its kind in Canada." When adopted, it would make it "contrary to public policy in Ontario to discriminate against men and women in respect of their employment because of race, creed, color, nationality, ancestry, or place of origin."[7]

In October 1951, McCallum had the honour of presiding over the eagerly awaited royal visit by Princess (soon to be Queen) Elizabeth and the Duke of Edinburgh. Escorting the popular royals as they arrived, McCallum scored a shrewd public relations coup, announcing to everyone that he would simply hand them a copy of his elaborately prepared 1,200-word formal greeting, then read a simple 100-word official welcome.

Also in October 1951, McCallum announced he would seek re-election for a fifth mayoral term. Although 367,000 were eligible to vote, and in what was seen as a stunning upset, McCallum was defeated by insurance executive Allan Lamport, who ran under the slogan "Toronto Needs a Fighting Mayor,"[8] and received 72,616 votes to McCallum's 59,511.

In October 1952, McCallum was appointed general manager of the 142-hectare CNE and also continued to serve the city in a senior role as a member of the all-important Planning Board from its inception in 1953 and as its chair in 1961–1962.

As CNE general manager, McCallum played a central role in finding a new site for the Hockey Hall of Fame. In August 1955, the Canadian Sports Hall of Fame opened on the CNE grounds in Toronto. It also included a section called the National Hockey Hall of Fame. With McCallum on hand, the new Hall of Fame was opened by Prime Minister John Diefenbaker and U.S. ambassador Livingston Merchant in August 1961.

McCallum retired as CNE general manager in 1964, and in semi-retirement was put in charge of a special new civic project: the CNE's 1967 Centennial Exhibition celebrating Canada's 100th birthday. Upon leaving the CNE project, McCallum led a quiet life out of the public eye, yet surfaced in a July 1974 *Toronto Star* op-ed piece in which he strongly defended the CNE's operations and funding from what he termed political interference.

In 1980, McCallum and his wife moved to Guelph, Ontario, and spent summers in the Kawarthas and winters in Florida. Two years later, he was interviewed by Florida's *Sarasota Herald-Tribune*, saying that he had been a winter visitor there since 1965. He noted that his proudest accomplishments as mayor had been the construction of the most modern of sewage treatment plants, calling it "water recycling," and the approval of the city's first subway. McCallum pointed out that there had been two stark choices: automobiles or transit. Detroit, he observed, was an auto-oriented city that opted for interstate highways, while Toronto had chosen subway transit.

McCallum was an active member of the Progressive Conservative Party, Kew Beach United Church, John Ross Robertson Loyal Orange Lodge, and Wilson Masonic Lodge 86 of the Ancient Free and Accepted Masons. He also served as president of the Beaches Lions Club and was a member of the Toronto Board of Trade, Canadian Red Cross Society, and National Society of Housing Officials. In addition, he was a member of the Toronto Flying, Scarboro Golf, Royal Canadian, Queen City, National Yacht, and West End Toronto Juvenile Football Clubs. He was also on the management committee of the East End Young Men's Christian Association.

In January 1989, McCallum died in Guelph General Hospital, leaving his wife, Margaret; son, Bruce; and daughter, Dorothy. His funeral took place at Harcourt United Church in Guelph, far from the bustle of Toronto's City Hall.

Mayoral Election in 1949

CANDIDATES	VOTES
Hiram McCallum	97,759
Ross Dowson	23,645

Mayoral Election in 1950 (Held on January 2, 1950)

SPECIAL NOTE: Instead of yearly civic elections being held on or close to New Year's Day, the annual election date was changed to the first week of December and the Council term itself began on January 1. As a result of this modification, there were two municipal elections held in 1950. One was in January for 1950, the other in December for the 1951 term of the Council.

Hiram McCallum	132,839
Charles Mahoney	19,733
Ross Dowson	15,576

Mayoral Election for 1951 (Held on December 4, 1950)

Hiram McCallum	86,672
Allan Lamport	85,065

Mayor Allan Lamport

1952–1954

The 50th mayor of Toronto

Occupations: Airline owner, insurance executive, Member of Ontario Legislative Assembly, Royal Canadian Air Force squadron leader, City of Toronto alderman and controller, Toronto Transit Commission vice-chairman and chairman, Maple Leaf Gardens public-relations associate, philanthropist
Residence While Mayor: 84 Harper Avenue
Birth: April 4, 1903, in Toronto
Death: November 18, 1999, in Toronto

——— • ———

The son of lawyer William Lamport and Alice Wood and one of four boys, Allan Austin Lamport was born in April 1903 in a house on Avenue Road near the tracks at Dupont Street. A few years later, the Lamports moved to Parkdale where Allan attended Queen Victoria Public School, and from 1917 to 1919, Central Technical High School. Parkdale is also where he met lifelong friend Harold Ballard, who became the high-profile millionaire owner of both the Toronto Maple Leafs and Maple Leaf Gardens.

From 1919 to 1923, Lamport attended the city's poshest private boy's school, Upper Canada College, where he was known as a talented and outgoing athlete who excelled in sports. Upon graduation, Lamport began a highly varied career that included football, construction, automobile sales, aviation, real estate, insurance, and politics. In 1923, he first tried out for the Toronto Argonauts football team, then moved to Thessalon, Ontario, to work with the Hope Lumber Company for two years before returning to the city. Back in Toronto, he worked as a sales manager with the Durant Automobile Agency.

Lamport also took up flying as a hobby, obtaining his pilot's licence, and soon after, founded the Century Airway Company, Toronto's first commercial airplane business. It was a modest firm involved with flight instruction and was one of the earliest air mail services. In 1929, he sold Century for a profit and also prospered with the establishment of Barker Airfield, then on Lawrence Avenue West.

He moved into the insurance business in 1930, establishing A.A. Lamport and Company, and also married Edythe Thompson. Settling in the leafy Moore Park area of North Toronto, he became active with the ratepayers' association, using it as a base to run for Toronto's Council. In 1932, he became a major community advocate for the long-discussed road link from Jarvis Street to St. Clair Avenue, an issue strongly supported in North Toronto.

Lamport was elected vice-president of the Moore Park Association in 1936, and though unsuccessful in his first Ward 2 Council race, later defeated the incumbent in 1937. That same year, Lamport was elected to

Ontario's Legislative Assembly as the Liberal MPP for St. David's riding from 1937 to 1943. While an MPP, "Lampy," as he was fondly known in his riding, served as a member of six standing committees in the assembly.

Always generous of heart, years later he recalled in the *Toronto Star*: "When I was first elected, people would come to me for help. There was no welfare. Times were hard. I couldn't see them not having coal. I'd buy them half a ton … I used to buy coal, rubber boots, a bag of groceries. Everyone has to be considerate of the other, this is the main teaching of life."[1]

While serving simultaneously on both Toronto's Council and at Queen's Park — allowed at the time — Lamport joined a key committee overseeing the planning, financing, and construction of new airports on the Toronto Islands and at Malton (today's Lester B. Pearson International Airport). In 1939, he also enlisted in the Royal Canadian Air Force (RCAF) where his pilot's experience, political savvy, and administrative abilities were put to good use.

In the Legislative Assembly, Lamport demonstrated a knack for grabbing headlines. Flying Officer Lamport rose in the assembly in 1941 to attack a "black-hearted American quisling,"[2] automobile manufacturer Henry Ford, for his total lack of sympathy for Canada's war effort, advocating a number of measures so that Ford would not enjoy any profits from his Canadian operations.

The RCAF magically transferred Lamport to the East Coast, whereupon he lost his St. David's seat to the union-supported Co-operative Commonwealth Federation candidate (and later Toronto mayor) William Dennison in 1943. Lamport left the air force in 1945 with the rank of squadron leader and again returned to municipal politics in 1946, serving three years as alderman in Ward 3.

In 1949 and 1950 Lamport was elected as a controller and took part in the hurly-burly of postwar development and expansion. Yet one issue was Lampy's alone: allowing sports in Toronto on Sundays. With strong opposition in the media, vocal denunciation from traditionalists and the deeply religious, and virtually no support from Council colleagues, he manoeuvred the question onto the 1950 election ballot. When asked if they supported making amateur, professional, and commercial sports legal on Sundays, Toronto's electorate defied conventional wisdom and agreed that it was time. Lamport was also re-elected to the Board of Control, setting the stage for a mayoral run the following year. But Lamport was defeated in 1951 for mayor by incumbent Hiram McCallum. His flamboyant, outgoing, populist style was pitted against the quiet reserve, steadiness, and conservatism of McCallum, and he fell short by only 1,600 votes.

When up against McCallum again in 1952, Lamport won the mayoralty this time with a surprising majority of more than 13,000 votes. With the catchy slogan "Toronto Needs a Fighting Mayor," he captured 72,616 votes to McCallum's 59,511, with another 24,797 going to veteran councillor Nathan Phillips.

In his 1952 inaugural address, Lamport called for a "closer unification of the greater Toronto area" and for the city to oppose any fare increase by the Toronto Transportation Commission (TTC). He proposed that parking tickets be paid at local police stations and declared that law and order would be "a constant aim" of his administration. In 1952, the city's first 11 parking meters were installed downtown, and within just a few weeks, a total of 1,300 were charging 10 cents for a half-hour stay.

Lamport won easily against Nathan Phillips, a courtly veteran alderman, in December 1952 (for the 1953 term). He noted in his inaugural

Members of Toronto's Council in the chambers of Old City Hall in 1952. Almost 120 years after the city's founding in 1834, the Council was still overwhelmingly made up of white, male, middle-class, Protestant homeowners.

address that he was pleased that electors had approved completion of the Regent Park housing project and that it was the first year that the Port of Toronto had met all financial obligations without seeking assistance. As mayor, Lamport helped bring in the city's first comprehensive zoning and planning bylaws and announced that Toronto would be one of nine cities in the world bidding to host the 1960 Summer Olympic Games.

In December 1953, Lamport won a tighter race, this time against school board trustee Arthur Brown. It proved far closer than anyone expected. Brown had never run for or held city-wide office yet came within 9,000 votes of winning. A key issue of the campaign was the introduction of rent controls, which Lamport opposed and Brown favoured.

Lamport reported on the progress of the Don Roadway (today's Don Valley Parkway), the Lakeshore Expressway (now the Gardiner Expressway), and the Spadina Road (later to become the ill-fated Spadina Expressway) in his 1954 inaugural address. He also called for a proper air terminal building on the Toronto Islands and a bridge over the Eastern Gap to make it more accessible.

Postwar Toronto was beginning to resemble the major North American cities, and in March 1954, Lamport officiated with Premier Leslie Frost at the opening of the Yonge Street subway. After five arduous years of construction, it soon carried 250,000 passengers per day. Torontonians were also thrilled to welcome a new monarch in 1953, and Lamport, accompanied by his family, represented the city at the coronation of Queen Elizabeth II.

Yet the most important development of Lamport's mayoralty was the introduction of a metropolitan system of government. While Toronto's Council had voted against it 19–1, Lamport was the lone vote in favour and later reminisced that the metro level of government was just an interim step toward amalgamation.

Always a bon vivant in the manner of legendary New York mayor Jimmy Walker, Lampy saw to it that the nickname "Toronto the Good" also meant a good life for its mayor. Over two years, from 1952 to 1954, he spent $46,000 ($502,000 today) on champagne, steaks, wine, cocktails, liqueurs, cigars, flowers, and room service in suite 1735 at the Royal York Hotel. Although entirely paid for by city taxpayers, it was without the prior knowledge, consent, or approval of Toronto's Council.

Lamport proudly claimed that the city's explosion of growth began during his term as mayor and pointed to improvements in street lighting, new underground wiring, the removal of telephone poles from Yonge Street, low-income housing, and the cleanup of crime. As mayor, Lamport also had a hand in ending some of the city's small-town bigotry by shunning hard-line Protestants and refusing to ride in the annual Orangeman's Parade.

On June 28, 1954, Lamport resigned as mayor to become a commissioner of the now-renamed Toronto Transit Commission (TTC), then a highly prestigious post. He served first as vice-chair, then as chair from 1955 to 1959, fought for a new TTC headquarters at Yonge Street and Davisville Avenue, and believed that increased development would come with subway lines, not through greater expressway building. During his chairmanship, he was instrumental in securing approval of the first section of the east-west Bloor-Danforth subway line and getting the Council to borrow $200 million ($2.1 billion today) to begin construction of the first stage.

In 1960, Lamport resigned from the TTC after repeated clashes over political interference with the commission, and again ran for mayor that December but was defeated by incumbent Nathan Phillips. A central election issue that also resonated decades later was the continued expansion of Toronto's subway system and how to pay for it.

Lamport was again elected to the Board of Control, serving for the 1963–1964 term. And after the sudden death of Don Summerville in November 1963 and Phil Givens succeeding him, Lamport once more chose to run for mayor, only to see Givens prevail with 82,696 votes to just 52,175 for Lamport.

In December 1966, Lamport captured the last spot on the four-member Board of Control, serving from 1967 to 1969. In the midst of the swinging sixties, he was a traditionalist who railed against birth control clinics and hippies. He helped chair a committee seeking to secure the 1976 Summer Olympics and actively fought the abolition of the city-wide Board of Control.

After the Board of Control's demise, Lamport ran successfully as an alderman for Ward 2 from 1970 to 1972 but was not selected for the newly created Executive Committee. As a Council veteran from eclectic Parkdale, he regularly faced off against a young, long-haired John Sewell, the new leather-jacketed downtown councillor and community activist.

In November 1972, Lampy announced his retirement from politics but remained active with Variety Village, the CNE, Canada's Baseball Hall of Fame, and the American Power Boat Association. In addition, he was a founding member and vice-commodore of the Canadian Boating Federation. In 1987, Lamport was given the city's highest local honour, the Civic Award of Merit, by Mayor Art Eggleton. In April 1993, a large 90th birthday party was organized for him, which raised money for Variety Village.

During his very busy personal life, Lamport was a member of a wide range of organizations: the Royal Canadian Yacht Club, the Granite Club, the Empire Club, the Royal Canadian Military Institute, the Air Force Association, the Canadian Legion, the Independent Order of Foresters, the Masons, the "Ulster Black Watch" Loyal Orange Lodge 675 of Toronto, the Fraternal Order of the Eagles, the Order of the Moose, the Upper Canada Old Boys' Association, the Toronto Flying Club, the Goodfellowship Club, Variety Club International, and the Argonaut Rowing Club.

In 1994, Lamport was named to the Order of Canada. As well, the city's Lamport Stadium was named in his honour. Always talking politics, the still fit, active, and very outgoing Lamport kept busy as the principal host at the iconic Hot Stove Club at Maple Leaf Gardens, a favourite watering hole for Toronto's corporate elite and keenest hockey fans. Lamport remained single after the death of his wife, Edythe, in 1965 and kept in close touch with his two daughters, Jane (Day) and Suzanne (Sievenpiper).

Allan Lamport died on November 18, 1999, in Sunnybrook Hospital, age 96, surrounded by family, after suffering a massive stroke. After visitations at the Ralph Day Funeral Home on Danforth Avenue, his funeral was held in St. Paul's Anglican Cathedral in Toronto.

Former mayor Art Eggleton called Lamport "an icon ... probably one of the greatest mayors of the millennium." Eggleton noted that "he ushered in a new era, and I think he was one of the most respected and beloved Torontonians."[3] Bob Macdonald of the *Toronto Sun* called him the "Mr. Toronto of the 20th century ... Lampy dragged Toronto kicking and screaming into the 20th century."[4] And as *Toronto Star* columnist George Gamester pointed out, "when one of his most distinguished successors, David Crombie, salutes Lampy as Toronto's 'mayor of the century' who will seriously argue?"[5]

Mayoral Election for 1952	
CANDIDATES	**VOTES**
Allan Lamport	72,616
Hiram McCallum	59,511
Nathan Phillips	24,797
Mayoral Election for 1953	
Allan Lamport	81,468
Nathan Phillips	41,907
Mayoral Election for 1954	
Allan Lamport	55,060
Arthur Brown	46,135

SPECIAL NOTE: Leslie Saunders was appointed mayor in 1954 when Allan Lamport resigned, then was defeated by Nathan Phillips in the 1955 election.

Mayor Leslie Saunders

1954

The 51st mayor of Toronto

Occupations: Rail worker, union leader, Town of North Bay councillor, printer, journalist, Orange Lodge official, Toronto Board of Education trustee, City of Toronto alderman and controller, mayor of East York, Metropolitan Toronto councillor, Imperial Grand Orange Council of the World president, author
Residence While Mayor: 62 Glenwood Crescent
Birth: September 12, 1899, in London, England
Death: March 30, 1994, in Toronto

——— • ———

T he second-last member of the Loyal Orange Lodge to become mayor of Toronto (William Dennison was the last), Leslie Howard Saunders counted the Orange Order, the British monarchy, the Protestant religion, and civic life as the passions of his life.

Saunders was born in London, England, on September 12, 1899, and with his family came to North Bay, Ontario, in 1906 where he attended public schools. "Les," as he was known, was the son of a rail worker for the Canadian Pacific Railway who had chosen to settle in the small lakeside Northern Ontario town. In his later autobiography, Saunders recalled how at nine years old he regarded kids from Catholic schools as "different" and would take another route home from school to avoid them.

In 1912, Saunders left school and began a career with the Temiskaming and Northern Ontario Railway (T&NO), which later became the Ontario Northland Railway. After the outbreak of the First World War, Saunders, just 16, joined the Canadian Army in February 1916, along with his father and two brothers. He served with the 97th Regiment, and later, overseas with the 1st Algonquin Regiment (159th Battalion). Saunders was wounded in action near Vimy Ridge in 1916 in a German attack that resulted in 38 casualties. Returning home to North Bay in 1917, he again worked for the T&NO.

After his war service, Saunders became secretary-general of the local Great War Veterans' Association, and from 1918 to 1926 was a member of the association's Provincial Command. From 1926 to 1930, he also served on the provincial executive of the Royal Canadian Legion in Ontario.

As a clerk with the T&NO, Saunders was an active trade unionist and became president of the local chapter of the Canadian Brotherhood of Railway Employees. He was also active with the Salvation Army and was a vocal anti-alcohol advocate. During these years, he became a fervent Orangeman and a rising star.

In 1921, he married Rose Clarke of Englehart, Ontario, in what was the first Salvation Army marriage performed in North Bay. Two years later, Saunders entered political life, becoming a member of North Bay's Council and beginning a 37-year-long political career. He served for four years before moving to Toronto in 1928 when he was hired by leading Orangeman and former Toronto mayor Horatio Hocken to become business manager of the Orange Order's influential twice-weekly *Sentinel* for the princely sum of $50 per week ($850 per week today).

For the next decade, Saunders was closely involved in the issues, policies, and business affairs of the Orange Order, acting as a provincial field agent, meeting with groups, organizing lodges across Ontario, and heading up the 34,000-member Grand Lodge of Ontario West from 1929 to 1931. Yet in 1936, believing that the *Orange Sentinel* was not taking a strong enough stand against Catholic schools, Saunders founded a rival publication, *Protestant Action*, that became the voice of militant Protestantism in Ontario.

Separate school funding, vehemently opposed by the Orange Lodge, was the pathway for Saunders to re-enter political life in 1938 as a candidate for school trustee in Toronto. Elected in 1939, he later served with the Public School Trustees' Association. As a very active spokesperson for the Orange Order, he also published a book in 1941, *The Story of Orangeism*, dedicated to "the Christian church, Canada, and the Empire."[1]

In January 1942, Saunders was elected to Toronto's Council as alderman for Ward 1, heading the polls after a campaign focused on Orange issues. He was attacked by the *Catholic Register*, which declared him "A Venomous [and] bigoted Anti-Catholic agitator."[2] Saunders proudly claimed that 16 of the 23 councillors were members of the Orange Order and gained wide notoriety for refusing to stand for "O Canada" due to his belief that "God Save the King" was the true national anthem. He retained his Ward 1 seat until the end of 1944.

In March 1943, upon the introduction of a motion by Jewish councillor Nathan Phillips protesting the persecution of Jews by the Nazis, Saunders observed that Canada's Jewish population was not contributing enough to the war effort. In 1945, he failed in his attempt to win city-wide election to the four-member Board of Control. That same year, he sought the Progressive Conservative Party nomination for the provincial riding of Riverdale but lost narrowly to an aldermanic colleague.

Saunders opened his own printing business, Britannia Printers, in 1946. That same year, he pointed out there was "strong opposition" to officially receiving James McGuigan, the Roman Catholic archbishop of Toronto, who had become the first English-speaking cardinal in Canada. When the cardinal was welcomed on the steps of City Hall by a Salvation Army official, Saunders protested publicly, calling for the official "to be reprimanded for his uncalled-for actions." Toronto was "a Protestant City,"[3] Saunders insisted, and Catholics had no right to parade through the streets.

Without the endorsement of any of the major dailies, Saunders failed to gain re-election to the Council in 1945 and 1946 but won back his former aldermanic seat in 1947, serving for two years before again trying for the Board of Control. In 1949, he finally won a seat there, capturing 57,745 votes; the following year he received 88,030 votes.

Saunders topped the race for the 1954 Board of Control, becoming its vice-chairman, and forged a political accommodation with Mayor Allan Lamport. A host of issues were discussed at the Council in 1954: the hiring of telephone operators for City Hall, traffic islands "on wide city streets," the men's hostel in St. Lawrence Hall, an upcoming major Dominion-Provincial Conference on Unemployment, winter boat service to the Toronto Islands, the awarding of formal "Certificates of Lunacy,"[4] the prohibition of neon signs, and quality control of all civic typewriters.

In presenting the budget estimates in June 1954, Saunders noted that with an increase in growth, assessment, taxation, and revenues, no services had been cut or lost funding. Upon the June 1954 resignation of Mayor Lamport to become a Toronto Transit Commission commissioner, a highly sought position at the time, Saunders was appointed to serve out the balance of the mayoral term. One of his first acts was to depart for Saskatoon where he was elected deputy grand master of the Orange Lodge in Canada.

At Toronto City Hall, controversy was always a constant, the result of Saunders's rabid ultra-Protestant views. He became widely known across the province for his strong opposition to Roman Catholic schools and to any form of bilingualism. As a devout Protestant, he also strongly opposed Sunday sports and cocktail bars in the city.

In his capacity as the new Orange deputy grand master, he caused immediate friction when his first public pronouncement as mayor was a letter to celebrate the July 12 Orangeman's Day, extolling King William III's 1690 victory over Catholics at the Battle of the Boyne and reminding Torontonians "of their British heritage" and how important the battle had been. The problem was that the letter was issued on the official stationery of the mayor of Toronto, with Saunders comparing the victory over Catholics to recent battles against "the Hun, the Nazi, and the Fascist."

The widely reprinted letter resulted in his vilification in the media, and by never apologizing, Saunders lost the support of a cross-section of the community. That controversy, as well as his anti-Catholic ramblings, were defining factors in his defeat by Nathan Phillips, who became the city's first non-Protestant mayor.

While Saunders proudly ran on "Leslie Saunders, Protestant," Phillips ran to be "Mayor of All the People." Another nail in Saunders's coffin came in the form of an election ad featuring prominent Torontonians supposedly supporting his campaign, yet several who were listed publicly declared they did not.

Saunders was opposed by a diverse range of interests: Sunday sports enthusiasts, Jews, communists, separate school supporters, Liberals, labour groups, devout Catholics, and both Toronto's *Telegram* and the *Toronto Daily Star*. With his 40,707 votes, the affable and courtly Phillips won the mayoral race, defeating Saunders, who received 36,751 votes, and veteran school trustee Arthur Brown with 36,648.

Refusing a formal concession, Saunders blamed the press and non-Orange population for engineering his electoral defeat and held Brown accountable for "splitting the Christian and Gentile vote."[5] For the 1956 term, Saunders captured the last spot on the four-member Board of Control, yet a year later failed to retain a board seat for the 1957–1958 term when Jean Newman became the first woman in Toronto to be elected to a city-wide position.

Saunders continued his high-profile involvement with the Orange Lodge and subsequently became politically active in East York where he operated a printing business. Running for reeve there in 1960, he was defeated but was elected to the East York Township Council in 1961 and became a political fixture, arguing against Canada's Flag Day celebrations because the prior Red Ensign had been removed as Canada's national flag.

In April 1976, he was chosen to be East York's chief magistrate as well as a member of Metro Council to complete the term of Willis Blair, who had been appointed to the Ontario Municipal Board. Then he was re-elected to East York's Council as an alderman for a final term before retiring in 1978.

On the Council, Saunders refused to support "Now Is Not Too Late," a major 1977 report on race relations prepared by the Ryerson Polytechnic Institute and Metro Toronto's Task Force on Human Relations. Saunders called it a waste of money, noting that the 1978 Orange Parade was composed of 4,000 members, 25 bands, and 150 participating lodges, and that the Orange Order was the second-largest fraternal society in Canada. He claimed that Mayor John Sewell had snubbed Toronto Orangemen in 1979 by ignoring a cenotaph ceremony, yet had time that year to attend what he called "a homosexual affair."

The title of his autobiography, *An Orangeman in Public Life*, summed up Saunders's personal, fraternal, religious, political, social, and business life. It detailed a range of stories: how separatists were keeping English out of Quebec, the "mistake" of the federal Commission on Bilingualism and Biculturalism, and Quebec's "tax evasion."

Over several decades, Saunders moved through the ranks of the Orange Order from his first initiation into Loyal Orange Lodge 876 in North Bay in 1918 to serving as the lodge's master in 1922. He became the grand master of the Lodge of Ontario West from 1929 to 1931, one of the youngest ever to serve in that position. At the time, the Orange Order was the strongest single voting bloc in civic politics.

Upon moving to Toronto, he joined Loyal Orange Lodge 375 where he remained a member until 1944 when he formed Loyal Orange Lodge 137. Shortly after stepping down as Toronto's mayor in January 1955, Saunders served as grand master of the Grand Orange Lodge of British America from 1957 to 1960 and also from 1964 to 1967. That was followed by a very rare distinction for a Canadian: appointment as the Orange Order's highest global official. From 1967 to 1970, he was president of the Imperial Grand Orange Council of the World.

In 1984, Saunders registered his strong opposition to the provincial decision to fund Roman Catholic high schools and supported the Orange Order's mounting of a legal challenge. In the late 1980s, he remained a faithful participant in the city's annual Orangeman's Parade to express his fervent objection to federal immigration policy, separate school funding, and the expansion of French-language services in Ontario.

During a busy life, Saunders was a member of the Empire Club of Canada, Rehoboam Masonic Lodge 65, the St. George's Society, the

Christian Businessmen's Association, the Canadian Legion, and Loyal Orange Lodge 1 in Brockville, Ontario.

Saunders died of cancer on March 30, 1994, in the Scarborough Salvation Army Grace Hospital, age 94. He was predeceased by his wife, Rose, in 1991, and survived by his four children: Howard, Margaret (Carter), Dorothy (Watkin), and Joy (Uden).

His funeral consisted of an Orange Order fraternal service at the House of Orange on Kennedy Road and St. Clair Avenue in Scarborough, followed by a funeral service at the Salvation Army's Agincourt Temple on Birchmount Road near Steeles Avenue.

Mayor Nathan Phillips
1955–1962

The 52nd mayor of Toronto

Occupations: Lawyer, City of Toronto alderman, Metropolitan Toronto councillor, community leader, philanthropist, author
Residence While Mayor: 26 Lauder Avenue
Birth: November 7, 1892, in Brockville, Ontario
Death: January 7, 1976, in Toronto

— • —

Nathan Phillips was born on November 7, 1892, in Brockville, Ontario, one of six children of shopkeeper Jacob Phillips and Mary Rosenbloom. The family then moved to Cornwall where he was educated at elementary and high schools. As Phillips later recounted in his autobiography, *Mayor of All the People*, "People knew each other and people were accepted for what they were. That was the only standard. I don't recall a single incident of prejudice or bigotry on account of race or religion."[1]

In 1908, Phillips articled as a law clerk to Cornwall lawyer Robert Smith, who later became a Supreme Court justice. He also supported himself by working as a photographer and moved to Toronto to attend Osgoode Hall, graduating in the spring of 1913. Phillips was forced to wait until his 21st birthday before being called to the bar in 1914, then entered the practice of law in the offices of William Laidlaw.

He married Esther Lyons in March 1917, and they had two children, Madeline and Howard (who served as a Toronto alderman from 1949 to 1956). In 1919, Phillips opened his own legal office in the Temple Building at Bay and Richmond Streets, gradually building a large general practice, though also admitting that he did enjoy the drama and oratorical flourish of the courts.

Phillips first entered local political life in 1923. Although a member of the Ward 4 Conservative Association, he ran for alderman without its support in a seat vacated due to the retirement of Ethel Small, then the city's second female member of Toronto's Council. In his first political campaign, Phillips spent $1,200 ($20,000 today) on his election effort, winning one of the ward's three aldermanic positions and serving as alderman in it for the next 28 years.

In 1929, Phillips was appointed a King's Counsel (KC) at age 36 in recognition of acting as Crown counsel at various assizes in the province. It was believed that he was the youngest KC in the British Commonwealth. A member of several Jewish organizations and the Masonic Lodge, Phillips was also active with the Conservative Party, yet on three separate occasions his ambition to reach higher office was thwarted. In 1935, he ran unsuccessfully in the Spadina riding during the 1935 federal election, and in both the 1937 and 1948 provincial campaigns, he lost in the neighbouring riding of St. Andrew's. Later, Phillips set his sights on the mayoralty: "I always considered the office of Mayor of the City of Toronto as one of the half-dozen important political positions in Canada."

In late 1951, age 59, Phillips lost his first bid for the mayoralty to Allan Lamport, a race in which he ran a poor third. As he later noted, "When it became public knowledge that I was to be a candidate for mayor, it wasn't received favourably by the regular establishment of Toronto. To them a mayor of Toronto of the Jewish faith was unpalatable."[2] Lamport again defeated him in the 1953 mayoral race. After Lamport resigned in mid-1954 to become a member of the Toronto Transit Commission, Phillips entered the 1955 mayoral race against controversial interim mayor Leslie Saunders and school trustee Arthur Brown.

Saunders publicly proclaimed that he was running for mayor as "Leslie Saunders, Protestant," pointing to a personal record as a key Orange leader and publisher of the monthly *Protestant Action* newspaper. His long-held and widely known anti-Catholic views and his public declaration that Toronto was "a Protestant city" triggered strong local reaction.

Phillips's electoral win marked a major change in staid Toronto: he was the first mayor in the city's history who was not a white Anglo-Saxon Protestant male with family roots in the British Isles. The *Globe and Mail* pointed out that Phillips's election reflected a spirit of religious and racial tolerance among the citizens of Toronto, noting that fewer than half of Canadians at that time were British by descent and that "for the first time in history Torontonians have chosen a member of the Jewish faith as their civic leader. Only a few years ago, such a selection would have been considered highly unlikely."[3]

He developed a strong hold on the mayor's office almost immediately, championing the construction of a new city cultural centre, which later opened in 1960 as the O'Keefe Centre. In March 1955, Phillips began *The Mayor Reports*, a weekly broadcast carried over three radio stations for the next eight years. He also called upon the federal government to loan the money to Toronto, interest-free, for the construction of the city's first east-west subway line.

After just a year in office, Phillips was easily re-elected for the 1956 term. He was opposed by Roy Belyea, a controller with whom he had been at odds all year. A ballot question to approve funds of $18 million ($191 million today) for the construction of a new City Hall was rejected by voters, with 32,640 voting against and just 28,497 in favour.

Ironically, that rejection led to the development of today's iconic new City Hall. University of Toronto architecture students called the original design "dull and uninteresting, a funeral home of vast dimensions" and comparable to the latest in Soviet Union architecture. After that, Phillips supported an international design competition.

By the end of 1956, his campaign for the two-year 1957–1958 mayoral term was a foregone conclusion. Phillips racked up 80,494 votes to limited opposition from the Communist Party's Ross Dowson. Another major change occurred when Toronto residents voted to extend the civic electoral franchise to all qualifying citizens over 21 who were British subjects. It was a major victory for boarders, tenants, and renters, with Phillips noting that it lifted the stigma of "second-class citizenship" from a large body of the city's population.

As mayor, Phillips was at the forefront of guiding the city through the late 1950s, a time of growth, modernization, industrialization, and increased immigration. An amendment to the city's zoning bylaw in 1957 proposed regulations governing the height, bulk, location, and spacing of buildings; the provision of off-street parking in conjunction with these buildings; and criteria for landscaped open space. Traffic was a major headache, with serious bottlenecks and more cars causing the mayor to declare it "one of the most vexing problems facing our community."[4]

Yet the signature issue of Phillips's mayoralty was the planning, selection, development, and construction of a new City Hall. In mid-September 1957, an international design competition was approved, with Eric Arthur, a respected professor of architecture at the University of Toronto, becoming the Council's professional adviser. By the April 1958 deadline, 510 architects from 42 countries submitted the required detailed plans and actual scale models for their visions of the new City Hall. In September, Phillips announced that the "breathtaking" design of Finland's Viljo Revell was the jury's final choice.

Phillips again sought re-election in 1958 for the 1959–1960 term. The *Toronto Daily Star* published a wide-ranging pre-election feature titled "'Nate'

Phillips: Social Butterfly or Mayor of All the People?" advising readers, "Here in a new and candid light is the ebullient and white-shocked man everyone calls Nate. His critics say he's a party-goer who doesn't know the score."[5]

Election issues included a major redevelopment of the south side of Queen Street, affordable housing at Moss Park, the creation of new parks, a bylaw proposing a parking space ratio for every new apartment unit, the escalating construction costs of the new City Hall, and whether Phillips spent too much time attending social engagements as mayor.

Phillips captured 53,834 votes, a greater number than both of his top two competitors combined. Priorities for the 1959–1960 term included slum clearance and new public housing, the commercial redevelopment of downtown, the push for Toronto to become a major convention city, and a much-needed east-west subway line.

A popular and highly social mayor, Phillips attended a never-ending series — sometimes up to six or seven per night — of civic receptions, banquets, conventions, testimonials, speeches, dinners, and social functions. The mayor considered all that to be important work, taking his job right out to the people.

The mayoralty race for the 1961–1962 term was a lively affair. Phillips, by then the city's six-year incumbent chief magistrate, faced a strong election challenge by two prominent, high-profile contenders — controller Jean Newman, the first woman elected city-wide, and the irascible yet still popular Allan "Lampy" Lamport, driven around the city in what the *Toronto Daily Star* referred to as a "Pied Piper" convertible "loaded with children's loot of 5,000 balloons and 300 pounds of peppermint kisses."[6]

Phillips easily prevailed, though, coming in almost 24,000 votes ahead of Lamport, yet the election foreshadowed changes to come: the popular up-and-coming young controller Don Summerville, elected with 112,226 votes city-wide, received 30,000 more than Phillips, then the incumbent mayor. Summerville was clearly the most popular elected official in Toronto.

For his part, Phillips pledged to push through new zoning regulations, a recently completed report on urban renewal, and anticipated recommendations on civic efficiency. "The next two years will be two of the most challenging"[7] in the city's history, he declared.

On November 7, 1961, his 69th birthday, Phillips received the best present of all: presiding over the sod-turning ceremony for the new City Hall and a major open square, which two months previously had been unanimously named Nathan Phillips Square by members of Toronto's Council. By December 1962, incumbent Nathan Phillips had served with distinction longer than any other mayor in the city's history, dealing with growth, expansion, redevelopment, and social change in a burgeoning metropolis emerging as a major global city.

Although Phillips at first appeared unbeatable for re-election to the 1963–1964 term, that proved not to be the case. Many political observers expected him to retire, yet he doggedly announced his determination to once more seek re-election. With no major daily newspapers supporting him this time, Phillips faced the younger Don Summerville, whom he later described as "the most aggressive member of council that ever sat with me. He had a natural ability to promote controversy and he always selected areas that had newspaper and election appeal."[8] The incumbent mayor's own platform was "Phillips gets the big jobs done — smoothly, efficiently, and without contention."[9]

In the end, Phillips suffered a crushing defeat, receiving just 48,163 votes for mayor to 118,196 for Summerville. "No one ever got a better shellacking,"[10] he said, thanking Toronto for the honour of being its mayor for the longest period in the city's history up to that time.

Yet his was an incredible legacy, with Phillips calling Toronto the "miracle city" of North America and predicting a rosy future, with a massive overhaul of sewage infrastructure, new freeways, and an underground subway system that would, he very prophetically said, "cost untold millions." And 30 years before it actually came to pass, Phillips predicted the amalgamation of the City of Toronto and Metro governments into "one geographic, social, economic, and political unit."[11]

In 1965, Phillips was again honoured when Toronto's new City Hall was officially opened to great fanfare. The former mayor credited it with sparking major downtown development, including the first phase of the Toronto-Dominion Centre and the new Robert Simpson Tower.

Phillips died of heart failure in January 1976 after three weeks in Toronto General Hospital. He was survived by his loving wife, Esther; son, Howard; and daughter, Madeline (Brodey). His funeral was at Holy Blossom Temple on Bathurst Street the following day, with interment at Holy Blossom Memorial Park on Brimley Road in Scarborough.

With great sadness, Metro chairman Paul Godfrey called Phillips the greatest politician of all time in Metro Toronto, while Mayor David Crombie observed that Phillips would be remembered with love because of his kindness, thoughtfulness, and also because he seldom had a bad word for anybody.

But the words of former East York mayor True Davidson captured it best when she said: "I think of his folksiness ... the time he was willing to spend with little people. I think of his broad tolerance, and I am convinced that the feature he likes best about Nathan Phillips Square is not that it bears his name or gives a suitable setting to his new City Hall, but that day and night it is full of people. His people. All the people."[12]

Mayoral Election for 1955	
CANDIDATES	VOTES
Nathan Phillips	40,707
Leslie Saunders	36,751
Arthur Brown	36,648
Alex MacLeod	4,892
Mayoral Election for 1956	
Nathan Phillips	70,702
Roy Belyea	26,629
Ross Dowson	2,349
Mayoral Election for 1957–1958	
SPECIAL NOTE: As of late 1956, election terms for Toronto's Council and mayor were changed from a one-year to a two-year term.	
Nathan Phillips	80,494
Ross Dowson	9,862
Mayoral Election for 1959–1960	
Nathan Phillips	53,834
Ford Brand	30,687
Joe Cornish	17,031
Mayoral Election for 1961–1962	
Nathan Phillips	82,319
Allan Lamport	58,783
Jean Newman	35,372
Ross Dowson	1,656
Harry Bradley	1,476

Mayor Don Summerville

1963

The 53rd mayor of Toronto

Occupations: Theatre manager, business association president, City of Toronto alderman and controller, Metropolitan Toronto councillor
Residence While Mayor: 16 Briar Dale Boulevard
Birth: August 4, 1915, in Toronto
Death: November 19, 1963, in Toronto

——— • ———

Donald Dean Summerville was born in Toronto in 1915, the son of William "Billy" and Alberta Dean Summerville. His father was a larger-than-life figure — a popular, colourful, high-profile east end community leader, Toronto Council member, and later Conservative MPP.

As a founder of the Danforth Businessmen's Association, Billy Summerville was often referred to as "Mayor of the Danforth" and was a man of many hats: a vaudevillian, songwriter, theatre owner, and real-estate developer. As a result, Don Summerville came to know political life and community affairs at a young age. He grew up in a dynamic environment, a world of business affairs, patriotic duty, Orange Lodge influence, Protestant church involvement, municipal affairs, theatrical and show business pursuits, sports, Conservative politics, and community affairs along the Danforth.

Attending local schools — Frankland Public, Danforth Technical School, and Shaw Business College — Summerville played organized hockey in both the junior and senior Ontario Hockey Association. He was also a reserve goaltender for the Toronto Maple Leafs in 1936. He then went to work for his father, helping to run Toronto's Prince of Wales Theatre.

During the Second World War, he was a pilot in the Royal Canadian Air Force, and after the war, returned to the theatre business, becoming a vice-president of Summerville Properties Ltd. and a managing director of Woodbine-Danforth Theatres Ltd. Like his father, he also became president of the Danforth Businessmen's Association. Active in the Variety Club, he was involved in its social, community, and fundraising efforts.

In 1955, age 40, Summerville ran for Toronto's Council for the first time, topping the polls as alderman for the east end's Ward 8. For four years, he established a reputation as a sometimes brash and headline-grabbing city councillor, clashing publicly with veteran city commissioner Harold Bradley, who sarcastically called him "sonny boy" one day when angrily leaving a meeting.

As a councillor, Summerville chaired the Metropolitan Civil Defence Committee from 1955 to 1958 and was also on the city's Waterfront

Committee. Early on, he was one of the strongest advocates of Toronto's municipal amalgamation. Elected to the city-wide Board of Control for the 1959–1960 term, Summerville captured the third spot on the four-member body and was so frugal that he was able to use 5,000 of his father's old campaign buttons rescued from a dusty box. The "Vote Summerville for Controller" had been ordered but not used in 1937 after his father was elected that year as a Tory member of Ontario's Legislative Assembly.

By the early 1960s, Summerville's crusading image proved to be a popular one. In the election for the 1961–1962 term, he gained the top spot as senior controller, polling 112,226 votes, and also became president of Toronto's Council and city budget chief. It was a foreshadowing of things to come: Summerville received 30,000 more votes than incumbent Nathan Phillips and was by far the most popular politician in Toronto.

With the retirement of Fred "Big Daddy" Gardiner, Summerville chose not to stand for the chair of Metro Toronto, deciding to support William Allen for the post. Instead, he waited until the next mayoral campaign to take a major gamble and challenge the long-serving Nathan Phillips.

By the end of 1962, Phillips had been in office for eight years but lost the mayoralty to the more energetic Summerville, whose intensive campaign focused on "strong, vigorous leadership." Summerville used an upbeat campaign slogan, "He Gets Things Done," to portray himself as a man of action for the 1960s. Toronto, he emphasized, needed a leader, not a social greeter, and he pledged to the electorate that if he were elected mayor, his program would be "Work, Work, and More Work,"[1] not knowing that indeed it was work that would soon kill him.

It was one of the largest mandates ever accorded a mayor of Toronto, and as a bonus, Summerville knocked off a tough incumbent. The *Toronto Daily Star* endorsed Summerville, saying he "has proved himself to be a hard-working, conscientious, and competent official. He has given his best to every post he has held and he has grown steadily in his grasp of civic affairs."[2]

Summerville approached his inaugural speech with great humility, urging immediate action on the redevelopment of Queen Street across from the new City Hall and inviting proposals from Canada, the United States, and Europe. He revealed he would soon sit down with Ontario premier John

Robarts to urge a better financial deal for the city and noted that a formal application for the amalgamation of municipalities in Metro Toronto had been filed with the Ontario Municipal Board.

Although a Conservative, Summerville was a Red Tory who showed compassion for those less fortunate. The new mayor called for private-sector involvement in low-cost housing, amendments to the Assessment Act, and a federal-municipal conference with Conservative prime minister John Diefenbaker, calling the British North America Act "weird, sad, and outdated."

Summerville also demanded reform of the Canadian National Exhibition, a new program of neighbourhood youth recreation centres, a 1 percent tax on bets placed at Woodbine Racetrack and a 3 percent tax on hotel rooms to raise $500,000 per year ($4.7 million per year today), and an end to speculative spot rezonings, saying residential areas deserved protection.

Known as an efficient, hard-driving administrator, Summerville kept a punishing pace as head of the often unwieldy 23-member Council and chair of the Board of Control while serving ex officio on all Council committees. If that wasn't enough, he was also on the board of another 15 external agencies.

In 1963, the Council dealt with a range of issues: the number of liquor outlets in west Toronto, asking the province for legislation to govern air-quality issues for the first time, the rehabilitation of the city's historic St. Lawrence Market building as a major centennial project, a brand-new city staff position (public relations officer for the mayor's office), and the final Toronto Transit Commission designs for the new Bathurst, Broadview, Coxwell, Donlands, Ossington, and Sherbourne subway stations.

The Council also discussed accommodating a press gallery in the new City Hall, the Toronto Parking Authority's first-ever parking facilities in neighbourhood retail areas, expanded seating inside Maple Leaf Gardens, and new safeguards to protect residential communities requiring a two-thirds vote of Council if zoning was made less restrictive. Councillors also considered the purchase of a new seven-passenger Cadillac limousine to replace the 1960 Lincoln that had already travelled 104,000 kilometres and required extensive repairs to its brakes, springs, and electrical system.

Summerville, it was noted, was not encumbered by any political credo and was impatient with those who were. Although a loyal member of the

Progressive Conservative Party, his political voting record was sometimes more liberal than that of the socialists on his Council.

Even though he was only the 53rd mayor of Toronto, Summerville officially welcomed Sir Ralph Perring, the 635th Lord Mayor of London. And with a flourish in October 1963, he opened The Colonnade on Bloor Street West, an exciting new mixed-use building with retail, residential, and commercial office space, a harbinger of things to come.

News articles began to appear observing that Toronto's mayor was spreading himself too thin, noting that to keep pace with his workload and social obligations, the new chief magistrate was working 14- to 18-hour days seven days a week. In addition to his extensive mayoral duties, Summerville was also in his private life a member of the Danforth Businessmen's Association, Variety Club International, the Lions Club (Beaches Branch), the Canadian Legion's British Empire Service League, the Toronto Board of Trade, and the 408 Wing of the Royal Canadian Air Force Association.

As his predecessor Nathan Phillips later observed in the *Toronto Daily Star*, "Summerville threw himself whole-heartedly into this schedule and it killed him,"[3] and true to form, his last hours on earth were spent thinking of others. His final act as mayor was to raise money for the victims of a major flood disaster in Longarone, Italy. On the night of November 19, 1963, the one-time practice goalie for the Maple Leafs donned his pads and skated onto the ice at George Bell Arena in the city's far west end for a charity hockey match between Toronto's Council and the city's press gallery.

Summerville, in fact, was scheduled to fly to Italy the following day to deliver the relief efforts in person. For about five minutes, he clowned a bit for the cameras, then complained of fatigue. Leaving the ice after a few minutes, he collapsed in the dressing room, causing an ambulance to be called. Yet because of municipal boundaries at the time, the nearest ambulance — one operated by the York Township Fire Department — was just a little more than a kilometre away but did not carry out the call. Instead, a city ambulance was dispatched from almost 16 kilometres away, and Summerville died while waiting for aid.

Soon after, a hushed crowd of more than 1,500 was informed that the mayor of Toronto had been pronounced dead at St. Joseph's Hospital at 9:06 p.m. For just the second time in Toronto's history, city staff had to organize a funeral for a sitting mayor. The next day, a huge *Toronto Daily Star* banner headline screamed: "Mayor Summerville Skates Off Ice to Die."[4]

Although just 48, the mayor had previously suffered a heart attack two years earlier. When a suggestion was made that Toronto engage some form of official representative, civic greeter, or host to help reduce the workload, Summerville had insisted on being available to organizations and community groups seeking the mayor's presence at their functions.

Ultimately, his death and recommendations arising out of the 1966 Goldenberg Report on municipal services resulted in a number of changes to services in Metro Toronto. One key proposal was for Metro Toronto to take over and operate all public ambulance services and set up a central ambulance dispatch to coordinate all ambulance calls.

Coming just a year after his election, his death was a tragic blow to the city and for the high expectations that had accompanied the "dynamo of the Danforth." After only 11 months in office, Summerville's intensive and sometimes unforgiving schedule had killed him.

The mayor was accorded a funeral with full civic honours. A wake was first held at former mayor Ralph Day's funeral home on Danforth Avenue, then his body lay in state in the Council chamber of what is now Old City Hall where an estimated 4,000 people paid their final respects.

It was noted that Summerville was "a victim of overwork and his own sense of duty." Known as a man of action and sometimes impatient with the machinery of government, he wanted to make decisions that others put off for weeks. Fellow Metro councillor Albert Campbell of Scarborough said: "This life has been very hard on him. He accepted his responsibilities and he was so conscientious about it that he worked day and night. It wore him down. He was showing signs of it."[5]

Ironically, during the funeral service at St. James Cathedral on the afternoon of November 22, 1963, news of the assassination of President John F. Kennedy in Dallas, Texas, rippled through the church in hushed tones from person to person. In the days and weeks that followed, comparisons were made between the two relatively youthful, charismatic leaders.

Summerville was survived by his wife, Alice Traschler, and their two sons, Dean and Wayne. Born in Hochdorf, Switzerland, in 1909, Alice had been dedicated to supporting her husband as he climbed the ranks of Toronto politics. As a gesture of the voters' affection after his shocking and unexpected death, she herself was elected in her own right as the Council member for the Ward 8 seat previously held by her husband, serving from 1964 to 1969.

Mayoral Election for 1963–1964	
SPECIAL NOTE: Don Summerville died in office on November 19, 1963.	
CANDIDATES	**VOTES**
Don Summerville	118,196
Nathan Phillips	48,163
Frank Nasso	4,995
Ross Dowson	1,120
Harry Bradley	826
Charles Mahoney	414

Mayor Phil Givens

1963–1966

The 54th mayor of Toronto

Occupations: Lawyer, City of Toronto alderman and controller, Metropolitan Toronto councillor, business executive, philanthropist, Member of House of Commons, Member of Ontario Legislative Assembly, Police Commission of Metropolitan Toronto chair, Provincial Court of Ontario judge
Residence While Mayor: 76 Caribou Street
Birth: April 24, 1922, in Toronto
Death: November 30, 1995, in Toronto

——— • ———

Philip Gerald Givens was born in Toronto in 1922, the son of Hyman Gewertz (later Givens) and Mary Grafstein. His parents had married just before his father immigrated in 1912 from Belce, Poland, to Canada. Givens's father sought to earn enough money that he could bring his wife to Canada but that took almost 10 years.

A tailor by profession, Hyman Givens first settled in the Euclid Avenue and Dundas Street neighbourhood, finding a job in a pants factory for $3 per week ($78 per week today). In 1921, Hyman and Mary Givens were finally reunited in Toronto, and a year later in April 1922, Philip was born. Growing up on Augusta and later Euclid Avenues, Givens was educated at Charles G. Fraser Public School and at Parkdale and Harbord Collegiates, then earned a bachelor of arts in political science and economics from the University of Toronto.

He then attended Osgoode Hall Law School where he was also a gold medallist debater. As a law student, Givens worked for eminent Toronto attorney David Peters, an ardent Zionist who became his mentor. Proud of his rich Jewish heritage, Givens was a graduate of the Talmud Torah Eitz Chaim on D'Arcy Street, and years later, was president of the Toronto Zionist Council and was on the board of several Jewish community organizations.

As a young boy, Givens's heroes were the public figures of the day. In a 1984 interview with Jewish historian Bill Gladstone, Givens recalled: "I loved oratory and my father used to take me to the public meetings at the Standard Theatre on Spadina." Yet, as he told Gladstone, he also experienced anti-Semitism first-hand as a boy in the 1930s, saying it was "particularly vicious … it was a time when you'd be chased through the streets of Toronto with epithets hurled at you." Givens remembered applying for many jobs when "the minute you said Jewish or Hebrew, you could see you were through."[1]

Givens worked summers at the Steel Company of Canada, shovelling coal into hot furnaces, and at Canada Packers cleaning out barrels of lard to earn university tuition. He married Minnie "Min" Rubin in June 1947, graduated from law school in 1949, age 27, and began practising law. It was also the year in which he started his political career.

As an early means of electioneering, Givens attended meetings of several non-partisan, ethnically mixed, left-wing Jewish fraternal organizations known as *landsmanshaftn* societies. They had been established to assist Eastern European Jews to integrate into the Jewish community, to help with finding work, and to lessen alienation and fear.

Although Givens first sought office in 1949 and then 1950, he failed to be elected as a school trustee. In 1951, he was elected alderman for Ward 5. When he ran for re-election, it was against the Communist Party's Stewart Smith. Givens won that contest and was re-elected to the Council eight times before becoming mayor. He also served on the Metro Council from 1953 to 1966, and in both 1957 and 1958, the ambitious Givens was an unsuccessful federal Liberal Party candidate in the Spadina riding.

In late 1960, he ran successfully for one of the four seats on the Board of Control for the 1961–1962 term. In what was a distinctly populist vein, he opposed a swanky 125-seat restaurant proposed for the top floor of the new City Hall under construction. Givens was appointed a Queen's Counsel in 1962, and later that year, sought re-election to the Board of Control, topping the polls with 87,051 votes. A strong supporter of Metro Toronto amalgamation, he was appointed as the Metro Council's president and city budget chief.

With Mayor Don Summerville's sudden death due to a massive heart attack, Givens was unanimously appointed mayor on November 25, 1963, by the 21 members of Toronto's Council. Staid, Protestant, British, Orange, and Conservative Toronto witnessed a second Jewish mayor take office, yet it was not the way Givens envisaged or wanted. His relationship with Summerville had been extremely warm, close, and personal, with Givens affectionately calling him "Donnie."

Tragically, one of his first acts as mayor in November 1963 was his appeal for citizens to fill city churches and synagogues to mourn slain U.S. president John F. Kennedy. He generated controversy soon after, saying the news media were endangering the lives of public figures by giving publicity to what he said were submarginal kooky characters.

The *Toronto Daily Star* described Givens as a "a stout, effervescent, outgoing man with an instinct for sizing up the flim-flam and the phonies who often surround the people in public office ... he gets huge enjoyment from the perquisites of the middle-class ... he lives comfortably in a house of modest size on a woodsy cul-de-sac just inside North York, likes Chinese food at Lichee Gardens, and is appalled at how few books his fellow politicians read." It noted the new mayor was "a lover of anecdote, but not of gossip," and described Givens as "the best phrase-maker in civic politics."[2]

Assuming the office under the most tragic of circumstances, Givens spoke of the need for continued "slum clearance" and a sales tax on hotel rooms to be imposed simultaneously with Montreal so that neither city lost convention business to the other.

In December 1964, Givens ran in his first full mayoral election, turning back a strong challenge from popular former mayor Allan Lamport. In a foreshadowing of Toronto's future diversity, he hailed the "mingling of countless races and creeds, people with intelligence, imagination, ingenuity, and the urge to work, create and succeed."[3]

His campaign was based on six key planks: an eased tax burden; smoother-flowing traffic, including low-cost transit and convenient parking; decent housing; maximized education and employment opportunities; new recreational facilities; and facilities for culture and social services. The 42-year-old son of poor Polish immigrants captured 82,696 votes, some 30,000 more than Lamport's, to head up what was then a $118 million ($1.1 billion today) city corporation. Givens pledged to make Toronto an "art city," and one of his immediate priorities was the completion of the St. Lawrence Centre for the Arts, a new home for theatre, opera, ballet, and music.

In his first inaugural address, he noted that the Council had seen "a liberal infusion of new blood, new ideas, and fresh points of view."[4] His top priority was the downtown area, which held "the key to Toronto's growth." Givens urged the appointment of a coordinator to expedite new construction, the immediate redevelopment of Queen Street across from City Hall, and a vast remake of the south end of Yonge Street. One newspaper referred to him as the "go-go mayor" who promoted change.

Indeed, the city was being transformed: by the mid-1960s drugs, "free love," the licensing of coffee houses in Yorkville, and an influx of young teenage "hippies" protesting automobile traffic there were big issues. As the *Toronto Daily Star* reported, hundreds routinely listened to rock bands, smoked marijuana, dropped acid, and burned incense.

Matters dealt with by the Council in 1964 and 1965 included the repeal of restrictions on sunbathing in public places, the proposed discontinuing of chauffeur-driven limousines for the Board of Control, and allowing for a major underground pedestrian mall in the financial district. The Council debated urban renewal funding, a heavy truck prohibition downtown, water pollution from detergents, the future of Old City Hall, the incineration of refuse, and air rights over subways. They also dealt with the establishment of provincial schools of technology, the holding of bicycle races on Sundays, the removal of railway tracks at Queen's Quay, and applying the same welfare benefits to women as to men.

A central highlight of Givens's term was the September 1965 official opening of the new $31 million ($281 million today) City Hall and the municipality's first major downtown square. To a crowd of some 50,000, Governor General Georges Vanier stated that the spirit and soul of a city were reflected through its architecture, which would "inspire its citizens to broader outlooks and nobler purposes." This new landmark, he added, "will serve as a constant reminder to every citizen of the overwhelming importance of a strong, inspired civic spirit."[5]

Yet, ironically, it was a new piece of public art in Nathan Phillips Square that contributed to Givens's defeat as mayor a year later when Henry Moore's *The Archer*, a new abstract, modern sculpture was initially rejected by the Council. Givens undertook a campaign to privately raise the $100,000 ($905,000 today) to purchase it, but it cost the mayor his job, since citizens were not quite ready for such artistic flare in the heart of staid old Hogtown.

In a lively three-way race, his successful opponent, William Dennison, consolidated support from labour, trade unions, socialists, grassroots community activists, and the New Democratic Party (formerly the Co-operative Commonwealth Federation) and emerged as the far more cautious candidate with "Respect for the Taxpayer's Dollar" as a slogan.

Givens was the recipient of the Jewish National Fund's prestigious Negev Award and re-entered politics again in 1968, running successfully for the federal Liberal Party in York West riding and replacing veteran Cabinet minister Robert Winters. In 1969, he served as a parliamentary observer with the Canadian delegation to the United Nations and became a member of the Canada–United States Inter-Parliamentary Group.

As an MP, Givens was a strong voice in championing urban issues, urging Prime Minister Pierre Trudeau's Liberals to pay more attention to cities and boldly declaring that Ottawa was not devoting sufficient attention to

City Halls Toronto Almost Had

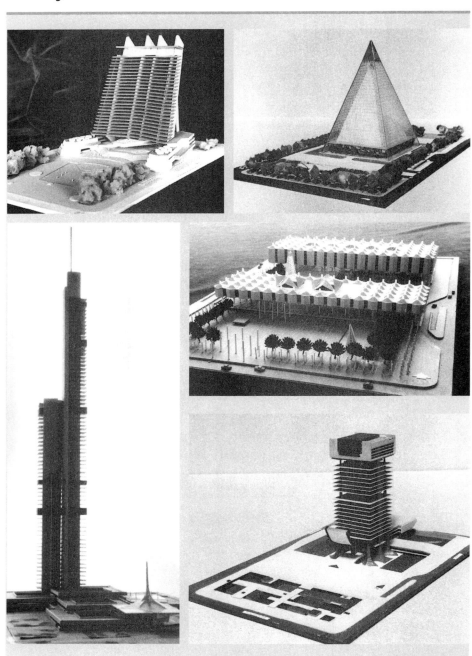

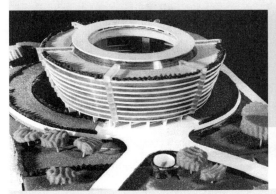

In 1946, Toronto voters approved the purchase of properties to create a new City Hall and civic square downtown. Uninspiring plans by a consortium of local architectural firms were defeated by voters in 1955.

Mayor Nathan Phillips (1955–1962) persuaded Toronto's Council in 1956 to hold an international design competition for a new City Hall, and in mid-September 1957, its terms were approved. Architecture professor Eric Arthur became its professional adviser, an eminent jury was selected, and the Council agreed to one very critical point: it would accept the jury's decision.

Soon, 1,500 inquiries were lodged, and by the April 1958 deadline, 510 architects from 42 countries submitted actual-scale models, enough to fill the Canadian National Exhibition's Horticultural Building. The anonymity of each entry was also assured. A first round of judging took place, and after six days of deliberation, eight finalists were chosen. In September 1958, judges returned for another four days of deliberation.

To use the words of Nathan Phillips, the "breathtaking" design of Finland's Viljo Revell was the jury's final choice, and on September 13, 1965, the City of Toronto's sparkling new City Hall building was officially opened.

Seven of the submissions that were rejected are shown here.

urban issues because of what Givens called "the clouded condition of the constitution." He urged a major federal role in urban affairs before Canada was swamped with the same big-city problems as the United States. At times, Givens openly criticized Trudeau, and as the friction grew, realized there was no future in being a backbencher in Ottawa "where government members 'must vote like a wooden soldier.'"[6]

Disappointed in never making the Cabinet, Givens announced in 1971 that he would run for the Ontario Legislative Assembly and became MPP for York–Forest Hill in the provincial election that year, though the Ontario Liberal Party went on to lose.

As an Opposition MPP, Givens spoke on a wide range of matters in the assembly: discrimination and human rights, low-cost housing, municipal land banking, vandalism, and urban development. He also tackled the newly created regional municipalities, the establishment of a greenbelt around Toronto, major sewage issues, urban poverty, GO Transit, federal-provincial co-operation, and the need for new subway and expressway construction (a popular position in the North York of the 1960s).

With redistribution in 1975, Givens ran in the Armourdale riding against Mel Lastman, the popular mayor of North York, who publicly (and incorrectly) declared that if he lost it would mean the end of his political career. Givens served in the Legislative Assembly until 1977 when Ontario premier Bill Davis appointed him chair of the Metropolitan Police Commission and a provincial court judge.

A member of the commission for more than a decade, Givens paid serious attention to the issues of victims' rights, keeping Toronto streets safe, and advocating an automatic death penalty for the killing of a police officer. "The police officer who goes out on the streets to fight crime should have the right to feel that a person who kills him will suffer the same fate," he insisted. And at times his remarks could be controversial. In 1984, he said, "We have to protect ourselves from the crackpots, nuts, and loonies out there."[7]

Givens was assigned as a trial judge in the Civil Division in 1985 and retired from the Police Commission and judiciary in 1989. It was during his tenure that Metro Police relaxed its height and weight restrictions, giving a host of new minority candidates an opportunity to apply. In 1988, Givens also joined the board of the 36,000-member Canadian Association of Retired Persons.

In his personal life, Givens was both vital and engaged, serving on the boards of the Canadian Council of Christians and Jews and the Toronto Symphony as well as being vice-president and general counsel of Atlantic Packaging. He was a member of the Mount Sinai Masonic Lodge, and for several years was a political commentator on CHUM Radio. A passionate sailor, Givens was a member of both the Royal Canadian and the Island Yacht Clubs in Toronto.

As a proud and ardent Zionist, Givens was a founder and the first president of the Upper Canada Lodge of B'nai Brith and chairman of the United Israel Appeal's Israel Emergency Fund in 1967. From 1973 to 1985, he was the national president of the Canadian Zionist Federation, and in the early 1990s was national chairman of the Canadian Jewish Congress's Yiddish Committee.

Givens died of a heart attack on November 30, 1995, while hospitalized at Sunnybrook Health Centre and was survived by his wife, Min; daughter, Eleanor; and son, Michael. In his eulogy at Beth Tzedec Synagogue, Rabbi Benjamin Friedberg remembered Givens's irrepressible personality and rich sense of humour. The flags of Canada and Israel were draped over his casket, a symbol of his "two loves." Friedberg recalled how Givens had been considered the "boy wonder of the Jewish community" and that "he reached for the heavens, but had his feet planted firmly on the ground."[8]

Mayoral Election for 1965–1966

SPECIAL NOTE: Phil Givens became mayor on November 25, 1963, after the death of incumbent Don Summerville. He then ran for election in 1964 and won the 1965–1966 mayoralty.

CANDIDATES	VOTES
Phil Givens	82,696
Allan Lamport	52,175
Ross Dowson	2,959
Charles Maloney	1,906

Mayor William Dennison
1967–1972

The 55th mayor of Toronto

Occupations: Realtor, teacher, beekeeper, speech therapist, Toronto Board of Education trustee, Member of the Legislative Assembly of Ontario, City of Toronto alderman and controller, Metropolitan Toronto councillor
Residence While Mayor: 23 Pricefield Road
Birth: January 20, 1905, in Westmeath, Renfrew County, Ontario
Death: May 2, 1981, in Toronto

The son of James Dennison and Margaret Sutherland, William Dennison was born in the front parlour of the family farm near Westmeath in the Ottawa Valley. A later family history described him as a "sturdy, handsome, and precocious little boy."[1] His early education was at Westmeath Public School, a log building with double desks and a wood stove. He also attended Renfrew Collegiate Institute 48 kilometres away, taking an early-morning train and returning on a 7:00 p.m. one each day. A combination of distance, age, and disability made high school "hell on earth," he later revealed.

A serious speech impairment proved to be a defining part of Dennison's life as well as a deeply personal triumph. In his self-published memoir, Dennison said, "In my youth I stammered terribly and for over twenty years the tormenting fear of stammering hung over my life."[2]

As a teenager, Dennison became a member of the populist United Farmers of Ontario in Renfrew County, working for it in the 1919 provincial election. Later, he joined the Co-operative Commonwealth Federation (CCF), the forerunner of today's New Democratic Party (NDP).

Dennison travelled to Saskatchewan to work on the grain harvests for $6 per day ($102 per day today) as a young man of 19 and 20. He then took a job with the Trick Lumber Company in Oshawa but left in 1927 to attend the Bassett School of Speech Correction in New York City to continue dealing with his speech impediment.

Returning again to Oshawa, he worked for General Motors and sold real estate until the stock market crash of 1929 when he began a speech therapy school in Oshawa. A severe stammerer, he then moved to Toronto, opening the Dennison School of Speech Correction in 1930. At the time, it was the only resident school of its kind in Canada for those suffering from speech disorders.

Originally based in the Dennison family home on Jarvis Street, the school offered up to 12 weeks of study, including daily one-on-one instruction, breathing exercises, the usage of vowels, and the preparation of speeches. In June 1931, Dennison married Dorothy "Do" Bainbridge, whose family roots were in Lancashire, England.

From 1934 to 1937, as a representative of the CCF, Dennison made several failed Toronto Council bids in Ward 2. In the 1935 federal election, he ran unsuccessfully as the CCF candidate in the Rosedale riding, and in 1937, suffered his sixth electoral defeat in a row, losing the race to become provincial MPP for St. David's riding to Liberal Allan Lamport.

Yet Dennison was also making a name for himself for sheer determination, and in 1938, finally entered public life as an elected school trustee, serving three successive one-year terms. He and his wife also bought their first home at 543 Jarvis Street. As the *Globe and Mail* recounted years later, "his first election campaigns were conducted on socialist planks. He fought for things that would help the 'little man' — a better deal for welfare recipients, municipal distribution of milk, bread and coal, city-owned low-cost housing, day care, and school meals."[3]

In 1941 and again in 1943, he successfully secured election to the Council as a CCF alderman for Ward 2, yet was forced to emphatically declare "I am not a Communist and never shall be one."[4] And in an era when it was possible to serve simultaneously on both Toronto's Council and at Queen's Park, he was elected provincially in 1943 for the CCF in the St. David's riding.

In the Legislative Assembly, Dennison was one of the earliest environmentalists. As a 1940s conservationist, he tried to stop the de Havilland aircraft factory's pollution of Black Creek and was an original founder of the Don Valley Conservation Association, established in 1946 to protect the Don Valley from proposed development and to carry out tree planting, public education, watershed protection, and early environmental advocacy.

On a personal side, during the Second World War, Dennison was contracted to do speech correction for both the U.S. and Canadian armies and also became president of the Stammerers Advisory Guild and the Association of Private Schools of Speech Correction (for the United States and Canada).

In the provincial general election in 1945, Dennison went down to defeat but regained his seat in the June 1948 provincial election. In 1946, he bought 20 hectares of property in Caledon East to use as an active farm and to plant the first of 40,000 trees.

At a time when just property owners and their spouses could vote in municipal elections, Dennison took on the issue of giving everyone over the age of 21, including all apartment renters and boarders, the right to vote.

He also championed better housing and hydro service. After again being defeated in the November 1951 provincial election, Dennison sought a return to Toronto's Council and successfully served as alderman from 1953 until 1958.

Well prior to the formal implementation of medicare in Canada, Dennison fought for the creation of a prepaid hospital insurance plan. On the Council, he was a champion for rent controls, better pensions, a heat bylaw, increased spending on education, the development of homes for the aged, and more effective conservation efforts.

In 1955, he ran once more provincially for the CCF but was defeated for a seat in the Legislative Assembly. Yet Dennison's prior political efforts to extend the civic franchise to all citizens were rewarded when voters approved it by a wide margin. And with a highly moralistic streak, he publicly denounced the popular movie *Blackboard Jungle*, calling it disgusting, since it showed public drinking, profanity, car theft, and an attack on a schoolteacher.

In late 1958, Dennison won election city-wide for the first time, serving on the 1959–1960 Board of Control. He campaigned with a meticulous system of index cards of everyone who had contacted him since entering public life in 1934. And with his tongue-twisting 1958 campaign slogan, "Vote Against the Tyranny of Expropriation for the Benefit of Speculators,"[5] he captured the fourth spot on the board.

He fought for tighter gun laws in 1959, seeking to prohibit the sale of them to anyone without a police permit. Dennison also began a campaign to restore the old St. Lawrence Market building, then slated for demolition. In 1961, he became a member of the newly created NDP, yet was also concerned about the influence of unions on the new party.

In December 1962, he was re-elected to the Board of Control and persuaded Toronto's Council to call for an increase in old-age pensions to $75 per month ($722 per month today). In 1964, years ahead of his time, he publicly advocated that women on social assistance be able to access free birth control pills. Dennison routinely interrogated senior city staff about their expense accounts, potential conflicts of interest, or relationships with companies doing business with the city. During the 1965–1966 Council term, he served as budget chief and was able to reduce the city tax rate.

After Dennison formally announced his decision to run for the 1967–1969 mayoral term, the *Globe and Mail* described him as "a funny kind of socialist, a former professional heckler, fender inspector and beekeeper ... a socialist with a conservative hue."[6] Key issues included the extension of the Yonge-University subway north of Eglinton and the proposed purchase of a controversial sculpture, Henry Moore's *The Archer*, with Dennison strongly objecting to modern art in such a prominent venue as the new City Hall.

The *Globe and Mail* noted that Dennison was "not an inspiring figure on a platform ... and somehow always manages to look awkward."[7] His mayoral campaign plank was boldly titled "He Will Do These Things for You"[8] and proposed no assessment increase for five years, increased provincial help, more public housing, and support for an elected Metro chair. Opposed for mayor by all three daily newspapers, Dennison became the first socialist mayor since 1935, winning with the backing of the city's Italian, Polish, and Ukrainian communities, as well as working-class neighbourhoods and NDP, socialist, and left-of-centre voters. He spent a grand total of $7,000 ($61,000 today) on his campaign.

At the Council's inaugural meeting in 1967, Dennison said he would seek more frequent meetings between the Board of Control, Ontario premier, and Cabinet ministers, saying "we must have a well-prepared case and carefully considered requests."[9] He urged the separation of the city's storm and sanitary sewer systems over a 25-year period and spoke of the richness of Canada's diversity.

Dennison was against the earliest plans for the Eaton Centre, which intended to demolish Old City Hall. Over time, he moved further into the centre of the political spectrum, becoming even conservative on some issues. Complaining about U.S. draft dodgers flocking to the city, he declared that "hippies and deserters are Toronto's only problem."[10]

By 1967, Yorkville and its cafés and small shops saw an eclectic combination of dreamers, students, artists, and beatniks congregating around the neighbourhood's meeting places. They were joined by a colourful assembly of rowdies, bikers, and hookers. Yorkville became linked, whether fairly or not, with a world of psychedelic music and drugs where upheaval, protest, and free love were the norms.

In late December 1967, the renovated St. Lawrence Hall at Jarvis and King Streets was officially reopened to the public, and a few days later,

Governor General Roland Michener held the official New Year's Day levee there. Dennison's personal frugality also caught on, with him claiming just $261 ($2,100 today) in expenses for two trips. In August 1968, Dennison proclaimed August 5 to 10 "Caribbean Week," and the following year its focus was expanded to include drama, dance, lectures, and social services. By 1970, it was the symbol of an increasingly more diverse Toronto.

On December 1, 1969, Dennison, the wily veteran socialist, was re-elected with a healthy margin of 13,000 votes ahead of his feisty challenger Margaret Campbell. A ballot question also confirmed overwhelming support by a vote of 101,163 in favour, to 22,390 against, for the amalgamation of Metro Toronto under a single municipal council. In his 1970 inaugural address, Dennison noted that Toronto was the fastest-growing city in North America and called for a new mechanism to unlock federal dollars.

On the personal side, Dennison and his wife downsized, and in August 1970, moved to a spacious apartment on Thorncliffe Park Drive in East York.

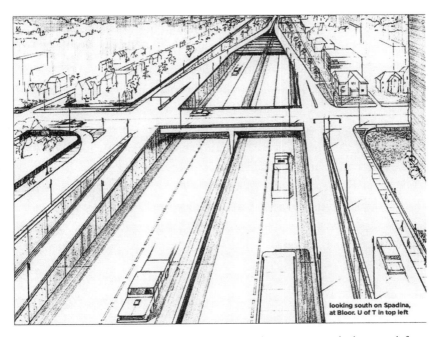

looking south on Spadina, at Bloor. U of T in top left

Rendering of the proposed four-lane, below-grade Spadina Expressway, looking south from Spadina Avenue and Bloor Street toward College Street.

A believer in physical fitness, he did not smoke and drank so little that he was viewed as a teetotaller.

In early 1971, Dennison welcomed revised plans for the massive Eaton Centre, and after hard-fought negotiations also announced a major rail lands redevelopment to the south. It would include a cultural site (later becoming Roy Thomson Hall), land on Front Street for a convention centre (today's Metro Convention Centre), and a telecommunications tower (today's CN Tower). In a foreshadowing of things to come, Dennison stated that "what is now the city's biggest eyesore is ensured to become its biggest attraction and most desired place to work and live."[11]

In May 1971 while on a municipal visit to Italy, Dennison learned that Ontario premier Bill Davis had cancelled the Spadina Expressway, calling the decision "a little hysterical" and later referring to it as a classic case of provincial meddling, noting the province had already spent $75 million ($546 million today) when it was abandoned.

Dennison retired from public life in June 1972. By the early 1970s, even Dennison himself noted that he was not as alert or active as he had once been and had developed a slight tremor, later diagnosed as Parkinson's disease. The one issue he was truly sorry to have lost was returning the Toronto Islands to public parkland, referring to the residents there as "squatters."

A congregant of the Unitarian faith, he was also a member of Enniskillen Loyal Orange Lodge 387, the Toronto Young Men's Christian Association, and the Glen Eagle Golf Club. His hobbies included golf, curling, swimming, carpentry, beekeeping, and tree planting. In retirement, the Dennisons divided their time between a condominium in Florida, a cottage on Lake Kasshabog, and their new condo in Mississauga.

William Dennison died in Toronto on May 2, 1981, after a long fight with Parkinson's and was survived by his wife, Dorothy, and daughter, Lorna Milne, who was appointed a Liberal Party member of the Canadian Senate in 1995 and served with distinction until 2009.

Mayoral Election for 1967–1969

SPECIAL NOTE: Ontario's electoral laws changed yet again. Municipal terms were expanded to three years rather than two, starting in the January immediately following the election.

CANDIDATES	VOTES
William Dennison	58,984
Phil Givens	54,525
William Archer	40,946
John Sara	1,217

Mayoral Election for 1970–1972

SPECIAL NOTE: In 1969, the Board of Control was abolished, as was its city-wide election. Toronto's Council was then expanded in size, and the term of office was slated to become a two-year term again, beginning after this election.

William Dennison	66,083
Margaret Campbell	52,813
Stephen Clarkson (under the Liberal Party banner)	31,927
John Riddell (under the League for Socialist Action)	2,337

Mayor David Crombie

1973–1978

The 56th mayor of Toronto

Occupations: Ryerson Polytechnical Institute lecturer and director of student services, City of Toronto alderman, Metropolitan Toronto councillor, Member of House of Commons, federal minister of national health and welfare, federal minister of Indian affairs and northern development, federal secretary of state, Royal Commission on the Future of the Toronto Waterfront commissioner, Waterfront Regeneration Trust chair, Canadian Urban Institute CEO, Toronto Lands Corporation chair

Residence While Mayor: 81 Glencairn Avenue
Birth: April 24, 1936, in Swansea, Toronto

———— • ————

No less an authority than former city archivist Victor Russell has stated that David Crombie was "the most popular and successful mayor in Toronto's history,"[1] and few would disagree. A combination of several factors, including issues, values, intelligence, drive, personality, and timing, all combined to give Crombie an almost iconic status decades after he stepped down as mayor.

David Edward Crombie was born in April 1936 in the Village of Swansea, a middle-class west end neighbourhood. His father was a manager with the Bilt-Rite Rubber Company, and with three brothers and a sister, he grew up in an upwardly mobile environment.

Crombie's family members were supporters of the Co-operative Commonwealth Federation (CCF), and as a young boy, he absorbed a mix of political issues, community affairs, and a deep love of nature. By the age of nine, Crombie was already trying to organize a Grade 5 student union. Family walks instilled in him a lifelong curiosity about landmarks, streets, public spaces, neighbourhoods, and people.

After a move to the suburbs, he attended Earl Haig Collegiate in North York, then the University of Western Ontario where he obtained a bachelor of arts in economics. Next, he began a degree in law at Osgoode Hall but quit after a year and a half to work as a salesman for General Foods.

In 1960, he married Shirley Bowden, a high school sweetheart, and they went on to have three children: Carrie, Robin, and the now-deceased Jonathan, known to millions of TV viewers for his role in the *Anne of Green Gables* television series. Crombie also began postgraduate studies at the University of Toronto that year, taking a master of arts in political science. In 1962, he joined the teaching staff at Ryerson Institute of Technology (now Toronto Metropolitan University), accepting an invitation to teach sociology, which led to a position as a lecturer in political science and urban affairs, a post he held for nine years.

By that time, he had moved to North Toronto, the area that served as his political base in the 1960s and 1970s. There, he became the central figure in a new urban reform movement as the co-founder of the Metropolitan Civic Action League (CIVAC).

Voters were starting to turn away from the high-growth, pro-development views of prior Toronto councils that encouraged more expressways, slum clearance, and mammoth high-rise blocks. In 1964, Crombie carried out a modest campaign for alderman in Ward 9, losing by a mere 403 votes. Although choosing not to run for the Council in late 1966, other CIVAC councillors were elected.

Also in 1966, he was appointed director of student services at Ryerson where he was responsible for several key areas, including food services, housing, athletics, student counselling, residences, and health services. As Victor Russell notes, Crombie "soon demonstrated an intellectual capacity for thoughtful decisions and, perhaps more important, superior adminis-trative and management skills."[2] In 1969, he was elected to one of the two Council seats of the new Ward 11 of North Toronto along with colleague David Rotenberg.

The issues facing Toronto were both numerous and complex, including the push for the so-called Spadina Expressway through the heart of midtown, as well as massive high-rises foisted upon stable residential neighbourhoods in High Park, St. Jamestown, and Trefann Court. Immense new downtown commercial projects included Metro Centre, Harbour Square, and the pro-posed Eaton Centre. The impact was huge, and a broad range of young urban professionals, community organizers, ratepayer groups, social activists, and tenant leaders became the voice of a new municipal reform movement.

Council colleague Anthony O'Donohue described Crombie as an ideal communicator with an ability "to talk to anyone and make them feel at ease … and a unique talent to smooth out the many little problems which beset our Council."[3] City Hall watchers noted that the words *negotiate, evaluate, conciliate* became watchwords of the day. As Jon Caulfield ob-serves in *The Tiny Perfect Mayor*, Crombie defined reform as "protection of neighbourhoods, common sense about the automobile, and concern for the style of development."[4]

As a member of the Council, Crombie served on the Planning Board and as chair of the Waterfront Committee. Also not shy about tooting his

own horn at times, in a 1972 news release, he declared it was "generally acknowledged" by the press and fellow aldermen that he was "an exceptional
member of Council."[5]

With the retirement of incumbent mayor William Dennison, Crombie's
final decision to contest the 1972 mayoral race came about in July while on
a family pilgrimage to Dundee, Scotland. His competitors were councillors Anthony O'Donohue and budget chief David Rotenberg. As Caulfield
writes, "He wanted very badly to be recognized as a leader ... to see Toronto

Published by the Crombie For Mayor Campaign.
Headquarters 887 Yonge Street, Toronto.
Telephone: 961-5130   This paper contains recycled, de-inked fibre

Campaign brochure from David Crombie's successful 1972 campaign for mayor of Toronto.

become a peaceful, attractive humane city, not the ugly sprawling mess which it threatened to become under old-guard policies."[6]

Crombie's campaign featured a snappy modern brochure asking voters to "Keep Caring About Toronto," with endorsements from a host of notable citizens. Central campaign messages were neighbourhood preservation, limited expressway construction, and control of development. They resonated with the public, and when combined with a well-orchestrated campaign, the support of city activists, and a lacklustre effort by political opponents, put him over the top.

On December 4, 1972, Crombie was elected mayor with 82,653 votes to 58,417 for O'Donohue and 35,219 for Rotenberg. In the end, he received 24,000 more votes than his nearest competitor.

As mayor, Crombie also became a member of the Metro Council, serving on its Planning Committee. As local historian Bruce Bell pointed out years later, Crombie "was the one who really started to think about saving downtown Toronto … he moved us away from a dull Victorian city, to becoming the great multicultural metropolis we have today. David had a vision to transform the downtown core, making it a place for people to live."[7]

With the mid-1960s demolition of several dozen buildings of historical interest, Crombie's plan for the St. Lawrence neighbourhood, an abandoned former industrial area, was to build mixed-use housing and avoid the creation of ghettos. For the first time in the city's history, Council members in 1973 were provided with an assistant and an individual office at City Hall. Crombie also transformed the mayor's office, becoming the first of 56 mayors to pick his own dedicated political staff.

Ignoring the howl of major development, real-estate, and construction interests, he announced, in September 1973, a two-year development freeze and a 13.7-metre height restriction on buildings downtown. While it was eventually thrown out by the Ontario Municipal Board, it had the precise and chilling effect that Crombie was seeking while also developing his reputation for astute mediation and skillfully maintaining an often shifting majority of votes on the Council.

Crombie's election also had a major effect on relations with Metro Toronto where four issues diverged: a debate on the route of a new subway line in the city's northwest, a contested race for Metro chair, the whittling away of city powers, and a war on the remaining homes on the Toronto

Islands. In mid-1974, *Time Magazine* (American edition) listed him among "100 leaders of tomorrow."[8] Heady stuff for a new mayor.

City elections were held in December 1974, and incumbent Crombie, with 102,807 votes, encountered no serious opposition. As Toronto Metropolitan University's Neil Thomlinson has observed, Crombie was a Conservative yet had Liberals and New Democrats on the same side. However, in second place was the race-baiting white supremacist Don Andrews, who is now leader of the ultra-right-wing Nationalist Party of Canada and has openly spoken of "niggers," "queers," and "commies,"[9] and whose platform advocated sending Toronto's Black population back to Africa.

In a 1975 *Time* (Canadian edition) cover story, Crombie said: "Commerce depends upon investment. Investment depends on stability. Stability flows from neighbourhoods, and neighbourhoods are based on roots. It's the domino theory in reverse."[10] He also ventured into international territory, travelling to Beijing (then known as Peking), China, in 1975, one of the earliest Canadian mayors to visit the emerging world power.

In December 1976, Crombie was re-elected with a massive 113,027 votes, ahead of nine other mayoral challengers, including, once again, notorious white supremacist Don Andrews in second place. A 1977 profile in the *Toronto Star*'s *The City* magazine paints a revealing picture of the political inner workings of Crombie's mayoralty: "Call a few reporters together, and, what the hell, get some aides and those petitioners hanging around the reception room, invite them in as well. Loosen your tie, pour some booze into a Styrofoam cup, and talk."[11]

Crombie resigned as mayor in 1978 to run for the Progressive Conservative Party in an October federal by-election in Rosedale riding. His opponent, Dr. John Evans, the former president of the University of Toronto, was Prime Minister Pierre Trudeau's hand-picked candidate. Crombie won convincingly with 18,732 votes to just 10,114 for Evans and was soon installed as a "Red Tory" in the House of Commons where Canada's political winds were changing. Under Joe Clark, the Conservatives won the May 1979 federal general election and Crombie was appointed minister of national health and welfare.

Years later, reports suggested that Crombie had never forgiven Clark for not naming him to the Cabinet's key priorities committee and Toronto's senior political minister. Yet his first Cabinet portfolio was short-lived, and though personally re-elected in the February 1980 general election, he spent four long years on the Opposition benches.

In 1983, Crombie became a candidate for the leadership of the federal Conservatives. It was widely felt that there was a strong reservoir of goodwill for Crombie, greater than that for several other candidates. He was viewed as a moderate Tory, a conciliator with broad appeal who had a base in Ontario where the party needed to win. Yet his consensus-building skills did not translate easily to the federal arena, "and he never seemed to gain the stature in Ottawa that those who admired his tenure as mayor hoped and expected he would."[12]

Although a member of the 1984 federal election campaign team, the popular ex-mayor was given no key role and was not a member of new leader Brian Mulroney's inner circle. Crombie won re-election in Rosedale with 53 percent to 26 percent for the Liberal Party's Bill Graham in what was a massive Conservative sweep across the nation.

Appointed to the Mulroney Cabinet as minister of Indian affairs and northern development, he served until June 1986, but the position was considered almost punitive, given Crombie's in-depth knowledge of planning, urban affairs, and big-city issues. Ottawa was also where he suffered a major heart attack.

In June 1986, he was appointed minister responsible for multiculturalism and secretary of state. Crombie himself defined his job as the minister of Canadian identity, linking Canadian citizenship with equality, diversity, inclusiveness, and community.

In 1988, he resigned his seat to accept an appointment as chair of the Royal Commission on the Future of the Toronto Waterfront. It was a good fit that saw him looking into federal land use, waterfront planning, environmental protection, the role of the Toronto Harbour Commission, and the future of the island airport. As Crombie noted, the position combined his interest in urban planning with being home again in Toronto, and he said it was "time for new interest in an old love, the Toronto waterfront."[13]

In 1992, he was appointed chair of the Waterfront Regeneration Trust with a mandate to implement his own royal commission report. The Province of Ontario also named him to head a special new panel called "Who Does What?" a significant task force examining the structure, competitiveness, and governance of the Greater Toronto Area.

By 1996, Crombie was serving as chancellor of Ryerson University (recently renamed Toronto Metropolitan University), helping to broker a bid for the Toronto Blue Jays, and chairing the Terry Fox Hall of Fame. He was also a director of the Laidlaw Foundation and served as CEO of the Canadian Urban Institute. When Toronto decided to pursue a 2008 Olympic bid, Mayor Mel Lastman tapped Crombie to head the city's high-profile 62-member bid committee.

In 2002, with business leader David Pecaut, Crombie helped convene the first Toronto City Summit, bringing together 150 of the municipality's leading urbanists to shape its future direction. He was also appointed by the federal government to oversee talks on Indigenous land claims and served as founding chair of the 800-kilometre Waterfront Trail along Lake Ontario. In 2004, Crombie was appointed an Officer of the Order of Canada, and in 2012 was made a member of the Order of Ontario.

Crombie has assisted in efforts to create a Toronto history museum as well as to have the Rouge Valley designated a national park. During the mayoral term of Rob Ford, he backed community efforts in support of Toronto's waterfront, and in December 2020, resigned as head of Ontario's Greenbelt Council to protest Premier Doug Ford's government rules that would gut environmental protections in the province.

Retired from active public life, Crombie is busier today than ever with requests for his sage advice, guidance, and input. Now living comfortably in Toronto's Dovercourt neighbourhood, he remains an inspiration for an entire generation and to this day is still known far and wide as Toronto's "Tiny Perfect Mayor."

Mayoral Election for 1973–1974	
CANDIDATES	VOTES
David Crombie	82,653
Anthony O'Donohue	58,417
David Rotenberg	35,219

SPECIAL NOTE: There were four other minor mayoral candidates.

Mayoral Election for 1975–1976	
David Crombie	102,807

SPECIAL NOTE: There were 10 other minor mayoral candidates, including second-place finisher Toronto white supremacist Don Andrews with 5,792 votes.

Mayoral Election for 1977–1978	
David Crombie	113,027

SPECIAL NOTE: There were nine other minor mayoral candidates, including the next in line, Toronto white supremacist Don Andrews with 7,129 votes.

Mayor Fred Beavis

1978

The 57th mayor of Toronto

Occupations: Roofing contractor, City of Toronto alderman and controller, Metropolitan Toronto councillor, philanthropist
Residence While Mayor: 1041 Logan Avenue
Birth: October 8, 1914, in Toronto
Death: July 11, 1997, in Toronto

——— • ———

Frederick Joseph Beavis was a veteran councillor who was briefly mayor in 1978, serving the second-shortest term in the city's history. Beavis had wanted to become mayor his entire political life, a dream shared by his wife and number one political supporter, Frances. When the city's popular David Crombie stepped down to run for the House of Commons, Beavis was faced with a stark choice: either throw his own hat in the ring to succeed Crombie, or seek the interim appointment as mayor and take his name out of the running.

In the end, the decision was a heartfelt one. By mid-1978, his wife, Frances, was racked with cancer and urged her husband to accept a short-term appointment and fulfill a long-held ambition, thus entering the city's history books.

At the time, the *Toronto Star*'s *The City* magazine described Beavis as "a big friendly man with an Irish potato face and a simple heart" and noted that "it wouldn't be right to call him anything but Fred."[1] The magazine pointed out that he was born and raised on Lewis Street in the neighbourhood of Queen Street East and Broadview Avenue where his family had lived since his grandfather emigrated from Ireland in the 1840s.

The son of Toronto roofer Ed Beavis and Jane O'Brien, the young Beavis was just 11 when his mother died, and the next year his father married Alice McInerney, a widow. Beavis was educated at St. Anne's School and Danforth Technical. At the time of his childhood in the mid-1920s, Danforth Avenue was still a mud road and the Beaches just a string of cottage settlements east of Toronto.

Beavis took courses in metalwork and drafting before going on to deliver beer six days a week for the O'Keefe Brewing Company. Raised a Roman Catholic in what was a very Orange Order city, Beavis later recalled the Toronto of a different era when "there were always confrontations, Catholic and Protestant boys fightin' each other …"[2]

At age 21, Beavis married Frances Wood and lost his father the same year. With his brothers, he took over Beavis Brothers Ltd., a local roofing and sheet metal contracting firm founded by their father in 1895. Through a combination of enterprise, business savvy, and sheer hard work, Beavis

Brothers saw its business expand from one truck to five while its workforce grew to more than 25 employees, operating from Windsor in the south to the Quebec border in the east.

In 1947, for the princely sum of $10,000 ($148,000 today), Beavis built a comfortable bungalow at 1041 Logan Avenue, a neighbourhood of modest single-family homes east of Broadview Avenue. Although comfortable but not wealthy, the family, including children Pam, Tom, and Michael, spent summers at their cottage at Young's Harbour on Lake Simcoe, with Dad coming up every weekend.

Beavis first entered public life in 1955 as the unsuccessful provincial Liberal Party candidate in the riding of Riverdale. He later recalled that his brother, Jack, suggested he run, since it might be good for business. Although he lost that race, Beavis got the political bug, and it was just the first election defeat in a three-decade career of public service.

Despite being an unsuccessful aldermanic candidate in 1956, Beavis persevered and was finally elected one of two councillors for Riverdale's Ward 1 in 1957. Appealing to a working-class, blue-collar base, he advocated free transportation for pensioners with no other means of support, the hiring of men over 50 years old for city jobs, and the building of a major new sports centre, stadium, and pool at Riverdale Park.

Toronto was changing, though. Nathan Phillips, the city's first-ever non-Anglo-Saxon Protestant mayor, was re-elected with an overwhelming margin, and Jean Newman became the first woman to gain election to a city-wide office. Beavis was comfortably re-elected for the 1959–1960 term and secured a seat on the Metro Council in 1961. By the early 1960s, Beavis was proving to be one of the city's more popular politicians, and in the 1964 election, was acclaimed.

A true practitioner of street-level, retail politics, Beavis later recounted: "I couldn't walk a block without somebody stopping to talk to me, and by my first name,"[3] estimating that he received about 40 phone calls per week. His campaign brochures trumpeted: "Fred Beavis is a man who thinks for himself and works for his fellow man."[4] In July 1967, he was selected by Toronto's Council to fill a vacancy on the Board of Control. When the city-wide body was later abolished, Beavis returned to being an alderman for the 1970–1972 term.

Never one to live a fancy life, Beavis was a self-made man of heartfelt generosity who lived for the simple pleasures of helping family members, whether paying for summer camp, helping with the purchase of a new car, or subsidizing a vacation in Florida.

For the 1973–1974 Council term under Mayor David Crombie, he served on the Parks and Recreation Committee and was a member of the Metro Council's Executive Committee on three separate occasions. Forced to temporarily leave the Metro Council in January 1975, he returned to both the city and the Metro position in 1977 as the senior alderman for Ward 8, remaining there until his defeat more than a decade later.

A profile of Beavis later said: "He has a way of disarming people with his gentle common-sense approach to everything. He certainly seduced the militants in his own community that way."[5] His campaign brochures in the 1970s listed a range of accomplishments: having the Royal York Hotel vastly increase the amount of taxes it paid, giving city employees the right to participate in civic elections, building new parking lots over subway rights-of-way, and a new Pape Recreation Centre.

Beavis put forward a mix of both populist and politically sellable propos-als such as a modern budgeting procedure and a city Finance Committee to control expenditures, the amalgamation of the six municipalities in Metro Toronto, the removal of pockets of blight, and action "to stop slum condi-tions before they exist."

In late August 1978, upon the resignation of David Crombie, Beavis was one of just two Council members nominated for the mayoralty. Thought at first to be a safe choice for the interim position, the Council deadlocked and Beavis found himself tied for support with fellow coun-cillor Anne Johnston.

The genial former roofer was backed by several members of the Executive Committee and the right wing of the Council but lost much-needed left-of-centre support due to prior boosting of the development industry, his seeking to revive the Spadina Expressway, and wanting to evict Toronto Islands residents from their homes. In the end, the mayoral selection was made during a tense 45-minute Council meeting. When the vote was tied, city clerk Roy Henderson deposited the two names in a box. The winner was Fred Beavis.

As the *Toronto Star* reported, Beavis always displayed a compassion-ate consideration for people of all political persuasions, noting that "he is the solid rock of the right but he also brings a warm sense of humour to politics."[6] However, that was not a view shared by everyone, and *Globe and Mail* columnist Dick Beddoes penned his own scathing assessment: "What Beavis has said that is intelligible in city affairs you could write on the head of a pin and have room left over for the entire 150 psalms ..."[7]

Even long-time political foe John Sewell, in a 1978 interview, described Beavis as "really nice, really easy to get along with. Fred is probably the best-liked member of council." Sewell observed that "[Fred] has a clear idea who he is representing, which is basically the development industry and the people who get jobs in the development industry."[8]

For Beavis, it was a badge he wore with pride, remarking that he was pleased when persons referred to him as the "old guard," supportive of large Toronto hotels, bank buildings, office towers, and shopping complexes. As alderman, he had opposed building the St. Lawrence Centre and recalled that he almost had a fit over *The Archer*, the Henry Moore sculpture in Nathan Phillips Square, saying, "We got culture up to our ears and this is the last straw."[9]

The personable Beavis fulfilled his mayoral duties with folksy accomplishment, yet it was not all clear sailing. The Council could not achieve a quorum for its last meeting and reversed itself on a controversial bylaw regarding dog ownership. A proposal to have candidates disclose the amounts and sources of campaign contributions was bounced around, and a decision on a new Ontario Hydro switching station to prevent power blackouts downtown was deferred until after the election.

After a hotly contested campaign against councillors Anthony O'Donohue and David Smith, it was John Sewell who captured the 1978 mayoralty election, succeeding Beavis as the city's 58th mayor. The dour Sewell — never one to enjoy the heavy social demands of the mayoral office — proposed the creation of a brand-new civic office, that of lieutenant governor of Toronto, with Fred Beavis as his choice to occupy the new position.

Following his brief service as mayor, Beavis was easily re-elected to the Council from Ward 8 in Riverdale in 1978, receiving 8,174 votes; by 1980, that climbed even higher. Beavis was re-elected for the 1982–1985 and 1985–1988 terms, serving on the Council that approved a rezoning for the massive new $550 million ($1.1 billion today) Canadian Broadcasting Corporation complex on Front Street West.

In 1985, Beavis, by now the 70-year-old dean of the Council and first elected in the 1950s, beat back a strong challenge by the New Democrats. He sent a small army of volunteers through his working-class neighbourhoods, staking out even bigger and flashier signs than in past years. The *Toronto Star* endorsed him, noting, "Incumbent Fred Beavis is the senior member of City Council's old guard and an unabashed supporter of development. His no-nonsense approach helps frame the debate over projects like the railway lands."[10]

In 1986, the *Toronto Star*'s municipal affairs columnist, David Lewis Stein, wrote, "I think of him as one of the last true gentlemen in municipal politics. He fights hard at council, but when meetings are over, he bears no grudges. Such grace is rare in these mean political times."[11] Ever the traditionalist, even Beavis was coming around on environmental issues, advocating that owners of properties polluted with dangerously high lead levels should be forced to make the contamination known should they plan to sell.

Beavis was a member of the 1986 Metro Council that gave the final go-ahead for the new Toronto Transit Commission Sheppard Avenue subway, and as the city's deputy mayor, also touted a possible 1996 Toronto Summer Olympic bid, insisting that it would also include low-cost housing post-Olympics.

In 1987, Toronto's Council overwhelmingly approved plans for a colossal new Bell Canada Enterprises development at Bay and Front Streets, yet Beavis objected when asked to approve $15,000 ($32,000 today) for a tenants' defence fund, calling it a disgrace and that tenants in his own ward did not use the service.

The Council granted itself a 30 percent pay raise in 1988, with Beavis voting in favour. For his east end ward, the right-of-centre councillor opposed a new energy plant, publicly explaining that in his re-election fight he now had to keep on top of environmental matters. Yet the pro-car Beavis also championed a six-month trial of one-way streets downtown: Yonge Street would become one way north and Bay Street one way south from Front Street to Davenport Road.

Beavis was known throughout Toronto as a more traditional "Mr. Fix-it" type of politician, and by the November 1988 municipal election, his time had come. He lost his seat to Marilyn Churley, an energetic young activist. A shift in ward boundaries, an intensive push by the New Democrats, and an influx of yuppies, students, gays, and young families all conspired to defeat him. Ousted by a young upstart, Beavis took his defeat quite hard at age 74: "It's an insult to the seniors when you tell them you're no longer useful. There's no substitute for experience."[12]

Immediately after his defeat, Beavis said he would use the $14,987 ($31,700 today) left over in his own campaign account to buy a new car and take a trip to Florida, perfectly legal at the time. In retirement, he helped St. Michael's Hospital with a $50 million ($106 million today) expansion campaign and assisted Riverdale United Church in setting up new services for its community centre.

In his personal life, Beavis was a member of the Ward 8 Ratepayer and Tenants' Association, the Yonge-Bloor-Bay Association, the Loyal Order of the Moose, the Riverdale Kiwanis Club, the Broadview Young Men's Christian Association, the Ward 7 Businessmen's Association, the Empire Club, and the Gerrard Businessmen's Association. He also served as a director of the Woodgreen Community Centre and St. Michael's Hospital.

In July 1997, Fred Beavis, the genial and well-regarded "honest roofer," died of pneumonia at St. Michael's Hospital, age 82. He was predeceased in April 1980 by his wife, Frances. A sombre funeral Mass was held at St. Joseph's Church on Leslie Street, and he was laid to rest at the Toronto Necropolis in Cabbagetown. Former mayor David Crombie recalled that Beavis was "the common sense of the east end" and noted that he was "a wonderful part of the history of Toronto … he was uneasy with ideologies but he understood the importance of Toronto growing.… He understood that as Toronto grew it would get better."[13]

Mayor John Sewell

1978–1980

The 58th mayor of Toronto

Occupations: Lawyer, activist, community organizer, City of Toronto alderman, Metropolitan Toronto councillor, Metro Toronto Housing Corporation chair, newspaper columnist, Provincial Commission on Planning and Development Reform chair, non-governmental organization executive, police reformer, author
Residence While Mayor: 205 Seaton Street
Birth: December 8, 1940, in Toronto

——— • ———

John Sewell was born in Toronto's Beaches neighbourhood on December 8, 1940, one of four children of William and Helen Sewell. He attended Balmy Beach Public School and Malvern Collegiate and then the University of Toronto, graduating with a bachelor of arts in English literature in 1961 and completing a law degree there in 1964. In 1965, he articled with the Toronto firm of Gordon, Elliott, Kelly and Palmer.

Sewell became a grassroots community organizer in 1966, working with the Toronto Community Union Project and with local residents seeking to stop further expropriations in their neighbourhoods. Following his call to the bar in 1966, he joined residents of the Trefann Court Urban Renewal Area to fight the levelling of their working-class, low-income neighbourhood.

From 1968 to 1971, he was a non-practising partner in the law firm of Sewell, Shuttleworth, Mackay-Smith and described the experience in his book *Up Against City Hall*. Two of the key ideas resonated far and wide across the city: that neighbourhood preservation was a priority and that urban planning must involve local residents.

Sewell was first elected as an alderman for Ward 7 in December 1969 in the predominantly working-class area of St. Jamestown, Regent Park, Don Vale, and Cabbagetown. He also worked with a small community-based, locally owned newspaper, *Seven News*, an alternative to large corporately owned dailies.

In a later *Globe and Mail* feature called "Saint John," John Barber described Sewell's arrival on the local political scene, noting that he was "an alderman with long stringy hair who wore cowboy boots and blue jeans.... Many of his new colleagues were absolutely convinced that John Sewell was a Communist.... But none of them could have predicted the stunning success of his revolution, let alone that this scruffy radical with the shrill, piping voice would someday be mayor."[1]

Barber also pointed out that Sewell "took elaborate pains to maintain his purity. His colleagues were 'the enemy.' He considered them corrupt and shunned them scrupulously, refusing all friendly gestures."[2] Once elected to the Council, Sewell broadened his scope, becoming active with attempts to protect historic buildings threatened with demolition, including the St. Lawrence Market, slated to be demolished for a parking structure.

Sewell proposed new planning measures to curb the height and size of structures downtown and insisted that Toronto's 1974 Central Area Plan put several new principles into effect: that downtown be a vibrant mix of residential and commercial uses, that new affordable housing should be built, that development should strengthen streetscapes, and that major new roads into the downtown not be built.

Anthony O'Donohue, a Council colleague who later ran against Sewell for mayor, described him as tall and lanky with thinning hair and dressed in the style of a hippie. "He seemed to be angry all the time," observes O'Donohue in his book *Front Row Centre*, also saying that he was "one of the most tenacious politicians I have ever met. He just never gave up.... He had that messianic fervour for his ideas and tried to convince the rest of us that his way was the only way."[3] For the next eight years, Sewell was a full-time councillor and was re-elected in 1972, 1974, and 1976. He also served on the Metro Council from 1974 to 1978 and later as mayor.

Sewell effectively became the de facto leader of the reform wing of Toronto's Council. He was widely viewed as controversial, articulate, intelligent, and committed, a man who championed low-income tenants, human rights, neighbourhoods, historic preservation, public transit, resident participation at City Hall, and the containment of urban sprawl.

He also had a knack for picking fights. In 1973, he declared his candidacy for Metro chair, publishing an inflammatory election-style pamphlet against eventual winner Paul Godfrey, declaring that Godfrey "would keep working with developers ... push for more expressways and wider roads [and] maintain the secret and closed position of the office of Metro Chairman."[4]

Involved in the earliest discussions around the creation of a new St. Lawrence neighbourhood, Sewell was an ardent advocate of core principles, including mixed uses, a street grid pattern, and a building form that reflected the existing area. He also fought almost single-handedly against proposals for a massive new downtown shopping complex (today's Eaton Centre), and yet, in one of the true ironies of political life, he later conducted its official opening as the new mayor of Toronto.

In 1976, the *Globe and Mail*'s Graham Fraser described Sewell as a political loner, noting "Sewell has always functioned best on his own ... more effective as an individual than as a difficult member of a collective."[5] By 1978, however, Sewell was contesting the mayoralty in a hard-fought campaign against Council veterans David Smith and Anthony O'Donohue.

While both O'Donohue and Smith were Liberals with links to the business community and major developers, Sewell was a reform-minded activist and the strongest critic of the "old guard." He was cast as a very left-of-centre, union-backed, New Democratic Party (NDP) radical, though he had never officially joined the party.

Sewell, who had previously been described as stubborn, private, often sullen, and at times self-righteous, began reshaping his image. In *Front Row Centre*, O'Donohue writes of Sewell: "He was no longer the raging maverick of olden days. He had discarded the jeans and beads for a suit and tie and his hair was much neater. He was also much more balanced in his approach to issues and appeared to be much calmer. It looked like he had gone to charm school."[6]

In the end, with the city's political centre divided, Sewell was able to win election as mayor in 1978 with support from tenants, activists, reformers, heritage supporters, unions, gays, and downtown residents, as well as a cross-section of progressive, community-based, left-wing, low-income, social justice, environmental, and anti-development groups. That said, the reaction was mixed. Media prognosticators said he would either be the best or the worst mayor Toronto had ever seen.

On December 4, 1978, the entire Sewell inaugural speech was just 20 paragraphs written in longhand and a foreshadowing of things to come. Sewell said that "this council has the potential to become a very fractious body."[7] There was not a single thank you to his immediate mayoral predecessors Fred Beavis or David Crombie, no recognition of the councillors or community members present, and no mention of city staff, invited guests, municipal partners, civic agencies, and stakeholders attending.

While in office, Sewell was vocal on greater public accountability for the Metro police and the need for an independent police-complaints commission. He also vocally championed heritage preservation, freezing Toronto Transit Commission fares, the introduction of a monthly transit pass, and allowing all homes on the Toronto Islands to remain. Mayoral accomplishments included the creation of a daycare within City Hall, efforts to redevelop Yonge Street, and being the first mayor in the city's history to publicly support the human rights of Toronto's gay and lesbian citizens.

Dubbed "Mayor Blue Jeans" by the *Toronto Sun*, Sewell, in many ways, ended up defeating himself in his bid for re-election. In March 1980, when Toronto police officer Michael Sweet was tragically shot and killed, Sewell pretended he could not attend the funeral due to a doctor's appointment, yet local media discovered that was not the case. He could have easily appeared. Although later changing his story to suggest that doing so could have caused discomfort among mourners, his absence was widely viewed as an anti-police snub.

Then, six weeks later on an official visit to Amsterdam to celebrate the 35th anniversary of the city's 1945 liberation from German occupation, Sewell paid $35 to see a live show featuring a man and a woman copulating, then spoke about it publicly, calling the live sex show "tasteful" and that "if you're a tourist in Amsterdam, you do what the tourists do ..." In terms of all the controversy, the unhappy Sewell said: "I think this is a joke."[8]

In May 1980, Sewell courted controversy yet again when he sought Council approval to send civic aid and staff to the People's Revolutionary Government of Grenada to aid Marxist prime minister Maurice Bishop, who had taken power in a violent overthrow the year before. The Council spent just 15 minutes debating a key city economic and jobs report, yet over four hours on the mayor's proposal to give foreign aid to Grenada.

Civic Affairs, a publication of the non-partisan Bureau of Municipal Research, reported that the key 1980 election issues were affordable housing, property tax reform, social services for single-parent families, unemployed youth, cuts to daycare, race relations, the need for a more effective police commission, and an industrial strategy for Toronto.

As reform colleague Karl Jaffary put it, "A lot of highly principled persons manage not to antagonize the electorate the way John did. In some ways he antagonized them needlessly. He seemed to like doing things that made people mad." Metro chair Paul Godfrey, with whom Sewell had been in an almost constant battle, stated bluntly that the central 1980 election issue would be Sewell and nothing else. As *Globe and Mail* bureau chief John Barber pointed out, "Sewell dwells on issues, not personality, but in every battle he fights, the issue becomes Sewell himself."[9]

After two years of almost non-stop controversy, Sewell lost the 1980 mayoral election. Although maintaining the support of some reform-minded Liberals and virtually all New Democrats, Sewell was defeated by city budget chief Art Eggleton who with 88,953 votes city-wide came in over 2,000 votes ahead. Sewell returned to the Council in a 1981 by-election as alderman for the adjacent downtown Ward 6. He was re-elected in 1982 but retired from municipal politics in 1984 to become a columnist on urban affairs for the *Globe and Mail*.

From his new perch, Sewell revealed that some of his strident, out-of-step views had not changed. In a 1986 *Globe* column titled "The CN Tower Has Got to Go," he called the landmark "a poor, inappropriate, belittling symbol" and said, "rarely do I favour demolishing existing structures, but this one has the city so wrong that I'm willing to make an exception."[10]

That same year, Sewell left the *Globe and Mail* to become the appointed chair of the Metro Toronto Housing Authority (MTHA), which managed 33,000 rent-geared-to-income units, including several notorious housing projects. In 1988, Ontario's housing minister unceremoniously fired Sewell for inserting himself into the MTHA administration and involving himself in day-to-day operations.

Following the 1990 election of the Bob Rae NDP government in Ontario, Sewell was appointed chair of the Provincial Commission on Planning and Development Reform, serving from 1991 to 1993. Final recommendations included prohibiting further development sprawl, building affordable housing in all new developments, protecting quality agricultural land, increasing energy conservation, protecting water quality, and enhancing major natural areas.

During the 1990s, Sewell, working with a number of consultants, was successful in winning a provincial competition that resulted in "A Plan for Seaton" on how a new city of 90,000 could be built in an environmentally and economically sustainable manner on lands in north Durham. From 1993 onward, he also began writing for several local community newspapers: *NOW* from 1993 to 1999, *Eye Weekly* (later *The Grid*) from 1999 to 2005, and *Post City* after 2000.

After the election of South African president Nelson Mandela, Sewell became involved in several international non-governmental organization consultations: as an adviser for the re-establishment of local government in Malawi and as part of an evaluation of local government programs for UN-Habitat. From 1994 to 1999, he worked with the municipal council of Buffalo City in South Africa's Eastern Cape Province during that municipality's transition from apartheid to democracy.

In the mid-1990s, Sewell was instrumental in the founding of Citizens for Local Democracy (C4LD), serving as a key leader in its unsuccessful attempts to fight the forced amalgamation of the City of Toronto and Metro municipalities into a single new megacity by Ontario premier Mike Harris's government. What started off as a dozen people with no real strategy erupted into a Metro-wide movement. And to further protest the new megacity, Sewell ran as an independent progressive candidate in the 1999 Ontario provincial election, placing third in the Toronto Centre–Rosedale riding.

From 1999 to 2006, Sewell managed a new website focused on government reform and headed the Toronto Police Accountability Coalition. In September 2002, he helped organize a Save Union Station committee to counter what he believed to be a flawed bidding process for the station's redevelopment.

Sewell sought election to Toronto's Council in Ward 21 in 2006, running against popular incumbent Joe Mihevc in that fall's municipal election. Strangely, he also took aim at the record of Mayor David Miller, someone who should have been considered a natural ally. Although billing himself as a former Toronto mayor, he was soundly defeated.

Appointed to the Order of Canada in June 2005, Sewell is the author of some 36 published reports, speeches, books, articles, and research papers. He resides today just south of St. Clair Avenue and Bathurst Street with his wife, Liz Rykert, and for several years maintained a small office on Beverley Street downtown in the 19th century home of George Brown, one of the Fathers of Confederation.

SPECIAL NOTE: Civic election dates in Ontario were moved from December to the second week of November. The term of Toronto's Council would begin on December 1 of that same year instead of January 1 the next year.

Mayoral Election for 1978–1980

CANDIDATES	VOTES
John Sewell	73,424
Anthony O'Donohue	63,496
David Smith	45,825

SPECIAL NOTE: There were nine other minor mayoral candidates.

Mayor Art Eggleton
1980–1991

The 59th mayor of Toronto

Occupations: Industrial accountant, City of Toronto alderman, Metropolitan Toronto councillor, Member of House of Commons, federal minister responsible for infrastructure, federal treasury board president, federal minister of international trade, federal minister of national defence, Canadian senator
Residences While Mayor: 14 Grenadier Heights
Birth: September 29, 1943, in Toronto

—— • ——

With solid working-class roots, Arthur "Art" Eggleton was born on September 29, 1943, at Women's College Hospital, the only child of Arthur and Louise Eggleton. His father was a stock clerk with Dominion Envelope, and the young Eggleton's earliest years were in Cabbagetown. As a later *Globe and Mail* campaign profile noted, "The family never owned its own home and lived in a succession of rented houses, flats, and apartments." Eggleton himself later said: "We had a very humble existence, and we knew the value of the dollar. Life was not easy …"[1]

The family moved often, and to earn money as a young boy, Eggleton worked at a number of jobs: delivering the *Globe and Mail* door to door, as a drugstore delivery boy, as a truck driver, and as a worker at the Canadian National Exhibition. He was educated at Lord Dufferin and Orde Public Schools and Harbord Collegiate. In 1959, the family moved to an apartment on Birchmount Road in Scarborough where he attended W.A. Porter Collegiate Institute and became a member of the school band.

At 18 and just short of finishing Grade 12, Eggleton went on to study business at Shaw Business College. After graduation, he joined Volvo Canada where he worked as an industrial accountant, rising to assistant head of accounting before leaving to become a full-time municipal councillor.

In 1965, he married Rita LeBlanc, and his daughter, Stephanie, was born in 1969. It was through friends that Eggleton first became active in political matters. A trip to Quebec in the mid-1960s had kindled a keen interest. Believing Canada should have its own flag and national anthem, Eggleton involved himself with the Spadina Liberal Association and also became the executive secretary of a fledgling new municipal party, the Metro Civic Action League or CIVAC.

Eggleton took the plunge in 1969 and was elected alderman on a platform of civic reform in west end Ward 4. At age 26, he was the city's youngest councillor. Re-elected in 1972, 1974, 1976, and 1978, he served on the city's influential Executive Committee from 1972 through to his election as mayor. During both the David Crombie and John Sewell administrations, he was chosen by colleagues to be the city budget chief. As the senior councillor for the dual-member Ward 4, he was on Metro's Executive Committee and served on the board of the Catholic Children's Aid Society, the Canadian National Exhibition, and the Non-Profit Housing Corporation.

In 1975, he separated from his wife, Rita, and they divorced in 1978. A close friend later said that it was Eggleton's heavy political involvement that contributed to the divorce. A later profile noted that it was also at that time that Eggleton entered into what some people called his "swinging bachelor" period. "I don't subscribe to that terminology," he explained in a personal interview. "That's all I'm going to say."[2]

Eggleton was the federal Liberal Party candidate in an October 1978 by-election in Parkdale but was defeated by the Progressive Conservatives, his only electoral defeat during the course of 13 election campaigns. Just weeks later, he ran again for the Council in Ward 4, finishing first among a field of 10 candidates to become the ward's senior councillor. In that election, the left-wing John Sewell, with 39 percent of the vote, won the mayoralty, setting the stage for what would be a vigorous race for mayor in 1980.

In 1979, Eggleton's personal appearance took on a whole new look when he had his mostly straight blondish hair restyled into a mop of fashionable curls. As he later pointed out, "the fuzzing" of one's hair had become popular, with both Metro chair Paul Godfrey and North York (and later Toronto) mayor Mel Lastman leading the way.

That same year Eggleton met his second wife, Brenda Clune, on a trip to Rome to mark the elevation of her uncle, Robert Clune, to become an auxiliary Roman Catholic bishop. Eggleton converted from the Anglican to the Catholic faith, and they dated for two years, awaiting the annulment of his first marriage. They were finally married at St. Michael's Cathedral in December 1981.

In March 1980, Eggleton announced his candidacy for mayor, pre-empting all other prospective challengers. His message was that Toronto needed a strong, clear, credible voice to articulate its needs and aspirations. However, he faced several obstacles from the very outset: first, the broad public did not know him; and second, both he and Sewell agreed on several issues, including police accountability, preservation of homes on the Toronto Islands, increased daycare, and new development on the waterfront. There was also the enormous difficulty of unseating an incumbent mayor.

With the support of former finance minister John Turner and some well-known Tories, a single Eggleton fundraising dinner raked in $70,000 ($242,000 today), while incumbent Sewell, by contrast, refused to accept campaign donations from corporations, developers, or political parties.

Eggleton accused the sitting mayor of demoralizing police officers through inflammatory remarks when Sewell referred to a "frightening record of shootings and killings established by Metro Police."[3] He campaigned on obtaining federal dollars to build affordable housing, a short takeoff and landing (STOL) air service at the island airport, and a lower-cost monthly Toronto Transit Commission Metropass. In the end, Eggleton won with 88,953 votes to Sewell's 86,919. As former mayor Crombie observed, it was because "Art has a style that the people are looking for right now."[4]

The victorious Eggleton attributed his victory to campaigning on seven substantive policy planks: housing, neighbourhood preservation, transportation, waterfront development, the elderly, police-community relations, and daycare. In his inaugural address, he stated emphatically: "This Mayor is going to move the city in only one direction — forward."[5]

Eggleton advocated job access for the disabled and proposed a new city economic development department, a mayoral Committee on Community and Race Relations, and a Toronto Economic Council made up of politicians, business, and labour to advise the Council on small business, tourism, and construction issues.

As Eggleton himself noted, his style was not one of conflict or confrontation. He was more of a conciliator and wanted to be thoroughly briefed on an issue before expressing an opinion. Yet, in early 1981, he faced significant anger from the gay community after a massive police raid on four downtown bathhouses, Canada's largest mass arrest since the 1970 War Measures Act. Eggleton called for a full review, and the Council commissioned a report on improved relations with the gay community, the first such initiative in the city's history.

In 1982, once more with the support of his winning coalition of Conservatives and Liberals, Eggleton competed for mayor with a small band of just 50 campaign workers, this time against the Hummer Sisters, a comedy team. Eggleton received 121,914 votes to 11,820 for his main opponent.

His 1982 inaugural address to the Council reflected the times. "People are hurting," he stated, pointing out that the economic distress had international roots and that his priorities included jobs, housing, safety, and social services. Eggleton said that "smokestacks and assembly lines are disappearing, replaced by a new generation of high technology, robotics, advanced computer-based manufacturing,"[6] and promised to hold any tax increase to no more than 5 percent in 1983. He pledged a crime-prevention coordinator for Toronto and called for better medical care for post-psychiatric patients.

The Office of the Mayor had also transformed into a highly effective political operation with a cadre of hand-picked advisers. Yet, at City Hall, Eggleton often kept a certain distance from his own councillors, and there was some criticism of his aloofness.

In 1985, he withstood a challenge from left-of-centre councillor Anne Johnston, a more populist fellow Liberal who campaigned on issues surrounding the $2 billion ($4.8 billion today) downtown rail lands development and did her best to have a proposed 60,000-seat domed stadium moved to Exhibition Place.

Eggleton was viewed as a hard worker with sound administrative skills and a well-rounded understanding of civic government. As the *Globe and Mail* noted, the city under Eggleton appeared to be under control, stable, and safe. When the final 1985 mayoral results came in, Eggleton swept in well ahead of Johnston by a vote of 93,938 to 60,010.

In a wide-ranging inaugural speech to the Council in the presence of Emmett Cardinal Carter, Eggleton described Toronto as a city of "deeply rooted human values, a centre for commerce and finance, a media capital, a city of learning and science," yet also pointed out that the poor were "the first constituency of the mayor and council."[7]

He stated that we "must crack homelessness"[8] and called for annual housing targets; a renewed focus on unskilled workers, minorities, and young people; and investments in the fashion, film, television, and computer software sectors. The newly re-elected mayor also requested major attention on the food, beverage, and tourism sectors and insisted that it was important to create an environmental protection office for the first time.

In November 1988, Eggleton faced little serious opposition in his bid for a fourth term. His closest opponent, community activist Carolann Wright, received just 24,662 votes to Eggleton's 92,043. In his final inaugural address, he outlined an agenda for increased daycare and environmental protection as well as a reduction in homelessness, improved social assistance, increased efforts to fight drugs, safer streets for women, help for seniors, and a new formula to equalize property taxes.

Over a period of 15 years, 60,000 low-income tenants were displaced from flats, apartments, and rooming houses, and Eggleton stated that "soaring land values cannot be allowed to eclipse basic human values."[9] He called for expanded apartment recycling, improved public transit, new beach cleanup efforts, and using existing rail corridors for transit.

The longest-serving mayor in Toronto's history retired from municipal politics in 1991, and the following year, Prime Minister Jean Chrétien appointed him the federal Liberal Party candidate in the stronghold of York Centre, a part of Chrétien's strategy to run "star candidates." In the 1993 federal election, Eggleton won and was soon appointed to the federal Cabinet where he served in several senior positions: president of the Treasury Board and minister responsible for infrastructure (1993 to 1996), minister for international trade (1996 to 1997), and minister of national defence (1997 to 2002).

At the Treasury Board, he was a key player in the program review process and was central to the success of Canada's new Infrastructure Works Program. In 1996, Eggleton became minister for international trade, a position he held until the 1997 election. The portfolio was responsible for Team Canada trade missions, relations with the World Trade Organization, and matters arising from the North American Free Trade Agreement.

Eggleton retained his seat in the 1997 election, increasing his share of the popular vote to 72 percent, and was appointed minister of national defence, overseeing Canada's involvement in a North Atlantic Treaty Organization campaign to prevent ethnic cleansing in Kosovo. Other issues included the North American Aerospace Defense Command, women in the military, and the lingering effects of the prior Somalia inquiry. As Jim Travers of the *Toronto Star* noted, Eggleton was "a good choice ... calm, quietly determined, and gifted at defusing difficult questions with the balm of bafflegab ..."[10]

Re-elected in the 2000 federal general election, Eggleton was reappointed minister of defence and had to deal with a host of new challenges: the fight against terrorism post-9/11, the war in Afghanistan, improvements to military health, and sweeping changes to military justice. Yet problems arose in 2002 when news stories surfaced that a former girlfriend of Eggleton was hired to do research for the minister's office, leading to the perception of non-tendered public contracts. Dubbed "a ladies' man" in the national press, Eggleton was forced to resign from the federal Cabinet, though no rules had been broken.

From 2002 to 2004, he was chair of the Greater Toronto Area federal Liberal Party caucus and chair of the Canada-Israel Inter-Parliamentary Group. In 2004, he announced he would not be a candidate in the next federal election.

Eggleton was appointed to the Senate in 2005 by Prime Minister Paul Martin. He identified several Senate priorities: affordable housing, income inequality, and the urban agenda, becoming one of the Senate's most productive members. As chair of the Senate Subcommittee on Cities, he oversaw a 2009 landmark report on poverty, housing, and homelessness. As Carol Goar of the *Toronto Star* pointed out, "Eggleton has become an outspoken and knowledgeable crusader for the 3.4 million Canadians living in poverty."[11] In 2011, he joined the executive of Liberal International, the global forum of liberal and progressive political parties.

By 2014, Eggleton had some blunt words for Mayor Rob Ford, saying the mayoral controversies had reached international notoriety and were an embarrassment. "It's a distraction for city council in dealing with issues that the city badly needs to deal with," said Eggleton. "It makes the only office in the city that deals with a city-wide vision, the mayor's office, dysfunctional."[12] He also stated: "It is time for the people of Toronto to decide who can best lead our city going forward. I will not be supporting Mayor Ford's re-election."[13]

In recent years, Eggleton has served as chair of the St. John's Rehabilitation Hospital's "Rebuilding Lives Campaign" and as chair of the Advisory Board for the World Council on City Data. In 2015, at the request of Mayor John Tory, he chaired a comprehensive review of the city's public housing authority. In 2018, the highly respected Eggleton retired from the Senate. He and his wife, Camille Bacchus, now live in Rosedale and actively support the Art Eggleton and Camille Bacchus Fund, a Toronto Foundation charitable trust that funds high-impact projects for youth at risk.

Mayoral Election for 1980–1982	
CANDIDATES	**VOTES**
Art Eggleton	88,953
John Sewell	86,919

SPECIAL NOTE: There were seven other minor mayoral candidates.

Mayoral Election for 1982–1985	

SPECIAL NOTE: After a period of two-year Council terms during the 1970s, Ontario returned to three-year Council terms in 1982.

Art Eggleton	121,914
A. Hummer (Hummer Sisters)	11,820

SPECIAL NOTE: There were nine other minor mayoral candidates.

Mayoral Election for 1985–1988	
Art Eggleton	93,938
Anne Johnston	60,010

SPECIAL NOTE: There were 12 other minor mayoral candidates.

Mayoral Election for 1988–1991	
Art Eggleton	92,043
Carolann Wright	24,662

SPECIAL NOTE: There were seven other minor mayoral candidates.

Mayor June Rowlands

1991–1994

The 60th mayor of Toronto

Occupations: Community advocate, research director, housing consultant, City of Toronto councillor, Metropolitan Toronto councillor, Metropolitan Police Commission chair
Residence While Mayor: 62 Wellesley Street West
Birth: May 14, 1924, in St. Laurent, Quebec
Death: December 21, 2017, in Toronto

——— • ———

orn in May 1924, June Pendock came to Toronto in 1928 with her father, a Bell Telephone Company supervisor, and her homemaker mother, who both had high expectations for their bookish daughter and who often talked to her about issues through the lens of old-style, left-wing politics and the perspective of the underdog. Rowlands remembered her father talking to a neighbour about the stock market crash and thinking to herself that when she grew up she wanted to study all about that.

She attended Bedford Park Public School and Lawrence Park Collegiate Institute, then enrolled at the University of Toronto to pursue political science and economics but was forced to drop out due to family illness. Rowlands started her work life in the customer service department of Bell Telephone where she met her husband, Harry, who had dropped into her office to make a then costly and rare long-distance call. They married in 1947 and soon began a family. As she told *Chatelaine* magazine later, they "were soon living in a comfortable, though not extravagant, life in Toronto's sedate well-scrubbed Rosedale."[1]

Her entry into community and political affairs was a gradual one. She and members of her bridge club in the 1950s created a group called the Tri-W's, whose slogan was "Where There's a Will, There's a Way," seeking to supply milk, vitamins, and financial donations to underprivileged families. Soon she was working on behalf of women's health, seniors, mothers needing daycare, disadvantaged tenants, and the mentally handicapped.

Rowlands was as a member of the Social Planning Council and the National Council of Welfare and was president of the Metro Family Service Association and the Association of Women Electors, a group of volunteers who monitored the municipal political scene. She was also a housing consultant for the Social Planning Council and dealt with the issues of homelessness and co-op housing. Active for many years with the North Rosedale Ratepayers' Association, she received a federal political appointment to the board of the federal Central Mortgage and Housing Corporation.

Prior to running for elected office, Rowlands was the director of the Provincial Liberal Caucus Research Office at Queen's Park under Liberal

Party leader Robert Nixon, and in 1975, attempted to win a seat in the provincial general election in the downtown St. David's riding, finishing third.

The next year, however, bitten by the political bug, Rowlands was first elected to Toronto's Council as alderman for the well-heeled Ward 10, which included Rosedale, Moore Park, Leaside, and North Toronto. It was a stable upper-income area of leafy trees and large single-family homes whose residents' main concerns were property taxes, market value assessment, and traffic congestion.

As a councillor, Rowlands was a moderate voice for a range of progressive causes, including pollution, better housing, and fighting body rub parlours and prostitution. A crowning achievement was the decidedly controversial 1977 first-ever bylaw to prohibit smoking in stores, theatres, hospitals, and office reception areas. Over significant local opposition, she supported giving group homes the right to locate in every area of the city.

In 1978, Ward 10 residents returned Rowlands with a vote of 16,006, and in topping the vote in her ward, she joined the Metro Council, as well. By 1980, Rowlands had increased her vote total to 17,465, but in 1982, it took a dip. She became the first woman appointed to the Toronto Transit Commission and served on the executive of Toronto's Council from 1978 to 1985 as well as holding the key post of city budget chief from 1980 to 1985 under Mayor Art Eggleton.

Rowlands ran for the Liberal Party in the 1984 federal general election, but it was both the wrong time and wrong location. The ethnically diverse suburban riding of York-Scarborough was geographically and socially far from her North Toronto base, and she was soundly defeated by Conservative Paul McCrossan.

Rowlands was a member of the incoming Ontario premier David Peterson's transition team, and for the November 1985 municipal election, she was acclaimed, serving until 1988 and helping to mediate a long-simmering Harbourfront dispute. In 1987, Rowlands sought the provincial Liberal nomination in the Eglinton riding, but in a major upset was defeated by law clerk Dianne Poole.

Back on Toronto's Council, she was instrumental in boosting the low wages of daycare workers as well as advocating housing for low-income single persons. She argued that a 25 percent cap for market value assessment was too high and that it should be no more than 10 percent. Rowlands championed safety and getting tough about poorly lit underground parking garages. As city budget chief, she steered millions of dollars in subsidies toward non-profit daycare centres. And in one of her proudest moments, she staged a lengthy filibuster to prevent the conversion of 10,000 rental units for sale as condominiums.

Rowlands served on the Council until 1988 when she chose not to run after accepting a major provincial appointment as chair of the Metropolitan Toronto Board of Commissioners of Police. With policing costing Metro taxpayers more than $1 million per day (equal to $2.1 million per day in today's dollars), a *Toronto Star* profile described Rowlands as "a feisty and outspoken politician with a long-time interest in policing issues such as domestic violence and juvenile prostitution," pointing out that she was a also a strong supporter of the civilian review of complaints against the police.[2]

The first woman to serve as chair, she was involved in a range of issues: improving police morale, relations with minority communities, a wave of extortion and robberies in the Chinese community, and preparations to host the G7 Economic Summit. Rowlands helped oversee the opening of the new $60 million ($128 million today) police headquarters on College Street and the 1989 selection of William McCormack as Toronto's new police chief.

In addition to navigating challenges posed by a first-ever New Democratic Party (NDP) provincial government and relations with an increasingly political police association, Rowlands had to deal with a new Police Services Act, the 1990 creation of the Special Investigations Unit, and the controversial case of Gordon Junger, a police constable moonlighting as a paid gigolo. Other issues included police misconduct, relations with the Black community, police training and recruitment policies, and a lack of diversity (out of 6,000 uniformed officers at the time, only 200 were from visible minorities). In the end, Rowlands's views were not in sync with the newly elected NDP government, and in 1991, Premier Bob Rae chose not to renew her as chair upon the expiration of her term.

With the surprise retirement of long-time incumbent Art Eggleton, pressure mounted on Rowlands to run for mayor, and as a result, Toronto saw its first truly competitive mayoral contest in 11 years, with her running against popular left-of-centre councillor Jack Layton, head of the progressive wing and the first-ever official candidate of the NDP for Toronto's mayoralty.

Fearing that 1978 might happen all over again, when a split in the right-of-centre and non-NDP vote had allowed the left-wing John Sewell to win, the city's corporate, business, legal, real-estate, and development communities rallied behind Rowlands. Her former campaign manager, John Laschinger, pointed out that her 1994 election day margin of victory of nearly two to one was because she followed "a carefully thought-out strategy that resisted the temptation to try and soften her views or make her candidacy more attractive to a larger number of voters." He called it "a tightly controlled, focused, strategic campaign."[3]

Toronto was changing demographically, and as police board chair, Rowlands was genuinely concerned about the problems of drugs, gangs, crime, and violence. Although candour was a strength, in this instance it was a political liability, since she voiced her opinion that Black youth were responsible for a disproportionate share of crime. She sought more drug treatment centres and to have Ottawa move forward on a series of changes, including tougher gun control, a clampdown on bogus refugees, and allowing local police to keep the proceeds of illicit drug dealing.

Unlike Layton, Rowlands backed Toronto's bid for the 1996 Summer Olympic Games and pledged not to reopen the development plan for the downtown railway lands, as Layton urged. In the end, at 67, she emerged the victor, winning with 58 percent of the vote to Layton's 23 percent. Rowlands was the first woman to become mayor of Toronto.

She is perhaps best remembered and unfairly blamed for banning the Toronto pop group Barenaked Ladies from performing at the major New Year's Eve City Hall function, claiming the group's name objectified women. Rowlands herself was out of town at the time, and the decision was made by three city staffers in charge of special events, not by Rowlands herself.

Rowlands lay low for much of her first year in office, explaining that she wanted to hunker down and get up to speed with the nuts-and-bolts issues and finances at City Hall. She helped streamline Toronto's 6,000-member bureaucracy, cutting almost 1,000 positions, and hired an economic czar to woo businesses to the city. Rowlands also launched an aggressive marketing campaign to extol the virtues of investing in Toronto.

Yet taking on key budgetary and financial matters also kept Rowlands further burrowed within City Hall, and her low-key personal style did not win fans among those desiring a more active political agenda. Her behind-the-scenes work was plodding, often complicated, and politically unrewarding, but it saved the city millions of dollars. As mayor, she was proud to bring forward Toronto's first-ever tax decrease of 0.5 percent, as well as a successful public-relations battle to oppose Metro's property tax reform plan. She also led a successful trade mission to China, netting several hundred million dollars of contracts for Toronto firms.

Still, city tax revenues continued to decline between 1991 and 1994 with no solution in sight. The recession left a fifth of Toronto office towers empty, and one city report predicted that The Bay department store chain might even close its flagship location downtown. The economic turbulence forced a cash-strapped city to approve a plan whereby city workers would forego seven days of pay in 1993, nine days in 1994 and 1995, and two in 1996.

Rowlands garnered negative attention in 1992 when she appeared to be uninformed, perhaps completely unaware, about a large-scale youth riot that shut down parts of Yonge Street near City Hall. The widely reported incident contributed to an image that Rowlands was out of touch. She noted that she had deliberately remained silent until she had had an opportunity to meet with leaders of Toronto's Black community, and in her own defence said, "A lot of healing has got to occur and that is not going to occur by somebody in my position making statements off the top of my head."[4]

She also angered some people by refusing to attend the Salvation Army's Red Shield fundraising ceremony in Nathan Phillips Square because of its position on homosexuality, one that was in conflict with the city's non-discrimination policy. Rowlands also became the first Toronto mayor to issue an official proclamation honouring gay pride. On other matters, she successfully fought the extension of Leslie Street below Eglinton Avenue and helped create a new organization of Great Lakes mayors to co-operate and work on water-quality issues and economic development matters.

Seeking re-election in 1994, Rowlands campaigned on a platform of fiscal responsibility, noting there was no tax increase in the first two years of her mandate, then a tax reduction for 1994, and pointed out her successful efforts to have the province kill a new corporate concentration tax. On the politically charged issue of a major casino in Toronto, Rowlands said she would need proof that casinos actually attracted tourist dollars. And at an all-candidates debate, she got into hot water when she called the Regent Park neighbourhood the "crack capital" of Metro.

Rowlands touted her efforts to defeat Metro's market value assessment scheme, downsize the city bureaucracy, modernize the municipality's Fire Department, and reform the Harbour Commission. She campaigned on a new official city plan, a "sister city" agreement with Chicago, and support for the film and biotech industries, and she backed a new basketball arena downtown and rezoning to allow a major expansion of the city's convention centre. She pointed to her lobbying efforts for tougher action on gun control, hate crimes, and violent young offender sentences, as well as mandatory prison time for using a gun during a crime.

Yet when the votes were counted, veteran councillor Barbara Hall emerged victorious with 70,248 votes to 58,952 for Rowlands. The third-place finisher, Gerry Meinzer, captured 20,868, mostly from pro-business and centre-right votes.

Post-retirement, Rowlands chose to remain out of the political lime-light. Her ex-husband had died in 1990, and in her personal and family time, Rowlands enjoyed hiking, cross-country skiing, the theatre, history books, and getting away as often as possible to the family cottage at Lake Kashwakmak in Eastern Ontario, but also pointed out that she was not a fan of television. Despite almost 20 years of public service, her annual civic pension was less than $30,000 per year ($53,000 today).

She was awarded a Woman of Distinction Award for public service, and in recognition of her decades of service to the citizens of Toronto, Davisville Park was renamed June Rowlands Park in 2004, a tribute to a woman who had worked tirelessly to promote and maintain park spaces.

Although rarely in the public spotlight post-retirement, Rowlands was emphatic about her successor, Rob Ford. In a January 2014 interview with the *Toronto Star*, she said: "I didn't vote for him. I've always considered him a political fraud and I'm afraid that's what he's turned out to be. He appears to have no sense of shame and no regard for the truth. His behaviour has really been quite disgraceful. I think he's done harm to the city.... His lack of any regard for the truth is fundamentally the worst. He should be forced to resign."[5]

Upon her death in December 2017, perhaps it is the words of her own family that best reflected her legacy: "June Rowlands was a true force of nature, a community activist, and a trailblazing politician."[6]

Mayoral Election for 1991–1994	
CANDIDATES	**VOTES**
June Rowlands	113,824
Jack Layton	63,854
Susan Fish	8,110

SPECIAL NOTE: There were six other minor mayoral candidates. Susan Fish's name remained on the ballot because she was too late to formally pull out of the race.

Mayor Barbara Hall

1994–1997

The 61st mayor of Toronto

Occupations: Social worker, lawyer, City of Toronto councillor, Metropolitan Toronto councillor, chief commissioner of the Ontario Human Rights Commission, adviser to Ontario's premier, community advocate
Residence While Mayor: 39 Amelia Street
Birth: May 9, 1946, in Ottawa, Ontario

—— • ——

I n what was the norm for a Canadian naval family of its time, Barbara Hall and her two sisters were raised in several different cities: Ottawa, Victoria, and Halifax, and also in London, England. Her father was a naval officer, while her mother was a social worker. Both were involved in the arts.

Hall obtained a bachelor of arts in psychology and sociology from the University of Victoria and later attended law school as a mature student. In 1966, she moved to Nova Scotia to volunteer with the Company of Young Canadians in Three Mile Plains, a rural community of 300 mainly Black families.

Upon moving to Toronto in the summer of 1967, she served as a frontline worker with the Elizabeth Fry Society, the Young Women's Christian Association, and the Central Neighbourhood House, working with poor, low-income, and marginalized youth. Between 1969 and 1971, she was also a co-founder and teacher with Toronto's Point Blank Alternative School.

From 1971 to 1974, Hall was married to an American classical musician, and from 1973 to 1975, lived in Cleveland where she was a youth probation officer with the Cuyahoga County Juvenile Court. It was while living there that she encountered violence and sexual assault first-hand. She was attacked while sunbathing in a park and was also twice held up at gunpoint. Ohio was also where Hall experienced her first political involvement, on the staff of the 1972 McGovern-Shriver U.S. presidential campaign. She returned to Toronto after the breakup of her marriage in 1974.

From 1975 to 1978, she attended Osgoode Hall Law School at York University and waited on tables at Lombard Street's Old Fire Hall, the original Toronto home of the Second City comedy troupe where Martin Short, Dan Aykroyd, John Candy, Eugene Levy, Catherine O'Hara, Mike Myers, and Gilda Radner all got their starts. As well as knitting sweaters to cover her rent, she also worked as a dressmaker, sewing wedding apparel for Yorkville boutiques to pay her way through school.

Working with Parkdale Community Legal Services, one of the first storefront law offices in the province, she was called to the bar in 1980, then opened a general law practice dealing with small business, family, and criminal law, as well as housing and tenant issues and human rights. Hall was also a member of the City of Toronto's Planning Board and a key supporter behind the revitalization of *Seven News*, one of the oldest community newspapers in the city.

She was a committed, visible champion of human rights at a time when they were being trampled on, and after the 1981 gay bathhouse raids — the second-largest police roundup of Canadian citizens since the Second World War — she worked with a group of criminal defence lawyers known as the Right to Privacy Committee.

Hall also served with Community Legal Education Ontario as well as Labour Community Services and taught at the Ontario Bar Admission Course. In May 1985, she ran for Ontario's Legislative Assembly as the New Democratic Party candidate in St. David's riding on a platform of quality daycare, tenant protection, better transit, an independent civilian review of policing, worker retraining, and affordable housing. Although Hall lost to noted Liberal Party lawyer Ian Scott, when she later ran for mayor in 1994, Scott was a strong and very public supporter.

In the fall of 1985, she ran for Toronto's Council in Ward 7, then taking in Cabbagetown, St. Jamestown, Regent Park, and Corktown. Serving from 1985 to 1994, she was city budget chief from 1988 to 1991, successfully keeping tax increases at or below the rate of inflation. Hall led housing and homelessness initiatives, working with front-line workers for more supportive housing and group homes. She was also a member of the Board of Health from 1988 to 1992 when the first public health AIDS budgets were put forward.

As the founder and later chair of the Safe City Committee, Hall put the issue of violence against women and children onto the national agenda for the first time, working on free self-defence courses for women, better lighting in underground garages, and design guidelines for city planners. She was also a director of the Toronto Arts Council, Harbourfront, and the Design Exchange. On the Task Force to Bring Back the Don, she sought an environmental river cleanup plan. In 1989, Hall married Max Beck, the former social planning director of the City of Vancouver, who later became general manager of Ontario Place.

Her voting record showed Hall to be more independent than given credit. The first reform councillor to support Toronto's bid for the 1996

Olympics, she also backed the Bay-Adelaide Centre rezoning as well as a change of street name to Blue Jays Way. In 1991, she was re-elected with 71 percent of the vote.

In November 1994, Hall entered a hard-fought three-way mayor's race against incumbent June Rowlands and past Board of Trade president Gerry Meinzer. It was also the first mayoral race in the city's history in which the two front-runners were women. Hall's platform included a rebuilding of the economy, safer streets, dealing with homelessness, and stopping polluters.

She spoke of a city drifting without leadership, saying red tape must give way to black ink. Her platform included support for the arts, tax reform, community policing, and improved city planning. She also backed the construction of four subway lines, not just the two Metro Toronto had approved. One key issue that drew a sharp distinction between the two female opponents was Rowlands's call for a crackdown on violent crime, extra-long sentences for gun offences, and increased deportations. Hall countered that law-and-order issues would "factor heavily in her bid" but added that she was not prepared to engage in "scare tactics and fear-mongering."[1]

The *Toronto Star* endorsed Hall, saying she had articulated "an inclusive vision for the city that combines a concern for the disadvantaged with a respect for entrepreneurship. She also has not hesitated to show leadership ... taking gutsy stands instead of ducking."[2]

In the end, city voters opted for Hall, who received 70,248 votes to 58,952 for Rowlands and 20,868 for Meinzer, who had pulled thousands of votes away from the incumbent right-of-centre mayor, bringing about her defeat. As City Hall columnist John Barber noted, it was Gerry Meinzer who had landed the heaviest blows: "On stages across the city ... Meinzer hammered relentlessly at the mayor's record."[3]

One of the very first things Hall did upon election was to hit the streets, touring the struggling Junction neighbourhood, having tea with Somali immigrants, and talking to business owners as she visited laundromats, variety stores, and automotive shops on Dundas Street West.

As mayor, Hall streamlined city bureaucracy, held the line on taxes for five years, fought for stronger gun control in the wake of the 1989 massacre at Montreal's École Polytechnique, worked to reduce city CO_2 emissions, and travelled abroad to sell Toronto. She vigorously fought Ontario premier Mike Harris's budget cuts, and in 1995 became the first big-city mayor in

Canada to march in a gay pride parade. Hall also led a major urban renaissance with construction of the Air Canada Centre, the development of
the multi-billion-dollar railway lands, and innovative new zoning changes.
She convinced the Council to approve two massive "re-investment areas,"
dubbed The Kings, for the King-Parliament and King-Spadina neighbourhoods. The two grubby industrial areas were made up of decrepit warehouses, rusting factories, surface parking lots, and boarded-up buildings,
which over time were transformed into what are today lively, thriving, vibrant neighbourhoods.

Hall forged a difficult consensus on a fixed link to the island airport,
improved frayed relations with Greater Toronto Area mayors, strove to develop new housing, supported the appointment of a children's advocate, and
brought in a survival fund to help the most vulnerable hurt by the province's
cuts. She fought for public health nursing, the passage of an anti-smog bylaw, and a ban on smoking in food courts.

Under what was a decidedly right-of-centre Harris Tory government at
Queen's Park, dozens of hospitals had been closed and monthly welfare payments cut. Mass demonstrations led to the October 1996 Days of Action, a
mass general strike and rally attracting almost 200,000 demonstrators. The
unilateral provincial decree that forced the creation of a new "megacity" also
led to one of the largest political mobilizations in postwar Toronto.

The direct political action culminated in March 1997 when 75 percent of
residents voted against the creation of a new megacity in a Metro-wide referendum. Yet only a month later, in April 1997, the province amalgamated
the City of Toronto with Metro Toronto and five suburban municipalities.

Although she opposed its creation, Hall ran for mayor of the new city,
and her 1997 campaign platform reflected a mix of high-profile issues, pragmatic concerns, and a future vision for the megacity. She outlined three
priorities: neighbourhood protection, economic competitiveness, and that
social needs must be met. Campaign materials trumpeted Hall's record:
fewer office building vacancies, a lower unemployment rate than in the 905
area code, and an increase in convention business and building permits.

Hall touted a new Raptors basketball arena as well as a billion dollars for
new development generated by lands once given up for dead. She took credit
for zero tax increases, the redevelopment of the Yonge-Dundas area, and a
less divisive Council, noting that of the 1,200 votes in the previous year, just

17 were decided by a close 9–8 vote. A detailed 15-point campaign platform included measures to attract tourism; revitalize the city; promote the arts; deal with homelessness; improve health, equity, and fairness; protect the environment; manage provincial downloading; and stand up for the city on both the provincial and national stages.

She received the endorsement of the *Toronto Star*, which observed that "we need a skilled conductor rather than a one-man band.... Hall naturally warms to people, is decent and inclusive and relates easily to all classes, creeds, colours, religions and political ideologies. She will be a good symbol of the new Toronto."[4]

Nevertheless, she lost the city-wide election to Mel Lastman, North York's mayor and a millionaire furniture retailer with a strong suburban base. Although starting far behind Lastman, she placed a strong second to him, capturing 346,452 votes to his 387,848.

In 1998, she received an Honorary Doctor of Laws from Ryerson (now Toronto Metropolitan) University, and from 1998 to 2002, Hall headed the federal government's National Strategy on Community Safety and Crime Prevention and was a member of the Crime Prevention Committee of the Canadian Association of Chiefs of Police.

She ran again for mayor in 2003, receiving strong support from Toronto's provincial Liberal Party caucus. Six years after amalgamation, she campaigned on political integrity, opening up city decision-making, restoring fiscal health, building better public transit, making Toronto the greenest city in North America, enhancing tenant protection, and keeping Toronto safe.

Although she was an early front-runner, Hall faltered in the home stretch. Election pundits noted her support was "a mile wide and an inch deep" and that it was based on high name recognition. An early campaign lead of 30 points evaporated a few weeks before election day to just seven points ahead of David Miller, who was boosted in part by the high-profile, paid-for celebrity endorsement of Robert Kennedy, Jr. The construction of a fixed-link bridge to the island airport became a defining issue, with Miller claiming it would destroy waterfront revitalization. In the end, the New Democratic Party–backed Miller rode to victory, capturing 299,385 votes to business executive John Tory's 263,189, with only 63,751 for Hall.

The defeated mayor then served on the Ontario government's new Health Results Team appointed by provincial health minister George Smitherman, and in November 2005 was chosen by Premier Dalton McGuinty to be chief commissioner of the Ontario Human Rights Commission, which has a responsibility to prevent discrimination and harassment in accommodation, housing, contracts, employment, and goods and services.

In 2007, the commission looked at bullying of Asians fishing on Lake Simcoe, with Hall noting that "these incidents are about racism.... It amounts to racial profiling because it assumes that people are doing something illegal based on who they are."[5] The following year, the commission considered a complaint from the Canadian Islamic Congress against *Maclean's* magazine. The publication was accused of publishing 18 Islamophobic articles between January 2005 and July 2007. Hall called the *Maclean's* articles an "explicit expression of Islamophobia" and said that "it fosters stereotypes and has a negative impact on the [Muslim] communities. It creates tension and conflict."[6] For its part, the magazine characterized Hall's press release as "a drive-by smear."[7]

During Hall's term, the commission dealt with a wide range of rights issues, including transgender protection, gender diversity, transit accessibility, mental health and addictions, the rights of employees experiencing mental illness, discrimination against religious minorities, racial profiling, and the practice of police "carding," as well as Indigenous reconciliation and working with municipalities on non-discriminatory zoning and licensing.

Hall retired as chief commissioner in February 2015, but "retirement" did not last long. The next month, Premier Kathleen Wynne, McGuinty's successor, asked her to chair a panel examining the governance of the Toronto District School Board and restore public confidence in Canada's largest school board after a series of scandals, spending problems, ethics controversies, and damning internal reports.

During the mayoral term of Rob Ford, at the formal ceremony to rename a city park in Hall's honour in 2014, Kristyn Wong-Tam, the downtown councillor who had proposed the renaming to the Council, said: "We are indeed going through some challenging times as a city right now, but one thing we all aspire to is a mayor we can be proud of. Barbara Hall was such a mayor ... a smart, intelligent, forward-looking mayor who governed with grace, style, dignity, and caring."[8]

In 2016, Hall was made a Member of the Order of Canada for leadership in human rights, and in 2018 was asked by Mayor John Tory to take on a very special task: to meet with the families, then allocate and distribute the $3.4 million that had been spontaneously raised in the community by the Toronto Strong Fund for the victims of the 2018 Yonge Street van rampage. She is an honorary witness of the Truth and Reconciliation Commission, and today lives with her husband Max Beck in Cabbagetown, the same community that gave her a political beginning.

Mayoral Election for 1994–1997	
CANDIDATES	**VOTES**
Barbara Hall	70,248
June Rowlands	58,952
Gerry Meinzer	20,868
SPECIAL NOTE: There were eight other minor mayoral candidates.	

Mayor Mel Lastman

1998–2003

The 62nd mayor of Toronto

Occupations: Retail merchant, community leader, Metropolitan Toronto councillor, North York controller and mayor, philanthropist
Residence While Mayor: 19 Wideford Place
Birth: March 9, 1933, in Toronto
Death: December 11, 2021, in Toronto

———— • ————

Mel Lastman was born in Toronto in March 1933. Raised in the busy, teeming neighbourhood of Kensington in a crowded apartment housing eight people, the young Lastman stored his clothes in a wooden crate once used to ship oranges.

Perhaps the most colourful account of his early life comes from a November 2000 *Toronto Star* profile by Moira Welsh. She describes Starkman's Fruit and Vegetables on Baldwin Street where a very young Lastman was hard at work, sizing people up as they walked into the store, then winning their confidence "by looking at them with his big shy eyes, or by telling funny stories and jokes. Before they knew it, they were buying."[1]

His family's Jewish life centred around the Minsk Synagogue just off Spadina Avenue, the city's largest downtown immigrant neighbourhood. Lastman attended Ryerson Public School and then Central High School of Commerce where he captained the basketball team and was elected president of the school council.

As legend has it, Lastman first noticed Marilyn Bornstein when he was 16, and they soon became inseparable, marrying five years later. Working at an appliance store on College Street, she approached her boss to see if they might hire Lastman. Employed in 1952, the die was cast, and the word on the street was that he was a genius for sales.

In 1955, he scraped together several hundred dollars, and with a used truck and a line of credit, opened his first retail storefront on Weston Road when major appliances were still a luxury. It was the era of home ice delivery, and Lastman followed an iceman making his rounds. The next day, he knocked on each door, pitching a new fridge with no money down. A retail legend was born, and by 1959, Lastman made his first million ($10 million today).

Adopting the "Bad Boy" nickname, he soon parlayed it into a host of colourful and attention-getting publicity stunts. In his signature black-and-white jailbird outfit, he set up on the corner of Queen and Yonge Streets, offering passersby a $2 bill in exchange for $1 and generating a wealth of free media exposure. As later reported in the *Toronto Star*, in 1965 he flew to Frobisher Bay (now Iqaluit) "to sell a refrigerator to an Eskimo."[2]

Yet, by 1969, a restless Lastman was thinking how his business savvy might apply to the public good, so he entered the race for one of four positions on the North York Board of Control. Once on the Council, Lastman was a populist and full of ideas, proposing an international trade centre on part of the Downsview air base and a hotline for complaints about air pollution. However, he did not always fit into the clubby world of North York politics, and some dismissed him politically. Lastman took on a host of causes: welfare cheats, deadbeat landlords, shoddy funeral homes, and tenant rights.

In 1972 when a veteran councillor was forced to drop out of the mayoral race, Lastman jumped in at the last minute, winning with 51,000 votes to 38,000 for his principal opponent. Ironically, although Lastman was viewed as an anti-development "reform" candidate, North York had just elected a mayor who wheeled around in a Rolls-Royce Silver Shadow, smoked several 15-centimetre-long cigars daily, and enjoyed instant recognition as a flashy millionaire furniture huckster with wide lapels and chunky gold rings.

However, his term started on a jarring note. In January 1973, presiding over his first Council meeting, the unthinkable happened. As widely reported, Marilyn Lastman, the mayor's wife, was abducted from the family home. Later released unharmed and without a ransom demand, the case was never solved.

The *Toronto Star* years later observed that "despite the jewels, the expensive hair transplants, the gangster chic suits of pinstripes and padded shoulders, the mayor kept the touch of the common man. He even answered his office telephone himself, and on the first ring. It was political gold...."[3] Lastman knew the North York of the early 1970s did not have what Toronto possessed — a vibrant, thriving business core — so he sought to change that. Over the next 15 years, Yonge Street north of Sheppard was transformed with a host of new high-rises, office towers, condominiums, and retail shops.

In 1975, the popular Lastman was persuaded by Bill Davis, the Tory premier, to run for the Legislative Assembly as the Progressive Conservative (PC) candidate in the Armourdale riding but lost to Phil Givens, a former Toronto mayor. It was the only election defeat of his entire career, and just a year later he was re-elected North York's mayor with more than 81,000 votes to just over 20,000 for his nearest challenger.

In the mid-1970s, his Bad Boy furniture chain was a key player in the appliance scene, yet trouble was looming. Profits had dropped, and in October 1976, he cashed out two-thirds of his family-owned shares. Ten months later, the new Bad Boy owners were petitioned into bankruptcy by an unsatisfied creditor.

As mayor, Lastman set up the first mayoral committees in Canada to deal with child abuse, drinking and driving, and community and race relations. He also came up with the "North York: The City with a Heart" campaign. A later inquiry into municipal procurement painted a vivid picture of the political culture of North York. Lastman was described as a "flamboyant, successful retailer and consummate showman" who enthusiastically promoted North York "and declared it open for business."[4]

On the personal front, the Lastmans put their 1,100-square-metre, 16-room mansion on Old Bridle Path on the market in 1985, and in 1987 paid $546,000 cash ($1.2 million today) for a new home on Wideford Place in the Bayview and Finch Avenue area.

The 1980s were made notable by the "Glitter Girls," a group of high-profile Toronto society wives, including Marilyn Lastman, whose sumptuous fundraising events raised millions of dollars for charity. But unknown to anyone then, it was also the time that North York's mayor contracted hepatitis C due to an operation and was affected by all of its symptoms, including tiredness, joint pain, and yellowish skin.

Nevertheless, Lastman was everywhere: fighting for a Sheppard subway, ensuring potholes were filled, and making the case for wide-open Sunday shopping. A 1989 profile in the *Globe and Mail*'s *Toronto* magazine noted that his power was based on "an ability to walk a public image tightrope between millionaire and man of the people, development advocate and protector of ratepayers, nouveau riche cigar-smoking tycoon and ordinary schlub."[5]

Yet his electoral popularity was real. In the November 1991 municipal election, he received 96,449 votes for mayor to 17,321 for his nearest challenger. In 1994, that rose even higher, with his 96,279 mayoral votes to just over 7,000 votes each from two minor challengers.

In late 1996, Ontario's PC government came up with a wide-ranging plan to amalgamate all of Metro's municipalities. A March 1997 referendum vote on the proposal resulted in 121,475 North Yorkers opposing it, with just

31,433 in support. With that, Lastman said a continued fight was a waste of money. "It's over," he insisted. "It's time to face reality."[6]

Lastman formally announced his bid for mayor in August 1997 at Bellevue Square in the heart of Kensington, just blocks from where he was born and raised. A first 1997 poll by Ekos Research showed Lastman out front with 54 percent to 25 percent for Barbara Hall. Key election issues included support for the arts, tourism promotion, Toronto Transit Commission fares, the pooling of social services, a new subway line to York University, the future of Downsview's air base, casinos, and tax hikes. Hall called for a major purge of crack houses, while Lastman urged greater job creation within the Black community.

Soon, Lastman was pegged as a Premier Mike Harris puppet, with he and Harris referred to as "Tweedledum and Tweedledee." Although his campaign had begun with a big lead, Lastman made a political gaffe that sent his team into a tailspin. He declared that there were no homeless residents in his city, yet only hours later a homeless woman died in a North York bus shelter. Opponents declared he was in over his head and out of touch.

When the final 1997 results were counted, Lastman was a clear winner with 53 percent city-wide support to 45 percent for Hall. Lastman had won both Etobicoke and Scarborough with 53 percent support, but what put him over the top was the 80 percent support from North York.

His first term got off to a rocky start. Angered by major provincial cuts, Lastman publicly called Premier Harris a liar. "You screwed Toronto, Mr. Premier,"[7] blasted the new mayor. Early issues included the creation of a major task force on homelessness; a 2008 Olympic bid; an overhaul of the taxi industry; promotion of the film, television, and creative sector; and a major revitalization of the Yonge-Dundas area downtown.

Transportation issues also topped the list, with the proposed subway extension to York University and a brand-new scheme to bury the Gardiner Expressway, financed by a special new toll, and a $16 million ($34 million today) bridge to the island airport. The Council also defeated a motion that called for the continued ban of jets.

By the end of 1998, the *Toronto Star* awarded the mayor praise, saying "Lastman's infectious spirit has added zip to this city."[8] Yet City Hall had still not shed all its excesses, including several chauffeur-driven limousines to drive councillors around and a private 12-seat executive box at the Air Canada Centre worth $230,000 ($386,000 today).

The year 1999 was marked by one of the worst weather catastrophes in Toronto's history. On January 16, the *Toronto Sun* reported that it was the snowiest January since records were first kept in 1840. Newspaper headlines tell the tale: "Reeling Toronto," "Snow Paralyzes Transit," "City Begs for Help." Waist-high drifts caused by a continuing series of storms shut down the subway and the airport, leaving the city hanging by a thread. Lastman asked for federal help, and 438 soldiers soon arrived, transporting the sick to hospitals and rescuing commuters and seniors trapped in their homes.

Personally, Lastman and his wife downsized at the end of 1999, purchasing a condo in the Yonge-St. Clair area. In April came an embarrassing episode when Marilyn Lastman, suffering from depression, was arrested by York Regional Police after being stopped in a shopping mall with an unpaid-for pair of designer slacks.

At Toronto's Council, a range of issues were under discussion in 1999 and 2000: protecting rental housing, the occupation of city parks by poverty activists, a budget for the Olympics, downsizing the 57-member Council, police chases, and the search for a new police chief. Lastman came up with a "Moose in the City" charitable fundraising campaign to sell 400 fibreglass moose at a cost of $6,500 each. The Council also froze taxes for three years in a row and approved a controversial plan to bury Toronto's garbage in an abandoned mine in Kirkland Lake, Ontario.

Lastman succeeded in bringing Prime Minister Jean Chrétien and Premier Mike Harris together to announce a major rehabilitation of the city's waterfront. The multi-year transformation of a gritty industrial lakeshore into a new mixed-use "clean-green" community would begin with $500 million ($800 million today) coming from each level of government.

He also became a fighter for the homeless and released a major task force report completed by Dr. Anne Golden. It was an effort that achieved significant results, with the federal government committing $754 million ($1.2 billion today) to new hostels and homelessness programs in Toronto.

Lastman's wide-ranging 2000 mayoral re-election platform included low taxes; a crackdown on waste; more effective police deployment, such as 15 percent more cruisers on the streets and a police helicopter; making red-light cameras a permanent fixture; and a major new investment in public transit rolling stock.

Although 25 other candidates contested the race, Lastman's 483,277 mayoral votes proved to be the highest total for an individual political candidate in Canadian history, which is still the case today.

Yet soon after the election, Lastman made a bombshell announcement. The flamboyant mayor was being sued for $6 million ($9.5 million today) by Kim and Todd Louie and their mother, Grace Louie, 68, as a result of a prior 14-year clandestine relationship. Personally admitting that he was both mortified and ashamed, Lastman went on to win the case after it was revealed that he had provided a financial settlement in 1974.

In 2001, Lastman caused a worldwide sensation. Just as he was about to travel to Kenya to pitch Toronto's Olympic bid, he said: "What the hell do I want to go to a place like Mombasa?" Yet the most damaging comment was this one: "I just see myself in a pot of boiling water with all these natives dancing around me."[9] It reverberated around the globe and shattered Toronto's bid efforts.

The mayor championed improvements in Toronto's waste diversion target, with a goal of 100 percent by 2010. In early 2002, another colourful event rocked the political world when at the King Street Holiday Inn Lastman publicly shook hands with members of the Hells Angels motorcycle gang, then claimed to be unaware of its distribution of illegal narcotics.

One piece of good news was the opening of the brand-new 6.4-kilometre Sheppard subway line, approved due to Lastman's formidable lobbying. As the *Toronto Star*'s Royson James recounted, Lastman had "pulled every trick in the book to deliver the subway. He begged, he whined, he cajoled, he lectured, he sulked, he came up with bogus financial plans."[10]

Lastman's final year in 2003 was not without challenges. Toronto was hit by the SARS epidemic and Lastman went on CNN to complain about the World Health Organization's global travel advisory, warning that Toronto was a "no-go" zone.

In 2006, Lastman retired and returned to an original love: his Bad Boy chain was formally rebranded as Lastman's Bad Boy, with him as honorary chair. Although rarely commenting on mayoral issues after leaving office, he urged Rob Ford to attend the city's gay pride celebrations, and by 2012, observed that Ford's inability to get along with the Council was harming Toronto. Ford, he noted, was making him "look like a genius."

In later years, the Lastmans enjoyed a quiet life, spending part of the year in West Palm Beach, and in 2018 celebrated their 65th wedding anniversary. Marilyn Lastman passed away on January 1, 2020, after a brief illness, while Mel died on December 11, 2021.

Mayoral Election for 1998–2000	
CANDIDATES	VOTES
Mel Lastman	387,848
Barbara Hall	346,452

SPECIAL NOTE: The newly amalgamated megacity's election in late 1997 was for a three-year term, starting on January 1, 1998. There were 18 other minor mayoral candidates, including white supremacist Don Andrews, who came in third with 1,985 votes.

Mayoral Election for 2000–2003	
Mel Lastman	483,277
Tooker Gomberg	51,111
Ezra Anderson	13,595

SPECIAL NOTE: There were 23 other minor mayoral candidates. To this day, Mel Lastman's total vote is the largest in Canadian history for a mayor.

Mayor David Miller

2003–2010

The 63rd mayor of Toronto

Occupations: Lawyer, City of Toronto councillor, Metropolitan Toronto councillor, environmental advocate, professor, author
Residence While Mayor: 46 Gothic Avenue
Birth: December 26, 1958, in San Francisco, California

— • —

Born on December 26, 1958, in San Francisco, California, David Miller is the only son of U.K.-born Joan Green and American teacher Joe Miller. His father died of leukemia in 1960, while his mother returned to England to live with relatives in Thriplow, a small farming village 85 kilometres north of London.

Miller's mother was a public school teacher who had begun work in 1940 at the height of the Nazi Blitz in London's East End. Seeing the war's devastation first-hand, she became a lifelong antiwar advocate. In 1967, she moved to Ottawa to be closer to her brother, Jim Green, who became a second father to the future mayor. Green had immigrated to Canada to work as an arbitrator with the federal Public Service Commission.

Although she was educated at the University of London and had taught in Britain for more than 25 years, Joan Miller was at first told she was not qualified to teach in Canada. Ultimately, she was able to obtain a certificate of equivalency and go on to become a teacher-librarian.

David Miller's first Canadian schooling was at Ottawa's Arch Street and Hawthorne Elementary Schools in Ottawa's south end, and it was there that his political interest began. It was, he recalled later, his way to understand the world and seek justice.

When the time came to attend high school, after checking out several boarding schools, the choice was Lakefield College School, an elite private school near Peterborough, Ontario. In September 1972, Miller enrolled there, and his mother took on two additional part-time jobs to pay the extra fees. On a scholarship at the school, Miller became involved in virtually every activity, including canoeing, rugby, soccer, cricket, acting, debating, the choir, and sailing. Lakefield formed him as an adult, he said later.

By Grade 13, the self-described pale and skinny Miller was overwhelmingly elected head boy (the same year Prince Andrew attended Grade 12). In his speech at the graduation ceremony, Miller floated the idea that the then all-male Lakefield become coed, a prospect not even on the radar at the time. (Today, the student body is almost half female).

Miller was encouraged to aim high and apply to an Ivy League college in the United States. Accepted at Harvard University with a scholarship in the fall of 1977, he studied economics. To support himself, he worked as a short-order cook, cleaned dormitory room toilets, and worked on a road-paving crew in Alberta in the summers. It was at Harvard that Miller further developed a strong sense of social justice, asking why there were such extremes of wealth and opportunity in society. In 1981, he graduated magna cum laude.

Yet it was a quest for justice, combined with the 1980 U.S. presidential election, that led to Miller's decision to return to Canada and attend law school at the University of Toronto. He later said that it was a very conscious decision to live in a country with socially progressive health care and environmental policies. To pay for law school, Miller relied on Ontario student aid and worked with Downtown Legal Services and the Union of Injured Workers, assisting those unable to afford a lawyer.

He articled with the firm of Aird & Berlis, learning about local politics in a very practical way through his work on behalf of the Toronto Islands Residents Association, winning a major victory that allowed them to remain in their island cottages. Miller also took on legal aid cases for refugee claimants from Iran, Sri Lanka, and Eastern Europe, and in 1989, he became a partner of the firm at age 30.

For Miller, it was also a politically exciting time in Ontario. The Liberal Party and New Democratic Party (NDP) had entered into a historic 1985 political accord to oust the Progressive Conservative government of 42 years. He joined the NDP where he fundraised, knocked on doors, and became part of the local riding executive.

In 1987, Miller met his future wife, Jill Arthur, who had grown up in Jamaica, Colombia, and Venezuela. For him, it was love at first sight; he said he knew at that moment he would get married. After several years of dating, they finally wedded in June 1991. The Millers bought a home on Gothic Avenue, a quiet leafy crescent off Bloor Street West, mere steps from the Toronto Transit Commission (TTC)'s High Park subway station, where they still live today.

Miller finally took the political plunge in 1991, receiving a leave of absence from his law firm to run as an NDP candidate for Metro Council in High Park against popular incumbent and Anglican minister Derwyn Shea, who had served since 1982. Ironically, several members of the local NDP riding did not believe Miller was a real New Democrat, given that he was with a major Bay Street law firm. In the end, he received a respectable 8,070 votes but was still more than 5,000 votes behind Shea's 13,706.

In 1993, Miller again ran for office, this time as the federal NDP candidate in the Liberal stronghold of Parkdale–High Park. Unfortunately, he fared even worse, placing fourth behind both the Reform Party and Conservative candidates, obtaining only 9 percent of the vote to MP Jesse Flis's 54 percent.

Miller faced a difficult choice as the fall 1994 municipal election approached, and after a lot of soul-searching, stunned colleagues by resigning a partnership at Aird & Berlis to run for Metro Council, coming 1,100 votes ahead of a former MP and 3,200 votes in front of well-known Conservative Tony Clement.

He threw himself into his work, focusing on jobs, fair taxes, safety and community policing, environmental issues, public transit, strong public services, reversing cuts to TTC accessibility programs, and stopping the Metro Toronto appeal of a court order that had granted same-sex benefits to two Metro employees. Miller was also vocal in his support of the Ontario NDP government's proposal to fund two new subway lines and extend two existing ones.

Although a councillor for just two years, Miller chose to run in 1996 in the York South provincial by-election for the seat vacated by former premier Bob Rae. Issues included the forced amalgamation of municipalities in Metro and a massive provincial downloading of services to the city. Yet he was not successful; popular food bank director Gerard Kennedy won for the Liberals.

However, the resilient Miller bounced back and was re-elected to serve on the newly amalgamated city's first Council in the dual-seat Ward 19 (High Park), receiving 13,665 votes to ward colleague Chris Korwin-Kuczynski's 13,115. In his 1997 campaign, Miller fought the further provincial downloading of social services and the creation of the new megacity itself.

Once elected, Miller pushed to have Toronto City Hall, not Metro Hall, become the new permanent seat of city government. He opposed the Toronto Police Association's Operation True Blue pro-police telemarketing campaign as well as a subway advertisement that many people considered anti-Hispanic. He forcefully led the opposition against shipping Toronto's garbage to Adams Mine in Northern Ontario, saying it risked polluting waters there for generations. As a result, the plan was ultimately defeated.

Miller's priorities on the Council included affordable housing, waterfront revitalization, and more responsible development. With new ward boundaries in 2000, Miller faced a challenge by Bill Saundercook, a popular incumbent with 15 years on the Council, yet Miller won easily.

Personally, he faced tragedy. His mother, fiercely independent and never missing a day of work, was diagnosed with cancer. With a tumour so close to her aorta, surgery was not an option. After a year of palliative care, Miller lost Joan Miller, his beloved mother and closest friend, holding her hand, just the two of them, on September 23, 2001.

In 2001, the Council unanimously supported Miller's motion to ask the federal government to dedicate gas tax revenues to Toronto's transit system. He also helped lead efforts to bring a major city disgrace to light: the tawdry MFP computer-leasing scandal, exposing corruption, bribery, and cash payoffs, as well as totally inappropriate gifts, relationships, and lobbying practices at City Hall. *Toronto Life* magazine awarded him an A-plus ranking, declaring that he was the best city councillor.

However, Miller tangled frequently with Mayor Mel Lastman, and during an angry 2002 debate, Lastman publicly shouted, "You will never be mayor of this city because you say stupid and dumb things!"[1]

Nevertheless, he ran for mayor in 2003, and to show his activist, waterfront, and environmental credentials, brought in noted U.S. environmentalist Robert Kennedy, Jr., for a speaking fee of US$25,000. An Environics poll, done during the popular Kennedy visit, put Miller in the lead for the first time. His campaign zeroed in on a proposed bridge to the island airport, making it a key election issue with his call for an end to backroom deals.

One controversial Miller ad showed a squadron of jets flying over Toronto's waterfront in a threatening manner, while the text of another proposed ad was "Kill birds. Kill fish. Kill tourism. Kill the island airport. You decide on November 10."[2] Miller was endorsed by the *Toronto Star*, and in the end prevailed with 299,385 votes to John Tory's 263,189. With her vote collapsing, Barbara Hall received just 63,751.

"We were elected on a mandate of reform, on an undeniable wind of change that is blowing across Canada's urban centres,"[3] Miller stated in his inaugural address, pledging to appoint an integrity commissioner, make City Hall more transparent, clean up municipal parks, and achieve increased, ongoing, and substantive funding from both Queen's Park and Ottawa.

He continued his campaign to keep Porter Airlines from flying out of the island airport, already declaring very publicly: "You cannot have a re-vitalized Port Lands and a busy commercial airport. It's impossible."[4] By a vote of 32–12, he persuaded the Council to reverse its approval of a bridge to the airport while at the same time Transport Canada was allowing Porter to expand its existing operations.

From 2003 to 2010, Miller led an activist agenda that included a range of environmental accomplishments: mandatory green roofs on large com-mercial buildings, new bike lanes, a major increase in the city's tree canopy, a reduction in greenhouse gas emissions, a significant boost in water rates to deal with aging sewer and water infrastructure, an expansion of deep lake water cooling, the purchase of a new landfill site, and a "clean and beautiful" initiative to tidy up city streets.

Miller brought forward a $60 vehicle registration tax and a new land transfer tax with a projected $354 million revenue potential. In response to several high-profile gang shootings, he publicly called for a nationwide ban on handguns and appointed Chief Justice Roy McMurtry to head a panel on safety and gun-related crime. Miller also brought a new $13 million youth and community safety initiative to 13 priority and underserviced neighbourhoods.

He implemented Canada's first municipal lobbying registry as well as Toronto's first integrity commissioner and ombudsman. A 2004 summit on affordable housing was convened, the comprehensive public housing renewal of Regent Park was approved, and a signature new Streets to Homes initia-tive was established to fight homelessness.

As mayor, Miller endorsed Prime Minister Paul Martin's federal New Deal for Cities, calling the new funding arrangement with senior govern-ment levels one of his proudest accomplishments, since it enabled Toronto to garner new powers, money, and respect.

In 2006, Miller handily won a renewed mandate with 332,969 votes to 188,932 for councillor Jane Pitfield and 8,078 for lawyer and former federal Liberal Party president Stephen LeDrew.

Under Miller, two new economic agencies, Invest Toronto (now Toronto Global) and Build Toronto (now Create Toronto), were created to attract external investment as well as generate prosperity by utilizing the city's real-estate assets. A new Transit City plan was unveiled, and sleek new air-conditioned, accessible, low-floor streetcars were approved to replace the aging TTC fleet.

In June 2008, Miller was appointed chair of the influential C40 Group of World Cities, an organization of leading major municipalities working together in the fight against climate change. He also continued work that resulted in the Mayor's Community Safety Plan, the new Clean and Beautiful City Initiative, the rejuvenation of parks and public spaces, and ongoing revitalization of the waterfront.

Citing family reasons, Miller publicly announced in September 2009 that he would not seek a third term as mayor. He had faced fierce criticism on how he had dealt with a six-week municipal strike, one largely seen as a victory for the unions. A post-strike Global News poll revealed that 79 percent of Torontonians wanted to see someone else as mayor.

In 2010, he co-authored *Witness to a City*, a vision of Toronto as a 21st-century metropolis, and in the 2010 municipal election, endorsed long-time Council ally and deputy mayor Joe Pantalone. However, Rob Ford was elected mayor with 47 percent of the popular vote to 35 percent for George Smitherman; Pantalone finished a distant third with 11 percent.

Miller rejoined the firm of Aird & Berlis, specializing in international business and sustainability, and accepted a three-year appointment as a Future of Cities Global Fellow at the Polytechnic Institute of New York University, leading courses in technological solutions to urban problems. In 2013, he became the president and CEO of World Wildlife Canada, the Canadian arm of the international World Wildlife Fund.

He also joined the advisory board of SAIL Capital Partners, an investment firm concentrating on emerging clean-tech energy projects, and provided strategic advice to the Organisation for Economic Co-operation and Development, the World Bank, and the environment program of the United Nations. "How do we, in cities, improve the economy and the environment at the same time," Miller said then. "It's the challenge of our times."[5]

In 2013, Miller and former mayor David Crombie very publicly opposed a possible major expansion and introduction of jets at the island airport, insisting it would threaten the environment and was counter to a sustainable waterfront meant to be used for multiple purposes.

At the end of 2017, Miller became the North American director for the C40 Cities Climate Leadership Group, whose founder was Michael Bloomberg, the former mayor of New York City. Today, Miller serves as managing director of the C40 Centre for City Climate Policy and Economy. He notes that 70 percent of the world's greenhouse gas emissions are from cities in four areas: generation of electricity, heating and cooling of buildings, transportation, and solid waste. In 2020, Miller authored *Solved: How the World's Great Cities Are Fixing the Climate Crisis*, outlining the initiatives cities have taken to control the climate crisis and what can be done today to mitigate our harmful emissions.

Mayoral Election for 2003–2006	
CANDIDATES	VOTES
David Miller	299,385
John Tory	263,189
Barbara Hall	63,751
John Nunziata	36,021
Tom Jakobek	5,277
SPECIAL NOTE: There were 39 other minor mayoral candidates.	
Mayoral Election for 2006–2010	
David Miller	332,969
Jane Pitfield	188,932
Stephen LeDrew	8,078
SPECIAL NOTE: There were 35 minor mayoral candidates. For the 2006 municipal elections, the Province of Ontario changed Council terms from three to four years.	

Mayor Rob Ford

2010–2014

The 64th mayor of Toronto

Occupations: Printing executive, volunteer football coach, City of Toronto councillor, philanthropist
Residence While Mayor: 223 Edenbridge Drive
Birth: May 28, 1969, in Toronto
Death: March 22, 2016, in Toronto

——— • ———

Robert "Rob" Bruce Ford was born at Etobicoke's Humber Memorial Hospital on May 28, 1969, the son of Doug Ford, Sr., and Diane Campbell, at a time when much of the borough was still undeveloped. Doug Ford, Sr., had founded Deco Labels in 1962, a company specializing in pressure-sensitive labels.

In the early 1970s, the Ford family moved to a sprawling six-bedroom California ranch–style home at 15 Weston Wood Road off Royal York Road. Its spacious backyard surrounded a saltwater pool and became a political gathering place for Toronto Conservatives. In his book *Ford Nation: Two Brothers, One Vision*, Doug Ford, Jr., later Ontario's premier, noted that the family home had hosted 200,000 attendees at political events over four decades.

Young Rob Ford attended Westmount Junior School, and in 1983, discovered a love of football while attending Scarlett Heights Collegiate in Etobicoke. Keen to have his son one day become a professional football player, Rob's father arranged for him to attend a training camp at the University of Notre Dame.

Ford attended Carleton University in Ottawa to study political science and business administration, and though his true goal was to play for the Carleton Ravens football team, he remained on the bench the whole year. Not liking Ottawa, he transferred to York University, continuing courses in economics and political science. He began coaching high school football, viewing it in the same way as politics: competitive, intense, demanding, and with the goal to win. He soon joined Deco Labels, working on both the factory floor and in the sales department.

In the June 1995 Ontario provincial election, the Ford family enthusiastically pitched in to get Doug Ford, Sr., elected the MPP for Etobicoke-Humber in Mike Harris's Progressive Conservative (PC) government. Rob Ford himself first ran for office in the 1997 Toronto election in Ward 3 (Kingsway-Humber), which elected two councillors. Placing fourth, he returned to Deco Labels and coaching football. He also served as a volunteer with the Heart and Stroke Foundation, the Terry Fox Foundation, the Salvation Army Red Shield Appeal, and the Rotary Club of Etobicoke.

In 2000, Ford married Renata Brejniak at Etobicoke's All Saints Roman Catholic Church and soon after ran again for the Council that November. Even the *Toronto Star* endorsed Ford, who was elected with some 5,700 votes in Ward 2 (Etobicoke North). Ford toiled for 10 years on the Council's backbench, very much outside the established power structure at City Hall. Concentrating on constituency service, he founded the Rob Ford Football Foundation to fund football programs at eight west end high schools. In 2003, he was handily re-elected with 79 percent of the vote.

On the Council, Ford sought to end a range of initiatives, including new homeless shelters, "green" initiatives, public art and commercial facade improvements, new community centres, the Don Valley Brick Works, and 13 library-expansion projects. His arch-conservative views were well received in his ward, and in 2006, he was again re-elected, this time with 66 percent of the vote.

Ford turned constituency service into a religion and also tackled politically incorrect causes. When a suicide barrier was proposed for the Bloor Street Viaduct, he stated the money would be better spent cracking down on pedophiles, since they caused people to commit suicide. He blamed the Walkerton water crisis on "people drinking on the job [who] weren't even competent at what they were doing"[1] and declared that if people were killed on their bikes, "it's their own fault at the end of the day."[2]

His right-wing, plain-talking, tight-fisted populism became the Ford Nation political brand, appealing to a broad coalition of conservative suburban voters and working-class, lunch-bucket, blue-collar workers. In March 2010 on AM 640 Radio, Ford announced his run for mayor with a clever four-word political pledge to "stop the gravy train." The populist Ford said that it gave "luxuries and perks to politicians and rich contracts to their friends."[3] The four-word slogan proved to be one of the most effective in Canadian political history.

Ford's platform included more contracting out, getting tough on unions, new subways, more police officers, privatized garbage collection, the removal of streetcars from city streets, an end to racing marathons clogging traffic, and an end to the "war on the car."[4] His principal mayoral opponent, former MPP and Liberal minister George Smitherman, was Ford's polar opposite.

Although initially dismissed as a long shot by Toronto's political elite, Ford prevailed in a field of 40 mayoral candidates, capturing 383,501 votes (47 percent) to Smitherman's 289,832 (36 percent) and 95,482 (12 percent) for third-place candidate Joe Pantalone. Ford swept suburban wards in Etobicoke, York, North York, and Scarborough. Yet, from the outset, his term was marked by confrontation when Canadian hockey icon Don Cherry, the invited guest speaker at his swearing-in, publicly attacked bicycle-riding "pinkos," "left-wing kooks," and "left-wing pinko newspapers."[5]

In office, Ford moved quickly, axing the city's $60 per vehicle registration tax, removing senior city housing officials, slashing councillors' office budgets, and narrowly approving a Scarborough subway extension. Yet his political support faltered due to a number of political missteps: an unpopular proposal to redevelop the Port Lands, closing public libraries, pushing for a downtown casino, and chaotic plans to slash the city budget.

Personally, cracks also began to appear: police were called to the mayor's home for domestic incidents, he was asked to leave a military ball after showing up incoherent and seemingly high, and on St. Patrick's Day in 2012, he was involved in a drunken fight during which he attempted to beat up one of his staff.

However, it was the 14 months from May 2013 to September 2014 that defined Ford's legacy, starting with the U.S. website Gawker showing him smoking what seemed to be crack cocaine. Ford's mayoralty and Toronto's civic affairs were thrown into a period of upheaval unlike anything experienced before.

Ford already had a fractious relationship with the city's media, but for months was an ever-present and daily fixture in the 24-hour news cycle. Former TV journalist Sean Mallen described it as a train wreck, noting that Ford "scrums were legendary, chaotic, unpredictable, and occasionally dangerous."[6]

In October 2013, Bill Blair, Toronto's police chief, publicly announced that the "crack video" had been recovered, and then a second video emerged of Ford in a drunken rampage. For the first time, a sitting Toronto mayor was forced to publicly answer questions about drug use. After months of denials, he finally admitted in November 2013 that he had indeed smoked crack cocaine in a "drunken stupor."[7]

It was simply too much for Toronto's Council. Unable to force him from office, it slashed the mayoral office budget, transferred most of his staff to Deputy Mayor Norm Kelly, and stripped him of all non-statutory powers. He was now mayor in name only, the only one to admit illegal drug use and consorting with known criminals and gang members.

Nevertheless, on January 2, 2014, he declared himself to be "the best mayor that this city's ever had" and filed for re-election, pushing his new "Ford More Years" slogan. In an editorial the next day, though, the *Toronto Star* proclaimed "Ford is first, and the worst"[8] in the 2014 campaign for mayor. In April 2014, Ford sought professional help for substance abuse at the Greenstone Clinic, returning to work in June and polling in second place for mayor.

On September 12, 2014, Toronto's incumbent mayor suddenly withdrew his candidacy after the discovery of a malignant liposarcoma, a rare form of soft-tissue cancer. He registered instead to run again as councillor in his former Ward 2 seat, while brother Doug Ford, Jr., replaced him on the mayoral ballot. The family's total combined donation of $779,000 toward the various Ford 2014 city races is the highest family contribution to any mayoral campaign in Canadian history.[9]

On October 27, 2014, John Tory was elected the city's 65th mayor, while Rob Ford continued with multiple rounds of chemotherapy, treatments that continued until March 2016 when he returned to hospital. On March 22, 2016, Ford died, age 46, surrounded by a loving family.

A full civic funeral was held, with visitations in the rotunda of City Hall and a formal service at the Anglican Cathedral Church of St. James. Perhaps the most poignant memory of Ford came from his young daughter, Stephanie Ford, who said: "What matters was that we're happy together.... I know my dad is in a better place." She noted that he was "the mayor of heaven now."[10] As the *National Post* observed, "Ford did accomplish a rare feat in Canadian politics. He built a movement based around his own identity."[11]

Mayoral Election for 2010–2014	
CANDIDATES	VOTES
Rob Ford	383,501
George Smitherman	289,832
Joe Pantalone	95,482
Rocco Rossi	5,012

SPECIAL NOTE: There were 36 minor mayoral candidates. Rocco Rossi dropped out of the election, but it was too late to have his name removed from the ballot.

The Mayor at Home: A Look at the Private World of Rob Ford

From Mark Maloney, "Who Lives Here? At Home with Toronto's Would-Be Mayors," Toronto Star, July 31, 2010, and an interview in June 2010 by Mark Maloney with Rob Ford. All Rob Ford quotations taken from these two sources.

Believe it or not, Toronto's 64th mayor loves doing laundry. Yes, laundry! Rob Ford says it's his favourite way to relax. "I know it sounds funny, but I do the laundry at our place. When I come home, I pick up all the clothes, go downstairs, divide the whites and the darks, hop on the phone, return my calls — and I get tons of calls — and I'll be folding clothes and doing laundry. I love it." But Ford does have one rule of thumb: "I never return calls after 11:00 p.m."

Ford's home is a modest yet tidy 1950s-style grey brick bungalow at 223 Edenbridge Drive in central Etobicoke, one of Toronto's more affluent neighbourhoods. Nestled between the St. George's and Lambton golf and country clubs, it's one of the smallest homes in a treed enclave of plush multi-million-dollar mansions with winding circular driveways, four-car garages, and imposing wrought-iron gates.

It's also no coincidence that Ford is also the 2010 mayoral candidate living the farthest away — almost 12 kilometres — from Toronto's trendy and left-of-centre downtown core. It also helps to explain his fervent campaign as an anti–David Miller, anti-tax, anti–City Hall, pro-business suburban outsider; and a gravy-hating, self-appointed champion of the little guy.

However, no taxpayer, journalist, or even "Ford Nation" supporter will ever see the inside of his residence, described even by Ford himself as "very messy." Unless you are a member of the family, an intimate friend, or a top mayoral aide, it is off limits.

The closest one will ever see is the Ford family's sprawling ancestral compound nearby, site of the Ford Fest political gatherings. It's where young Rob grew up and honed his political ambitions. The sprawling six-bedroom ranch-style home with its high-end finishes, sloped stone terraces, designer landscaping, screened patios, and shimmering salt-water pool is on Weston Wood Road.

Ford himself has lived in just three other homes. Attending Carleton University in the 1990s, he lived in a well-known Lees Avenue high-rise filled with immigrants, students, and blue-collar workers. Returning to Toronto, he resided for 10 years at 600 Rexdale Boulevard across from Woodbine Racetrack before marrying Renata Brejniak, a receptionist at his family's printing firm. And then, in 2002, he purchased his current bungalow "from an 80-year-old hermit" for $499,000. [Note: In 2018, following Rob Ford's death, his wife listed the property for sale for $2.5 million.]

Although buying it for what he calls "a steal," convincing his wife to move in was another matter. "There were cobwebs in the whole house … the downstairs wasn't used, the kitchen wasn't used … the couch in one area was black."

Ford openly notes that he could never live in older parts of Toronto: "I need space. I like my own driveway. I like my own backyard." And he is fiercely protective of his family's privacy. In Ford's case, all political work and entertaining is done elsewhere.

"I wouldn't bring anybody here, right now … it's all toys for the kids here. It's old … it has to basically be redone," he says. Ford plans to tear down this home and build new on the same site but will wait several years until his children are older.

While his passions include politics, the family printing business, and coaching football, it is the time spent with his young children, Dougie Junior and Stephanie, that truly relaxes him. The kids love going with him to City Hall on weekends where they can run in the wide hallways. Although not a big traveller, Ford enjoys quiet time at his cottage on Fawn Lake near Huntsville because no one can find him there. Emphatic when saying he is no cook, Ford prefers to dine out, yet claims to make a mean rice pudding, and on weekends will whip up bacon and eggs for the family. "While I'm not a chef, I do like eating," he says, and Chinese food, veal parmesan, and a good steak top his list.

What restaurants would he recommend? His favourites are Mississauga's "phenomenal La Castile restaurant," Rosa's Place in Woodbridge, the Asian Buffet on Rexdale Boulevard, and the "amazing" Mayflower Chinese restaurant on Royal York Road. For steak, it's Harbour Sixty or Ruth's Chris, though both are, he mentions, "way too pricey." And he asks every Italian restaurant to please take note: he is searching for the city's best veal parmesan.

At home Ford likes to relax with a game of Ping-Pong, though he admits "it's hard to find someone to play it with," and though holding season's tickets to the Toronto Maple Leafs and Toronto Argonauts, he is not a big fan of basketball or soccer.

As for his entertainment tastes? Old repeats of *Seinfeld*, *Three's Company*, and *Cheers* are favourites. He's not a real fan of cop shows such as *Law & Order* or *CSI*, though he loves *America's Most Wanted*. Ford loves to unwind with a good documentary, a fishing show, or a comedy. A big fan of Julia Roberts, Eddie Murphy, Gene Wilder, and Richard Pryor, Ford counts the 1980 classic *Stir Crazy* as his all-time favourite flick.

When not returning calls on his cellphone, Ford will crank up a CD of Supertramp classics while driving around the city. Rounding out his musical tastes are the Beatles, Led Zeppelin, and early disco. While his radio loyalties include *680 News*, the *John Oakley Show*, and *Leaf Talk* on AM 640, it's no surprise that CBC-FM is not a favourite.

For exercise, Ford used to run "religiously," he claims. Eight kilometres every night at a nearby track. And while now 136 kilograms, up from a once "108 kilos of solid muscle," he notes it is impossible to jog out in the street. "People are honking, people are pulling over, people are stopping me," all wanting to talk, he says.

While now running for mayor, Ford reveals that it has been 15 years since he has read any non-fiction books, and his current reading centres around just three things: his Council-related agenda materials, the financial statements of his family's printing firm, and information about his own personal investments.

Although always wanting to be in the know, Ford proudly observes that he's "not online all that much." And "forget email," says Ford. He prefers the grassroots, face-to-face, very personal touch.

Mayor John Tory

2014–2023

The 65th mayor of Toronto

Occupations: Radio journalist, political adviser to Ontario's premier, lawyer, corporate executive, Canadian Football League commissioner, Member of Ontario Legislative Assembly, Ontario Progressive Conservative leader, community leader, radio talk show host, philanthropist
Residence While Mayor: 1 Bedford Road
Birth: May 28, 1954, in Toronto

—— • ——

A true son of Toronto, John Tory has made a career of giving back to the city he loves. Taking office after the unprecedented turbulence of Rob Ford's single-term mayoralty, he brought stability and direction back to an office rocked by chaos, addiction, turmoil, and scandal.

The eldest of four children, Tory was born in Toronto on May 28, 1954, the son of Elizabeth Bacon and John A. Tory, the highly regarded president of Thomson Investments and a director of Rogers Communications.

A politically engaged young Conservative from the age of 13, Tory attended the University of Toronto Schools, a high school then affiliated with the university. His first summer job was at age 17 for Toronto radio stations CHFI and CFTR, then owned by cable magnate Ted Rogers, a family friend. He cleared wire copy, served coffee, and even filled parking meters for newsroom staff before graduating to more substantial jobs such as reading the news and reporting on City Hall.

In 1975, he received a bachelor of arts in political science from the University of Toronto and a bachelor of laws in 1978 from Osgoode Hall Law School. Upon graduation, Tory joined the family's influential Bay Street law firm, known as Tory Tory DesLauriers & Binnington (now Torys LLP), founded by his grandfather in 1941.

From 1981 to 1985, he served in his first political role as principal secretary to Ontario premier Bill Davis. After Davis's 1985 retirement, Tory briefly worked as an adviser to the Canadian Special Envoy on Acid Rain, then a top political issue of Prime Minister Brian Mulroney's federal administration.

Tory returned to the family's powerhouse Bay Street law firm from 1985 to 1995, specializing in government relations and serving as managing partner. In 1990, he supported Dianne Cunningham, not Mike Harris, for the provincial Progressive Conservative (PC) leadership campaign.

He was also a volunteer adviser to Mulroney and to Kim Campbell, Mulroney's successor. As a co-manager of the Conservatives' 1993 federal campaign, just days before the election, Tory authorized two infamous campaign ads that ridiculed Liberal Party leader Jean Chrétien's face, partially paralyzed due to a childhood disease. After a major national outcry, the ads were withdrawn by Campbell and the PCs were decimated in the federal election.

Possessing a strong legal track record but no senior experience as chief executive officer of a major corporation, Tory was nevertheless entrusted by Ted Rogers to become head of Rogers Media in 1995 after the firm's $3.1 billion acquisition of Maclean-Hunter. As Rogers grappled with the arrival of high-speed internet service while several billions of dollars in debt, one of Tory's greatest challenges was Ted Rogers himself, who was known for his mercurial temper.

In a 2014 profile in the *Toronto Star*, Tory recalled that the relationship was close and that Ted Rogers had placed a lot of trust in him. Graham Savage, a former Rogers chief financial officer, said Tory "was always prepared, always hard-working"[1] and contributed greatly to executive decision-making.

In 1999, Tory was chosen to lead Rogers Cablesystems, the precursor to Rogers Cable, where he remained until his first run for mayor in 2003. The firm went through a major business transformation from cable monopoly to an open marketplace. As CEO, Tory inherited a portfolio of 2.2 million cable subscribers and achieved a significant increase in operating income.

Tory served as a co-chair of Mel Lastman's 1997 and 2000 mayoral campaigns and was a member of the mayor's highly influential "kitchen cabinet." And for just a dollar per year, he also served from 1996 to 2000 as the ninth commissioner of the Canadian Football League and was later credited with saving the league from going under.

When Lastman retired from politics, Tory ran to succeed him in the November 2003 election for mayor. His principal opponents were veteran NDP councillor David Miller and former mayor Barbara Hall, while controversial former MP John Nunziata and former councillor Tom Jakobek were given zero chances of winning.

Tory campaigned aggressively to become known city-wide, and while Miller and Hall split the left-of-centre progressive vote, Tory appealed to conservatives, pledging more police officers, opposing tolls on the Don Valley Parkway, tackling the issue of panhandlers more effectively, and implementing new state-of-the-art incineration technology to deal with garbage. Miller, on the other hand, had two central concerns: the cleanup of

City Hall in the wake of the MFP computer-leasing scandal under Lastman's watch, and the halting of a bridge to the island airport.

Tory's campaign ended up moving into second place, and though he had never held elected office, he garnered a respectable 263,189 votes (38 percent) to Miller's 299,385 (43 percent) and Hall's 63,751 (9 percent).

Having been bitten by the political bug, Tory soon turned his sights on the provincial scene, announcing in May 2004 that he would seek the leadership of the Ontario PCs to succeed Ernie Eves, who had lost the 2003 Ontario election to Liberal Dalton McGuinty. With the support of eight former provincial Cabinet ministers, Tory defeated former Ontario minister of finance Jim Flaherty by a vote of 54 percent to 46 percent on the second ballot.

In March 2005, Tory ran in a by-election in Dufferin-Peel-Wellington-Grey, a safe PC riding just an hour northwest of Toronto, and was elected as an MPP with 56 percent to the Liberal's 16 percent. As party leader, he served as head of a fractious and sometimes divided caucus. In June 2007, Tory released *A Plan for a Better Ontario*. His election platform included using gas taxes for public transit improvements, putting scrubbers on coal-fired power plants, dealing with the land occupations in Caledonia, advancing Ontario's nuclear energy, and implementing public funding for faith-based schools.

In the end, Tory was forced to backpedal on his $400 million campaign pledge to extend funding to private Christian, Jewish, Sikh, Hindu, and Muslim religious schools. Although running in a Toronto riding, he failed to win a seat against Minister of Education Kathleen Wynne in Don Valley West.

Later, in what was his fourth election in six years, Tory attempted to reclaim a seat in the Legislative Assembly in a 2009 provincial by-election in Haliburton-Kawartha-Lakes-Brock, a rural central Ontario riding. However, in a stunning upset, Liberal Rick Johnson prevailed with 43 percent to Tory's 41 percent. After the devastating setback, Tory resigned immediately as PC leader.

He soon turned to the broadcasting world. In October 2009, Canada's largest talk radio station, CFRB Newstalk 1010, moved Tory into its prized late-afternoon slot with *Live Drive with John Tory* weekdays from 4:00 to 7:00 p.m., a job he held until 2014. In addition, he served as the volunteer high-profile chair of Greater Toronto CivicAction, an urban affairs advocacy group in which he was viewed as a community builder with a broadly inclusive approach.

Tory was a first-hand witness to the turmoil of the Rob Ford years. When the Council stripped Ford of key mayoral powers after he admitted to smoking crack while in office, Tory had seen enough. In February 2014, he declared his candidacy for mayor, pledging to end the toxicity, polarization, and division at City Hall, and to work effectively with councillors and senior levels of government.

One Toronto, Tory's election platform, included modernizing City Hall, new smart city technology, more effective trade promotion, and making Toronto a global magnet for research and development. The 2014 mayoral campaign was a gruelling 300-day effort, with Tory focused on better transit, tackling congestion, a dynamic arts and cultural policy, bringing new jobs to Scarborough, action on youth unemployment, property taxes lower than the rate of inflation, and the rehabilitation and expansion of public housing.

Yet, after Tory spent seven busy months running against incumbent Rob Ford, the entire mayoral campaign unexpectedly changed when Toronto's sitting mayor was forced to withdraw due to a cancer diagnosis mere hours before the election's nomination deadline. At the last minute, his brother, Doug Ford, stepped in to replace him as the candidate for mayor. In the end, the Ford family collectively spent $779,000 in personal family funds to try to keep Ford Nation in power.

The October 27, 2014, results were closer than expected, with Tory garnering 395,124 votes (40 percent) to 331,006 (33 percent) for Doug Ford and 227,003 (23 percent) for former councillor and New Democratic Party MP Olivia Chow. Another 62 minor candidates captured the rest. For Tory, it was a crowning achievement, and as journalist Theresa Tedesco noted, he was "arguably the bluest Blue Chip mayor that has ever taken office in this country."[2] He was also the first Toronto mayor since William Howland (1901–1902) not to have first served on the city's Council.

Tory won early praise for restoring civility at City Hall and for a disciplined professional approach to the mayor's office. He carried out several new initiatives: allowing children under 12 to ride the Toronto Transit Commission (TTC) free, action to achieve his SmartTrack surface transit plank, a monthly meeting of key officials to coordinate road construction, a major new effort to improve public housing, meeting regularly with Greater Toronto Area mayors, and renewing the city's participation in the Big City Mayors' Caucus of the Federation of Canadian Municipalities.

The newly elected mayor brought a fresh new personal style to the office: arriving at the office most days by 6:45 a.m., releasing his schedule to the media, holding regular news conferences, and rebuilding the morale of Toronto's public service after the chaos of the Ford era.

Tory also dealt with controversial issues such as "carding," in which police disproportionately stop Black youth and demand personal information. Calling it "illegitimate, disrespectful, and hurtful," he said it had "eroded the public trust."[3] He supported rehabilitation of the Gardiner Expressway instead of tearing it down in favour of a wide new surface boulevard, pushed through an extension of the Bloor-Danforth Line 2 subway to Scarborough Town Centre, and proposed a major new 8.5-hectare Rail Deck greenspace above the western downtown rail corridor.

In September 2017 at the annual Ford Fest event held at his mother's home in Etobicoke, former councillor and mayoral candidate Doug Ford announced that in the 2018 municipal election he would again oppose Tory. "Transit in this city is a mess, traffic has ground to a halt, and your taxes have never been higher," said Ford, also taking aim at Tory for road tolls and SmartTrack.[4] For his part, Tory reminded Ford voters that three years before, the previous Council had been dysfunctional and relationships with the other governments were in tatters.

Due to an unrelated and unforeseen political development — the sudden and unexpected resignation of Patrick Brown as leader of the Ontario PCs — Ford shifted his political sights and announced at the end of January 2018 that he would instead run for the leadership of the Ontario PCs, leaving the Toronto mayoralty without its highest-profile challenger.

On May 1, 2018, Tory registered for the October 2018 mayoral campaign in what was to become a crowded field of 35 mayoral candidates. Pledging to continue work on prior campaign commitments rather than make daring new ones, Tory saw his main opposition come in the form of a last-minute, left-of-centre bid by progressive challenger Jennifer Keesmaat, Toronto's former chief planner, who campaigned on affordable housing, a rent-to-own program, fact-based transit planning, and replacing the east Gardiner Expressway with a broad new boulevard.

Yet, in the middle of the 2018 campaign, Ford, who by then had become the premier of Ontario, unexpectedly brought in legislation to slash the size of Toronto's Council from a planned 47 to just 25 seats to match Toronto's federal and provincial electoral boundaries. The city's ward election process was thrown into turmoil, with many candidates halting their campaigns. For his part, Tory proposed a referendum to decide the Council's size while also expressing doubt about the success of any legal challenge.

Promising four more years of cautious and conservative "balanced" rule, Tory easily beat Keesmaat on October 22, 2018, taking 63.5 per cent of the vote. Keesmaat received 23 percent, while controversial white supremacist Faith Goldy came third with 3 percent. After four years in office, Tory could take comfort in the fact that he won every ward in Toronto, and in 19 of the city's 25 wards, captured more than 60 percent of the vote. It was also a 23 percent improvement over his previous 2014 vote total.

In his second term, Tory dealt with a diverse range of issues facing the city: cybersecurity, an end-to-end review of the development process, confronting anti-Black racism, a freight-and-goods movement strategy, the regulatory framework of scooters in Toronto, strengthening the municipality's nighttime economy, significant new climate change initiatives, securing substantial new funding for affordable housing projects, the uploading of major TTC subway projects to the province, measures to combat gun violence, approval of a new 10-year cycling plan, a strategy for the future of Ontario Place, the licensing of Airbnb, and new waterfront development. Yet for Tory, the ultimate goal was "a place where no neighbourhoods are left out. Where no groups of people are left out."[5]

Things were going well, and in February of 2020, the City of Toronto passed one of its smoothest municipal budgets in years, with Tory gaining praise from all sides of the aisle. As the *Toronto Star* noted, the $13.53 billion operating budget passed in a record six hours "without the typical in-fighting or late-night crises," while Tory called it "a good, responsible, realistic, forward-looking budget for a very fast-growing and successful city."[6]

Yet just weeks later, in March 2020, Tory's second mandate was completely upended when he was unexpectedly forced to deal first-hand with the social, economic, public health, and budgetary devastation caused by Covid-19, the most serious pandemic in the city's history, causing more than 15,800 confirmed deaths in Ontario.

The City of Toronto was forced to shut down counter services and in-person meetings, order staff to work from home, declare a public health emergency, bring in a mask mandate, and mount the largest mass vaccination

program in Toronto's history. After Health Canada's authorization, the first
Covid-19 vaccine in the city was administered in mid-December 2020, in
what medical officer of health Dr. Eileen De Villa called "a miracle."[7] In
January 2021, Toronto Public Health launched its Covid-19 mass vaccination campaign to immunize residents. More than 7.8 million vaccine doses
and booster shots were administered, reaching over 90 percent of residents
age 12 and older with two doses.

On May 2, 2022, Tory registered to run for a third term, which if it had
been completed in 2026 would have seen him become the longest-serving
mayor in Toronto's history. Again championing tax increases below inflation, Tory and his 2022 campaign focused on just six key areas: the economy, parks, climate change, transit safety, traffic, and housing affordability.
Included were a host of promises: growing the city's film industry; a new
landmark city park downtown, advancing the TransformTO climate plan,
fighting for stronger gun control, incentivizing rental housing, increasing
non-police alternatives for mental health calls, and finally getting the $28
billion transit plan accomplished.

The mayor's principal election opponent in 2022, renowned left-of-
centre urban affairs advocate Gil Penalosa, hammered Tory on Toronto's
housing crisis and crumbling infrastructure during mayoral debates. "In the
last eight years, the city has been less affordable, less equitable, less sustainable,"[8] Penalosa said.

But Tory's easy win did not mean that easy days were ahead. Toronto
still faced an unprecedented budget shortfall, the largest in the city's history,
while in early 2023, rampant drug use and opioid deaths, increasing street
homelessness, random violent attacks, carjackings, youth swarmings, and
transit stabbings led to a city on the edge and a strong perception of danger.
Globe and Mail city columnist Marcus Gee wrote that there was "a growing
sense that things in Toronto are spinning out of control"[9] and that the new
2022–2026 term of Toronto's Council was off to a sombre beginning.

What would become Tory's final weeks as mayor were dogged by three
major issues: changes to provincial legislation, the Council's passage of the
2023 city budget, and the mayor's sudden and totally unexpected resignation due to a personal affair.

The province had introduced the Strong Mayors, Building More Homes
Act (2022), which granted Tory, and indeed all future Toronto mayors,

The Catastrophe of Covid-19

On January 23, 2020, 15 months after John Tory (2014–2023) was re-elected mayor with 63 percent of the vote, a lethal, unknown virus — later named Covid-19 — entered Toronto when a 56-year-old man who had recently travelled to Wuhan, China, was admitted to Sunnybrook Health Sciences Centre. He was Canada's first Covid-19 patient, but the full impact of the virus was not evident yet.

Just weeks later, in February 2020, Toronto's Council approved a 2020 operating budget of $13.53 billion, and City Hall watchers noted it had been the smoothest budget approval in years. And then, a week before March break, Premier Doug Ford urged Ontarians to "go away, have a good time." Yet, on March 16, Toronto's medical officer of health broke the news that Toronto had seen a surge of cases of the new virus, "some of which are unlinked and thus indicate community transmission."

It was the beginning of a social, economic, and budgetary catastrophe that crippled the city for more than two years. On March 23, 2020, Tory declared a local state of emergency, and by May 2020, two months later, the Toronto Transit Commission saw an 86 percent decrease in ridership, resulting in a $300 million loss by Labour Day 2020.

Covid-19 quickly resulted in school closures and online learning, business lockdowns, the cancellation of virtually all major events, the closure of City Hall to the public, and the largest mass vaccination campaign in the city's history. It also derailed Tory's entire political agenda and resulted in a multi-billion-dollar budgetary shortfall, the largest ever in Toronto, affecting all city departments, programs, and services.

On May 9, 2022, Tory announced the termination of Toronto's Covid-19 state of emergency, which had been in effect for 777 days.

considerable new powers: the power to appoint the city manager and department heads, reorganize entire departments, set the city's budget, choose the chairs of Council committees, and even veto Council decisions. In addition, the new Better Municipal Governance Act (2022) allowed bylaws to be passed with just one-third of Council in favour if the mayor declared it to be in line with provincial priorities.

The new legislation was denounced in November 2022 by the five living former Toronto mayors: David Crombie, Barbara Hall, Art Eggleton, David Miller, and John Sewell. They harshly criticized Tory's stand, calling it an "attack" on democracy and majority rule and urging Tory to "soundly reject" the new Bill 39.[10]

Although Tory was widely regarded as a good steward of city finances, Toronto still hadn't recovered financially from the revenue losses of the global pandemic. And generating further controversy were Tory's plans to allocate an additional $48 million to the police budget for the hiring of 200 more officers for priority-response units. Activists urged him to spend less on policing and more on community service programs targeting the roots of crime. In the end, Toronto councillors adopted a 7 percent property tax hike and a $16 billion spending package, with its controversial increases to the police budget and service cuts to the Toronto Transit Commission.

On February 10, 2023, the *Toronto Star* broke a story about the mayor's personal life in which a months-long affair with a 31-year-old former staffer came to light. Although the relationship had ended, Tory agreed that it was a "serious error of judgement,"[11] and at a hastily called press conference that same evening, unexpectedly announced he would resign as mayor. Residents of Toronto were stunned.

As Tyler Griffin of the Canadian Press reported, it was "a blowout ending to the straight-laced, button down moderate conservative's otherwise uneventful tenure in the city's top job,"[12] noting that he had served two drama-free terms at City Hall. With Tory's resignation, Toronto's respected deputy mayor, Jennifer McKelvie, assumed both the function and responsibility of the mayor's office, yet without the actual title itself.

Despite Tory's sudden departure from the mayoralty in a way that no one had expected, he spoke of his time in office with appreciation. In his final public remarks as mayor, he said that it broke his heart to leave the job, but quitting was the right decision,[13] also acknowledging that his legacy will be tarnished.

Tory said he had tried to be a mayor whose energy and drive matched that of the city itself, pointing to new housing and transit currently under construction, keeping taxes low, improved city services, and dealing with the pandemic as signal accomplishments. Being Toronto's mayor "is the best job anyone could ever have," he said, and that he was leaving "with great hopes, high spirits, deep humility, and ever deeper gratitude."[14]

Declaring he would spend time rebuilding trust with his family, Tory said he would then look for other ways to contribute to Toronto. Indeed, in a professional career spanning decades, John Tory already has one of the most extensive records of philanthropic and community service of any Toronto mayor. He has served with the United Way, the Toronto International Film Festival's Bell Lightbox Theatre, and as chair of Greater Toronto CivicAction and chair of fundraising for St. Michael's Hospital. Tory has also held leadership positions with the African Canadian Achievement Awards, the Canadian Paraplegic Association, the Canadian Football League, Crimestoppers, the Association for Community Living, the Women's Legal Education and Action Fund, and the Salvation Army's advisory board.

In 2011, he was awarded a Harry Jerome Award by the Black Business and Professional Association for his work as co-chair of DiverseCity, an award-winning training program for rising city builders. Tory was honoured in 2012 with an appointment to the Order of Ontario, recognizing him as a "consummate champion for the Greater Toronto Region."[15]

A member of the United Church of Canada, Tory was born and raised in North Toronto's Lawrence Park area where he and his wife, Barbara Hackett, a Toronto home renovation contractor, also brought up their four children: John Junior, Chris, Susan, and George. Today, he lives in a comfortable Annex condominium, has a family cottage on Lake Simcoe, and owns a winter home in North Palm Beach, Florida.

Mayoral Election for 2014–2018	
CANDIDATES	**VOTES**
John Tory	395,124
Doug Ford	331,006
Olivia Chow	227,003
SPECIAL NOTE: There were 62 minor mayoral candidates.	
Mayoral Election for 2018–2022	
John Tory	479,659
Jennifer Keesmaat	178,193
Faith Goldy	25,667
SPECIAL NOTE: There were 32 minor mayoral candidates. Faith Goldy was an acknowledged white supremacist.	
Mayoral Election for 2022–2026	
John Tory*	342,158
Gil Penalosa	98,525
Chloe-Marie Brown	34,821
SPECIAL NOTE: There were 28 minor mayoralty candidates.	

*Mayor John Tory resigned from office on February 17, 2023.

Advice to Future Mayors of Toronto

interviewed the six living former mayors of Toronto to ask them the following:

- What are some key learnings from your own mayoral term that you would like to convey to Toronto's next mayor?
- Having done the job, what is some personal advice you would like to convey to all future mayors of Toronto?
- As we approach Toronto's 200th anniversary as a city, what thoughts do you have about Toronto's future?

Barbara Hall (Mayor 1994–1997)

Key Learnings for Toronto's Next Mayor

It's important to bring people with different views together to explore possibilities or solutions to problems. And if you can get a lot of different folks to support an idea, then you can usually get broader community support, and ultimately, Council support, because in a sense they can't afford not to, since a broad base is already there. You also need to inspire and give people hope.

Personal Advice to Future Toronto Mayors

Be ready for a new life. Being mayor isn't a job; it's really a life. Look after yourself. Go out and listen to very different groups. Don't just depend on your own personal staff or city staff. Go and hear what people are really thinking. People appreciate the fact that you come out to even very simple events.

Thoughts About Toronto's Future

I have mixed feelings. I have some real concerns but also some positive belief in our ongoing potential. The housing issue is so destructive to life in the city: it pushes away a lot of people who want to be here; it makes us more elitist. It also means people are living in our ravines, parks, and sidewalks. That's terrible for them and is demoralizing. It's an issue that all levels of government, the civil society, and the corporate world will have to work on. We do have a lot of very progressive city pieces: strong neighbourhoods and very diverse populations that are more and more moving into positions of influence and inclusion. We also have a lot of good infrastructure that we need to protect and expand.

Art Eggleton (Mayor 1980–1991)

Key Learnings for Toronto's Next Mayor

When I ran for mayor, I remember the phrase: "Listen, learn, leave." That's important for someone to do when they get into the job of mayor. Listen to people, councillors, and officials. Learn from that and do the necessary research to develop the programs and services that need to be advanced, then take the leadership role to make it happen. Always keep in touch with the members of City Council. To get support for your issues, you have to know where they stand, you have to be able to talk to them and work with them. You have to cobble together a majority. Don't just rush in with "Here's what I want to do, so please support me." You have to work with the Council.

Personal Advice to Future Toronto Mayors

You have to find a balance, not only in the job but in your life, as it's affected by the job. You shouldn't spend all the time in the office shuffling papers. You need to get out in the neighbourhoods, communities, and different organizations to meet people. You learn a lot that way. It also provides a diversity in the performance of your job. You have to find a balance in your personal life in terms of your family and friends. Don't neglect the parts of your life that are really important. And keep fit. When I went to City Hall, I opened a gym for all city staff, and it's still there. I would work out there every morning. It was a good way to start the day.

Thoughts About Toronto's Future

The city has lost a lot of its spark due to Covid, so we need to focus on getting that back. There's been a considerable drop of ridership on the transit system and a lack of pedestrian traffic in the downtown core. A lot of people may continue to work from home and may come in for just part of the week. We have to be concerned about the vitality of the downtown core. It needs to be a place where people live, work, and enjoy a wide range of cultural and recreational activities, and it has to be safe day and night. The city is known as a "city that works," and we have to get it back to the way it was before Covid. When I first ran for mayor, my theme was "Safe, Clean, and Livable." We have to strive to keep the city livable and affordable for all income brackets. To focus on that is the best way to celebrate the 200th anniversary of the city.

David Crombie (Mayor 1973–1978)

Key Learnings for Toronto's Next Mayor

If you're running for mayor, then have something to say. Really tell it like it is. Yes, there are all sorts of advice you can get from all sorts of people, but as mayor, no one is in your shoes. Be unafraid to go forth with what you have to say. And, at the same time, recognize that other people have different ways of looking at things. In city politics, unlike other levels, you never know who will be your new partner at the dance. Do stand for what you really think is important and know what you want to do, but also remember the old saying: "All things are possible if you give the other guy the credit." Unfortunately, today, people don't listen; they just wait until it's their turn to speak. As mayor, I actually listened to what people had to say and knew where their hearts were. Learning to listen isn't just a cliché; it's a good skill.

Personal Advice to Toronto's Future Mayors

For politicians who are busy, it may sound like an old cliché, but "to thine own self be true." At the end of the day, you're the only person around. You have to be really clear while you're taking positions. You have to have three or four persons whose judgment matters and who you can go to. And in terms of events, I didn't do Friday nights, or Sundays, and if I went to anything on a Sunday, it would be something my kids would want to go to. But I won't sugar-coat it; you're out and about a lot.

Thoughts About Toronto's Future

We have nothing holding us back but ourselves. We need a strong, strong community life. One great thing we've done and that great cities need to do is a sense of social peace in the midst of constantly growing diversity. We have done well in terms of the economy, and we've also rediscovered the environment. Increasingly, that's one of the most powerful things to worry about. Ecology, economy, and community are the three things cities require. I really am hopeful about Toronto's future. We have to find the things that are important for social peace. And we're one of the few countries that understands that immigration makes money. That's because every immigrant works hard and wants their kids to get ahead.

John Sewell (Mayor 1978–1980)

Key Learnings for Toronto's Next Mayor

First, define the issues in a good and clear way. Spend a lot of attention on them. That's one thing the mayor can do that really no one else can. Second, it's really important to speak to all the city department heads on a regular basis. Very early on, I spent an hour with every department head. I got a sense of what they were up to and told them what I was interested in. It's really important to keep in touch with them. They have a lot of power. Third, make sure you're always available for councillors. Wander through "councillor alley" at City Hall. See what's going on and have informal chats. Often, mayors don't worry about that, but they should because you have to get councillors' votes and their attention. And fourth, it's important that the mayor forms alliances with the economic leaders in the city: the financial, union, and development leaders.

Personal Advice to Future Toronto Mayors

Limit the amount of time you spend on personal appearances. It's very easy to spend a lot of time going around and doing this, and this, and this. Limit your personal appearances to places where you can actually do something important, like make an important public speech or recognize an initiative that's not getting the proper attention. Concentrate on a few issues you really understand and can actually resolve. Don't be too scattergun. If you get too scattered, you aren't going to get anything done.

Thoughts About Toronto's Future

The future of Toronto is relatively bleak at the moment. The premier of Ontario doesn't like the city and is willing to try to destroy its ability to govern itself. The problem with Toronto and every other big city in Canada is that we're all caught in a 19th-century constitution. We have to get out of that, which will be very, very difficult to do. That will be a serious priority for Toronto mayors in the next decades. Inequality is a major problem and will have to be addressed, as well, but the city doesn't have the money or the legislative ability to actually address those kinds of issues.

David Miller (Mayor 2003–2010)

Key Learnings for Toronto's Next Mayor

If you include the people properly and structurally in a robust discussion of the city's future, they'll be with you. You can count on that, even when hard decisions have to be made. An example is the land transfer tax. People want this city to succeed. You can get them on your side, but they need to be involved from the beginning. They need to be engaged. If they are, it's immensely powerful.

Personal Advice to Future Mayors

First, listening is the most important skill you have. It got you to where you are today. Keep using it. Find opportunities to listen. Have coffee at Tim Hortons. Have a beer at a local pub and find other informal settings. It's the biggest thing. People know their neighbourhoods and their communities. You have a responsibility to listen. Second, prioritize your own health and fitness. The demands are 18 hours per day. If you neglect yourself, you're not doing the city a service. The time to prioritize is first thing in the morning. Finally, be home for dinner with your family at least three nights a week.

Thoughts About Toronto's Future

First of all, Toronto faces a massive opportunity because of migration from across Canada and around the world. The inner suburbs were built for cars. Our next mayors will have to deal with how to ensure this migration brings people into Toronto and not into the Greenbelt or Oak Ridges Moraine. The inner suburbs need to dramatically increase density to provide affordable housing opportunities. Housing needs to be developed around higher-order transit. How does the city grow inside Toronto in a way that leaves no one behind? To do that, you need neighbourhoods that give people the option to not own a car. Second, the recent governance changes from the province are profoundly anti-democratic. Imposing minority rule is shocking. It disempowers people from their local governments. If you want to solve big-picture problems, such as how to accommodate a million people coming to this area in the next 15 to 20 years in a way that actually works, people need to be both involved in that decision and have the feeling they're involved and therefore trust how the government leads. Finally, Toronto is bankrupt. The last six years have seen a decline in services. It has a structural deficit of over $1 billion. In a year or two, you can't use the reserves anymore. What do you do then? It's a fundamentally profound challenge.

John Tory (Mayor 2014–2023)

Key Learnings for Toronto's Next Mayor

Always remember the paramount responsibility of a mayor in a city as complex and diverse as Toronto is to unify and to represent the entirety of the city. We are so lucky to have brought together the best of the world and many of the brightest people, and we have combined those things with respect and compassion. Smart people able to achieve their full potential are our most important building blocks. That will never change. So it's crucial that unity and respect for everyone, without exception, must be maintained, and this requires vigilance and hard work. A mayor must constantly focus on the role of unifier, using leadership skills but also arts and culture, education, and civic pride to bring people together. A real and present threat to that unity is the increasing marginalization of a number of communities within our city. So solid, constructive partnerships with other governments are necessary to address this challenge. Mayors must understand the critical importance of their personal presence as a demonstration of respect and recognition for all. Consistent, meaningful presence in the geographic and demographic communities of Toronto is as important as any City Hall briefing in keeping Toronto on track. Show respect at all times for the public service. Lonely as the job can sometimes seem, no mayor can do it alone. Work with councillors and the pubic service but remember the role leaders, including mayors, have in moving big organizations away from inertia, which is a feature of any big organization. Finally, never forget the importance of the economy and enterprises big and small. The most effective way to improve the lot of people is through secure, well-paying jobs in the private or public sectors. It's that job creation that in turn creates the wealth and quality of life in Toronto.

Personal Advice to Future Toronto Mayors

Most wisdom is actually *not* found within City Hall. Public servants and elected officials know a lot, but the people collectively know more. Get out and listen to them. From the simplest encounters with people in the community can come the greatest insights and wisdom. Even the structured public input processes of city government can become predictable and not necessarily representative. Communicate proactively and consistently. The city and the world are complex, and people leading busy lives want to be kept informed. The media aren't to be feared or despised. They're there to hold public officials accountable, but even in today's opinionated world, they offer the best chance to keep three million Torontonians informed in an increasingly fast-moving environment. Work at consensus-building every day. That doesn't have to mean compromising yourself, but it must mean building support for your chosen direction and decisions. The realities of the Council structure and an incredibly diverse city make this job one part of unifying the city. Don't allow those with extreme views of any kind to paralyze you. Even some people who cloak themselves in righteous causes are sometimes not really interested in dialogue and solutions, and they find greater attraction in controversy. Be rigid in setting aside time for yourself and for your friends and family. This wasn't a strength of mine. It's necessary for a mayor to do both because it's considerate of family members who themselves bear the burden of your public service but also because a life away from City Hall helps relieve stress and maintain a better balance.

Thoughts About Toronto's Future

I'm hugely optimistic about the future of Toronto even as we face some of the most daunting challenges of the entire 200 years. Our foundational values, including respect, compassion, and enterprise, will keep us in a position that will continue to be the envy of the world and the reason people flock here. We must continue our focus on equity, the quality of life, the environment, arts and culture, sports and recreation, and education, among other things, as great unifiers. We must push back with commitment against those who would divide or discriminate. The legal, political, and financial shackles that continue on larger local governments are causing serious harm to people. It's up to the mayors of Toronto, and those of other large cities, to work with other governments to overcome politically based resistance to change. We live in a world of profound change. Why would we ever think a model of local governance put in place in 1867 would still work effectively in the 21st century? While there were many negative consequences of the pandemic, our world-leading success in dealing with it showed what we can do together, as well as the effectiveness of local government and local service delivery. It also showed that strong and healthy neighbourhoods are still the essential building blocks for a robust city. Two hundred years on, Toronto is still a crucial work in progress.

Final Thoughts

oronto Mayors offers a brief glimpse into our city's past: where we came from and how we got to where we are today.

But where is Toronto headed next?

In 2034, Toronto will celebrate its 200th anniversary as a city. It will be a time to celebrate what is great about our city, but the anniversary should also be used to challenge ourselves on how to do better.

Better in terms of racial equity, climate change, arts and culture, policing reform, transit, opportunities for our next generation, housing, and how we deal with homelessness.

Let's use the decade leading up to 2034 to create a broad community partnership to set concrete and measurable goals and track their progress as we approach the 200th anniversary. Let's call it Toronto 2034.

Acknowledgements

Writing a book is a unique journey and at times a very solitary experience: hours of archival research and time spent in libraries or in front of a computer monitor, so my sincere thanks to friends, work colleagues, City Hall watchers, and to those who love Toronto's history for their encouragement, support, and friendship, especially to Virginia Williams, a gentle soul who reflects the best of Toronto.

Toronto Mayors came to be due to several influences. As a high school student in the classroom of teacher Tom Taylor, I had a love of history come alive, which was further nurtured at the University of Ottawa by professor Micheline D'Allaire and the eminent Canadian historian Marcel Trudel. And later, my coming across a book by former City of Toronto archivist Victor Loring Russell about Toronto's first mayors sparked a profound curiosity: *What were the others like?* I wondered.

I would like to thank Dundurn Press for being such a very special part of Toronto's rich cultural fabric. In particular, special thanks to Kwame Scott Fraser, Kathryn Lane, Chris Houston, Elena Radic, Rajdeep Singh, Alyssa Boyden, Erin Pinksen, Megan Beadle, Julia Kim, Laura Boyle, Karen Alexiou, Kendra Martin, Maria Zuppardi, and my extraordinary editor, Michael Carroll, a veritable Dundurn treasure. Thank you for your thoughtful and wise input.

Thank you, as well, to the superb staff at the City of Toronto Archives and Toronto Reference Library, where so much of our city's incredible history is kept, awaiting to be discovered.

In an incredible career, I had the wonderful opportunity to work full-time for three Toronto mayors — Barbara Hall, Mel Lastman, and John

Tory — in either a mayoral campaign position or at Toronto's City Hall. In addition, I have also been fortunate to have worked closely on community-related projects with two other renowned former mayors — Art Eggleton and David Crombie. I would also like to thank David Crombie for writing the foreword for this book.

I have learned so much from each of you and am a better person as a result.

I would like to thank a former chief of staff in the Mayor's Office, Rod Phillips, who hired me to work with Mayor Mel Lastman and who later went on to become Ontario's finance minister. Rod was the best boss I have ever had and was succeeded by a beloved colleague, the late Alan Slobodsky, a true mensch who left this world far too young.

Special thanks go out to Barbara Hall and Max Beck for their advice, friendship, and counsel over many years.

I would also like to thank former mayor John Tory for the enormous contribution to our city and province over four decades.

I am grateful for the support, input, and encouragement of Mark O'Neill, the former CEO of the Canadian Museum of History, who has contributed so much to our nation.

The office of the mayor of Toronto is an honourable calling and an important position in the public life of our city, province, and nation. The past, present, and future mayors of Toronto deserve our sincere thanks for their service, dedication, passion, and commitment to the well-being of our city — and for appealing to our better angels.

Appendix

Mayors of the City of Toronto from 1834 to Present

- **From 1834 to 1858:** Mayors were not elected directly by the public. Municipal elections were held every year on January 1, not by a secret ballot but by voting in the open at a large public meeting, often in a bar. After each election, the new Council members chose the mayor for that year.
- **From 1859 to 1866:** In a major reform, Toronto mayors were for the very first time elected city-wide by the voting public, who were at that time overwhelmingly male property owners. Until the 1920 civic election, women were actually barred by law from running for municipal office.
- **From 1867 to 1873:** The above reform ended. Toronto mayors were once again chosen by members of the Council and were not directly elected by the public. Municipal elections were held each January 1, and after each, the assembled Council chose one of its own to be mayor for just one year.
- **1874 to the present:** Once again, Toronto mayors were directly elected by popular vote, but at first only by male property owners. In eight cases since 1834, a mayor was

appointed by the Council to fill a mayoral term. Only two
Toronto mayors have died in office. Over the years, the
City of Toronto has changed dramatically due to the annexation of 50 adjacent municipalities, communities, and
neighbourhoods from 1883 until 1967. In 1953, a number of key City of Toronto services, including regionally
focused planning, major roads, housing, transit, welfare,
and, later, policing, were hived off by the province and
put under a new regional corporation, the Municipality of
Metropolitan Toronto, or Metro, as it was best known. In
1985, the Metro Council became a directly elected body,
and in 1998, the final and most sweeping amalgamation
of local municipalities and of Metro itself was ordered by
the Province of Ontario, taking effect on January 1, 1998,
as the megacity of Toronto, then comprising 2.4 million
citizens.

Mayoral Facts

- Of Toronto's 65 mayors (from 1834 to the present), 25
  have been from Toronto, 21 from outside Canada (all
  but two from the British Isles), 17 from other parts of
  Ontario, and 2 from Quebec.
- Of Toronto's 65 mayors, 59 have been white, Anglo-
  Saxon, English-speaking, Protestant, middle-class,
  property-owning males; three were Jewish; and just two
  were women. No one born Roman Catholic has ever been
  elected Toronto's mayor. The single Catholic, Fred Beavis,
  was appointed by the Council for three months.
- Despite all of its supposed diversity, the City of Toronto,
  in its almost 19 decades as a city, has not been diverse
  at all. For 62 of its years, the Council had a Board of
  Control made up of four Council seats elected on a
  city-wide basis. During that 62-year period, there were
  236 opportunities in which one could run and be elected

across the entire pre-amalgamation city, yet in all that time only a single non-white member of the Council, William Hubbard, was ever elected on a city-wide basis.

- The facts also show a shocking lack of diversity on Toronto's Council: when changes to both the size and also the length of various Council terms over the past 18 decades are taken into account, there have been 3,485 opportunities in which a citizen could run for the Council. Yet between 1834 and 2023, Toronto has seen just 25 non-white city councillors, and several were appointed on a temporary basis, not elected.

- During its first 40 years as a city, no women in Toronto were permitted to vote. By the mid-1870s, only property-owning widows and single women — or "spinsters," as they were called — were allowed to vote. Married women were not able to, since the rationale of the time was that it was the husband and not the wife who made all major decisions in a family.

- Women were actually barred from running for Toronto's Council until the 1920 municipal election. That year, Constance Hamilton, Toronto's first female councillor, was elected. Indeed, she was also the very first woman in Ontario to be elected at either the federal, provincial, or municipal level.

- Of Toronto's 65 mayors, 60 have been either Conservative, Liberal, or were non-affiliated. Just five were considered "lefties" or "socialists," having either a prior membership in and/or political support from organized labour and the New Democratic Party or its predecessor, the Co-operative Commonwealth Federation. They are Jimmy Simpson (1935), William Dennison (1967–1972), John Sewell (1978–1980), Barbara Hall (1994–1997), and David Miller (2003–2010).

	The mayor was selected by members of Toronto's Council from 1834 to 1858		
Number	**Term**	**Mayor**	**Address While Mayor**
1	1834	William Lyon Mackenzie	19 Richmond St. (at Church St.)
2	1835	Robert Sullivan	Duke St. (now Adelaide St. E.)
3	1836	Thomas Morrison M.D.	57 Newgate St. (now Adelaide St. E.)
4	1837 and 1848–50	George Gurnett	119 King St. E.
5	1838–40	John Powell	William St. (now St. Patrick St.)
6	1841	George Monro	Palace St. (now Front St.)
7	1842–44	Henry Sherwood	Yonge St.
8	1845–47 and 1858	William Boulton	The Grange (John St. N.)
9	1851–53 (appointed by Council) and 1861–63 (elected)	John Bowes	296 Front St. W.
10	1854	Joshua Beard	212 Jarvis St.
11	1855	George Allan	Moss Park (Queen St. E.)
12	1856	John Beverley Robinson, Jr.	College Avenue
13	1857	John Hutchison	51 Church St.
14	1858 (Nov. 11 to Dec. 31, 1858)	David Read	510 Queen St. W.
	The mayor was directly elected by the general public of Toronto from 1859 to 1866		
15	1859–60	Adam Wilson	Spadina Ave. (north of College St.)

	Prior Service on Council?	Born	Primary Occupation	Religion
	No	Scotland	Journalist	Protestant
	No	Ireland	Lawyer	Protestant
	Yes	Quebec City	Physician	Protestant
	Yes	England	Journalist	Protestant
	Yes	Niagara, Upper Canada	Lawyer	Protestant
	Yes	Scotland	Merchant	Protestant
	No	Augusta Township, Upper Canada	Lawyer	Protestant
	Yes	York (Toronto)	Lawyer	Protestant
	Yes	Ireland	Merchant	Protestant
	Yes	England	Businessperson	Protestant
	Yes	York (Toronto)	Lawyer	Protestant
	Yes	York (Toronto)	Lawyer	Protestant
	Yes	Scotland	Merchant	Protestant
	Yes	Augusta Township, Upper Canada	Lawyer	Protestant
	Yes	Scotland	Lawyer	Protestant

16	1864–66 and 1874–75	Francis Medcalf	448 and 506 King St. E.

The mayor was once again selected by members of Toronto's Council from 1867 to 1873

17	1867–68	James Smith	42 Wood St.
18	1869–70	Samuel Harman	308 King St. W.
19	1871–72	Joseph Sheard	14 Magill St. (now McGill St.)
20	1873 (appointed by Council) and 1885 (elected)	Alexander Manning	63 Wellington St. W.

The mayor was again directly elected by the general public of Toronto from 1874 to the present

21	1876–78	Angus Morrison	2 Windsor St.
22	1879 and 1880	James Beaty, Jr.	305 Church St.
23	1881 and 1882	William McMurrich	55 Beverley St.
24	1883 and 1884	Arthur Boswell	230 Wellington St. W.
25	1886 and 1887	William Howland	7 Queen's Park Cres.
26	1888–91	Edward Clarke	10 Harbord St.
27	1892–93 and 1896–97	Robert Fleming	325 Parliament St.
28	1894 and 1895	Warring Kennedy	200 Beverley St.
29	1897–99	John Shaw	222 Bloor St. W.
30	1900	Ernest Macdonald	35 Grenville St.
31	1901–02	Oliver Howland	21 Isabella St.
32	1903–05	Thomas Urquhart	136 Major St.

Yes	Ireland	Foundry owner	Protestant
Yes	England	Merchant	Protestant
Yes	England	Lawyer	Protestant
Yes	England	Architect	Protestant
Yes	Ireland	Contractor	Protestant
Yes	Scotland	Lawyer	Protestant
Yes	Halton County, Upper Canada	Lawyer	Protestant
Yes	Toronto	Lawyer	Protestant
Yes	Cobourg, Upper Canada	Lawyer	Protestant
No	Lambton Mills (now Etobicoke), Canada West	Businessperson	Protestant
No	Ireland	Editor	Protestant
Yes	Toronto	Merchant	Protestant
Yes	Ireland	Merchant	Protestant
Yes	Toronto	Lawyer	Protestant
Yes	Oswego, New York	Developer	Protestant
No	Lambton Mills (now Etobicoke), Canada West	Lawyer	Protestant
Yes	Wallacetown, Canada West	Lawyer	Protestant

33	1906–07	Emerson Coatsworth	218 Carlton St.
34	1908–09	Joseph Oliver	598 Sherbourne St.
35	1910–12	Reginald Geary	Alexandra Apartments, 184 University Ave.
36	1912–14	Horatio Hocken	340 Palmerston Ave.
37	1915–21	Thomas Church	98 Binscarth Rd.
38	1922–23	Alfred Maguire	74 Oriole Rd.
39	1924	William W. Hiltz	682 Broadview Ave.
40	1925–27	Thomas Foster	20 Victor Ave.
41	1928–29 and 1936 (died in office)	Sam McBride	351 Palmerston Ave. and 335 Inglewood Dr.
42	1930	Bert Wemp	45 Playter Blvd.
43	1931–34	William Stewart	309 Kennedy Ave.
44	1935	Jimmy Simpson	91 Indian Rd.
45	1936–37	William Robbins	750 Logan Ave.
46	1938–40	Ralph Day	4 Castle Frank Dr.
47	1941–44	Fred Conboy	1043 Bloor St. W.
48	1945–48	Robert Saunders	15 Melgund Rd.
49	1948–51	Hiram McCallum	1501 Queen St. E
50	1952–54	Allan Lamport	84 Harper Ave.
51	1954	Leslie Saunders	62 Glenwood Cres.
52	1955–62	Nathan Phillips	26 Lauder Ave.
53	1963 (died in office)	Don Summerville	16 Briardale Blvd.
54	1963–66	Phil Givens	76 Caribou Rd.
55	1967–72	William Dennison	23 Pricefield Rd.

Yes	Toronto	Lawyer	Protestant
Yes	Erin, Canada West	Lumber merchant	Protestant
Yes	Strathroy, Ontario	Lawyer	Protestant
Yes	Toronto	Editor	Protestant
Yes	Toronto	Lawyer	Protestant
Yes	Toronto	Insurance executive	Protestant
Yes	Wellington County, Ontario	Builder	Protestant
Yes	York Township, Canada West	Businessperson	Protestant
Yes	Toronto	Lumber merchant	Protestant
Yes	Tweed, Ontario	Journalist	Protestant
Yes	Toronto	Funeral director	Protestant
Yes	England	Union leader	Protestant
Yes	England	Union leader	Protestant
Yes	Toronto	Funeral director	Protestant
Yes	Toronto	Dentist	Protestant
Yes	Toronto	Lawyer	Protestant
Yes	Caledon, Ontario	Commercial printer	Protestant
Yes	Toronto	Businessperson	Protestant
Yes	England	Printer	Protestant
Yes	Brockville, Ontario	Lawyer	Jewish
Yes	Toronto	Theatre manager	Protestant
Yes	Toronto	Lawyer	Jewish
Yes	Pembroke, Ontario	Speech therapist	Protestant

56	1973–78	David Crombie	81 Glencairn Ave.
57	1978 (appointed by Council)	Fred Beavis	1041 Logan Ave.
58	1978–80	John Sewell	205 Seaton St.
59	1980–91	Art Eggleton	14 Grenadier Heights
60	1991–94	June Rowlands	62 Wellesley Ave. W.
61	1994–97	Barbara Hall	39 Amelia St.

Mayors of the new amalgamated megacity of Toronto

62	1998–2003	Mel Lastman	19 Wideford Place
63	2003–10	David Miller	46 Gothic Ave.
64	2010–14	Rob Ford	223 Edenbridge Dr.
65	2014–23	John Tory	1 Bedford Rd.

Yes	Toronto	Educator	Protestant
Yes	Toronto	Roofer	Catholic
Yes	Toronto	Activist	Protestant
Yes	Toronto	Accountant	Protestant
Yes	Montreal	Police Board chair	Protestant
Yes	Ottawa	Lawyer	Protestant
Yes	Toronto	Merchant	Jewish
Yes	San Francisco, California	Lawyer	Protestant
Yes	Toronto	Businessperson	Protestant
No	Toronto	Lawyer	Protestant

Notes

Mayor William Lyon Mackenzie (1834)

1 John Sewell, *Mackenzie: A Political Biography* (Toronto: James Lorimer, 2002), 26.
2 Sewell, *Mackenzie*, 46.
3 Sewell, *Mackenzie*, 47.
4 Sewell, *Mackenzie*, 59.
5 Sewell, *Mackenzie*, 48.
6 Sewell, *Mackenzie*, 98.
7 Sewell, *Mackenzie*, 115.
8 Sewell, *Mackenzie*, 118.
9 Sewell, *Mackenzie*, 145.
10 John Charles Dent, *The Story of the Upper Canadian Rebellion* (Toronto: C. Blackett Robinson, 1885), 184.
11 Frederick H. Armstrong and Ronald J. Stagg, "Mackenzie, William Lyon," *Dictionary of Canadian Biography*, vol. 9 (Toronto: University of Toronto Press, 1976), biographi.ca/en/bio/mackenzie_william_lyon_9E.html.

Mayor Robert Sullivan (1835)

1 *Commemorative Biographical Record of the County of York, Ontario* (Toronto: J.H. Beers, 1907), 29.
2 Minutes of Toronto City Council, 1836.
3 Minutes of Toronto City Council, 1836.
4 Minutes of Toronto City Council, 1836.
5 Victor Loring Russell, Robert Lochiel Fraser, and Michael S. Cross, "Sullivan, Robert Baldwin," *Dictionary of Canadian Biography*, vol. 8 (Toronto: University of Toronto Press, 2003), biographi.ca/en/bio/sullivan_robert_baldwin_8E.html.
6 David Read, *The Lives of the Judges of Upper Canada and Ontario: From 1791 to the Present Time* (Toronto: Rowsell & Hutchison, 1888), 244.
7 Russell, Fraser, and Cross, "Sullivan, Robert Baldwin."
8 Russell, Fraser, and Cross, "Sullivan, Robert Baldwin."
9 Russell, Fraser, and Cross, "Sullivan, Robert Baldwin."
10 Read, *The Lives of the Judges of Upper Canada and Ontario*, 244.

Mayor Thomas Morrison (1836)

1 William Canniff, *The Medical Profession in Upper Canada 1783–1850* (Toronto: W. Briggs, 1894), 522.
2 Canniff, *The Medical Profession in Upper Canada*, 522.
3 Canniff, *The Medical Profession in Upper Canada*, 522.
4 Minutes of Toronto City Council, 1836.

5   Claire Mackay, *The Toronto Story* (Toronto: Annick, 2002), 34.
6   Mackay, *The Toronto Story*, 33–34.
7   Minutes of Toronto City Council, 1836.
8   Minutes of Toronto City Council, 1836.
9   Canniff, *The Medical Profession in Upper Canada*, 523.

Mayor George Gurnett (1837 and 1848–1850)
1   *The Examiner*, January 6, 1841.
2   A "rotten borough" was a House of Commons seat held by a patron who controlled the voting rights in that constituency: Michael Kaczorowski, "Parliamentary Government in the Age of Populism," *Canadian Parliamentary Review* 43, no. 4 (January 2021).
3   Maximilian Smith, "The World Outside These Walls: Toronto's Provincial Lunatic Asylum in Context, 1830–1882" (Ph.D. dissertation, York University, Toronto, September 2019), 117.
4   Richard W. Pound et al., eds., *The Fitzhenry and Whiteside Book of Canadian Facts and Dates*, 3rd ed. (Markham, ON: Fitzhenry & Whiteside, 2005), 190.
5   Pound et al., *Canadian Facts and Dates*, 215.
6   Mackay, *The Toronto Story*, 46.
7   Mackay, *The Toronto Story*, 43.
8   Victor Loring Russell, *Mayors of Toronto: Volume 1, 1834–1899* (Toronto: Boston Mills, 1982), 26.
9   Frederick H. Armstrong, "Gurnett, George," *Dictionary of Canadian Biography*, vol. 9 (Toronto: University of Toronto Press, 1976), biographi.ca/en/bio/gurnett_george _9E.html.
10 *Globe*, November 18, 1861, 2.

Mayor John Powell (1838–1840)
1   William Kilbourn, *The Firebrand: William Lyon Mackenzie and the Rebellion in Upper Canada* (Toronto: Dundurn, 2008), 204.
2   Russell, *Mayors of Toronto*, 30.
3   "Extract of a Despatch from Lieutenant Governor Sir George Arthur to Lord Glenelg, December 13, 1838," in Charles Grant Glenelg, *British North America: Copies or Extracts of Correspondence Relative to the Affairs of British North America* (London: HMSO, 1839).
4   Minutes of Toronto City Council, 1838.
5   Anna Jameson, *Winter Studies and Summer Rambles in Canada* (London: Saunders and Otley, 1838), 2.
6   Jameson, *Winter Studies and Summer Rambles in Canada*, 267, 269.
7   Jameson, *Winter Studies and Summer Rambles in Canada*, 256.
8   Minutes of Toronto City Council, 1840.
9   *The Canadian Biographical Dictionary and Portrait Gallery of Eminent and Self-Made Men* (Toronto: American Biographical Publishing Company, 1880–81), 160.
10 *The Canadian Biographical Dictionary and Portrait Gallery of Eminent and Self-Made Men*, 161.

Mayor George Monro (1841)
1   Edwin C. Guillet, *Toronto from Trading Post to Great City* (Toronto: Ontario Publishing Company, 1934), 47.
2   Minutes of Toronto City Council, 1841.
3   Catherine Slaney, *Family Secrets: Crossing the Colour Line* (Toronto: Dundurn, 2003), 46.

4   William R. Wilson, "Crime Is Timeless," *Historical Narratives of Early Canada*, 2013, uppercanadahistory.ca/lteuc/lteuc16.html.

5   Victor Loring Russell, *Forging a Consensus: Historical Essays on Toronto* (Toronto: University of Toronto Press, 1984), 49.

6   K.I.K. Davidson, "Monro, George," *Dictionary of Canadian Biography*, vol. 10 (Toronto: University of Toronto Press, 1972), biographi.ca/en/bio/monro_george _10E.html.

7   Jamie Bradburn, "'Dereliction of Duty': The Rise and Fall of Toronto's First Police Force," *TVO Today*, June 20, 2020, tvo.org/article/dereliction-of-duty-the-rise-and -fall-of-torontos-first-police-force.

8   Mackay, *The Toronto Story*, 46.

9   Davidson, "Monro, George."

10   J. Ross Robertson, *Robertson's Landmarks of Toronto* (Toronto: Mika, 1974).

11   Minutes of Toronto City Council, 1878.

Mayor Henry Sherwood (1842–1844)

1   Donald Robert Beer, "Sherwood, Henry," *Dictionary of Canadian Biography*, vol. 8 (Toronto: University of Toronto Press, 1985), biographi.ca/en/bio/sherwood_henry _8E.html.

2   Taylor, "When Dickens Visited Toronto," *Toronto Star*, December 20, 2007, thestar.com /news/gta/2007/12/20/when_dickens_visited_toronto.html.

3   Orville Luther Holley, *The Picturesque Tourist: Being a Guide Through the Northern and Eastern States and Canada* (New York: J. Disturnell, 1844), 218.

4   *Globe*, April 10, 1855, 3

Mayor William Boulton (1845–1847 and 1858)

1   Russell, *Mayors of Toronto*, 42.

2   Graeme Mercer Adam and Charles Pelham Mulvany, *History of Toronto and County of York, Ontario* (Toronto: C. Blackett Robinson, 1885), 367.

3   Hereward Senior, "Boulton, William Henry," *Dictionary of Canadian Biography*, vol. 10 (Toronto: University of Toronto Press, 2003), biographi.ca/en/bio/boulton_william _henry_10E.html.

4   Senior, "Boulton, William Henry."

5   Minutes of Toronto City Council, 1847.

6   J.T.H. Connor, *Doing Good: The Life of Toronto's General Hospital* (Toronto: University of Toronto Press, 2000), 48.

7   Senior, "Boulton, William Henry."

8   Senior, "Boulton, William Henry."

9   George P. Ure, *The Hand-Book of Toronto: Containing Its Climate, Geology, Natural History, Education Institutions, Courts of Law, Municipal Arrangements* (Toronto: Lovell and Gibson, 1858), 150.

10   Minutes of Toronto City Council, 1858.

11   Minutes of Toronto City Council, 1858.

12   Minutes of Toronto City Council, 1858.

Mayor John Bowes (1851–1853 and 1861–1863)

1   William G. Ormsby, "Bowes, John George," *Dictionary of Canadian Biography*, vol. 9 (Toronto: University of Toronto Press, 2003), biographi.ca/en/bio/bowes_john _george_9E.html.

2   Victor Russell, "Toronto's Run of Amazing Mayors," *Toronto Sun*, May 25, 2013, torontosun.com/2013/05/25/torontos-run-of-incredible-mayors.

3 Mackay, *The Toronto Story*, 48.
4 Mackay, *The Toronto Story*, 48.
5 Ormsby, "Bowes, John George."
6 Minutes of Toronto City Council, 1861.
7 Minutes of Toronto City Council, 1861.
8 Minutes of Toronto City Council, 1863.
9 *Globe*, May 21, 1864, 2.

Mayor Joshua Beard (1854)

1 Julia Roberts, "Taverns and Tavern-Goers in Upper Canada, the 1790s to the 1850s" (Ph.D. dissertation, University of Toronto, 1999).
2 Guillet, *Toronto from Trading Post to Great City*, 456.
3 Henry Christmas, *The Emigrant Churchman in Canada* (London; Richard Bentley, 1849), 71.
4 Minutes of Toronto City Council, 1854.
5 Minutes of Toronto City Council, 1854.
6 Minutes of Toronto City Council, 1854.

Mayor John Beverley Robinson, Jr. (1856)

1 Dent, *The Canadian Portrait Gallery*, 231.
2 George M. Rose, *A Cyclopædia of Canadian Biography: Being Chiefly Men of the Time* (Toronto: Good Press, 1886), 450.
3 Minutes of Toronto City Council, 1856.
4 Minutes of Toronto City Council, 1856.
5 Minutes of Toronto City Council, 1856.
6 Patrick Brode, "Robinson, John Beverley," *Dictionary of Canadian Biography*, vol. 12, (Toronto: University of Toronto Press, 2003), biographi.ca/en/bio/robinson_john _beverley_12E.html.
7 *Industries of Canada: Historical and Commercial Sketches of Toronto and Environs, Its Prominent Places and People, Representative Merchants and Manufacturers, Its Improvements, Progress and Enterprise* (Toronto: M.G. Bixby, 1866), 89.
8 Brode, "Robinson, John Beverley."
9 Brode, "Robinson, John Beverley."

Mayor John Hutchison (1857)

1 Russell, *Mayors of Toronto*, 62.
2 Charles Mackay, *Sketches of a Tour in the United States and Canada in 1857–1858* (New York: Harper and Brothers, 1859), 374.
3 Mackay, *The Toronto Story*, 53.
4 Minutes of Toronto City Council, 1857.
5 Minutes of Toronto City Council, 1857.
6 Adam and Mulvany, *History of Toronto and County of York, Ontario*, 267.
7 Minutes of Toronto City Council, 1857.
8 *Globe*, July 8, 1863, 2.

Mayor David Read (1858)

1 Minutes of Toronto City Council, 1858.
2 Minutes of Toronto City Council, 1858.
3 *Globe*, December 6, 1858, 2.
4 *Globe*, January 5, 1859, 2.
5 *Globe*, May 12, 1904, 6.

Mayor Adam Wilson (1859–1860)

1　*Commemorative Biographical Record of the County of York, Ontario*, 140.
2　*Globe*, January 4, 1859, 2.
3　*Globe*, January 7, 1860, 2.
4　Minutes of Toronto City Council, 1859.
5　Minutes of Toronto City Council, 1859.
6　Minutes of Toronto City Council, 1859.
7　*Globe*, January 4, 1860, 2.
8　Minutes of Toronto City Council, 1859, 1860.
9　*Commemorative Biographical Record of the County of York, Ontario*, 141.
10　*Globe*, January 2, 1892, 18.

Mayor Francis Medcalf (1864–1866 and 1874–1875)

1　Minutes of Toronto City Council, 1864.
2　Minutes of Toronto City Council, 1865.
3　Minutes of Toronto City Council, 1866.
4　*Globe*, December 23, 1865, 2.
5　Minutes of Toronto City Council, 1874.
6　Minutes of Toronto City Council, 1874.
7　*Globe*, December 31, 1874, 2.
8　*Globe*, January 2, 1875, 2.
9　Minutes of Toronto City Council, 1875.
10　*Globe*, July 13, 1875.

Mayor James Smith (1867–1868)

1　*Globe*, March 10, 1892, 8.
2　William Kilbourn, ed., *The Toronto Book: An Anthology of Writings Past and Present* (Toronto: Macmillan of Canada, 1976), 41.
3　Minutes of Toronto City Council, 1867.
4　Minutes of Toronto City Council, 1867.
5　Mike Filey, *Toronto Sketches 8: "The Way We Were"* (Toronto: Dundurn, 2004), 259–60.

Mayor Samuel Harman (1869–1870)

1　Minutes of Toronto City Council, 1869.
2　Minutes of Toronto City Council, 1869.
3　Minutes of Toronto City Council, 1869.
4　Mackay, *The Toronto Story*, 56.
5　Minutes of Toronto City Council, 1870.
6　Minutes of Toronto City Council, 1888.

Mayor Joseph Sheard (1871–1872)

1　Joseph Sheard, "Personal Family Biography," City of Toronto Archives, Mayors' Files, 1.
2　Sheard, "Personal Family Biography," 1.
3　Sheard, "Personal Family Biography," 2.
4　Sheard, "Personal Family Biography," 3.
5　Sheard, "Personal Family Biography," 4.
6　Sheard, "Personal Family Biography," 4.
7　Lorna Poplak, *The Don: The Story of Toronto's Infamous Jail* (Toronto: Dundurn, 2021), 12.
8　*Globe*, January 17, 1871, 4.

9   Minutes of Toronto City Council, 1871.
10 Minutes of Toronto City Council, 1871.
11 Minutes of Toronto City Council, 1872.
12 Sheard, "Personal Family Biography," 5.
13 Minutes of Toronto City Council, 1883.

Mayor Alexander Manning (1873 and 1885)
1   Russell, *Mayors of Toronto*, 93.
2   Desmond Morton, *Mayor Howland: The Citizens' Candidate* (Toronto: Hakkert, 1973), 11.
3   Minutes of Toronto City Council, 1873.
4   Minutes of Toronto City Council, 1885.

Mayor Angus Morrison (1876–1878)
1   Victor Loring Russell, "Morrison, Angus," *Dictionary of Canadian Biography*, vol. 11 (Toronto: University of Toronto Press, 1982), biographi.ca/en/bio/morrison_angus _11E.html.
2   Russell, "Morrison, Angus."
3   Donald Swainson, "Wilkes, Robert," *Dictionary of Canadian Biography*, vol. 10 (Toronto: University of Toronto Press, 1972), biographi.ca/en/bio/wilkes_robert _10E.html.
4   Minutes of Toronto City Council, 1876.
5   Minutes of Toronto City Council, 1876.
6   *The Canadian Biographical Dictionary and Portrait Gallery of Eminent and Self-Made Men*, 420.
7   Minutes of Toronto City Council, 1876.
8   Minko Sotiron, "Robertson, John Ross," *Dictionary of Canadian Biography*, vol. 14 (Toronto: University of Toronto Press, 1998), biographi.ca/en/bio/robertson_john _ross_14E.html.
9   Minutes of Toronto City Council, 1876.
10 Minutes of Toronto City Council, 1876.
11 *The Canadian Biographical Dictionary and Portrait Gallery of Eminent and Self-Made Men*, 420.

Mayor James Beaty, Jr. (1879 and 1880)
1   *The Canadian Biographical Dictionary and Portrait Gallery of Eminent and Self-Made Men*, 427.
2   Minutes of Toronto City Council, 1880.
3   Minutes of Toronto City Council, 1880.
4   Minutes of Toronto City Council, 1880.
5   *The Canadian Biographical Dictionary and Portrait Gallery of Eminent and Self-Made Men*, 429.
6   "Beaty Family History," City of Toronto Archives.

Mayor William McMurrich (1881 and 1882)
1   Rose, *A Cyclopædia of Canadian Biography*, 611.
2   Minutes of Toronto City Council, 1881.
3   Minutes of Toronto City Council, 1881.
4   Minutes of Toronto City Council, 1881.
5   Minutes of Toronto City Council, 1881.
6   Minutes of Toronto City Council, 1881.
7   Minutes of Toronto City Council, 1882.

8   Minutes of Toronto City Council, 1882.
9   George Monro Grant, ed. *Picturesque Canada: The Country as It Was and Is* (Toronto: Belden Bros., 1882), 408.

Mayor Arthur Boswell (1883 and 1884)

1   *Globe*, January 2, 1883, 6.
2   Jesse Edgar Middleton, *The Municipality of Toronto: A History* (Toronto: Dominion Publishing Company, 1923), 320.
3   Minutes of Toronto City Council, 1883.
4   Minutes of Toronto City Council, 1883.
5   Minutes of Toronto City Council, 1883.
6   Minutes of Toronto City Council, 1883.
7   Minutes of Toronto City Council, 1883.
8   Minutes of Toronto City Council, 1884.
9   Russell, *Mayors of Toronto*, 110.
10   Minutes of Toronto City Council, 1884.
11   *Globe*, May 18, 1925, 11.

Mayor William Howland (1886 and 1887)

1   Minutes of Toronto City Council, 1886.
2   Graeme Mercer Adam, *Toronto, Old and New: A Memorial Volume, Historical, Descriptive, and Pictorial* (Toronto: Mail Printing Company, 1891), 42.
3   Morton, *Mayor Howland*, 5.
4   Morton, *Mayor Howland*, 37.
5   Minutes of Toronto City Council, 1887.
6   Minutes of Toronto City Council, 1887.

Mayor Edward Clarke (1888–1891)

1   *Commemorative Biographical Record of the County of York, Ontario*, 99.
2   *Commemorative Biographical Record of the County of York, Ontario*, 100.
3   Gregory S. Kealey, *Toronto Workers Respond to Industrial Capitalism, 1867–1892* (Toronto: University of Toronto Press, 1980), 263.
4   Minutes of Toronto City Council, 1888.
5   Minutes of Toronto City Council, 1888.
6   Minutes of Toronto City Council, 1889.
7   Minutes of Toronto City Council, 1890.
8   Minutes of Toronto City Council, 1890.
9   *Commemorative Biographical Record of the County of York, Ontario*, 100.
10   *Toronto Daily Star*, March 4, 1905, 1.
11   *Globe*, March 8, 1905, 10.

Mayor Robert Fleming (1892–1893 and 1896–1897)

1   Middleton, *The Municipality of Toronto*, 518.
2   Donald Jones, "Truly a Career Key to the City," *Toronto Star*, February 15, 1986, M3.
3   Minutes of Toronto City Council, 1892.
4   Minutes of Toronto City Council, 1892.
5   Middleton, *The Municipality of Toronto*, 349.
6   Minutes of Toronto City Council, 1893.
7   Middleton, *The Municipality of Toronto*, 518.
8   Minutes of Toronto City Council, 1896.
9   Minutes of Toronto City Council, 1897.
10   Minutes of Toronto City Council, 1925.

Mayor Warring Kennedy (1894 and 1895)

1   *The Canadian Biographical Dictionary and Portrait Gallery of Eminent and Self-Made Men*, 414.
2   *The Canadian Biographical Dictionary and Portrait Gallery of Eminent and Self-Made Men*, 414.
3   Legislative Assembly of Ontario, Legislative Library, Research and Information Services, "Referendums in Ontario: An Historical Summary," Research Paper 07-01 (July 2007), 3.
4   Minutes of Toronto City Council, 1894.
5   Minutes of Toronto City Council, 1895.
6   Minutes of Toronto City Council, 1904.

Mayor John Shaw (1897–1899)

1   *Commemorative Biographical Record of the County of York, Ontario*, 576.
2   *Toronto Evening Star*, January 3, 1899, 4.
3   Minutes of Toronto City Council, 1897.
4   Minutes of Toronto City Council, 1897.
5   Minutes of Toronto City Council, 1899.
6   Donald Jones, "A Great Mayor's Dreams and Promises," *Toronto Star*, November 1, 1986, M3.
7   Minutes of Toronto City Council, 1899.
8   Middleton, *The Municipality of Toronto*, 101.

Mayor Ernest Macdonald (1900)

1   *Globe*, December 19, 1902, 12.
2   Middleton, *The Municipality of Toronto*, 344.
3   *Globe*, January 2, 1900, 6.
4   Minutes of Toronto City Council, 1900.
5   K.G. Ghanem and E.W. Hook, "Syphilis," in *Goldman-Cecil Medicine*, 26th ed., eds. L. Goldman and A.I. Schafee (Philadelphia: Elsevier, 2020), chapter 303.
6   *Globe*, January 2, 1900, 6.
7   Jay W. Marks, "Definition of Neurosyphilis," RxList, March 6, 2021, rxlist.com /neurosyphilis/definition.htm. Ernest Macdonald died a long, slow, agonizing death due to paresis, a stage of syphilis. Neurosyphilis is a neurological complication in the third and final phase of syphilis that involves the central nervous system and can include psychosis, pain, and loss of physical control over a variety of bodily functions.
8   Charles Patrick Davis, "General Paresis," RxList, March 29, 2021, rxlist.com /general_paresis/definition.htm. General paresis is a progressive dementia and generalized paralysis due to chronic inflammation of the covering and substance of the brain (meningoencephalitis). It is part of third-stage syphilis and occurs a decade or more after the initial infection. The symptoms include memory problems, decreased mental function such as problems with thinking and judgment, mood changes, and personality changes such as delusions, hallucinations, irritability, and inappropriate behaviour.
9   *Globe*, January 2, 1900, 6.
10 *Globe*, December 19, 1902, 6.

Mayor Oliver Howland (1901–1902)

1   Minutes of Toronto City Council, 1901.
2   Minutes of Toronto City Council, 1902.
3   Minutes of Toronto City Council, 1905.

Mayor Thomas Urquhart (1903–1905)

1   *Toronto Daily Star*, January 6, 1903, 6.
2   *Toronto Daily Star*, January 2, 1904, 1.
3   Mackay, *The Toronto Story*, 65.
4   Nancy J. White, "Cyberspace Swallows Toronto's Phone Book," *Toronto Star*, May 28, 2010, thestar.com/life/2010/05/28/cyberspace_swallows_torontos_phone_book.html.
5   *Toronto Daily Star*, December 31, 1904, 4.
6   Minutes of Toronto City Council, 1905.
7   Minutes of Toronto City Council, 1905.
8   Minutes of Toronto City Council, 1905.
9   Middleton, *The Municipality of Toronto*, 373.

Mayor Emerson Coatsworth (1906–1907)

1   Minutes of Toronto City Council, 1906.
2   Alexander Fraser, *A History of Ontario: Its Resources and Development*, vol. 1 (Toronto: Canada History Company, 1907), 586.
3   Minutes of Toronto City Council, 1907.

Mayor Joseph Oliver (1908–1909)

1   *Toronto Daily Star*, January 2, 1908, 1.
2   *Toronto Daily Star*, January 2, 1908, 1.
3   Minutes of Toronto City Council, 1908.
4   Minutes of Toronto City Council, 1908.
5   *Toronto Daily Star*, January 6, 1909, 6.
6   Minutes of Toronto City Council, 1909.
7   Minutes of Toronto City Council, 1909.

Mayor Reginald Geary (1910–1912)

1   Minutes of Toronto City Council, 1910.
2   Minutes of Toronto City Council, 1910.
3   Minutes of Toronto City Council, 1910.
4   Minutes of Toronto City Council, 1910.
5   *Globe*, December 31, 1910, 4.
6   Minutes of Toronto City Council, 1911.

Mayor Horatio Hocken (1912–1914)

1   *Toronto Daily Star*, October 22, 1912, 6.
2   Ann Marie F. Murnaghan, "The City, the Country, and Toronto's Bloor Viaduct, 1897–1919," *Urban History Review* 42, no. 1 (Fall 2013): 3–63.
3   Minutes of Toronto City Council, 1914.
4   Donald Jones, "Crusader for Social Reforms," *Toronto Star Saturday Magazine*, December 19, 1987, M3.
5   Jones, "Crusader for Social Reforms," M3.
6   Jones, "Crusader for Social Reforms," M3.

Mayor Thomas Church (1915–1921)

1   *Toronto Daily Star*, February 8, 1950, 6.
2   *Globe and Mail*, February 9, 1950, 6.
3   Minutes of Toronto City Council, 1916.
4   Minutes of Toronto City Council, 1919.

5   Minutes of Toronto City Council, 1919.
6   Minutes of Toronto City Council, 1919.
7   *Globe and Mail*, February 8, 1950, 1.
8   *Globe and Mail*, February 8, 1950, 1.

Mayor Alfred Maguire (1922–1923)
1   Minutes of Toronto City Council, 1923.
2   Minutes of Toronto City Council, 1923.
3   Middleton, *The Municipality of Toronto*, 405.
4   Minutes of Toronto City Council, 1949.

Mayor William W. Hiltz (1924)
1   *Toronto Daily Star*, February 27, 1936, 3.
2   W.W. Hiltz election advertisement, City of Toronto Archives, Mayor's Files.
3   *Toronto Daily Star*, December 24, 1923, 1.
4   Minutes of Toronto City Council, 1922.
5   Minutes of Toronto City Council, 1922.
6   *Toronto Daily Star*, January 14, 1924, 4.
7   *Toronto Daily Star*, February 27, 1936, 4.

Mayor Thomas Foster (1925–1927)
1   Minutes of Toronto City Council, 1925.
2   Minutes of Toronto City Council, 1925.
3   Minutes of Toronto City Council, 1926.
4   Minutes of Toronto City Council, 1927.
5   Donald Jones, "The 'Old Vagabond' Was Our Millionaire Mayor," *Toronto Star*, November 17, 1984, M3.

Mayor Sam McBride (1928–1929 and 1936)
1   Donald Jones, "Two-Fisted Mayor McBride Earned Toronto's Respect," *Toronto Star*, April 30, 1983, H6.
2   *Toronto Daily Star*, December 30, 1919, 5.
3   *Toronto Evening Telegram*, December 29, 1926, 14.
4   *Toronto Daily Star*, November 14, 1936, 6.
5   Minutes of Toronto City Council, 1928.
6   Minutes of Toronto City Council, 1929.
7   Minutes of Toronto City Council, 1936.

Mayor Bert Wemp (1930)
1   Donald Jones, "When One Word Lost the Race for Mayor," *Toronto Star Saturday Magazine*, February 4, 1989, M4.
2   Minutes of Toronto City Council, 1931.
3   Bruce West, *Toronto* (Toronto: Doubleday Canada, 1979), 283.
4   Bruce West, "Chit Chat," *Globe and Mail*, February 9, 1976, 27.

Mayor William Stewart (1931–1934)
1   *Globe*, December 25, 1930, 4.
2   *Globe*, December 29, 1930, 4.
3   Clare A. Dale, *Whose Servant I Am: Speakers of the Assemblies of the Provinces of Upper Canada, Canada, and Ontario, 1792–1992* (Toronto: Ontario Legislative Library, 1992), 242.

4   *Globe*, January 2, 1934, 4.
5   Dale, *Whose Servant I Am*, 242.
6   Dale, *Whose Servant I Am*, 242.
7   Dale, *Whose Servant I Am*, 242.

Mayor Jimmy Simpson (1935)
1   *National Encyclopedia of Canadian Biography* (Toronto: The Dominion Publishing Company, 1935), 368.
2   *Toronto Daily Star*, December 27, 1930, 6.
3   Minutes of Toronto City Council, 1935.
4   John Brehl, "When Toronto Had a Socialist Mayor," *Toronto Star*, February 4, 1966.

Mayor William Robbins (1936–1937)
1   Minutes of Toronto City Council, 1937.
2   Minutes of Toronto City Council, 1937.
3   Minutes of Toronto City Council, 1938.
4   Minutes of Toronto City Council, 1952.
5   *Globe and Mail*, March 26, 1952, 6.

Mayor Ralph Day (1938–1940)
1   Minutes of Toronto City Council, 1938.
2   Minutes of Toronto City Council, 1938.
3   Minutes of Toronto City Council, 1940.

Mayor Fred Conboy (1941–1944)
1   Minutes of Toronto City Council, 1949.
2   Fred Conboy election brochure, City of Toronto Archives.
3   Minutes of Toronto City Council, 1941.
4   Minutes of Toronto City Council, 1941.
5   Citations from the Toronto tabloid *Hush*.
6   Minutes of Toronto City Council, 1944.
7   *Toronto Daily Star*, March 30, 1949, 6.
8   Minutes of Toronto City Council, 1949.

Mayor Robert Saunders (1945–1948)
1   Minutes of Toronto City Council, 1945.
2   *Time*, January 22, 1945.
3   Allan Anderson, "Toronto Mayor Saunders," *The Standard*, December 14, 1946, 3.
4   Minutes of Toronto City Council, 1955.

Mayor Hiram McCallum (1948–1951)
1   *Toronto Calling* 1, no. 8 (January 1951).
2   Minutes of Toronto City Council, 1950.
3   Minutes of Toronto City Council, 1950.
4   Minutes of Toronto City Council, 1951.
5   Minutes of Toronto City Council, 1951.
6   *Toronto Daily Star*, February 19, 1951, 6.
7   *Toronto Daily Star*, February 19, 1951, 6.
8   "Alan Lamport for Mayor, 1951," election brochure, City of Toronto Archives, Election Files.

Mayor Allan Lamport (1952–1954)

1 Warren Gerard, "Boisterous Mr. Toronto Thriving at 90," *Toronto Star*, March 28, 1993, A1.
2 *Globe and Mail*, November 20, 1999, 26.
3 *Globe and Mail*, November 20, 1999, 26.
4 *Toronto Sun*, April 4, 1993, 11.
5 *Toronto Star*, March 29, 1993, 2.

Mayor Leslie Saunders (1954)

1 Leslie H. Saunders, *The Story of Orangeism* (Toronto: The Grand Lodge of Ontario West, 1941), foreword.
2 Leslie H. Saunders, *An Orangeman in Public Life: The Memoirs of Leslie H. Saunders* (Toronto: Britannia Printers, 1984), 81.
3 Saunders, *An Orangeman in Public Life*, 96.
4 Minutes of Toronto City Council, 1944.
5 Saunders, *An Orangeman in Public Life*, 127.

Mayor Nathan Phillips (1955–1962)

1 Nathan Phillips, *Mayor of All the People* (Toronto: McClelland & Stewart, 1967), 23.
2 Phillips, *Mayor of All the People*, 91.
3 *Globe and Mail*, December 7, 1954, 3.
4 Minutes of Toronto City Council, 1957.
5 Robert Nielsen, "'Nate' Phillips: Social Butterfly or Mayor of All the People?" *Toronto Daily Star*, November 21, 1958, 7.
6 *Toronto Daily Star*, December 3, 1960, 8.
7 Minutes of Toronto City Council, 1961.
8 Phillips, *Mayor of All the People*, 125.
9 Nathan Phillips election advertisement, City of Toronto Archives, Election Files.
10 Phillips, *Mayor of All the People*, 130.
11 Phillips, *Mayor of All the People*, 139.
12 *Toronto Star*, January 8, 1976, A11.

Mayor Don Summerville (1963)

1 Minutes of Toronto City Council, 1963.
2 *Toronto Daily Star*, December 1, 1962, 6.
3 *Toronto Daily Star*, November 20, 1963, 1.
4 *Toronto Daily Star*, November 20, 1963, 1.
5 *Globe and Mail*, November 20, 1963, 4.

Mayor Phil Givens (1963–1966)

1 Bill Gladstone, former president of the Jewish Genealogical Society of Toronto, "Phil Givens in Conversation, 1984," billgladstone.ca/phil-givens-in-conversation-1984.
2 *Toronto Daily Star*, November 21, 1963, 7.
3 Minutes of Toronto City Council, 1965.
4 Minutes of Toronto City Council, 1965.
5 *Toronto Daily Star*, September 13, 1965, 1.
6 *Globe and Mail*, May 21, 1971.
7 *Toronto Star*, December 1, 1995, A4.
8 *Toronto Star*, December 4, 1995, A3.

Mayor William Dennison (1967–1972)

1 Lorna Milne, *A Fighting Politician* (Toronto: Self-published, 1987), 84.
2 William D. Dennison, *The Correction of Stammering* (Toronto: Self-published, 1941).

3   *Globe and Mail*, May 4, 1981, 20.
4   *Toronto Daily Star*, December 28, 1940, 4.
5   Milne, *A Fighting Politician*, 40.
6   *Globe and Mail*, February 15, 1966, 5.
7   *Globe and Mail*, February 15, 1966, 5.
8   Election advertisement, City of Toronto Archives, Election Files.
9   Minutes of Toronto City Council, 1967.
10 Minutes of Toronto City Council, 1967.
11 Minutes of Toronto City Council, 1971.

Mayor David Crombie (1973–1978)

1   Victor Loring Russell, "David Crombie: Remaking Toronto," in *Your Worship: The Lives of Eight of Canada's Most Unforgettable Mayors*, ed. Allan Levine (Toronto: James Lorimer, 1989), 100.
2   Russell, "David Crombie: Remaking Toronto," 102.
3   Anthony O'Donohue, *Front Row Centre: A Perspective on Life, Politics, and the Environment* (Toronto: Abbeyfield, 2000), 165.
4   Jon Caulfield, *The Tiny Perfect Mayor: David Crombie and Toronto's Reform Aldermen* (Toronto: James Lorimer, 1974), 21.
5   David Crombie for Mayor Campaign News Release, 1972, City of Toronto Archives, Election Files.
6   Caulfield, *The Tiny Perfect Mayor*, 143.
7   Author interview with Bruce Bell, August 1, 2022.
8   Caulfield, *The Tiny Perfect Mayor*, 143.
9   Don Andrews, "Don Says," the website of the White Nationalist Party of Canada, 2013, natparty.com/DSA-2011.htm.
10 "The Greening of Toronto," *Time*, June 23, 1975.
11 *Toronto Star, The City: The Toronto Star Sunday Magazine*, October 16, 1977, 19.
12 *Globe and Mail*, March 3, 1988, A1.
13 *Toronto Star*, March 31, 1988, A4

Mayor Fred Beavis (1978)

1   Warren Gerard, "Leave It to Beavis," *Toronto Star, The City: The Toronto Star Sunday Magazine*, 1978, 11.
2   Gerard, "Leave It to Beavis," 13.
3   Gerard, "Leave It to Beavis," 13.
4   Fred Beavis election brochure, City of Toronto Archives, Election Files.
5   Gerard, "Leave It to Beavis," 14.
6   *Toronto Star*, November 11, 1978, 6.
7   *Globe and Mail*, September 5, 1978, 6.
8   Gerard, "Leave It to Beavis," 11.
9   *Toronto Star*, April 15, 1990, C6.
10 *Toronto Star*, November 9, 1985, B2.
11 *Toronto Star*, November 28, 1986, A25.
12 *Toronto Star*, November 15, 1988, A1.
13 *Toronto Star*, July 12, 1997, A6.

Mayor John Sewell (1978–1980)

1   John Barber, "Saint John," *Globe and Mail*, November 25, 1988, 46.
2   Barber, "Saint John," 46.
3   Anthony O'Donohue, *Front Row Centre: A Perspective on Life, Politics, and the Environment* (Toronto: Abbeyfield, 2000), 164.
4   John Sewell election brochure, City of Toronto Archives, Election Files.

5 *Globe and Mail*, August 23, 1976, 5.
6 O'Donohue, *Front Row Centre*, 195.
7 Minutes of Toronto City Council, 1978.
8 *Globe and Mail*, May 12, 1980, P5.
9 Barber, "Saint John," 46.
10 John Sewell, "The CN Tower Has Got to Go," *Globe and Mail*, May 6, 1986, A8.

Mayor Art Eggleton (1980–1991)
1 *Globe and Mail*, November 6, 1985, A13.
2 Author's interview with Art Eggleton, October 2018.
3 *Globe and Mail*, November 8, 1980, 4.
4 *Globe and Mail*, November 11, 1980, 1.
5 Minutes of Toronto City Council, 1980.
6 Minutes of Toronto City Council, 1982.
7 Minutes of Toronto City Council, 1985.
8 Minutes of Toronto City Council, 1985.
9 Minutes of Toronto City Council, 1985.
10 *Toronto Star*, September 29, 2001, K02.
11 *Toronto Star*, March 3, 2010, A25.
12 "Rob Ford Ducks Questions on Drug Video as New Ones Emerge, *CBC-TV News*, May 29, 2013, cbc.ca/news/canada/toronto/rob-ford-ducks-questions-on-drug-video-as-new-ones-emerge-1.1359522.
13 Marco Chown Oved, "We Asked the City's Leaders to Break Their Silence: Here's What They Said," *Toronto Star*, January 11, 2014, IN4.

Mayor June Rowlands (1991–1994)
1 *Chatelaine* 65, no. 6 (June 1992), 48.
2 *Toronto Star*, April 7, 1988, A22.
3 John Laschinger and Geoffrey Stevens, *Leaders and Lesser Mortals: Backroom Politics in Canada* (Toronto: Key Porter, 1992), 186.
4 *Toronto Star*, May 6, 1992, A6.
5 *Toronto Star*, January 11, 2014, IN4.
6 "Obituary for June Rowlands," the website of Aftercare Cremation & Burial Service, December 18, 2017, aftercare.org/obituaries/June-Rowlands/#!/Obituary.

Mayor Barbara Hall (1994–1997)
1 *Globe and Mail*, May 26, 1994, A14.
2 *Toronto Star*, November 12, 1994, B2.
3 *Globe and Mail*, November 15, 1994, A1.
4 *Toronto Star*, November 9, 1997, F2.
5 *Toronto Star*, October 6, 2007, AA7.
6 *London Free Press*, April 10, 2008, C3.
7 *National Post*, April 19, 2008, A10.
8 Remarks by City Councillor Kristyn Wong-Tam at the Barbara Hall Park dedication ceremony, July 16, 2014.

Mayor Mel Lastman (1998–2003)
1 *Toronto Star*, November 11, 2000, 1.
2 *Toronto Star*, November 11, 2000, 1.
3 *Toronto Star*, November 11, 2000, 1.
4 Denise E. Bellamy, *The Toronto Computer Leasing Inquiry, Volume 1: Facts and Findings* (Toronto: City of Toronto, 2005), 43.

5　Stephen Brunt, "But Seriously, Folks," *Toronto Magazine*, January 27, 1989, 29.

6　*Toronto Star*, April 23, 1997, A6 and A22.

7　*CTV National News*, CTV, December 12, 1997.

8　*Toronto Star*, December 31, 1998, 1.

9　*Toronto Star*, June 20, 2001, C09.

10　*Toronto Star*, November 16, 2002, B1.

Mayor David Miller (2003–2010)

1　*Globe and Mail*, December 3, 2003, A15.

2　*Toronto Life* 38, no. 1 (January 2004), 64–76.

3　Minutes of Toronto City Council, 2003.

4　*Toronto Star*, November 5, 2003, A1.

5　Michael Kolberg, "Q&A with David Miller: The Intersection of Economy and Environment," *Toronto Standard*, September 17, 2012.

Mayor Rob Ford (2010–2014)

1　Don Wanagas, *National Post*, March 10, 2001, nationalpost.com/toronto/don-wanagas -the-odd-rantings-of-young-rob-ford.

2　"Rob Ford on Cyclists," YouTube, youtube.com/watch?v=nySs1cEq5rs.

3　Rob Ford, "Saving Our City Plan," YouTube, September 27, 2010, youtube.com /watch?v=ry1-xZIx_Zw.

4　*CTV News*, "Ford Says Ending the 'War on Cars' a Top Priority," December 1, 2010, toronto.ctvnews.ca/ford-says-ending-the-war-on-cars-a-top-priority-1.580604.

5　David Rider, "Don Cherry Rips 'Left-Wing Pinkos' at Council Inaugural," *Toronto Star*, December 7, 2010, thestar.com/news/city_hall/2010/12/07/don_cherry_rips_leftwing _pinkos_at_council_inaugural.html.

6　Sean Mallen, "The Mayor Who Won't Shut Up. And Shouldn't," Sean Mallen Communications, June 12, 2015, linkedin.com/pulse/mayor-who-wont-shut-up -shouldnt-sean-mallen/?trk=mp-reader-card.

7　Allan Black, "Can Rob Ford Remain as Mayor of Toronto?" *CTV National News*, November 5, 2013, ctvnews.ca/ctv-national-news/can-rob-ford-remain-as-mayor -of-toronto-1.1529418.

8　"Toronto Mayor Is the First, and the Worst, in 2014 Election: Editorial," *Toronto Star*, January 3, 2014, A18, thestar.com/opinion/editorials/2014/01/02/toronto_mayor _rob_ford_is_the_first_and_the_worst_in_2014_election_editorial.html.

9　"2014 Municipal Election — Financial Disclosures," City of Toronto, app.toronto.ca /EFD/jsf/main/main.xhtml?campaign=9.

10　*Globe and Mail*, March 31, 2016, A3.

11　*National Post*, March 23, 2016, B4.

Mayor John Tory (2014–2023)

1　*Toronto Star*, October 23, 2014.

2　Theresa Tedesco, "The Mayor of Bay Street: John Tory Sharpens His Boardroom Skills for Toronto's City Hall," *Financial Post*, November 29, 2014, financialpost.com /news/fp-street/the-mayor-of-bay-street-john-tory-sharpens-his-boardroom-skills -for-torontos-city-hall.

3　*CBC News*, "John Tory Calls for End to 'Illegitimate, Disrespectful' Practice of Carding," June 7, 2015, cbc.ca/news/canada/toronto/john-tory-calls-for-end-to -illegitimate-disrespectful-practice-of-carding-1.3103855.

4　Nick Westoll, "Doug Ford Joining 2018 Toronto Mayoral Race, Says 'Enough Is Enough,'" *Global News*, September 8, 2017, globalnews.ca/news/3729974/doug-ford-2018 -toronto-mayors-race.

5   Jennifer Pagliaro, David Rider, and Francine Kopun, "Smooth Sailing for $13.53-Billion Operating Budget at Toronto City Council," *Toronto Star*, February 19, 2020.

6   Pagliaro, Rider, and Kopun, "Smooth Sailing for 13.5-Billion Operating Budget at Toronto City Council."

7   Chris Fox, "Toronto's Top Doctor on the Three-Year Anniversary of COVID in Ontario and Whether an End Is in Sight," CP24.com, January 25, 2023, cp24.com/news /toronto-s-top-doctor-on-the-three-year-anniversary-of-covid-in-ontario-and-whether-an-end-is-in-sight-1.6245544.

8   Michael Talbot, "Tory Wins Third Term as Toronto Mayor in Predictable Election," CityNews 680, October 24, 2022, toronto.citynews.ca/2022/10/24/tory-wins-third -term-toronto-mayor-election.

9   Marcus Gee, "It's Not Just the TTC: There's a Growing Sense That Things in Toronto Are Spinning Out of Control," Globe and Mail, January 27, 2023, theglobeandmail.com/canada/toronto/article-its-not-just-the-ttc-theres-a-growing -sense-that-things-in-toronto-are.

10   Shawn Jeffords, "Former Toronto Mayors Call on Tory to Reject Expanded 'Strong Mayor' Powers," *CBC News*, November 21, 2022, cbc.ca/news/canada/toronto/former -mayors-tory-strong-mayor-powers-1.6658788.

11   Transcript of John Tory's resignation announcement, *Toronto Star*, February 10, 2023, thestar.com/news/gta/2023/02/10/in-his-own-words-transcript-of-john-torys -resignation-announcement.html.

12   Tyler Griffin, "John Tory's Affair, Resignation Blow Up Mayor's Legacy as Calm, Stable Leader: Political Analysts," Canadian Press, *CBC News*, February 12, 2023, cbc.ca/news/canada/toronto/john-tory-toronto-mayor-affair-resignation-1.6745947.

13   Ben Spurr, "'It Breaks My Heart to Leave,' Says John Tory in His Final Remarks as Mayor," *Toronto Star*, February 17, 2023, thestar.com/news/gta/2023/02/17/john-tory -jennifer-mckelvie-speaking-at-city-hall-on-friday-afternoon.html.

14   Spurr, "'It Breaks My Heart to Leave,' Says John Tory in His Final Remarks as Mayor."

15   "27 Appointees Named to Ontario's Highest Honour," Ontario Ministry of Citizenship and Immigration, January 20, 2012, news.ontario.ca/en/release/20117/27-appointees -named-to-ontarios-highest-honour.

Bibliography

Adam, Graeme Mercer. *Toronto, Old and New: A Memorial Volume, Historical, Descriptive, and Pictorial.* Toronto: Mail Printing Company, 1891.

Adam, Graeme Mercer, and Charles Pelham Mulvany. *History of Toronto and County of York, Ontario.* Toronto: C. Blackett Robinson, 1885.

Armstrong, Frederick. "Gurnett, George." *Dictionary of Canadian Biography*, vol. 9. Toronto: University of Toronto Press, 1976. biographi.ca/en/bio/gurnett _george_9E.html.

Armstrong, Frederick H., and Ronald Stagg. "Mackenzie, William Lyon." *Dictionary of Canadian Biography*, vol. 9. Toronto: University of Toronto Press, 1976. biographi.ca/en/bio/mackenzie_william_lyon_9E.html.

Beer, Donald Robert. "Sherwood, Henry." *Dictionary of Canadian Biography*, vol. 8. Toronto: University of Toronto Press, 1985. biographi.ca/en/bio/sherwood _henry_8E.html.

Bellamy, Denise E. *Toronto Computer Leasing Inquiry, Volume 1: Facts and Findings, The.* Toronto: City of Toronto, 2005.

Bradburn, Jamie. "'Dereliction of Duty': The Rise and Fall of Toronto's First Police Force," *TVO Today*, June 20, 2020. tvo.org/article/dereliction-of-duty -the-rise-and-fall-of-torontos-first-police-force.

Brode, Patrick. "Robinson, John Beverley." *Dictionary of Canadian Biography*, vol. 12. Toronto: University of Toronto Press, 2003. biographi.ca/en/bio/robinson _john_beverley_12E.html.

Bureau of Municipal Research, Toronto. *Civic Affairs Bulletins (1914–1983)*.

Canadian Biographical Dictionary and Portrait Gallery of Eminent and Self-Made Men, The. Toronto: American Biographical Publishing Company, 1880–81.

Canniff, William. *The Medical Profession in Upper Canada 1783–1850.* Toronto: W. Briggs, 1894.

Caulfield, Jon. *The Tiny Perfect Mayor: David Crombie and Toronto's Reform Aldermen.* Toronto: James Lorimer, 1974.

Christmas, Henry. *The Emigrant Churchman in Canada.* London: Richard Bentley, 1849.

Clark, C.S. *Of Toronto the Good: A Social Study.* Montreal: Toronto Publishing Company, 1898.

Colton, Timothy. *Big Daddy: Frederick G. Gardiner and the Building of Toronto.* Toronto: University of Toronto Press, 1980.

Commemorative Biographical Record of the County of York, Ontario. Toronto: J.H. Beers, 1907.

Connor, J.T.H. *Doing Good: The Life of Toronto's General Hospital.* Toronto: University of Toronto Press, 2000.

Dale, Clare A. *Whose Servant I Am: Speakers of the Assemblies of the Provinces of Upper Canada, Canada, and Ontario, 1792–1992.* Toronto: Ontario Legislative Library, 1992.

Davidson, K.I.K. "Munro, George." *Dictionary of Canadian Biography*, vol. 10. Toronto: University of Toronto Press, 1972. biographi.ca/en/bio/monro_george _10E.html.

Dent, John Charles. *The Canadian Portrait Gallery*, vol 3. Toronto: John B. Magurn, 1881.

_____. *The Story of the Upper Canadian Rebellion.* Toronto: C. Blackett Robinson, 1885.

Doolittle, Robyn. *Crazy Town: The Rob Ford Story.* Toronto: Penguin Canada, 2014.

Filey, Mike. *Toronto Sketches 8: "The Way We Were."* Toronto: Dundurn, 2004.

Filey, Mike, and Rosalind Tosh. *Toronto Then and Now.* Toronto: Magic Light Publishing, 2000.

Filion, John. *The Only Average Guy: Inside the Uncommon World of Rob Ford.* Toronto: Random House Canada, 2015.

Ford, Rob, and Doug Ford. *Ford Nation, Two Brothers, One Vision: The True Story of the People's Mayor.* Toronto: HarperCollins Canada, 2016.

Fraser, Alexander. *A History of Ontario: Its Resources and Development.* Toronto: Canada History Company, 1907.

Grant, George Monro, ed. *Picturesque Canada: The Country as It Was and Is.* Toronto: Belden Bros., 1882.

Guillet, Edwin C. *Toronto from Trading Post to Great City.* Toronto: Ontario Publishing Company, 1934.

Holley, Orville Luther. *The Picturesque Tourist: Being a Guide Through the Northern and Eastern States and Canada.* New York: J. Disturnell, 1844.

How Rob Ford Happened: A History of the Toronto Mayor from the Pages of the National Post. Toronto: HarperCollins Canada, 2013.

Individual News Clippings File of Each Mayor of Toronto (1834–2022). Research Hall, City of Toronto Archives.

Industries of Canada: Historical and Commercial Sketches of Toronto and Environs, Its Prominent Places and People, Representative Merchants and Manufacturers, Its Improvements, Progress and Enterprise. Toronto: M.G. Bixby, 1866.

Jameson, Anna. *Winter Studies and Summer Rambles in Canada.* London: Saunders and Otley, 1838.

Kealey, Gregory S. *Toronto Workers Respond to Industrial Capitalism, 1867–1892.* Toronto: University of Toronto Press, 1980.

Keenan, Edward. *Some Great Idea: Good Neighbourhoods, Crazy Politics and the Invention of Toronto.* Toronto: Coach House Books, 2013.

Kilbourn, William. *The Firebrand: William Lyon Mackenzie and the Rebellion in Upper Canada*. Toronto: Dundurn, 2008.

Kilbourn, William, ed. *The Toronto Book: An Anthology of Writings Past and Present*. Toronto: Macmillan Company of Canada, 1976.

Lamport, Allan, and John Robert Colombo. *Quotations from Chairman Lamport: Metro's Goldwyn Mayor*. Vancouver: Pulp Press, 1990.

Laschinger, John, and Geoffrey Stevens. *Campaign Confessions: Tales from the War Rooms of Politics*. Toronto: Dundurn, 2016.

____. *Leaders and Lesser Mortals: Backroom Politics in Canada*. Toronto: Key Porter, 1992.

Levy, Sue-Ann. *Underdog: Confessions of a Right-Wing Gay Jewish Muckraker*. Toronto: McClelland & Stewart, 2016.

Mackay, Charles. *Sketches of a Tour in the United States and Canada in 1857–1858*. New York: Harper and Brothers, 1859.

Mackay, Claire. *The Toronto Story*. Toronto: Annick Press, 1991.

Middleton, Jesse Edgar. *The Municipality of Toronto: A History*. Toronto: Dominion Publishing Company, 1923.

____. *Toronto's 100 Years*. Toronto: The Centennial Committee, Corporation of the City of Toronto, 1934.

Miller, David. *Witness to a City: David Miller's Toronto*. Toronto: Cormorant Books, 2010.

Milne, Lorna. *A Fighting Politician*. Toronto: Self-published, 1987.

Minutes of Toronto City Council (1834–2022). Research Hall, City of Toronto Archives.

Morton, Desmond. *Mayor Howland: The Citizens' Candidate*. Toronto: Hakkert, 1973.

Mulvany, C. Pelham. *Toronto, Past and Present: A Handbook of the City*. Toronto: W.E. Caiger, 1884.

Murnaghan, Ann Marie F. "The City, the Country, and Toronto's Bloor Viaduct, 1897–1919." *Urban History Review* 42, no. 1 (Fall 2013).

O'Donohue, Tony. *Front Row Centre: A Perspective on Life, Politics, and the Environment*. Toronto: Abbeyfield, 2001.

Ormsby, William G. "Bowes, John." *Dictionary of Canadian Biography*, vol. 9. Toronto: University of Toronto Press, 2003. biographi.ca/en/bio/bowes_john _george_9E.html.

Phillips, Nathan. *Mayor of All the People*. Toronto: McClelland & Stewart, 1967.

Poplak, Lorna. *The Don: The Story of Toronto's Infamous Jail*. Toronto: Dundurn, 2021.

Pound, Richard W., et al., eds. *The Fitzhenry and Whiteside Book of Canadian Facts and Dates*, 3rd ed. Markham, ON: Fitzhenry & Whiteside, 2005.

Read, David. *The Lives of the Judges of Upper Canada and Ontario: From 1791 to the Present Time*. Toronto: Rowsell & Hutchison, 1888.

Richmond, John, and Bruce West. *Around Toronto: A Look at the City with John Richmond and Bruce West*. Toronto: Doubleday Canada, 1969.

Robertson, J. Ross. *Old Toronto: A Selection of Excerpts from Landmarks of Toronto*, edited by E.C. Kyte. Toronto: Macmillan Company of Canada, 1954.

____. *Robertson's Landmarks of Toronto*. Toronto: Mika Publishing Company, 1974.

Rose, George M. *A Cyclopædia of Canadian Biography: Being Chiefly Men of the Time*. Toronto: Good Press, 1886.

Russell, Victor Loring. "David Crombie: Remaking Toronto." In *Your Worship: The Lives of Eight of Canada's Most Unforgettable Mayors*, edited by Allan Levine. Toronto: James Lorimer, 1989.

____. *Mayors of Toronto: Volume 1, 1834–1899*. Toronto: Boston Mills, 1982.

____. "Morrison, Angus." *Dictionary of Canadian Biography*, vol. 11. Toronto: University of Toronto Press, 1982. biographi.ca/en/bio/morrison_angus _11E.html.

Russell, Victor Loring, ed. *Forging a Consensus: Historical Essays on Toronto*. Toronto: University of Toronto Press, 1984.

Russell, Victor Loring, and Robert Lochiel Fraser and Michael S. Cross. "Sullivan, Robert Baldwin." *Dictionary of Canadian Biography*, vol. 8. Toronto: University of Toronto Press, 2003. biographi.ca/en/bio/sullivan_robert_baldwin_8E.html.

Saunders, Leslie. *An Orangeman in Public Life: The Memoirs of Leslie Howard Saunders*. Toronto: Self-published; Britannia Printers, 1980.

____. *The Story of Orangeism*. Toronto: The Grand Lodge of Ontario West, 1941.

Scadding, Henry. *Toronto of Old: Collections and Recollections Illustrative of the Early Settlement and Social Life of the Capital of Ontario*. Toronto: Willing and Williamson, 1878.

Senior, Hereward. "Boulton, William Henry." *Dictionary of Canadian Biography*, vol. 10. Toronto: University of Toronto Press, 2003. biographi.ca/en/bio/boulton _william_henry_10E.html.

Sewell, John. *How We Changed Toronto: The Inside Story of Twelve Creative, Tumultuous Years in Civic Life, 1969–1980*. Toronto: James Lorimer, 2015.

____. *Mackenzie: A Political Biography of William Lyon Mackenzie*. Toronto: James Lorimer, 2002.

Slaney, Catherine. *Family Secrets: Crossing the Colour Line*. Toronto: Dundurn, 2003.

Smith, Maximilian. "The World Outside These Walls: Toronto's Provincial Lunatic Asylum in Context, 1830–1882." Ph.D. dissertation, York University. Toronto, September 2019.

Stanford, Geoffrey Hunt. *To Serve the Community: The Story of Toronto's Board of Trade*. Toronto: University of Toronto Press, 1974.

Taylor, Conyngham Crawford. *Toronto Called Back, from 1886 to 1850*. Toronto: William Briggs, 1886.

Tossell, Ivor. *The Gift of Ford: How Toronto's Unlikeliest Man Became Its Most Notorious Mayor*. Toronto: Random House Canada, 2012.

Towhey, Mark, and Johanna Schneller. *Mayor Rob Ford: Uncontrollable: How I Tried to Help the World's Most Notorious Mayor*. New York: Skyhorse, 2015.

Unknown Torontonian and Rob Ford. *The Little Book of Rob Ford*. Toronto: Anansi, 2011.

Ure, George P. *The Hand-Book of Toronto: Containing Its Climate, Geology, Natural History, Education Institutions, Courts of Law, Municipal Arrangements*. Toronto: Lovell and Gibson, 1858.

West, Bruce. *Toronto*. Toronto: Doubleday Canada, 1969.

Wilson, William R. "Crime Is Timeless." *Historical Narratives of Early Canada*, 2013. uppercanadahistory.ca/lteuc/lteuc16.html.

Image Credits

All mayor images courtesy of City of Toronto Archives.

15   Toronto Public Library.

95   (*left*) City of Toronto Archives, Fonds 1498, Item 16; (*right*) City of Toronto Archives, Fonds 1498, Item 1.

170   Toronto Public Library, Baldwin Collection of Canadiana, R-2314.

206   Toronto Public Library, Baldwin Collection of Canadiana, R-3940.

226   City of Toronto, Culture Division, Art Collection, A75-29.

227   City of Toronto Archives, Fonds 1244, Item 2.

254   City of Toronto Archives, Series 372, Subseries 32, Item 187.

260   City of Toronto Archives, Series 372, Subseries 10, Item 841.

277   Toronto Public Library, Baldwin Collection of Canadiana, R-5241.

289   Toronto Public Library, *Evening Telegram*, December 29, 1926.

346   City of Toronto Archives, Series 381, File 31, Item 6650-6.

354   City of Toronto Archives, Fonds 1257, Series 1057, Item 1228.

386   Toronto Public Library, Baldwin Collection of Canadiana.

387   Toronto Public Library, Baldwin Collection of Canadiana.

395   City of Toronto Department of Public Works, Bloor Street West to College Street Metropolitan Proposal (March 1970).

401   David Crombie.

Index